Learning ASP.NET 2.0 with AJAX

Other Microsoft .NET resources from O'Reilly

Related titles

ASP.NET Cookbook™   Programming ASP.NET
Essential Silverlight   Programming ASP.NET AJAX
Learning ASP.NET   Programming C#
Learning JavaScript

.NET Books Resource Center

dotnet.oreilly.com is a complete catalog of O'Reilly's books on .NET and related technologies, including sample chapters and code examples.

ONDotnet.com provides independent coverage of fundamental, interoperable, and emerging Microsoft .NET programming and web services technologies.

Conferences

O'Reilly & Associates bring diverse innovators together to nurture the ideas that spark revolutionary industries. We specialize in documenting the latest tools and systems, translating the innovator's knowledge into useful skills for those in the trenches. Visit *conferences.oreilly.com* for our upcoming events.

Safari Bookshelf (*safari.oreilly.com*) is the premier online reference library for programmers and IT professionals. Conduct searches across more than 1,000 books. Subscribers can zero in on answers to time-critical questions in a matter of seconds. Read the books on your Bookshelf from cover to cover or simply flip to the page you need. Try it today for free.

Learning ASP.NET 2.0
with AJAX

Jesse Liberty, Dan Hurwitz, and Brian MacDonald

O'REILLY®

Beijing · Cambridge · Farnham · Köln · Paris · Sebastopol · Taipei · Tokyo

Learning ASP.NET 2.0 with AJAX

by Jesse Liberty, Dan Hurwitz, and Brian MacDonald

Published by O'Reilly Media, Inc., 1005 Gravenstein Highway North, Sebastopol, CA 95472.

O'Reilly books may be purchased for educational, business, or sales promotional use. Online editions are also available for most titles (*safari.oreilly.com*). For more information, contact our corporate/institutional sales department: (800) 998-9938 or *corporate@oreilly.com*.

Editor: John Osborn
Production Editor: Rachel James
Production Services: Octal Publishing, Inc.

Cover Designer: Karen Montgomery
Interior Designer: David Futato
Illustrator: Jessamyn Read

Printing History:

September 2007: First Edition.

 This book uses RepKover™, a durable and flexible lay-flat binding.

ISBN-10: 0-596-51397-6
ISBN-13: 978-0-596-51397-9
[M]

This book is dedicated to truth tellers and rational thinkers; our nation depends on them, especially now.

Table of Contents

Cheat Sheets

VB Cheat Sheets

SQL Cheat Sheets

Preface

ASP.NET 2.0 with AJAX is arguably the fastest, most efficient, most reliable and best supported way to create interactive web applications available today. Combined with the development tools available from Microsoft, both free and commercial, it is incredibly easy to create web sites that look great and perform well. Best of all, most of the "plumbing" (security, data access, layout, and so on) is taken care of for you by the .NET Framework.

About This Book

This book will teach you how to build professional quality, interactive, robust datadriven web applications using Visual Basic 2005. In addition, your applications will be highly interactive and data driven—must-have features in today's feature-rich web world.

ASP.NET is not difficult. All of the concepts are straightforward, and the Visual Studio and Visual Web Developer environments simplify the process of building powerful web applications. The difficulty in ASP.NET is only that it is so complete and flexible that there are many pieces that must be woven together to build a robust, scalable, and efficient application. This book cuts to the heart of the matter, showing in clear, easy-to-follow steps, how to understand and build a web site.

Because there are three authors' names on this book, you might be concerned that the tone will be uneven. Every possible measure has been taken to avoid this. Although each chapter was originally written by one author, they were edited by all three. Every chapter was then extensively edited and rewritten by me, Jesse Liberty, to give the book a single voice. If that weren't enough, the chapters were subsequently edited by O'Reilly editors as well as independent tech editors, and once more by the authors. The bottom line is that while three individuals wrote this book, you should find it reads as if written by just one. This system has worked well with my previous books. If not, please be sure to let me know by dropping a note in my support forum (*http://forums.delphiforums.com/JesseLiberty*).

About This Series

O'Reilly Learning books are written and designed for anyone who wants to build new skills and who prefers a structured approach to studying. Each title in this series makes use of learning principles that we (with your help) have found to be best at equipping you with the knowledge you need for joining that new project, for coping with that unexpected assignment from your manager, or for learning a new language in a hurry.

To get the most out of any book in the Learning series, we recommend you work your way through each chapter in sequence. You'll find that you can get a quick grasp of a chapter's content by reading the instructional captions we've written for its examples and figures. You can also use the chapter Summary to preview its key takeaways and to review what you have learned. Most chapters feature a sample application, and, if you learn best by reading code, you can turn to the complete source listing that appears just before the Summary. To bridge any gaps in your knowledge, check out the Cheat Sheets. Finally, to help you test your mastery of the material in each chapter, we conclude with a Brain Builder section, which includes a short quiz and some hands-on exercises.

Learning books work with you as you learn—much as you would expect from a trusted colleague or instructor—and we strive to make your learning experience enjoyable. Tell us how we've done by sending us praise, brickbats, or suggestions for improvements to *learning@oreilly.com*.

Learning or Programming?

We have written two ASP.NET books: the one you are currently reading and another named *Programming ASP.NET 2.0*. This book, *Learning ASP.NET 2.0 with AJAX* is intended for beginning ASP.NET developers, and answers the question: "What is the quickest way for me to build real web applications with the least handcoding?"

Our other book, *Programming ASP.NET* is for developers who are saying: "Help me learn—in depth; show how everything works, and then help me put it to work in web applications." The key difference is this book is aimed to make you productive quickly, while the second book is designed to explore the technology in detail. They complement each other, but if you are starting out and want to get to work fast, *this* is the one for you.

Learning ASP.NET 2.0 with Ajax assumes you know some HTML and have either some familiarity with Visual Basic 2005 (VB) or C#, or can pick up what you need along the way. (Or you're willing to run right out and buy *Programming Visual Basic 2005* by Jesse Liberty, although for what you'll be doing here, you won't really need it). To help with this, we have included VB Cheat Sheets throughout the book to explain and clarify some of the VB topics for newbies.

VB Versus C#

A quick note on Visual Basic versus C#: Some people choose a .NET book based on what language the examples are given in. That's a natural reaction, but it's really not necessary, and here's why: There is very little actual VB or C# code in any given ASP.NET program, and what there is, you can easily translate from one to the other "on inspection." Besides, the two languages are strikingly similar. If you know one, it's quite simple to learn the other. In fact, there are software tools that can convert one language to the other with amazing accuracy. Finally, ASP.NET programmers benefit terrifically by being "bilingual"—that is, having the ability to read VB and write C# (or vice versa).

How This Book Is Organized

Chapter 1, *Getting Started*, walks you through creating your first web site, *HelloWorld*.

Chapter 2, *Building Web Applications*, goes over the fundamentals of web sites and covers the basic controls available to you in ASP.NET.

Chapter 3, *Snappier Web Sites with AJAX*, shows you how to integrate this powerful client-side technology into your pages.

Chapter 4, *Saving and Retrieving Data*, shows you how to make your site interact with data stored in a database. You have controls to retrieve data, allow your users to interact with that data, and then save it back to the database.

Chapter 5 looks at *Validation*. ASP.NET provides extensive support for data validation, including ensuring that a choice has been made, checking that values are within a range, and matching regular expressions.

Chapter 6, *Style Sheets, Master Pages, and Navigation*, shows you how to make web sites that are professional quality, good looking, consistent, and easy to navigate.

Chapter 7 examines *State and Life Cycle* in ASP.NET. Understanding how, and in what order, a page and its controls are created on the server and rendered to the browser is crucial for building successful interactive web sites. State is the current value of everything associated with the page. This is mostly handled automatically, but this chapter shows you how useful it can be to the developer.

Poop happens. Chapter 8, *Errors, Exceptions, and Bugs, Oh My!*, shows you how to deal with unexpected problems, and also how to debug your application.

Chapter 9, *Security and Personalization*, shows how you can protect your web site from malicious users. A related topic is personalization, which allows your end users to customize the look and feel of the web site according to their personal preferences. You will see how to use themes and skins to accomplish this.

Chapter 10, *Putting It All Together*, is a single, large example that integrates everything you have learned throughout the book.

Appendix A, *Installing the Applications*, tells you what hardware and software is required to run the examples in this book, and helps you set up your environment.

Appendix B, *Copying a Web Site*, describes the process of copying a web site to a new web site. This is a technique used often throughout this book when building up examples.

Appendix C, *Answers to Quizzes and Exercises*, presents detailed solutions to all the quiz questions and practice exercises found at the end of each chapter.

Conventions Used in This Book

The following font conventions are used in this book:

Italic
> Used for pathnames, filenames, program names, Internet addresses, such as domain names and URLs, and new terms where they are defined.

`Constant Width`
> Used for command lines and options that should be typed verbatim, and names and keywords in program examples. Also used for parameters, attributes, expressions, statements, and values.

`Constant Width Italic`
> Used for replaceable items, such as variables or optional elements, within syntax lines or code.

`Constant Width Bold`
> Used for emphasis within program code examples.

Pay special attention to notes set apart from the text with the following icons:

> This is a tip. It contains useful supplementary information about the topic at hand.

> This is a warning. It helps you solve and avoid annoying problems.

Support: A Note from Jesse Liberty

I provide ongoing support for my books through my web site. You can obtain the source code for all of the examples in *Learning ASP.NET* at:

> *http://www.LibertyAssociates.com*

There, you'll also find access to a book support discussion group that has a section set aside for questions about *Learning ASP.NET*. Before you post a question, however, please check my web site to see if there is a Frequently Asked Questions (FAQ) list or an errata file. If you check these files and still have a question, then please go ahead and post it to the discussion center. The most effective way to get help is to ask a precise question or to create a small program that illustrates your area of concern or confusion, and be sure to mention which edition of the book you have (this is the first edition).

Using Code Examples

This book is here to help you get your job done. In general, you may use the code in this book in your programs and documentation. You do not need to contact us for permission unless you're reproducing a significant portion of the code. For example, writing a program that uses several chunks of code from this book does not require permission. Selling or distributing a CD-ROM of examples from O'Reilly books *does* require permission. Answering a question by citing this book and quoting example code does not require permission. Incorporating a significant amount of example code from this book into your product's documentation *does* require permission.

We appreciate, but do not require, attribution. An attribution usually includes the title, author, publisher, and ISBN. For example: "*Learning ASP.NET 2.0 with AJAX*, by Jesse Liberty, Dan Hurwitz, and Brian MacDonald. Copyright 2007 Jesse Liberty and Dan Hurwitz, 978-0-596-51397-9."

If you feel your use of code examples falls outside fair use or the permission given above, feel free to contact us at *permissions@oreilly.com*.

We'd Like to Hear from You

Please address comments and questions concerning this book to the publisher:

O'Reilly Media, Inc.
1005 Gravenstein Highway North
Sebastopol, CA 95472
800-998-9938 (in the United States or Canada)
707-829-0515 (international or local)
707-829-0104 (fax)

We have a web page for this book, where we list errata, examples, and any additional information. You can access this page at:

http://www.oreilly.com/catalog/9780596513979

To comment or ask technical questions about this book, send email to:

bookquestions@oreilly.com

For more information about our books, conferences, Resource Centers, and the O'Reilly Network, see the web site:

http://www.oreilly.com

Visit the O'Reilly .NET DevCenter:

http://www.oreillynet.com/dotnet

Safari® Books Online

 When you see a Safari® Books Online icon on the cover of your favorite technology book, that means the book is available online through the O'Reilly Network Safari Bookshelf.

Safari offers a solution that's better than e-books. It's a virtual library that lets you easily search thousands of top tech books, cut and paste code samples, download chapters, and find quick answers when you need the most accurate, current information. Try it free at *http://safari.oreilly.com*.

Acknowledgments

From Jesse Liberty

I am particularly grateful to John Osborn who has shepherded all my work through O'Reilly as well as the editors and production folk at O'Reilly who (as always) made this book so much more than what we originally created.

From Dan Hurwitz

In addition to the people mentioned by Jesse, as always I especially want to thank my wife for being so supportive of this project. It sounds trite and repetitious, but it would not be possible without her help.

From Brian MacDonald

My thanks, first and foremost, go to Jesse and Dan for inviting me to be a part of this project. My deepest appreciation goes to John Osborn for getting me involved with O'Reilly in the first place, many years ago now. Thanks as well to Dan Maharry for his technical feedback, especially on the exercises. Finally, thanks to my wife, Carole, who provided technical as well as emotional support, and to my son, Alex. You both put up with a lot of my absences while I worked on this book, and I thank you for it.

CHAPTER 1

Getting Started

Learning ASP.NET 2.0 with Ajax will teach you everything you need to know to build professional quality web applications using Microsoft's latest technology, including ASP.NET 2.0 and AJAX. ASP.NET is Microsoft's tool for creating dynamic, interactive web pages and applications. Using plain vanilla HTML, you can make a web page that has some great content, but it's *static*. The content doesn't change, no matter what the user does. You can even use Cascading Style Sheets (CSS) to make it the most visually impressive thing on the Web, but if what you really need is for users to be able to leave comments, or browse your inventory, or buy things from you, then HTML alone won't get it done.

That's where ASP.NET 2.0 comes in. Within these chapters, you'll find out how to do all the great tricks that you see on the most popular commercial web sites. Order forms? We've got that. Interact with a database? You'll do that too. Dynamic navigation tools? It's in here. Personalized appearance that the user can customize? No problem.

The best part is, you'll do it all with minimal coding. You can make ASP.NET pages in your favorite text editor if you want, but that's a bit like using a hammer and chisel to write the Great American Novel. If you use Visual Studio 2005, or its free counterpart, Visual Web Developer, adding features to your page is as simple as dragging and dropping. The tools generate most of the code for you. If you're an old-school type who cringes at the idea of letting someone else write your code, it's all still there, and you can tweak it to your heart's content. Consider this, though: would you rather spend your time writing the code for another radio button list, or figuring out what to do with the data that you gather using it? In short, the tools do the tedious chores for you, so you can get to the good stuff.

On top of all this, you can enhance your ASP.NET 2.0 site with AJAX, which is more than just résumé enhancement; it's a genuine improvement in the user experience. When a user is browsing your product catalog, and she clicks on one of your thumbnail images to view the product's details in another panel, she simply expects it to *work instantly*. She doesn't want to wait while the page contacts your server, reloads, and then redraws itself with the new information. With AJAX, she won't see any of that. The update is seamless, and the user never has to slow down. You'll see AJAX tools used throughout this book. In fact, Chapter 3 is dedicated solely to just that topic, so you can use AJAX with everything else we'll show you.

One of the wonderful characteristics of the tools (Visual Web Developer or Visual Studio) and the technology you'll be using (ASP.NET and ASP.NET AJAX) is that you'll be able to create your applications with drag and drop programming and just a little bit of hand coding to handle "events" (such as what happens when the user clicks a button). Not *toy* applications—meaningful business applications.

By the time you've finished this book, you'll be able to do all of that and more, and you'll learn about it by doing it yourself—hands-on. If you don't have Visual Studio or Visual Web Developer installed yet, turn to Appendix A now for detailed instructions on how to install and set it up. Once you've done that, it's time to dive right in and create your first application, "Hello World."

Hello World

One of the most difficult problems in beginning any programming technology is the "bootstrap" problem. That is, writing your first program requires using techniques that you haven't learned yet, but learning those techniques in a vacuum is not only boring, but to some degree pointless because there's no context, and thus no way to integrate that which you learned.

The traditional solution to this dilemma is to create the canonical "Hello World" program. Our Hello World web site will allow us to demonstrate many useful aspects of ASP.NET without overwhelming you with detail. We promise we will explain every aspect of this web site in detail, as we go along.

 According to Wikipedia (*http://en.wikipedia.org/wiki/Hello_World*), the tradition of a Hello World program dates back to a 1974 Bell Laboratories memorandum by Brian Kernighan.

This introductory web site will have only a Button and a Label control. Initially the Label will display the text "Label." When the user clicks the Button, the Label text becomes "Hello World." Very cool, eh? You can see the finished product in Figure 1-1, after the user clicked the button.

Creating a New Web Site

To get started, open the Integrated Development Environment (IDE), which for these purposes is either Visual Web Developer or Visual Studio. (Throughout this book, we will use the acronym IDE for both, specifically using VS or VWD only where they are different.)

Figure 1-1. This is what the HelloWorld web site will look like after the user clicks the Button.

To create a new web site, click on the menu item File → New Web Site..., or alternatively, use the Create: Web Site... link on the Start Page. Either way, you should see the New Web Site dialog, like the one shown in Figure 1-2.

In this book, we will be using Visual Basic as our default language, although it is the profound belief of the authors that Visual Basic and C# are really a single language, just with slightly different syntax.

We will be showing many of our screen shots from Visual Web Developer, because it is freely available from Microsoft, however, anything that can be done in Visual Web developer can also be done in Visual Studio.

Take another look at Figure 1-2, and we'll examine it in some detail. In the upper part of the window, you are offered various Visual Studio templates (though yours may vary). Select the ASP.NET Web Site template, because that is the kind of site that you are going to create (shown circled in this figure).

In the Location drop-down box at the bottom of the dialog box, select *File System* (the other options are HTTP or FTP; we'll explain this selection later in the next section).

The Location drop-down in Figure 1-2 covers up another drop-down in which we have set the language to Visual Basic (rather than to Visual C# or Visual J#). Finally, you need to specify where on your disk you would like this web site to be placed—in this case, in the *LearnASP* directory on the C drive.

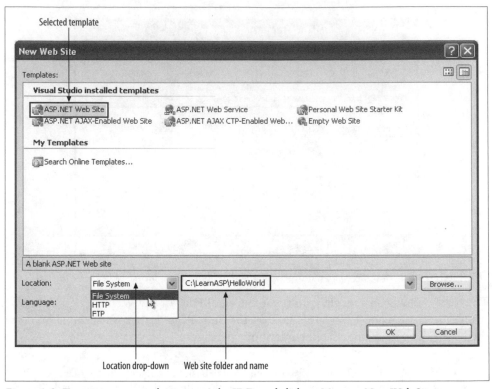

Figure 1-2. To create a new web site, open the IDE, and click on Menu → New Web Site to open the New Web Site dialog box. The Templates and My Templates panels show you the types of sites supported by your version of Visual Studio.

The name of the new web site will be *HelloWorld* (with no space character). The site will be fully contained in a subdirectory named *HelloWorld* within the directory *LearningASP*.

Click OK; the IDE will create the directory for you, put the needed default files for your site within it, and then open the IDE.

You can confirm that the files are in the right place by navigating to the specified directory using Windows Explorer, as shown in Figure 1-3. When you work on your site, however, you'll most likely access these files through the Solution Explorer window located on the right-hand side of the IDE window.

The Location field in Figure 1-2 is really comprised of two parts: a drop-down with three possible values, and a text box for the folder name and path. The drop-down choices are File System, HTTP, and FTP.

File System is the default choice for new web sites and the only choice we'll be using in this book. It creates a new web site folder somewhere on the physical file system, either on your local machine or your network. One important feature of ASP.NET is

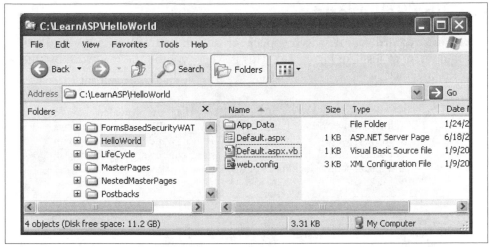

Figure 1-3. *Visual Studio creates a new web site directory for you, complete with the default files it requires.*

that an entire web site can be contained within a directory. This is extremely convenient not only for deploying your web site to a web server, but as a side benefit, it allows us to easily place samples from this book onto our web site for you to download and try on your local machine.

When you create your web site, you can use the Browse button (lower-right corner in Figure 1-2), and its associated drop-down, to browse the file system as you would with Windows Explorer, and select any desired folder as the "home" for your new web site folder.

When you run your file system-based web application from within the IDE, the development environment runs the application using its own internal web server, rather than a web server program such as Microsoft Internet Information Server (IIS). This means that you can easily develop web sites on your machine without the necessity of installing IIS.

The alternatives to hosting your site in your file system are named HTTP and FTP. HTTP indicates that IIS will be serving the pages, and requires that the web application be located in an IIS virtual directory. If you choose HTTP, the IDE will automatically create this virtual directory for you and the web site will be served by IIS.

FTP allows you to develop your web site on a remote location accessible via the FTP protocol. You will be presented with an FTP Log On dialog box with a checkbox to allow Anonymous Log in, and textboxes for login user name and password, if necessary.

Creating HelloWorld

After you've named your new web application and chosen a place to host it, the IDE will look more or less like Figure 1-4. This is where you do the real work of putting your site together.

 Which exact windows you see and how they are presented may be influenced by options you've chosen. In your IDE, you can always open new windows from either the View or Window menu and you can undock, move, and redock the various windows using the mouse and the on-screen docking indicators.

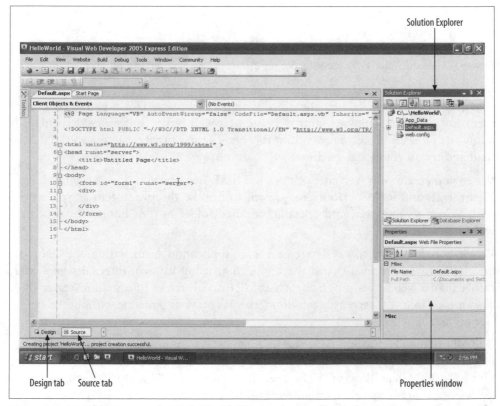

Figure 1-4. Initial IDE screen for HelloWorld. This is what you'll see after you've named your web site, chosen a language, and created a directory for it.

In Figure 1-4, you see the main window, which shows the page markup: HTML plus ASP.NET declarations and controls. Also note the two tabs at the bottom of this pane, labeled Design and Source. You'll be using these two tabs a lot as you create your pages.

To start, click on the Design tab. When you click this tab, the middle window of your IDE becomes the *design surface*. On the design surface, you can drag and drop items such as buttons, text fields, labels, and so on from the Toolbox, which you'll see in a moment, where they automatically become part of your application. Each item that you can drag onto the design surface is called a *control*. You'll be reading more about controls in Chapter 2 and throughout this book.

Next, click on the Source tab. This view allows you to see the same controls, but displayed as HTML and ASP.NET markup. When you drag a control onto the design surface, the IDE automatically adds the appropriate markup to make that control part of the page. You can view and adjust that markup from the Source tab and even drag controls from the Toolbox directly onto the Source view. As you switch back and forth between Source and Design view, they will remain consistent with one another as they are two views of the same information.

 Many working programmers and even Microsoft itself will refer to markup as source code. Other programmers draw a distinction between markup (HTML, ASP.NET controls, XML, etc.) on the one hand, and source code (C#, VB.NET, JavaScript) on the other. This can, and does cause confusion, and all ASP.NET programmers learn to differentiate as best we can by context. The Source tab shows markup or HTML source code. The "code-behind" page, discussed below, shows C# or VB.NET source code. Not a perfect naming system, but there you have it. In practice, markup and ASP.NET source code have become synonymous.

Again, referring to Figure 1-4, the window at the right edge of the screen displays the Solution Explorer, which is used for navigating and working with the files that make up your web site. The Database Explorer tab (at the bottom of the Solution Explorer window) allows you to create and work with data connections.

Below the Solution Explorer window is the Properties window, which displays the *properties* for the currently selected object on the page. Properties are settings that are specific to each control, so the content of this window changes, depending on what control you've clicked on. You'll be reading a lot more about properties in the discussion on controls in Chapter 2.

On the left edge of the Main window, click on the Toolbox tab to display the Toolbox. Inside the Toolbox, you'll find a number of expandable categories that contain just about every control you'd want to use on your web page. If the Toolbox tab is not visible, click on View → Toolbox to display it. Initially it will be displayed in expanded view, as shown on the left side of Figure 1-5. Click on the + or − icon to collapse or expand each section.

Figure 1-5. The Toolbox provides quick access to just about everything you'd want to put on your page. Here, the Toolbox is shown expanded on the left, and collapsed on the right.

You can "pin" any of the auxiliary windows in place, keeping them visible, by clicking the pushpin icon in the title bar of the window. When "unpinned," they will auto-hide, showing only their tab. Clicking on a tab while unpinned will make them temporarily visible.

Making the HelloWorld Web Site Interactive

You've created your web page, but it doesn't do much of anything right now. To make your page come alive, you need to add some *controls* to it. Everything that you'll find in the Toolbox is a control, and you can add controls to your pages simply by dragging them onto either the design surface or into the Source view.

For this first program, you'll add a button and a label to your page, making it look like what you saw back in Figure 1-1. Follow these steps:

1. Click the Design tab at the bottom of the main window to ensure that you are in Design view.

2. If the Toolbox window is not already pinned in place, click on the pushpin icon in its title bar to pin it in place.

3. If the Standard category of the Toolbox is not expanded, click on the plus symbol and expand it. You should be able to see a number of basic controls listed in the Toolbox, such as "Label," "TextBox," and "Button."

4. Click on a Button control in the Toolbox, and drag it onto the design surface.

5. Click on a Label control in the Toolbox, and drag that onto the design surface next to the button.

At this point, your IDE should appear similar to Figure 1-6.

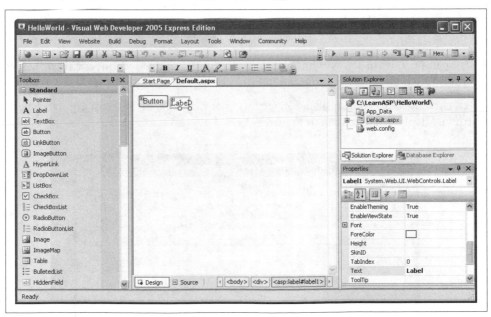

Figure 1-6. After you've added the button and label to your HelloWorld application, the design view should look like this.

This is a good time to stop and run your program, to see what it does so far. There are three ways to do so:

- Click on the menu item Debug → Start Debugging
- Press the F5 keyboard shortcut
- Click on the Start Debugging icon (▶) on the toolbar

Because this is the first time you've run the program, the IDE will detect that your *web.config* file is not set to allow debugging and will offer to make that adjustment for you, as shown in Figure 1-7.

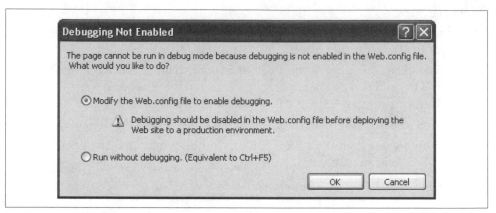

Figure 1-7. You'll see this Debugging Not Enabled dialog box the first time you run your application. Just select the first option and click OK to keep going.

It's not important to know what a *web.config* file is right now, but we'll explain it later. For now, click OK to allow the IDE to modify the configuration file.

After clicking OK, your application begins, your default browser opens, and your button is displayed, as shown in Figure 1-8.

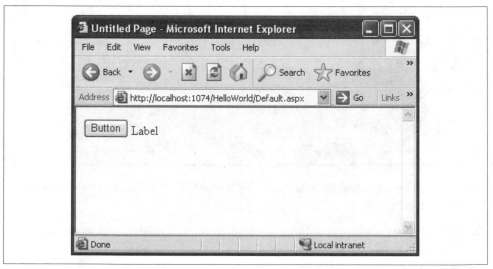

Figure 1-8. This is what HelloWorld looks like in the browser before you do any coding. The button doesn't do anything yet, though.

Click the button. Unfortunately, nothing happens. In the status bar of the browser, you may see evidence that the page is sent back to the server—this is called a *post back*, which we'll describe in Chapter 2. For now, close the browser to end the application; then return to the Design view in the IDE.

All web applications are "event-driven," meaning that for anything to happen—for any of your controls to take any action in the page—an *event* must *fire*. Then, behind the scenes, a block of code called an *event handler* is *called* to handle that event. All of this firing of events and calling event handlers is automatically wired in by ASP.NET, and is far easier to set up than it is to describe, so *don't panic!*

Not surprisingly, all buttons have a built-in event called Click. The Click event is automatically fired whenever the user clicks a button. At the moment, when you click the button on your web page, the event is fired, but there's no event handler yet, so nothing happens.

Creating the event handler for the Click event is easy. In Design view, double-click the button control. This instructs the IDE to create an event handler and name it. The IDE will name your event handler as follows: the ID of the control, followed by an underscore, followed by the name of the event. If you do not explicitly name the ID for this button (we'll discuss naming events and event handlers later), the IDE will apply the default ID of Button1. Thus, the name of the event handler will be set to Button1_Click.

The IDE then displays the *code-behind* page and an event handler stub for you to complete. Here you can add your own custom code to specify the operations you want the handler to perform when it's called.

Give it a try. Switch to Design view and double-click on the button. The code-behind file containing your newly created event handler will open, as shown in Figure 1-9.

Because the IDE gave your button a default name of Button1, the click event handler is named Button1_Click by default. Later you'll see how to name your own buttons, and if you wish, name your own event handlers.

In this event handler, whenever the user clicks the button, you want to set the Text property of the Label control, which the IDE named Label1, to the phrase "Hello World." To do that, you need to assign that string of letters to the Text property of the Label. The event handler for Button1_Click appears as shown in Example 1-1.

Example 1-1. The Button1_Click event handler in HelloWorld, before you change it

```
Protected Sub Button1_Click( _
      ByVal sender As Object, _
      ByVal e As System.EventArgs) _
      Handles Button1.Click
End Sub
```

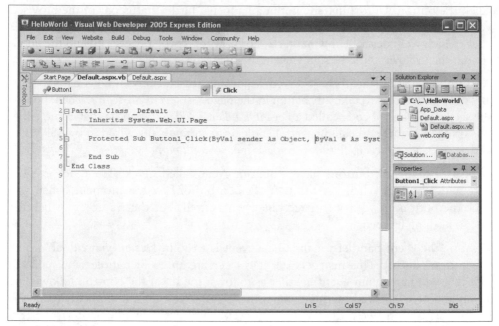

Figure 1-9. When you double-click the button in HelloWorld, you'll be taken to the code-behind page, where you can modify the event handler yourself.

 Please note that in this listing, and in other listings throughout this book, we've reformatted the code to fit the width of the printed page. In Visual Basic, the line continuation character is the underscore (as seen at the end of the first three lines, used here and elsewhere to make legal VB code). Your IDE, or you, may place many of these commands on a single line without the continuation character(s).

To assign the text string to the label, click inside the event handler, and then type the following code:

CODE

```
Label1.Text = "Hello World"
```

When you're done, the event handler should look like Example 1-2.

Example 1-2. The Button1_Click event handler, after your addition

```
Protected Sub Button1_Click( _
      ByVal sender As Object, _
      ByVal e As System.EventArgs) _
      Handles Button1.Click
          Label1.Text = "Hello World"
End Sub
```

After you've added the code to your event handler, run the program again. When the page opens in your browser, click the button. Your event handler is working now, so you should see the text label change to "Hello World," as displayed back in Figure 1-1.

What has happened is that when you click the button, the page is sent back to the server, where your event handler is evaluated, and the string "Hello World" is assigned to the Text property of the Label control. A new page was created by the server and sent back down the "wire" to the browser as pure HTML, and then displayed on your screen. Close your browser to stop the application and return to the IDE.

What You Just Did

When you follow step-by-step instructions as if following a recipe, it's easy to lose sight of what you've done. Here's a quick review:

- You created a new web site on your file system.
- You dragged a Button and a Label into the design surface.
- You double clicked on the Button to create an event handler.
- In the event handler, you assigned "Hello World" to The Text property for the Label control.
- You ran your application and clicked on the Button, causing the page to be sent back to the server where the event handler code was evaluated. The text "Hello World" was assigned to the Label and the page was sent back to the browser.

Congratulations! You've just built your first bona fide web page—and it's interactive, too. Pretty easy, isn't it? You've seen how to use the IDE, you've worked in Design view and in the code-behind file, and most important, you saw how to create a page that actually responds to user input.

Summary

- ASP.NET 2.0 lets you create interactive web pages and applications. With dynamic pages, you can interact with your users and create a richer experience for them.
- Visual Studio 2005, or the free Visual Web Developer, supplies the tools that make creating a web page as easy as dragging and dropping, minimizing the code you need to manually write.
- AJAX is a set of tools that you can use to make the user's experience more seamless, by reducing the number of page flickers caused by the entire page posting back.

- You can create a new web site, or open an existing one from the Start Page in Visual Web Developer or Visual Studio.

- In ASP.NET, you can store your entire web site within a single directory, which in this book will always be on your local hard drive, but you can also store them at a remote location and serve them using IIS.

- The main window of the IDE has two views: Design and Source. Design view allows you to see the visual design of your web page; Source view shows the HTML and ASP.NET markup instead. You can switch between the two views on the fly.

- The items that you add to your web page are called controls. Controls are stored in the Toolbox, which by default appears on the left side of the IDE. You add controls to the page simply by dragging them from the Toolbox onto the appropriate spot on the page, in either Design view or Source view.

- The Solution Explorer, located on the right side of the IDE, displays the files in your web site. Below the Solution Explorer is the Properties window, which lets you adjust the properties of any control you select. On a separate tab is the Database Explorer for access to the databases and servers that support your web site.

- You can run your application by clicking Debug → Start Debugging from the menu, pressing F5, or clicking the Start Debugging button.

- Web applications are event-driven, meaning that the controls raise events, which are handled by code blocks called event handlers.

- When you double-click on a control, you're automatically taken to the code-behind file, where the IDE will create a handler for the control's default event.

- The code for the server controls resides in another file called the code-behind file.

- The user interface of your page is made up of controls, such as buttons, text fields, and radio buttons, although many controls are more complex. HTML controls are available to any HTML page. ASP.NET server controls include more powerful controls provided by Microsoft, in addition to server versions of the HTML controls. .NET AJAX server controls resemble ASP.NET server controls, but are implemented with JavaScript, and run on the browser, not the server. User controls and custom controls are created by developers.

You've come a long way in just one chapter. Sure, "Hello World" is a trivial page, as web pages go, but it's interactive, which is the point of the book. You can close out the chapter with some quiz questions to see how much you've learned, and then a simple exercise to let you practice your skills. Even though you've come this far, you've just scratched the surface of what's available to you in ASP.NET. Just glancing at the Toolbox shows you that there are many more controls than you've used in this chapter. In Chapter 2, we'll show you how to use some of them, and you'll build an order form to see how they all work together.

Quiz

1. How do you create a new web site in the IDE?
2. What are the two views of your page that you can use in the IDE?
3. What's the name for the settings that are specific to each control?
4. Where in the IDE will you find the controls that you can place on your page?
5. How do you run your application?
6. What event is raised when you click on the Button control?
7. Where is the code for the event handler located?
8. What's one way to access the default event handler's code?
9. What property of the Label control do you use to set its content?
10. Every ASP.NET web site has at least one web page. What is the extension for the file that contains this page?

Exercises

Exercise 1-1. This is your first exercise, so we'll take it easy on you—you'll make some changes to *HelloWorld*. Open the example again. Recall there are a few ways to do this:

- Select File → Open Web Site.
- Click the Start Page tab at the top of the main window to display the Start Page, and click the Open Web Site link, or select it from the Recent Projects list, if it's there (and it should be, if you've just finished this chapter).

With the file open, select the code-behind file, either from the tab at the top of the window, or in Solution Explorer. Go to the Click event handler, and change the "Hello World" text to a message of support for your favorite sports team (or band, or movie, or whatever you like).

Now switch back to the *.aspx* file. Select the label control, and check out the Properties window. There's more here than just setting the text, as you've seen. Go to the Appearance section of the Properties, and play around with them to your liking. Click the + sign next to the Font property, and you'll find lots of options with which you're probably familiar. Try changing the font, the text size, and the color. You can also play with the border of the label too. Note that if you change the Text property here, you're changing the initial text of the label. After you've kicked the tires a bit, run your application to see how it looks. You can see an example in Figure 1-10, although this is the affiliation of only one of the authors.

Figure 1-10. The results of Exercise 1-1, for at least one of the authors. Your page may look different, depending on your sports loyalties.

CHAPTER 2

Building Web Applications

You've built your first web site, and you've gotten your feet wet, which is great. But so far, you've only used two controls: Label and Button. You've seen the Toolbox in the IDE, and it's stuffed with controls just waiting for you to experiment with. That's exactly what you're going to do in this chapter. You'll build a functional order form for a fictional business, even though you won't do anything just yet with the data your form will collect. You'll get to try out many of the basic controls in both Design view and Source view, you'll learn about web site fundamentals and selection controls and their collections of items, and you'll see how to display the results retrieved by one control in another control somewhere else on the page.

Mastering Web Site Fundamentals

The difference between a web *page* that simply displays information and a web *application* that interacts with your user is the application's ability to gather data from the user, process it on the server, and take action accordingly. The core of a web application is the page and its interactive controls. This part of the chapter will introduce the web page and the types of controls that you'll use throughout the remainder of this book, and throughout your ASP.NET programming career. We will also introduce the mindset that will move your applications from being a "brochure" that displays information, into an interactive application delivered over the Web.

The Page

Every ASP.NET web site consists of at least one web page stored in a single file with the extension *.aspx*. There is usually more than one file, as you will see as we go along. The *.aspx* file is called a *content* file. Some developers call it the *markup* file, which makes sense when you remember that HTML stands for HyperText Markup Language.

The contents of the page itself are comprised of "server controls" and "normal" HTML. Server controls are simply controls with code that runs on the server. Normal HTML is sent to the browser "as is." For technical details on how these pages are processed by the web server, see the sidebar below, "How Pages Are Processed on the Server."

How Pages Are Processed on the Server

When a user enters the URL for a page into a browser, the browser requests that page from the web server. If the page being requested is an *.aspx* page, the server processes the page before returning it.

The *.aspx* page serves as a set of instructions to the server on how to create a standard HTML page to return to the browser. If this is the first time that the *.aspx* page has been requested since the web application started, then the ASP.NET runtime compiles, from the page, a Page class that derives from the base System.Web.UI.Page class. The compiled class contains all the control declarations and code that make up the page, including properties, event handlers, and other methods. This compiled class is cached in server memory for faster response on subsequent requests.

In order for an *.aspx* file to be processed by the ASP.NET runtime, it must have a *page directive* as the first line in the file. Directives provide information to the compiler, such as the language in use, the name of the code-behind file, if any, and the name of the Page class. Visual Studio automatically generates the page directive for you when you create a new web page. The page directive for your *HelloWorld* web page (which can be seen in Figure 1-9) looks like the following:

```
<%@ Page Language="VB" AutoEventWireup="false"
    CodeFile="Default.aspx.vb" Inherits="_Default" %>
```

With all this information, the server is able to run all of the server-side code, translate all of the server-side controls into standard HTML and JavaScript, and assemble an HTML page that will be returned to the calling browser. If the page that is returned includes client-side script, that script will be run on the client-side machine, by that browser, when the page is rendered.

The *.aspx* files can also contain *script blocks*, usually written in JavaScript, to be executed on the client. Remember, server-side code is executed on the server; client-side script is executed on the client's machine by the browser.

The normal structure for an ASP.NET with AJAX application is this: the markup (content) file will contain controls. Some of the controls will be server controls. Their code (which will execute on the server) is written in a second file called the *code-behind file*. Other controls are AJAX controls, and their code is sometimes written in script blocks in the markup file, or more commonly, it is buried in *.dll* files provided to you by Microsoft (and thus not visible to you as script code), but which is interpreted by the browser on the client machine.

There are also HTML controls that are passed "as is" to the client machine's browser: such as tables, and
 (the line break tag), and so on.

 ASP.NET also allows you to create so-called HTML-server controls, which are HTML controls with the tag runat="server" but these are not commonly used, and won't appear in this book.

Once again, this book assumes you have a passing familiarity with HTML, but even if you do not, you should find the examples self-explanatory.

If a markup file is named *Welcome.aspx*, its associated code-behind file will be named *Welcome.aspx.vb*, indicating that the code-behind file is written in Visual Basic (*.vb*) (or *Welcome.aspx.cs* if you are writing in C#).

Controls

As you saw in the HelloWorld example, *controls* are the building blocks of the web page's graphical user interface (GUI). Some controls that you are probably familiar with include buttons, checkboxes, and list boxes.

Controls allow a user to indicate a preference, enter data, or make selections. They can also provide support for validation, data manipulation and security, or help to ensure a uniform look and feel to the application.

There are several types of web controls:

HTML controls
> The original controls available to any HTML page, such as input (for entering data), a (anchor), div (for separating and applying format to a section), and more. These all work in ASP.NET exactly as they work in other web pages. HTML controls will be used where appropriate in this book, but will not be discussed in detail. For a good resource on HTML controls, see *HTML & XHTML: The Definitive Guide*, by Chuck Musciano and Bill Kennedy (O'Reilly).

ASP.NET server controls
> Microsoft created the ASP.NET server controls to accomplish two complementary aims. First was to "normalize" the HTML controls so that the programmer would have a more consistent interaction with the control, and second, to add an extensive and rich set of powerful new controls such as calendars, ad rotators, and more.

.NET AJAX server controls
> These new controls look and feel like traditional ASP.NET server controls. However they implement JavaScript that is run by the browser on the client side to greatly enhance the performance of the application. AJAX provides two key benefits to the ASP.NET programmer: client-side functionality and asynchronous updates of data, allowing the page to update a segment of data without page

flicker. That is quite a mouthful and we will cover this in much more detail later in the book.

User controls and custom controls

Controls created by the developer or third parties (that is, not Microsoft). This topic is beyond what we'll cover in this book, but for a full discussion of creating these user-defined controls please see our more advanced text, *Programming ASP.NET*, also published by O'Reilly.

The heart of ASP.NET programming is the ASP.NET server control. With the exception of tables, the use of the vast majority of traditional HTML controls is replaced by their equivalent ASP.NET control both for convenience and flexibility. Thus rather than using a traditional HTML input control, you will use instead an ASP. NET TextBox control. Not only will this allow the TextBox to run server-side code, but it is easier to use, being more intuitive and consistent.

 There is an ASP.NET Table server control, but unless you really need some of its features for a specific reason, the majority of developers use HTML tables most of the time as they are simply easier to use.

ASP.NET AJAX server controls enjoy all the benefits of ASP.NET server controls, such as drag-and-drop operation and a declarative programming model. However, they also include added client-side functionality, helping you to create a smooth and snappy user interface.

In addition to standard form elements, such as text boxes, labels, buttons, and checkboxes, ASP.NET controls include several broad categories that provide rich functionality with very little code. These include:

Validation controls

Often, a given field requires a specific format or range of data to be valid. Many of these validation routines are similar and used in many places (making sure there is an entry), that two entries match (such as when setting a password), that an entry falls within a predetermined range of values, (which can help protect against malicious code injection attacks). Microsoft provides a full range of built-in validation controls. Chapter 5 discusses these controls in detail.

Data source controls

Data binding to a variety of data sources, including Microsoft SQL Server and Access and other relational databases, XML files, and classes implemented in code. Data source controls are covered in Chapter 4.

Data view controls

Various types of lists and tables that can bind to a data source for display and editing. Data view controls are also covered in Chapter 4.

—VB CHEAT SHEET—
Classes

Although we've said that you don't need to know much VB to make ASP.NET pages, you need to know a bit of the vocabulary to understand the background discussion in this section. You may have heard that VB.NET is an *object-oriented* language, which means that everything you make with the language is an *object*—every control, every label, even the page itself is an object. Each object is a specific instance of what's called a *class*, or to put it another way, a class is a general case that defines each object. Using the classic example, if Dog is a class, then your own dog Sparky is an object — he's an *instance* of the Dog class. You can't see or touch Dog, but you can see and touch Sparky. In ASP.NET, you can't put the Label class on your page, but you can create a Label object that's an instance of the Label class, and put it on your page.

So what's the point of the class, then? The class defines the qualities that the object *has* (called *properties*), and the things that the object *does* (called *methods*).

Dog might have properties called color and size, for example. Each object might have different values for each property, but by definition they all must have the property. So Sparky might have a color of brown and a size of large, whereas Frisky has a color of white and a size of small, but they're both still members of Dog. In ASP.NET, a Label control has properties for Text and Font.

Methods, on the other hand, tend to be actions which all objects in the class can perform. If Dog has a method for Bark( ) and Eat( ), then both Sparky and Frisky can bark and eat. The Label control, for example, has methods of ApplyStyle( ) and Focus( ) so you can *call* those methods on any Label control to apply a style to the label, or set the focus to that control.

You *invoke* both properties and methods with what's called *dot notation*. It's pretty simple; you give the object's name, followed by a period, followed by the method or property name you want to use, like this:

CODE ▶
```
sparky.color = white
lblMyLabel.Text = "The text for the label"
lblMyLabel.ApplyStyle(MyStyle)
```

Login & Security controls

Handle the common chores of logging in to a site and maintaining user passwords. Login and Security controls are covered in detail in Chapter 9.

Personalization controls

Allow users to personalize their view of a site, including rearrangement of the page itself. User information can be saved automatically and transparently, and retained from one session to the next. Personalization is also covered in detail in Chapter 9.

Master pages
> Create web sites with a consistent layout and user interface. Master Pages are covered in Chapter 6.

Rich controls
> A subset of ASP.NET controls that implement complex features such as menus, tree views, and wizards.

AJAX controls
> A new set of controls that provide client-side asynchronous and partial-page postbacks, including the `ScriptManager`, `UpdatePanel`, `UpdateProgress`, and `Timer`. AJAX is covered in detail in the next chapter.

AJAX Toolkit Controls
> An expanding set of controls based on AJAX that provide enhanced client-side functionality without the need to write JavaScript, such as watermarks, collapsing panels, and pop ups.

Code-Behind Files

Although you can put your content and your code in a single file, it is strongly discouraged and we will not do so in this book. The preferred method is to put your content (HTML, server controls, and AJAX controls) into a markup file with the extension *.aspx*, and to put your server-side code into a code-behind file with the extension *.aspx.vb*. You saw this separation of content from code-behind in the "Hello World" example in Chapter 1.

Events and Postbacks

In the *HelloWorld* program you created earlier, the page was sent back to the server when you clicked the button. When the page returned to the browser, it was displayed with new text, specifically with the words "Hello World."

As we described in the example, clicking on the button raised the `Click` event. It turns out that many controls have a `Click` event, and each control may also have other events specific to itself. For example, lists typically have an event for when the selected item changes, while text boxes have events for when the text they contain is changed.

The code that responded to the button's `Click` event in *HelloWorld* (the control's *event handler*), was a method of the `Page` class, specifically the page that contained the button. As is often the case, this is more confusing to explain than to see in action. To the user, it simply appeared that clicking the button changed the contents of the page.

What is important to keep in mind however, is that when you click the button, the page is "posted back" to the server. A *postback* is an instruction to the page to return to the server to have event handlers evaluated, then to have the *same* page sent back to the browser after the code in the event handlers is run.

 When you return to the server and a new page is sent to the browser that is not a postback. When you return to the server, processing is done, and the same page is returned to the client, that is a postback.

Not all controls automatically post back every time you click on them. Buttons do, but just changing the selection in a list box, for example, normally does not. (You can, if you want, set a list box to post back every time its selection is changed, as you will see later in this chapter.)

Synchronous and Asynchronous Postbacks

In ASP.NET with AJAX, there are actually two types of postbacks:

Normal

In a normal postback, the entire page is sent back to the server for processing. As just noted, some events do not cause an automatic postback. These events are stored up until a postback occurs, and then they are all handled together. When all of the event handlers have been run, a new HTML page is generated and sent back to the browser.

A normal postback is *synchronous*—nothing else will happen in your application until the server processing is complete and the response is sent back to the browser. The typical time for such an update is less than one second, but this can be dramatically affected by database interactions, network speed and other factors, some of which are beyond your control. In any event, the user will see the page flicker when the browser redraws it.

Partial page, Asynchronous

AJAX allows an asynchronous postback in which the developer designates an area of the page to be updated, while the rest of the page remains unaffected. The user usually perceives no page flicker and may be unaware that processing is happening on the server at all. This can make for a dramatically more responsive application.

 Be careful with event handling in postbacks. A common bug is caused by assuming that event handler A will run before event handler B. The best way to discover such bugs is by putting break points into your event handlers, which we will explore in Chapter 8, and stepping through the postback, seeing which event handlers are called, and in what order.

The next example will demonstrate both a normal postback and an AJAX asynchronous (partial) post-back with two labels: one will update every time the full page updates; the other will update asynchronously.

To start, create a new web site named Postbacks. If necessary, refer back to Figure 1-2, and create the new web site just as you did in the *HelloWorld* example, but this time select the ASP.NET AJAX-Enabled Web Site template instead of ASP.NET Web Site. Be sure to name the web site folder *Postbacks*, to give that name to the site. When the project is open, switch to Design view by clicking on the Design tab at the bottom of the editing surface.

Because you chose the AJAX-Enabled Web Site template, you'll notice that the IDE inserted a `ScriptManager` control onto your page. We'll discuss the `ScriptManager` in detail in Chapter 3, but be assured that it will not be visible when your application is running; its job is to work behind the scenes to coordinate the AJAX controls on the page.

Press the Enter key once to move the cursor below the `ScriptManager` control, then type in the text:

CODE▶
```
Page Loaded at:
```

Drag a `Label` control from the Toolbox onto the design surface next to the text you just typed. Click on the `Label` control to select it, so that the Properties window shows the properties for the Label. You'll know if you've selected the right control because its name will be listed at the top of the Properties window—in this case, `Label1`. Before proceeding, change the ID of the `Label` to something more meaningful. In the Properties window, scroll up or down until you find the (ID) property in the left column. Click in the right column, delete `Label1`, and then type in `lblPageLoad`. Now find the `Width` property in the left column, and change its value to `200px` in the right column.

Drag a button onto the page, to the right of the label. Select the button, and in the Properties window, change the button's ID to `btnPostback` and the `Text` property to `Postback`, in the same way that you changed the label's properties.

Your page should now look pretty much like that shown in Figure 2-1.

In Solution Explorer, click on the plus sign next to *Default.aspx* to expand the list of files. You will see the code-behind file created for you, named *Default.aspx.vb*. Double-click on the code-behind file to display that file in the editing window, as shown in Figure 2-2.

You can also open the code-behind window by right-clicking on the markup window and choosing "View Code."

Naming Conventions

Microsoft's .NET naming guidelines prohibit the use of Hungarian notation for all "public" identifiers. Hungarian notation is the practice of prepending variable names with letters that indicate the type of the identifier (e.g., prepending a variable of type integer with "i"). (You can read about the history of Hungarian notation at *http://en. wikipedia.org/wiki/Hungarian_Notation*. Apropos of nothing, the namesake of Hungarian notation, Charles Simonyi, recently visited the International Space Station as a tourist aboard a Russian space vehicle.)

Because the guidelines do allow the use of Hungarian notation in private member variables, two schools of thought have arisen about using this notation, especially when referring to controls on a page. Many developers will refer to a text box, for example, as txtLastName, while others will name the same text box LastName. The authors of this book represent vociferous advocates of both camps. (In fact, one of the authors is himself a strong advocate on both sides of this issue depending on his mood.) You will, therefore, stumble across both notation in this book. This is not a bug, it is a feature, intentionally included to help you become used to both approaches. Honest.

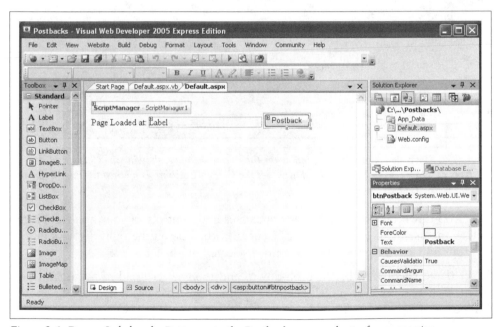

Figure 2-1. Drag a Label and a Button onto the Postbacks page and set a few properties.

The Page Load event and synchronous postback

Every time an ASP.NET page is displayed, the Page's Load event is fired. You'll use that event to display the time that the page was loaded. To do so, you need to create an event handler for the Page Load event.

At the top of the code window are two context-sensitive drop-down controls, as indicated in Figure 2-2.

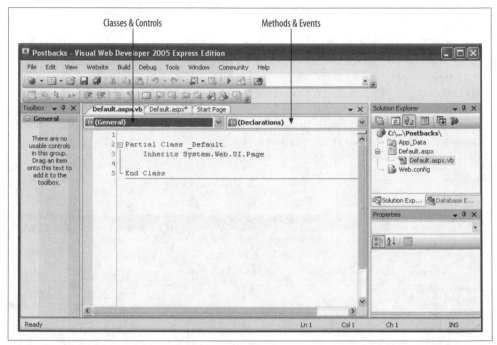

Figure 2-2. The code-behind editing window for the Postbacks page, showing the Classes & Controls and Methods & Events drop-downs. Set the Classes & Controls method to (Page Events), and the Methods & Events drop-down to Load.

The drop-down on the left displays the classes and controls in your application (as well as the useful all-purpose setting [General]); the one on the right displays all the methods and events for the class or control selected on the left.

Select (Page Events) in the left drop-down, and then select Load in the right drop-down. This will bring up a code skeleton for the Page_Load event handler, as shown in Figure 2-3.

Type the highlighted code from Example 2-1 into the Page_Load event handler.

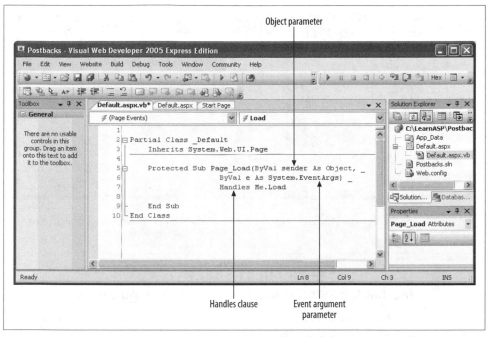

Figure 2-3. After you select Page Events and Load from the code-behind page drop-down, a code skeleton for the Page_Load event handler is inserted automatically.

Example 2-1. Page_Load for Postbacks example

```
Protected Sub Page_Load( _
            ByVal sender As Object, _
            ByVal e As System.EventArgs) _
            Handles Me.Load
    lblPageLoad.Text = DateTime.Now
End Sub
```

Run the application. If it is the first time the web site has been run, the IDE will offer to modify the *web.config* file to enable debugging. Click OK to that. A browser should open with text similar to that shown in Figure 2-4.

Buttons post back to the server even if you do not implement an event handler for their Click event. Click the button a few times. As you can see, each time you click the button, the page is posted back. Take a look at the status bar to see the change to the page being sent back to the "server" (in quotes because in this case the server is your local machine). For each postback, the page is reloaded, triggering a Page_Load event. This in turn causes the Load event handler to run and the Label's text to be updated with the current time.

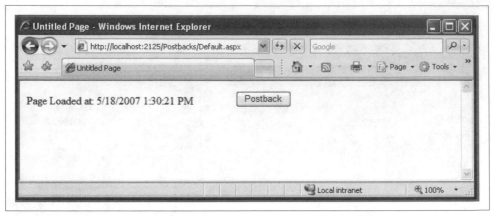

Figure 2-4. When you run the Postback page for the first time, you see a normal postback like this.

—VB CHEAT SHEET—
Methods, Event Handlers, Parameters, Arguments

In Visual Basic.NET, a method is implemented either as a sub (which returns no value) or a function (which returns a value).

Methods may declare values that are "passed into" the method and used as if they were declared as local variables. In VB.NET you must declare the type of the value to be passed in. When the method is called you must pass in a value. The declaration and the value passed in are called either *parameter* or *argument*. Some old-school computer scientists distinguish between these terms, but we will use them interchangeably.

Event handlers are special methods that are designated to run when an event is raised by a control, or by the operating system, or by something else happening in your program that requires a response. By convention, event handlers in ASP.NET always take two arguments. The first, marked as type object, is the object that caused the event, and is named, by convention, sender. The second is marked as type EventArgs or a type that derives from EventArgs. (Derivation is a concept from object oriented programming. It can be summarized as "specialization." When you derive a Cat from Animal, you say that a Cat is an animal, but a special type of animal, with special characteristics or special behaviors.) This second parameter, the EventArgs, is called e.

Event handlers in VB.NET are marked with the event that they handle. Thus, you might mark the method Page_Load with the keywords Handles Load or Handles Me.Load where Me is a keyword that refers to the object itself (in this case, the page) signaling .NET that this method handles the Load event of the page.

If you are adventurous, you can put a breakpoint in the PageLoad event handler. Open the code behind page, navigate to the Page_Load method, and then click on the line where you want the debugger to stop the program execution. Press the F9 key, and then F5 to run the app in debugging mode. You will see this break point stop the application each time the page is about to run. We will cover debugging in detail in Chapter 8, but we couldn't resist showing you that this really works.

You can achieve the same result by clicking the refresh button on your browser, which forces a refresh of the current page, and thus a post back to the server. When you're done, close your browser to stop the application.

Adding asynchronous postbacks

With traditional postback code in place, you'll modify this application to add the ability to make an *asynchronous* postback using AJAX.

Return to *default.aspx* by clicking on it in Solution Explorer, then switch to design view. by clicking the Design tab. Bring up the Toolbox and pin it in place. Expand the AJAX extensions section in the Toolbox. Place the cursor after the button control and press the Enter key to move the cursor down to the next line. Drag an UpdatePanel from the Toolbox onto the design surface.

The AJAX UpdatePanel control is the key to asynchronous updates. Any controls that you place within the UpdatePanel will be updated asynchronously, including both standard ASP.NET and HTML controls. The panel acts as an asynchronous portal back to the server.

To display the time the UpdatePanel was updated, add the following text inside the UpdatePanel:

```
Partial-Page Update at:
```

Scroll back up within the Toolbox to the Standard controls and drag another Label control into the UpdatePanel. Be sure this control is inside the UpdatePanel or this example won't work. Make sure the new label is selected, and update its properties. Change its ID to lblPartialUpdate and set its Width property to 200px.

 You can also add these controls in Source view, either typing the code by hand, or by dragging a control from the Toolbox. You can then set properties in the Properties window or type in attributes directly in the code window.

Drag a Button control into the UpdatePanel. In the Properties Window, change the ID of that Button to btnPartialUpdate, and set the Text property to "Partial Update." The Design view should look something like Figure 2-5.

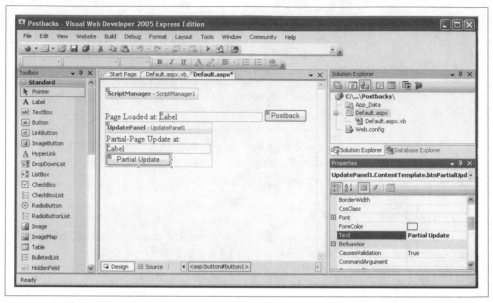

Figure 2-5. After you've added the UpdatePanel and the Partial Postback controls, your Design view should look like this.

Next, you need to add an event handler for btnPartialUpdate's Click event. Double-click on btnPartialUpdate. The default event for a button is its Click event, and when you double-click on a control, the default event handler is created for you. The code behind file will open within the default event handler. As you have already seen, the event handler inherits its name from the control and the event, separated by an underscore, in this case btnPartialUpdate_Click.

Enter the highlighted line of code from Example 2-2 in the click event handler for btnPartialUpdate.

Example 2-2. Click Event Handler for btnPartialUpdate

```
Protected Sub btnPartialUpdate_Click( _
        ByVal sender As Object, _
        ByVal e As System.EventArgs)
    lblPartialUpdate.Text = DateTime.Now
End Sub
```

Once you've made the change, run the updated application. After the page loads, click on the Partial Update button. You will see something similar to Figure 2-6.

Depending on which region your computer is in and how your region options are set, you may see the date and time displayed using a different format.

Figure 2-6. After you click the Partial Update button, the label in your UpdatePanel refreshes, but the label outside the UpdatePanel does not.

Now try clicking each of the buttons and notice how the labels change. When you're done, close the browser.

Note the following results:

- Clicking on Partial Update button updates the label in the UpdatePanel control, but not the label outside the UpdatePanel.
- Clicking on the Postback button updates the label outside the UpdatePanel but not the one inside.
- The UpdatePanel is invisible to the user (though its effects are not).
- We work too late.

What's great about updating just a portion of a page this way is that it not only eliminates "flicker" but your entire application will *seem* faster and more responsive to the end user.

Controls

As you've seen in both the examples so far, when you drag a control from the toolbox onto the design surface, it is generally represented as a visible widget to the user. Some controls, however, are used less for display than for manipulating other objects (for example, database manipulation controls) and these are displayed in a special area at the bottom of the main window.

In any case, every control is identified by a unique ID property. Both Visual Web Developer and Visual Studio will automatically assign an ID to your control as you drag it onto your page. These automatically generated IDs are rarely meaningful, and we suggest that you rename them. For example, while the IDE might name your label "Label2," you will probably find it much more useful to rename that label lblPartialUpdate.

When you click on a control in either Design or Source view, its properties are shown in the Properties window. You can change any property value in the Properties window or directly in Source view, and any changes you make will be reflected in both places immediately.

Organizing the Properties Window

Within the Properties window, you can group properties by category or alphabetically. Figure 2-7 shows the Accessibility, Appearance, and Behavior categories of a button, though there are others. You can click the appropriate buttons in the menu bar to toggle between the Categorized and Alphabetical views. (When organized alphabetically, the ID of the Control is placed, out of order, at the top of the list, for convenience.)

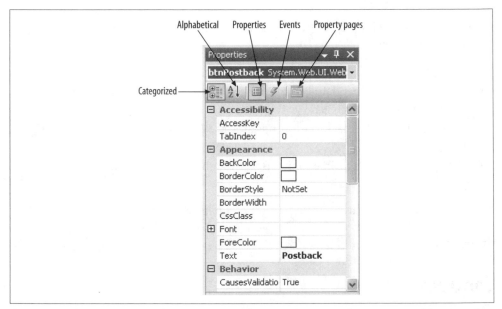

Figure 2-7. The Properties window, as you would expect, shows you the properties of the control you select. You can organize the properties by category, as shown here or alphabetically. You can also view the events associated with the control.

Virtually every control has events associated with it. To view a control's events, click the lightning bolt button. To switch back to properties click the Properties button.

Finding properties with IntelliSense

If you prefer to work in Source view rather than Design view, you can enlist IntelliSense to help you find both the properties and events for any given control. As you press the spacebar, the list of members for the control will be displayed. As you type,

IntelliSense will help you fill in the appropriate property or event, as shown in Figure 2-8.

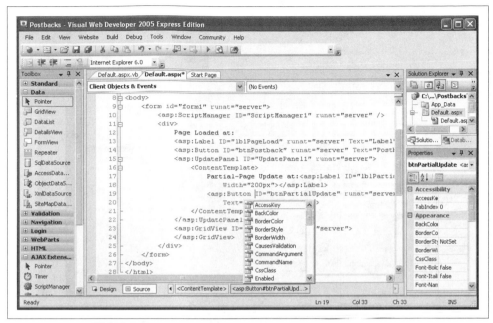

Figure 2-8. Intellisense provides a drop-down as you type, so that you can select the property or event you want to use.

Basic Controls

We could simply review the basic controls in a vacuum, but that's not very interesting. Instead, in this section you'll create a meaningful business application using the ASP.NET and AJAX controls in context. The application will be for a fictitious company called AdventureWorks, a recreational equipment retailer. You may remember the name AdventureWorks from Chapter 1; it's the name of the fictional company used in the sample databases you downloaded and installed there. You won't need the databases now, but you'll see them again in Chapter 4. To begin, create a new web site using the ASP.NET AJAX-Enabled Web Application template (similar to what you did in the previous chapter). Name your new project AdventureWorks.

For this version of the program, you'll use hardcoded data. In later chapters you will add dynamic content with data retrieved from a database.

The first page you're going to build is the order form. The finished page will look something like Figure 2-9, where all the types of controls are labeled. This somewhat contrived web page (see the sidebar "Good Sites Look Good") is intended to demonstrate many of the available ASP.NET controls for various applications.

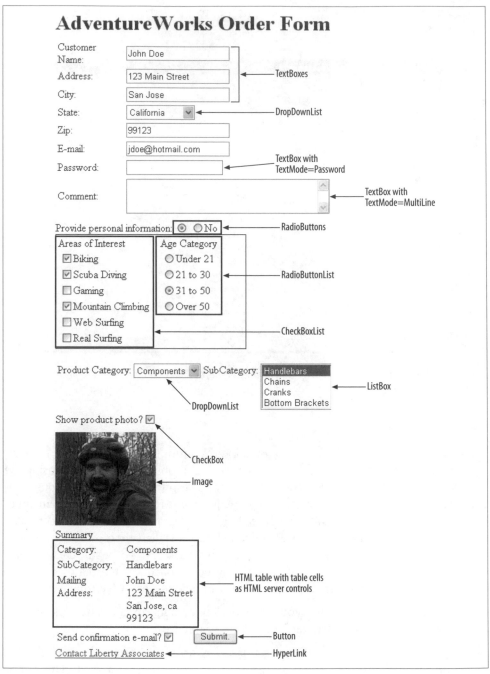

Figure 2-9. This is what the AdventureWorks Order Form in this example will look like when it's finished. It's not the prettiest page, but it uses lots of the controls you'll be using in this book.

In Solution Explorer, rename *default.aspx* to *OrderForm.aspx* by right-clicking on the file name and selecting Rename. The code-behind file is automatically renamed, as well as *almost* all the internal references.

 When you use automatic renaming, be careful about names that are used in text or in page directives (at the top of HTML files)—they will not be renamed for you. Also, the name of the class in the code-behind file will not be updated automatically.

In this example, you'll work in both Design and Source view, moving back and forth depending on which is most convenient for the task at hand.

Open *OrderForm.aspx* and select Source view. Change the text between the <title> tags from Untitled Page to AdventureWorks, and then run the application. At this point, an empty browser will come up with AdventureWorks in the title bar.

That was fun. Now, add some substance to the page, beginning with header text. Close the browser. In Source view, type in the following HTML between the `<div>` tags:

CODE ▶

```
<h1>AdventureWorks Order Form</h1>
```

Notice how Intellisense helps by entering the closing tag for you.

Alternatively, in Design view, you can just type in the text on the design surface and then highlight the text and click on the Block Format drop-down menu in the Formatting toolbar, as shown in Figure 2-10.

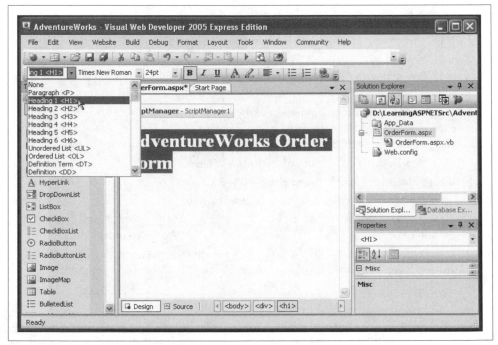

Figure 2-10. You can enter this heading in Source view, or you can enter it in Design view, and apply the formatting with the Block Format drop-down menu.

Creating Tables

To position the controls on your page, you'll need to create a table. If you're comfortable with HTML, you can certainly insert your table row and column tags manually in Source view and receive assistance from IntelliSense as you go. If you prefer, however, both VS and VWD offer an insert table wizard.

To see this at work, switch to Design view (some of the procedures that follow cannot be done in Source view) and position the cursor immediately below the heading you just entered. Click on the Layout → Insert Table menu item to bring up the insert table dialog box and enter, for this example, eight rows and two columns, as shown in Figure 2-11.

Tables, Page Layouts, and the HTML/CSS Debate

To lay out an *.aspx* page with the necessary precision, you have a number of options. The two most common and successful of methods are to use either HTML tables or Cascading Style Sheets (CSS).

Many CSS aficionados believe that HTML should only be used to describe "content," and cascading style sheets should be used to describe layout. It would be their position that HTML tables should be used only to create tabular data, and never as a tool for manipulating the layout of the page. Certainly it is true that when using HTML tables for layout, you will find yourself forced to use "nested tables," that is, tables within tables (within tables, ad infinitum) to get the level of precise control your page might need. It is argued that this is not only inefficient but difficult to maintain.

Whatever the theoretical or practical merits of this argument, few would disagree that the use of HTML tables for layout is a well-established tradition, and is certainly easier to demonstrate than using CSS. In any case the layouts we will be using for our sample applications will be simple enough that we will be satisfied with HTML tables for layout.

ASP.NET provides an ASP.NET Table control, which you can drag onto your form from the Toolbox. We believe it is more inconvenient than it is worth though because it does not size properly in design view and it is generally easier, faster, and less resource-intensive on the web server to use HTML tables.

Figure 2-11 demonstrates how you can use this dialog to set various attributes for the table, although you can also adjust these attributes later in the Source view. Click OK to create the table.

You'll use this table to align all of the prompts in the left column, and the user input in the right column. As is typical with most ASP.NET pages, you'll use HTML to generate the display text for your prompts, and ASP.NET TextBox controls for most of the user input. Figure 2-12 shows the end result.

Type in the text shown in the left column in Figure 2-12, and then add the controls to the right column. For the Customer Name, Address, City, Zip, and E-mail fields, the controls are simple TextBoxes, so you can just drag them from the Toolbox into the appropriate table cells. The Password and Comment fields are special TextBoxes that we'll cover in the next section. The State field is a drop-down list that we'll get to a bit later in this chapter. You can leave those cells empty for the moment. Every ASP.NET control must have a unique ID, and when you drag your text boxes onto the page, the IDE will assign a simple default ID for you. We strongly recommend however, that you rename each text box with a meaningful name to make your code easier to read and maintain. It is far easier to understand code that refers to txtName than code that refers to the same field as TextBox1.

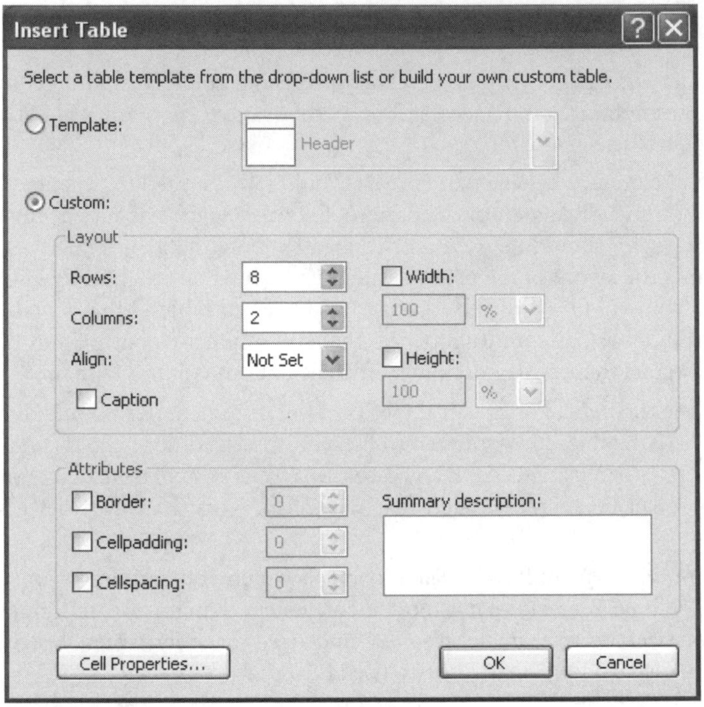

Figure 2-11. For this example, enter 8 rows and 2 columns in the Insert Table dialog box.

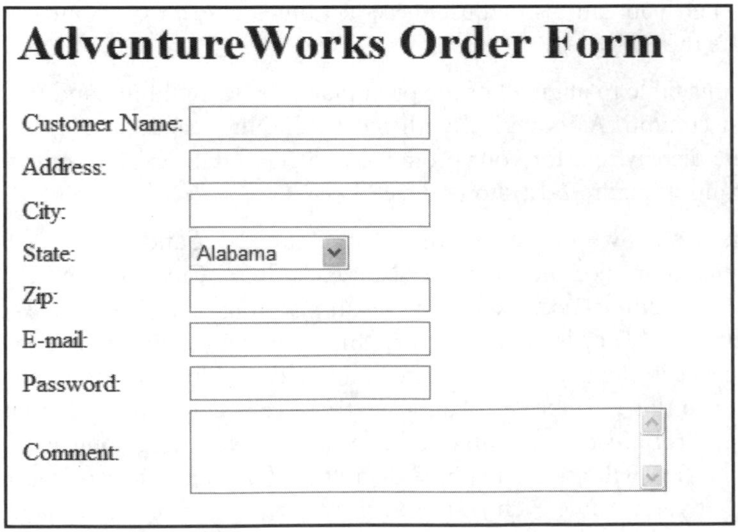

Figure 2-12. You'll use a two-column table to hold the user prompts and input fields in this example.

The TextBox control has a Text property. You can set this property either declaratively in your markup page or programmatically in your code behind page. You can also read from that property programmatically. For example you might write:

```
Dim city as string
City = txtCity.Text
```

Setting Properties

There are three ways to set the properties of your controls: in the markup, in the Properties window, or through a wizard. For example, you can set the font characteristics for text in a text box in the markup or, again, in the Properties window, as shown in Figure 2-13.

Figure 2-13. Use the Font section of the Properties window to set the font characteristics of the TextBoxes in your page.

The TextMode property for text boxes allows you one of three settings: single line, multi-line, or Password. If you choose password, the text that is entered will appear as asterisks. Select the TextBox for the password, and change the TextMode property to Password.

> ASP.NET controls treat the font family, or individual character attributes such as bold, as a property of the TextBox class, while for HTML controls it would be more typical to use styles, set most typically from a style sheet. We cover style sheets in Chapter 6.

Now set the TextMode property on the comment text box to MultiLine. Set the Rows property to 3 to create a three-line comment field. Run your application again to see how these special text fields work.

Selection Controls

ASP.NET offers a number of different controls to create lists from which the user can make a selection. These include: the *ListBox*, the *DropDownList*, *RadioButtons* and *RadioButtonLists*, *CheckBoxes*, and *CheckBoxLists*. All of these controls work more or less the way you'd expect them to.

While not used for selection, ASP.NET has one more kind of list used for organization: the *BulletedList*. BulletedLists have a BulletStyle property, which can be set to numbered, lower- or uppercase alphabetic, lower- or uppercase Roman numeral, disk, circle, square, or a custom image.

Radio button lists and checkbox lists are convenient for creating and grouping more than one radio button or checkbox at a time. Table 2-1 reviews the use of each of these different types of selection controls.

Table 2-1. Summary of selection controls

Control type	Selection	Best for?
CheckBox	Multiple	Short lists
CheckBoxList	Multiple	Short lists
RadioButton	Single	Short lists
RadioButtonList	Single	Short lists
DropDown	Single	Long lists
ListBox	Multiple	Long lists

Just below the table that gathers the user's name and address, you want to add a control to prompt the user to decide whether to provide certain personal information. Since the decision is either yes or no—a mutually exclusive choice—we will use two radio buttons. In Source view, just below the first table, insert the text "Provide personal information:" Following the text, drag two radio buttons onto your Source view. Edit the properties for the two radio buttons so they look like this:

```
<asp:RadioButton ID="rbYes" runat="server" AutoPostBack="True"
    Checked="True" GroupName="grpPersonalInfo"
    Text="Yes"
    ToolTip="Click Yes to gather personal information - no to skip that step" />

<asp:RadioButton ID="rbNo" runat="server" AutoPostBack="True"
    GroupName="grpPersonalInfo"
    Text="No"
    ToolTip="Click Yes to gather personal information - no to skip that step" />
```

Each radio button has a unique ID; the first, rbYes, and the second, rbNo. You'll also notice that they both have the attribute runat="Server". You'll see this attribute on all controls that are evaluated at the server; it's inserted for you automatically.

The text that is displayed next to the RadioButton is assigned in the Text attribute. The attribute AutoPostBack="True" signals that every time this RadioButton is clicked, the page will be sent back to the server for processing. RadioButtons are mutually exclusive within their own grouping, meaning that only one button of the group can be checked at once. The group is established by assigning each radio button a group name, with the GroupName property, in this case grpPersonalInfo.

Finally, each of these buttons is assigned a tool tip. In this case the tool tip for each button is the same, though that need not be true.

 Radio buttons get their name from old-fashioned automobile radios which had mechanical buttons to select the station unlike modern electronic ones that can be used to select more than one station depending on other settings on the radio. These old-fashioned radio buttons physically adjusted the tuner to the desired location. This design was so standardized across all automobiles, that setting and using radio buttons in a car required no more thought than using a water fountain.

For more on this curious idea about self evident design, we highly recommend the seminal work *The Design of Everyday Things* by Donald A. Norman (Basic Books), which along with *Don't Make Me Think* by Steve Krug (New Riders) should be required reading for all web application programmers and designers.

Panels

The personal information that you will be gathering will be clustered together within an ASP.NET Panel control. Panels give you the opportunity to provide a background color if you choose, or to make the panel itself visible or invisible as a whole.

Begin by dragging a Panel control from the Standard section of the Toolbox into your Source view and giving it the ID and properties as shown here:

```
<asp:Panel ID="pnlPersonalInfo" runat="server"
    BorderWidth="1px" Width="300px" BackColor="beige">
```

Selection Controls

Create an HTML table within the panel, like this:

```
<table>
    <tr valign="top">
        <td>
```

The valign property in your first row sets the vertical alignment for all elements within that row to be top-aligned helping ensure that all of the contents will align properly.

Create the first cell by inserting the <td> tag, and type "Areas of Interest." Next, drag a CheckBoxList control into the cell—after the <td> tag and after the text you just added. Switch to Design View; the display should look something like Figure 2-14. Notice the small arrow on the CheckBoxList control; this is a *Smart Tag*. Smart Tags are convenient helpers that provide fast access to essential properties for many controls. Clicking on the arrow opens a small menu.

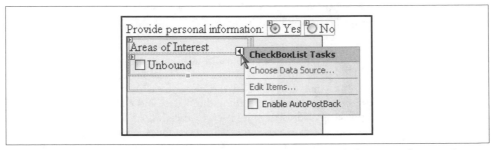

Figure 2-14. The CheckBoxList you just added shows a Smart Tag to help you set the critical properties of the control.

Adding controls with the Item editor

Click the Smart Tag arrow and select the *Edit Items...* option to add items to the CheckBoxList control.

With the exception of CheckBox and RadioButton, all the list controls in Table 2-1 hold a collection of ListItem objects. Each ListItem has a Text property, which is what is displayed to the user, and a Value property, which you can access programmatically.

This allows you to display text to the user—"Scuba Diving," for example—but when the user selects that option, you'll return a different value to your program—"SC" perhaps, or "4," or whatever value will be meaningful in your application.

 The ability to tie a "value" to a "Text property" becomes particularly useful when displaying values retrieved from a database, as we'll see later in this book. You can retrieve, for example, all your vendors, and display them by name, but when one is selected, you can retrieve the vendorID from the value field.

To add items to your list, click on the Smart Tag, and then on Edit Items... to open the ListItem Collection Editor, shown in Figure 2-15. The list is empty when you start, so click the Add button to insert an item. As soon as you add an item, you'll see some familiar-looking properties in the box on the right. Click in the Text field and type "Biking." Notice that you can set the Text and Value properties separately if you choose. If you don't, the Wizard defaults to the same name for both. You can also set the Selected property to True (causing that item to show as checked). For this specific example, add all the items shown in Figure 2-15, set the Text and Value properties to the same value, and leave all the items unselected and enabled.

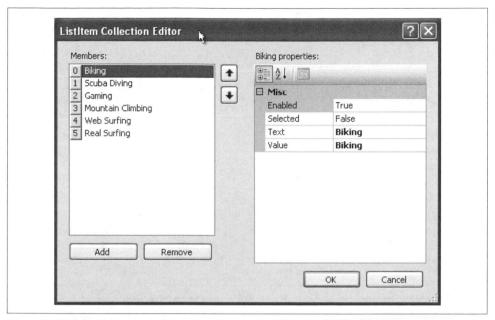

Figure 2-15. When you select "Edit Items" from the Smart Tag, you'll see the ListItem Collection Editor, where you can enter each item in the list.

Once you've added all the items to your list, click OK to close the dialog box. Return to the properties dialog and change the ID property of the CheckBoxList to cblAreas. Set AutoPostBack to True so that each time a checkbox item is checked or unchecked the page will be sent back to the server for processing.

Adding items in Source View

Click Source view to see the markup. Press Ctrl-F to bring up the Find dialog, and enter "pnlPersonalInfo" in the Find what box to locate the Panel control. You should see something like that shown in Figure 2-16.

Notice the CheckBoxList declaration with its end tag. Between the opening and closing tags are a series of ListItem declarations.

Let's go back to constructing our table and add a second set of cell tags (<td> </td>) in the same row as our first cell. Press Enter to create a new line, then use the Tab key to indent. Type in the following HTML to form a heading:

CODE▶
```
Age Category
<br />
```

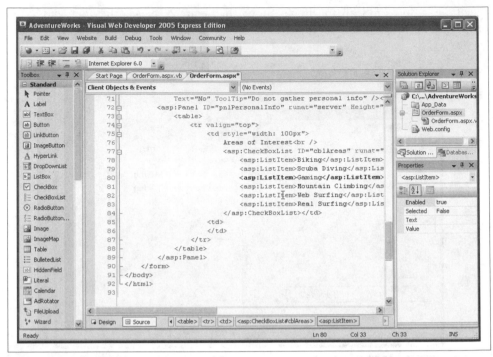

Figure 2-16. The Source view shows the markup for the Panel control, showing the table and the list items you added.

Drag a RadioButtonList control from the Toolbox onto the source view, directly after the `<br />` tag. Set the ID for the new RadioButtonList to rblAge, AutoPostBack to True, and the Width to 150. This time, you'll add ListItems to the radio button list by hand. Between the opening tag and the closing tag of the radio button list, type `<asp:ListItem>`. IntelliSense will help you, as shown in Figure 2-17.

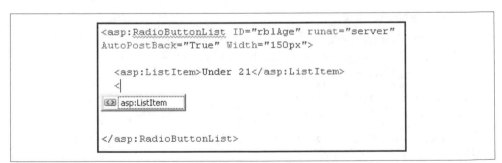

Figure 2-17. Creating A RadioButtonList by hand. Intellisense completes the ListItem entry for you.

You have now added one list item, Under 21, and opened the angle bracket for a second ListItem. IntelliSense knows the only possible control that can go in this location is an ASP.NET ListItem, and so it offers that option to you. You can click on the ListItem offered by IntelliSense to explicitly select it, or simply press tab to accept it.

When you enter the closing angle bracket (>), the IDE will immediately create a closing tag for you:

```
<asp:ListItem></asp:ListItem>
```

You need only put your new value between the tags. Thus you can quickly build the contents of your radio button list. Add the rest of the ListItems now, so the Source view looks like this:

```
<asp:RadioButtonList ID="rblAge" runat="server"
AutoPostBack="True" Width="150px">
    <asp:ListItem>Under 21</asp:ListItem>
    <asp:ListItem>21 to 30</asp:ListItem>
    <asp:ListItem>31 to 50</asp:ListItem>
    <asp:ListItem>Over 50</asp:ListItem>
</asp:RadioButtonList>
```

Now switch back to Design view. You should see something like Figure 2-18.

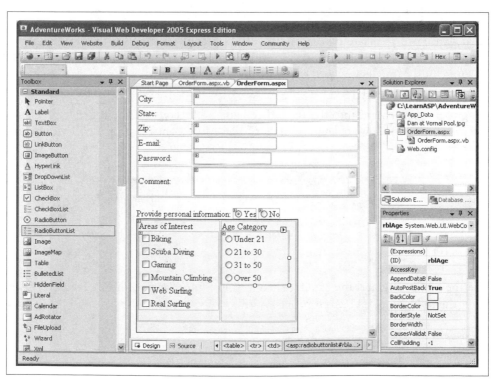

Figure 2-18. Design view with personal information controls in place in a Panel control.

In the first table, you gathered the user's name and address. You'll remember that we planned to use a drop-down list for the state field. It would be convenient to display the full name of the state while setting the corresponding value property to the two letter postal abbreviation.

Go back up to the first table and drag a DropDownList control into the cell for State, and name the control ddlState. At this point, you have two options for setting the text and value property: you can either use the ListItem Collection Editor in Design view, or you can fill in the list items by hand in Source view. Add the following four items to the DropDownList now, so the Source view looks like this:

```
<asp:DropDownList ID="ddlState" runat="server">
    <asp:ListItem Value="AL">Alabama</asp:ListItem>
    <asp:ListItem Value="AK">Alaska</asp:ListItem>
    <asp:ListItem Value="CA">California</asp:ListItem>
    <asp:ListItem Value="CT">Connecticut</asp:ListItem>
```

 In a production environment, you would probably retrieve both the text and the value from columns in a database table.

More Selection Controls

Next, you need to create two more list selection controls, one for the product category and one for the subcategory. Begin by inserting a new layout table just as you did previously, but below pnlPersonalInfo. Give the table one row and four columns. In the first cell, type "Product Category:"; in the third cell, type "SubCategory:".

Drag to a DropDownList into the second cell and a ListBox into the fourth cell. Using the Properties window, change the IDs of these two controls and set the following properties:

Property	DropDownList	ListBox
ID	ddlCategory	lbSubCategory
SelectionMode		Single
ToolTip	Select a category	Select a sub-category
AutoPostBack	True	True

Use the Smart Tag and the ListItem Collection Editor, as you did in Figure 2-15 to enter the following ListItems for each control:

DropDownList	ListBox
Bikes	Brakes
Components	Handlebars
Clothing	Chains

DropDownList	ListBox
Accessories	Cranks
Scuba	Bottom Brackets
Parasailing	Tires
	Wheels
	Seats
	Derailleurs

One final layout tweak: go to Source view, find the HTML `<table>` currently under construction, then add a valign attribute to the row tag, `<tr valign="top">` to top align all the elements in the row to the top of the table.

Let's look at this section of the page in Design view. Figure 2-19 shows how the product table should appear at this point.

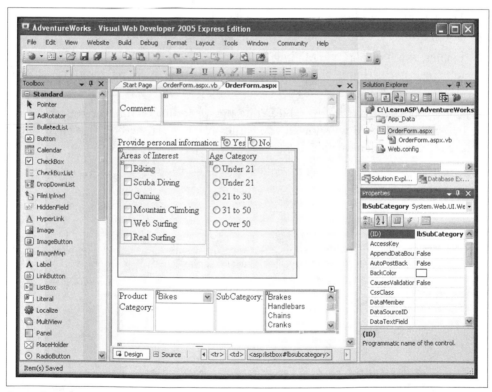

Figure 2-19. Design view of the product category lists after adding the last set of selection controls.

Displaying Text

So far, you've created controls that provide choices to the user, but you haven't seen how your page knows what items the user selected, or how to do anything with them. The answer lies in the properties. The DropDownList control, and all of the other list controls in Table 2-1 (except CheckBox and RadioButton) provide three properties for retrieving selections: SelectedIndex returns the zero-based index of the currently selected item, SelectedItem return the Text property of the currently selected item, and SelectedValue returns the Value property of the currently selected item.

When a user submits this form, you want to provide feedback regarding the selected product category, subcategory, and the mailing address to which the purchase will be sent. A Summary table is the solution.

To demonstrate three different ways of displaying text:

- You'll display the chosen Category in a label.
- You'll display the chosen Subcategory in a read-only text box.
- Finally, you'll display the Mailing Address by modifying the *inner HTML* of the table cell itself. (Inner HTML is the content between the opening and closing tags.)

To begin, you need to create the table. You can type it directly into the source, or use the Insert Table Wizard we showed you earlier. Whichever method you choose, the table should end up looking like this in Source view:

CODE
```
Summary<br />
<table>
   <tr valign="top">
      <td>
         Category:
      </td>
      <td>
          <asp:Label ID="CategoryLabel" runat="server" Text="" />
      </td>
   </tr>
   <tr valign="top">
      <td>
         SubCategory:
      </td>
      <td>
         <asp:TextBox ID="SubCategoryTextBox" runat="server"
         ReadOnly="true" />
      </td>
   </tr>
   <tr valign="top">
      <td >
         Mailing Address:
      </td>
```

```
        <td id="tdAddress" runat="server" style="width:200px">
        </td>
     </tr>
   </table>
```

This is a fairly straightforward HTML table. In the left column, type "Category" in the first row, "SubCategory" in the second, and "Mailing Address" in the third row.

In the right column, place a Label control in the first row with an ID but with its Text property set to an empty string. You'll fill that at run time. In the second row, insert a TextBox control that has its ReadOnly property set to true, so that the user cannot type into the text box (you're using it for display only). The third row's second column is a bit unusual; the <td> itself has both an id and a runat attribute, meaning that you can modify the column itself programmatically.

If you want to populate the Summary table, you'll need to perform a postback to evaluate and process the code (as discussed in Chapter 1). To do that, you'll need a Submit button. In Design view, drag a Button control onto the page just below the Summary table. Change its ID to btnSubmit, and its text to "Submit."

The Submit button's Click event handler will populate the Text of the Label and of the text button, and will set the inner HTML of the third row's second column. Double-click the Submit button from Design view, and you'll be automatically taken to the Click event handler in the code behind file. Add the following code to wire up the functionality:

CODE

```
    Protected Sub btnSubmit_Click( _
        ByVal sender As Object, _
        ByVal e As System.EventArgs) _
        Handles btnSubmit.Click

        CategoryLabel.Text = ddlCategory.SelectedItem.Text

        SubCategoryTextBox.Text = lbSubCategory.SelectedItem.Text

        Dim strMailingAddress As String
        strMailingAddress = txtName.Text + "<br/>" + _
                            txtAddress.Text + "<br/>" + _
                            txtCity.Text + ", " + _
                            ddlState.SelectedValue + " " + _
                            txtZip.Text
        tdAddress.InnerHtml = strMailingAddress
    End Sub
```

Let's take a closer look at this code. The event handler retrieves the selected item from the drop down list for Categories (ddlCategory) and asks it for its Text property, which it then assigns to the Text property of the CategoryLabel:

CODE

```
    CategoryLabel.Text = ddlCategory.SelectedItem.Text
```

Similarly, the text is retrieved from the SelectedItem property of the ListBox that holds the SubCategory, and that text is assigned to the Text property of the read-only TextBox:

CODE

```
    SubCategoryTextBox.Text = lbSubCategory.SelectedItem.Text
```

Finally, and this is a bit tricky, the text of the various address fields are retrieved (including the selected value from the state drop-down), concatenated into a single string, and assigned to the local variable strMailingAddress. That value is then assigned to the InnerHtml property of tdAddress. This is, you'll remember, the ID assigned to the second <td> tag of the third row. The net result is that the cell is filled with the address string.

CODE▶

```
Dim strMailingAddress As String
strMailingAddress = txtName.Text + "<br/>" + _
                    txtAddress.Text + "<br/>" + _
                    txtCity.Text + ", " + _
                    ddlState.SelectedValue + " " + _
                    txtZip.Text
tdAddress.InnerHtml = strMailingAddress
```

—VB CHEAT SHEET—
Variables and Strings

In the first two examples in this section, you simply assigned the Text property of one control to the Text property of another control; that's easy enough. But for the third control, you took the Text properties of several controls, joined them together, and assigned them as a whole.

The trick to this is using a *variable*. Simply put, a variable is like a bucket in your code, which can be used to hold a value. You can retrieve the value later, change it, or replace it with another value. You don't need to worry about what the value is when you're writing your code; you just need to know the name of the variable. In this case, you're using a variable called strMailingAddress to hold the text of the user's address.

In VB, you create a new variable using the Dim statement, followed by the name you want to give the variable:

CODE▶

```
Dim strMailingAddress As String
```

You then need to give the variable a *type*, which tells the compiler what kind of data it can expect to find in the variable. In this example, the variable consists of text, and in VB a sequence of text is called a *string*. You use the keyword As to declare a variable named strMailingAddress, of type String. The important thing to know about strings is that all string values are surrounded by double quotes ("").

One of the useful things about strings is that you can take two strings and put them together into a single, longer string. This is called *concatenation*, and it's very easy to do in VB; you just use the + operator. Look at this bit of code:

CODE▶

```
txtName.Text + "<br/>" + txtAddress.Text + "<br/>"
```

All this does is take the string in txtName.Text, add to it the string that represents a line break in HTML (<br/>), add the string from txtAddress.Text, and then add another line break. All of that gets assigned to the variable strMailingAddress, which in turn gets assigned to the inner HTML of the <td>.

The final result is shown in Figure 2-20. Run your application and try it out. When you enter text in the textboxes and make selections in the category fields, and then click the Submit button, the Summary table updates with the text you've entered.

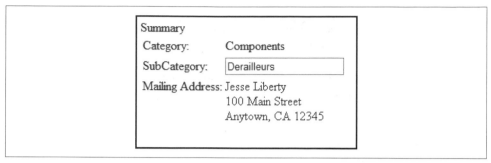

Summary
Category: Components
SubCategory: Derailleurs
Mailing Address: Jesse Liberty
                 100 Main Street
                 Anytown, CA 12345

Figure 2-20. This is what the Summary Table of the page looks like after the user has entered values in the top part of the page.

Images

Images are an important addition to any web site. An image can be a photograph, a drawing, a logo—any graphic.

ASP.NET provides several controls to work with images.

- An Image control is used to display an image. We will demonstrate this momentarily.

- An ImageButton is used to create an image that can be clicked, thus giving it the behavior of a normal button.

- An ImageMap control provides an image with multiple clickable hotspots. Each of the hotspots behaves like a separate hyperlink.

Let's insert an Image control into the form. To do so, insert some room between the layout table and the Summary table by hitting the Return key a few times, and drag on a CheckBox and an Image control. In the properties window, set the CheckBox ID to cbDisplayPhoto and be sure to set AutoPostBack to True, Checked to True and Text to "Show product photo?" Also set the TextAlign property to Left.

Set the ID for the image to imgPhoto and the ImageURL to "Dan at Vernal Pool.jpg."

The Image control has only three essential properties: the ID (so that you can address the control programmatically), the ubiquitous runat="server", and the ImageUrl that identifies the location of the image. Since this image is in the base directory of the application, you do not need a pathname, only the name of the file itself.

In this example, we are using an image of Dan on a bike ride. You can download that image along with the source code for this example from *www.LibertyAssociates.com*, or use any image file you happen to have handy.

In this form, the CheckBox control offers the user the opportunity to make the image visible or not. It has its AutoPostBack property set to true, to force a postback every time the Checked property changes. To make use of this, of course, you must write an event handler for the CheckedChanged event. Double-click the CheckBox to create an event handler for CheckChanged, and add the following highlighted line of code:

CODE▶

```
Protected Sub cbDisplayPhoto_CheckedChanged( _
        ByVal sender As Object, _
        ByVal e As System.EventArgs) _
        Handles cbDisplayPhoto.CheckedChanged
    imgPhoto.Visible = cbDisplayPhoto.Checked
End Sub
```

This event handler changes the Visible property of the Image. When the property is set to false, the image isn't rendered. Go ahead and try it out. You'll see that when you uncheck the box, the page posts back, and the image vanishes.

—VB CHEAT SHEET—
Booleans

The *Boolean* variable is a special type of variable that can have only one of two values: true or false. They're very useful for evaluating simple conditions, and taking an action based on whether the condition is true. In this case, cbDisplayPhoto.Checked is a Boolean—if the box is checked, cbDisplayPhoto.Checked is equal to true; false if the box isn't checked. The imgPhoto.Visible property is also a Boolean, that controls whether the image is displayed. When you set the value of imgPhoto.Visible to be equal to whatever cbDisplayPhoto.Checked is, you link the two controls, so that they're always true or false together. You'll see this technique used a lot in this book.

Links

Hyperlinks provide immediate redirection to another page in the application or to a location elsewhere on the Internet. We'll use a HyperLink control to provide a link to Jesse's home page, serving here very much the same function as an <a> tag would do in HTML.

At the bottom of your form, type "For help contact" and then drag on a HyperLink control. Set the ID to hypContact, its NavigateURL to *http://www.LibertyAssociates. com*, and its text (which will become its inner HTML) to Liberty Associates, Inc. Finally, set the target to "_blank" (we'll explain this property in just a moment).

Switch to Source view, and you'll see that the markup produced looks like this:

```
<br />
For help, contact
<asp:HyperLink ID="hypContact" runat="server"
    NavigateUrl="http://www.LibertyAssociates.com"
    Target="_blank">
    Liberty Associates, Inc.
</asp:HyperLink>
<br />
```

This last property, `Target`, specifies in which window or frame the new page will open. You can specify a window by name, or use one of the special values listed in Table 2-2.

Table 2-2. Special values of the Target attribute

Target value	Description
_blank	Renders the content in a new unnamed window without frames.
_new	Not documented, but behaves the same as _blank.
_parent	Renders the content in the parent window or frameset of the window or frame with the hyperlink. If the child container is a window or top-level frame, it behaves the same as _self.
_self	Renders the content in the current frame or window with focus. This is the default value.
_top	Renders the content in the current full window without frames.

By setting the value of `Target` to `_blank`, clicking on the link instructs the target page to open in a new browser window.

One significant advantage of using this control over an `<a>` tag is the ID and `runat="server"` properties, which allow you to address the control programmatically. For example, you could set the `NavigateUrl` to a different location from within a method, based on conditions established while the program is running.

LinkButtons

Remember that a hyperlink redirects immediately and does not post back first; thus there is no server-side processing possible when the user clicks the link. If you want the *appearance* of a hyperlink but need to perform server-side processing before departing for the new page (e.g., to save data to a database) then use a `LinkButton` control. The `LinkButton` behaves like a `Button` but looks like a `HyperLink`, and the behavior is to post back to the server, do its work and then redirect the user to a new location.

In order to accomplish the redirection to the new page, you'll need to use the `Response.Redirect` method, as shown in the following click event handler:

```
Protected Sub MyLinkButton_Click( _
    ByVal sender As Object, _
    ByVal e As System.EventArgs) _
```

```
            Handles MyLinkButton.Click
                'Save data to db
                Response.Redirect("http://www.LibertyAssociates.com")
        End Sub
```

Source Code

For your convenience (in case you are away from your computer) the complete source code is shown below. The OrderForm markup is shown in Example 2-3. The code behind file is shown directly after in Example 2-4. Note that although this first example is set up to use AJAX, it does not actually contain any AJAX controls except for the ScriptManager that is added by the IDE; we'll add AJAX starting in the next chapter.

Example 2-3. OrderForm.aspx

```
<%@ Page AutoEventWireup="true" CodeFile="OrderForm.aspx.vb" Inherits="_Default"
    Language="VB" %>

<!DOCTYPE html PUBLIC "-//W3C//DTD XHTML 1.1//EN"
"http://www.w3.org/TR/xhtml11/DTD/xhtml11.dtd">
<html xmlns="http://www.w3.org/1999/xhtml">
<head runat="server">
    <title>AdventureWorks</title>
</head>
<body>
    <form id="form1" runat="server">
        <asp:ScriptManager ID="ScriptManager1" runat="server" />
        <div>
            <h1>
                AdventureWorks Order Form
            </h1>
            <table>
                <tr>
                    <td >
                        Customer Name:
                    </td>
                    <td >
                        <asp:TextBox ID="txtName" runat="server"></asp:TextBox>
                    </td>
                </tr>
                <tr>
                    <td >
                        Address:
                    </td>
                    <td >
                        <asp:TextBox ID="txtAddress" runat="server" />
                    </td>
                </tr>
                <tr>
                    <td >
                        City:</td>
```

Example 2-3. OrderForm.aspx (continued)

```
        <td >
           <asp:TextBox ID="txtCity" runat="server"
           Font-Bold="True" Font-Names="Arial Black" />
        </td>
    </tr>
    <tr>
        <td >
           State:</td>
        <td >
           <asp:DropDownList ID="ddlState" runat="server">
              <asp:ListItem Value="AL">Alabama</asp:ListItem>
              <asp:ListItem Value="AK">Alaska</asp:ListItem>
              <asp:ListItem Value="CA">California</asp:ListItem>
              <asp:ListItem Value="CT">Connecticut</asp:ListItem>
              <asp:ListItem Value="FL">Florida</asp:ListItem>
              <asp:ListItem Value="PA">Pennsylvania</asp:ListItem>
              <asp:ListItem Value="TX">Texas</asp:ListItem>
              <asp:ListItem></asp:ListItem>
           </asp:DropDownList></td>
    </tr>
    <tr>
        <td >
           Zip:</td>
        <td style="width: 100px">
           <asp:TextBox ID="txtZip" runat="server"></asp:TextBox></td>
    </tr>
    <tr>
        <td >
           E-mail:
        </td>
        <td >
           <asp:TextBox ID="txtEmail" runat="server"></asp:TextBox>
        </td>
    </tr>
    <tr>
        <td >
           Password:
        </td>
        <td >
           <asp:TextBox ID="txtPassword" runat="server"
              TextMode="Password" />
        </td>
    </tr>
    <tr>
        <td>
           Comment:</td>
        <td >
           <asp:TextBox ID="txtComment" runat="server"
           Rows="3" TextMode="MultiLine" Width="300px" />
        </td>
    </tr>
```

Example 2-3. OrderForm.aspx (continued)

```
      </table>
   </div>
   <br />
   Provide personal information:
   <asp:RadioButton ID="rbYes" runat="server" AutoPostBack="True   "
      Checked="True" GroupName="grpPersonalInfo"
      Text="Yes"
      ToolTip="Click Yes to gather personal information - no to skip that step" />

   <asp:RadioButton ID="rbNo" runat="server" AutoPostBack="True"
      GroupName="grpPersonalInfo"
      Text="No"
    ToolTip="Click Yes to gather personal information - no to skip that step  " />
   <asp:Panel ID="pnlPersonalInfo" runat="server"
          BorderWidth="1px" Width="300px" BackColor="beige">
      <table>
         <tr valign="top">
            <td>
               Areas of Interest<br />
               <asp:CheckBoxList ID="cblAreas"
                  runat="server" AutoPostBack="True" Width="150px">
                  <asp:ListItem>Biking</asp:ListItem>
                  <asp:ListItem>Scuba Diving</asp:ListItem>
                  <asp:ListItem>Gaming</asp:ListItem>
                  <asp:ListItem>Mountain Climbing</asp:ListItem>
                  <asp:ListItem>Web Surfing</asp:ListItem>
                  <asp:ListItem>Real Surfing</asp:ListItem>
               </asp:CheckBoxList></td>
            <td>
               Age Category
               <br />
               <asp:RadioButtonList ID="rblAge" runat="server"
               AutoPostBack="True" Width="150px">
                 <asp:ListItem>Under 21</asp:ListItem>
                  <asp:ListItem>Under 21</asp:ListItem>
                  <asp:ListItem>21 to 30</asp:ListItem>
                  <asp:ListItem>31 to 50</asp:ListItem>
                  <asp:ListItem>Over 50</asp:ListItem>

               </asp:RadioButtonList>
            </td>
         </tr>
      </table>
   </asp:Panel>
   <br />
   <table>
      <tr valign="top">
         <td>
            Product Category:</td>
         <td style="width: 100px">
            <asp:DropDownList ID="ddlCategory" runat="server"
              ToolTip="Select a category">
```

Example 2-3. OrderForm.aspx (continued)

```
                <asp:ListItem>Bikes</asp:ListItem>
                <asp:ListItem>Components</asp:ListItem>
                <asp:ListItem>Clothing</asp:ListItem>
                <asp:ListItem>Accessories</asp:ListItem>
                <asp:ListItem>Scuba</asp:ListItem>
                <asp:ListItem>Parasailing</asp:ListItem>
            </asp:DropDownList></td>
        <td>
            SubCategory:</td>
        <td >
            <asp:ListBox ID="lbSubCategory" runat="server"
            ToolTip="Select a sub-category">
                <asp:ListItem>Brakes</asp:ListItem>
                <asp:ListItem>Handlebars</asp:ListItem>
                <asp:ListItem>Chains</asp:ListItem>
                <asp:ListItem>Cranks</asp:ListItem>
                <asp:ListItem>Bottom Brackets</asp:ListItem>
                <asp:ListItem>Tires</asp:ListItem>
                <asp:ListItem>Wheels</asp:ListItem>
                <asp:ListItem>Seats</asp:ListItem>
                <asp:ListItem>Derailleurs</asp:ListItem>
            </asp:ListBox></td>
    </tr>
</table>
<br />
<asp:CheckBox ID="cbDisplayPhoto"
runat="server"
AutoPostBack="True"
Checked="True"
Text="Show product photo?"
TextAlign="Left" />
<asp:Image ID="imgPhoto"
runat="server"
ImageUrl="Dan at Vernal Pool.jpg" />
<br /><br />

Summary<br />
<table>
    <tr>
        <td style="height: 21px" >
            Category:</td>
        <td>
            <asp:Label ID="CategoryLabel" runat="server" Text="" />
        </td>
    </tr>
    <tr>
        <td >
            SubCategory:</td>
        <td>
            <asp:TextBox ID="SubCategoryTextBox" runat="server"
            ReadOnly="true" />
        </td>
    </tr>
```

Example 2-3. OrderForm.aspx (continued)

```
        <tr valign="top">
           <td style="height: 21px" >
              Mailing Address:</td>
           <td id="tdAddress" runat="server" style="width:100px; height: 21px;">
           </td>

        </tr>
     </table>
     <br />
     <asp:Button ID="btnSubmit" runat="server" Text="Submit" />
     <br />
     <br />
     For help, contact
     <asp:HyperLink
     ID="hypContact"
     runat="server"
     NavigateUrl="http://www.LibertyAssociates.com"
     Target="_blank">
     Liberty Associates, Inc.
     </asp:HyperLink>
     <br />
  </form>
</body>
</html>
```

Example 2-4. OrderForm.aspx.vb

```
Partial Class _Default
    Inherits System.Web.UI.Page

    Protected Sub btnSubmit_Click( _
        ByVal sender As Object, _
        ByVal e As System.EventArgs) _
        Handles btnSubmit.Click

        CategoryLabel.Text = ddlCategory.SelectedItem.Text
        SubCategoryTextBox.Text = lbSubCategory.SelectedItem.Text
        Dim strMailingAddress As String
        strMailingAddress = txtName.Text + "<br/>" + _
                            txtAddress.Text + "<br/>" + _
                            txtCity.Text + ", " + _
                            ddlState.SelectedValue + " " + _
                            txtZip.Text
        tdAddress.InnerHtml = strMailingAddress
    End Sub

    Protected Sub cbDisplayPhoto_CheckedChanged( _
    ByVal sender As Object, _
    ByVal e As System.EventArgs) _
    Handles cbDisplayPhoto.CheckedChanged
        imgPhoto.Visible = cbDisplayPhoto.Checked
    End Sub

End Class
```

Summary

- A *postback* occurs when an event happens on your page that causes the page to return to the server, handle the events, and then send the same page back to the browser. The contents of the page may have changed, but the page object itself is the same.

- With AJAX, postbacks can be either synchronous, in which case the entire page is returned to the server, or asynchronous, in which case only part of the page is returned to the server.

- A *control* is a tool that lets your web page take an action. It could be as simple as displaying some text, or as complicated as interacting with a database. Most controls have some visual representation that the user sees, although not all do.

- Placing a control in your web page is as simple as dragging it from the Toolbox onto your page; the IDE inserts the appropriate markup for you. Controls all come with at least a few properties and methods, which you can use to customize their appearance and behavior, respectively.

- Every control has a unique identifier, its ID property. The IDE assigns a default ID automatically, but you can (and usually should) rename them to be more meaningful.

- Almost every control has associated events, as well as properties. You can access these by clicking the Events button in the Properties window.

- You can create tables by hand in Source view, or you can use the Insert Table Wizard by selecting Layout → Insert Table in Design view.

- The TextBox control is a relatively simply control that allows the user to enter text that you can retrieve later. You can change the TextMode property of a TextBox to create single-line entry fields, multiline fields, or to hide the text for a password field.

- ASP.NET has a number of *selection controls*, including the ListBox, DropDownList, RadioButton, RadioButtonList, CheckBox, and CheckBoxList, which display various options for the user to choose from. You decide which control to use based on its appearance, and whether you want the user to be able to make only one selection from within a list or multiple selections.

- If the AutoPostBack property of a control is set to True, the page is posted back to the server whenever that control's value changes.

- Radio buttons can be assigned to a group, by setting each button's GroupName property. That ensures that only one button in a group can be checked at a time. You can also use a RadioButtonList to accomplish the same thing.

- You can use a Panel control to group other controls together, and also to make the content in the panel visible or invisible as a group.

- Many controls have a Smart Tag, which is a small menu that provides quick access to the most common tasks for that control. In the case of selection controls, the Smart Tag lets you access the ListItem editor.

- The selection controls each contain a collection of ListItem objects, which you use to offer the user choices to select from. The Value property of the ListItem can be different from the Text property that you display to the user, and you can retrieve the selected value for later use. The ListItem Collection Editor makes it easy to add ListItems, but you can also add them by hand in Source view.

- There are three properties that let you retrieve the items that users select from a selection control: SelectedIndex gets the index of the selected item, SelectedItem gets the Text property, and SelectedValue gets the Value property. You can use these values to display the selected item in another control, or to use it in other ways.

- There are several ways to display dynamically generated read-only text in your page: among others, you can set the property of a Label control, you can use a read-only TextBox control, or you can set the inner HTML of an HTML element.

- You use an Image control to display an image or graphic. The ImageButton control displays an image, and acts like a button. An ImageMap control displays an image that has multiple areas that the user can click, each acting like a hyperlink.

- The Visible property of a control determines whether that control is rendered on the page. You can change the value of this property programmatically, and cause the control to appear or disappear with a postback.

- A HyperLink control works like an <a> tag. You can set the NavigateURL property and the text of the hyperlink separately. You can also specify if the link's target will open in a new page or a new frame with the Target property.

You've got a lot of things in your toy box now, and you can do a lot more than just the label and button from *HelloWorld* in Chapter 1. In fact, in this chapter you've just seen the more common controls—there are many others out there that are more specialized, such as the Calendar and AdRotator controls, and that's not even leaving the General tab of the Toolbox. Feel free to experiment with them. Now that you have a base to work from, in the next chapter we'll show you how you can use AJAX to do some clever things with the plain-vanilla controls you just learned about.

Quiz

1. What is a postback?
2. What are the two types of postbacks in AJAX, and what is the difference between them?
3. What property is found on every control?
4. What control would you use to have the user enter a password, but keep the text hidden?
5. What control would you use if you have a list of 20 items, and the user can select as many as they want?
6. How do you make single radio buttons mutually exclusive?
7. What can you use a `Panel` control for?
8. What does the `SelectedItem` property retrieve?
9. How do you include a control on the page, but not render it?
10. What do you do to make the target of a `HyperLink` control open in a new window?

Exercises

Exercise 2-1. Now that you've played with *HelloWorld*, you're going to make a change to the Postbacks example, so you can see how flexible the `UpdatePanel` control is. Open the Postbacks web site, similar to how you opened *HelloWorld* in the previous exercise. In Design view, drag another `UpdatePanel` control inside the first one, after the button. Drag another `Label` control inside the new `UpdatePanel`. In the Properties window, set the label's name to `lblOtherPartialUpdate`, and set its width to `200px`. (Note that you can't give this label the same name as the other label—or any other control on the page—or you'll get an error.) Now add another Button to the new `UpdatePanel`, under the label, set its name to `btnOtherPartialUpdate`, and change the text to "Another partial-page update:".

Now you need the event handler for your new button, so double-click it, and you'll be taken to the code-behind file. You'll see the event handlers for the two existing buttons already there, and the skeleton for the new event handler. Add the following line of code to this new event handler so it will update with the current time, like the other two buttons do:

CODE ►
```
lblOtherPartialUpdate.Text = DateTime.Now
```

Run your application, and click the buttons. If all went well, you'll see that each label updates independently from the others, and that the two buttons in the update panels don't cause any page flicker. Your page should look something like Figure 2-21.

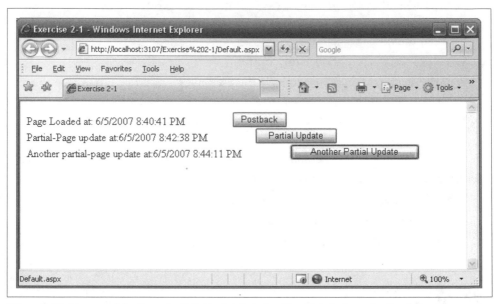

Figure 2-21. Your goal for Exercise 2-1. Each label should update independently of the others.

Exercise 2-2. When you're creating a web page, often knowing which controls to use is a bigger challenge than using the controls properly. That's what you're going to practice here. Imagine a page for a busy ice cream shop that lets you preorder an ice cream cone so it will be ready for you when you get to the counter. The page should have three controls. The first control asks the user to select the type of ice cream from the following list: Vanilla, Chocolate, Strawberry, Mint, Butter Pecan, Coffee, Pistachio, Coconut, Bubble Gum, and Cotton Candy. Only one type of ice cream is allowed per order. The second control asks the user to select the toppings they want: chocolate sprinkles, rainbow sprinkles, hot fudge, caramel, cookie dough, Oreo cookies, pretzel bits, walnuts, coffee beans, or crushed candy bars. It's a gourmet ice cream shop, so customers can have as many toppings as they like. The third control asks users to choose a cone or a dish for either ice cream. Obviously, only one is allowed. Make sure to include a way for users to submit their order.

Exercise 2-3. Now that you've made a working page with different controls, it's time to try retrieving a value. Create a page with a simple TextBox that asks the user to enter his or her password. The password should be disguised as the user types it.

Then, with shocking disregard for security, use a label control to repeat the user's password back to him. The page should look something like Figure 2-22.

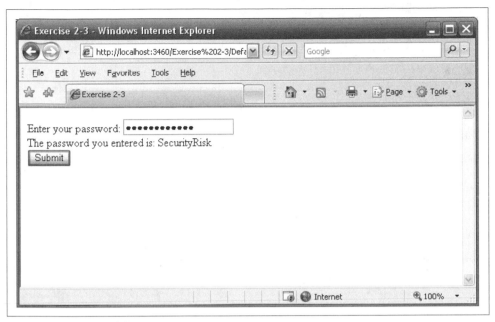

Figure 2-22. Your goal for Exercise 2-3.

Exercise 2-4. Now you're ready to try a slightly more complicated example. Create a drop-down list that presents a number of fine books from your authors; call it ddlBookList. This time, the Text and Value properties of the ListItems in the drop-down should be different, according to the following table:

Text	Value
Programming ASP.NET	00916X
Programming C#	006993
Programming Visual Basic.NET	004385
Learning C# 2005	102097

These values are part of each book's ISBN, and were you a bookstore or a warehouse, you would probably use a database with these numbers to help keep track of the books you have in stock. In this case, though, you'll just show the user what they selected, including the value. Add two labels to show the results, as shown in Figure 2-23.

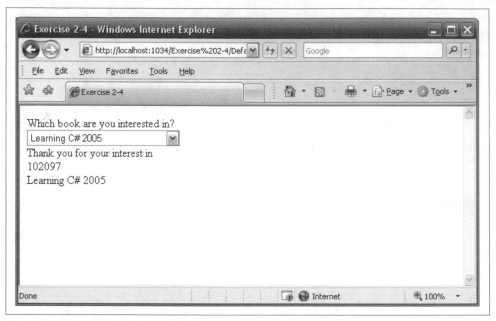

Figure 2-23. Your goal for Exercise 2-4.

CHAPTER 3

Snappier Web Sites with AJAX

AJAX has revolutionized ASP.NET, and from this moment forward most ASP.NET applications will routinely integrate AJAX controls. AJAX moves ASP.NET applications from being 99% server-side code, to offering the option for a great deal of the processing to happen on the user's browser. The net effect is a tremendous increase in both real and perceived performance of ASP.NET applications.

To demonstrate how much more dynamic and responsive AJAX is, you'll rewrite the order form from Chapter 2, applying Ajax techniques. You'll enhance the site by adding a watermark to user entry fields. A watermark is a bit of text that appears in the text field itself, but disappears as soon as the user starts typing. It serves as an elegant prompt to the user. You will also create a pop-up panel to hide controls until the user needs them, and you'll add a collapsible text field to display product information in a very space-efficient manner.

Take a Walk on the Client Side

While server-based web applications have wonderful advantages, they have the obvious disadvantage that any time you want to run any code (or retrieve any data) you must endure the cost of a "round trip" from the browser to the server and back, and the page must be redrawn from scratch. Round trips can be slow (though the Internet is getting faster all the time) and redrawing the page causes a noticeable flicker.

AJAX (which more accurately should be spelled AJX, but that's harder to pronounce) is an acronym for Asynchronous JavaScript and XML—that is, it is a technique for combining well established (some might say *old*) Internet technology in new ways to greatly enhance the performance of web applications. AJAX enabled applications are very hot—they out-perform server-based applications in ways that would make your jaw drop.

Microsoft, realizing this was not a technology they could ignore, and having learned the lesson that they must leave open standards open, chose to take this very good idea and make it much *much* better, without making it proprietary.

AJAX Doesn't Exist

There really isn't any such thing as AJAX. It isn't a product or a standard; it isn't even a technology. It is just a way to refer to a set of existing technologies used together in new ways, to do cool things.

The first use of the term as an acronym for "Asynchronous JavaScript and XML" was by Jesse James Garrett in February 2005. Garrett thought of the term while in the shower (if you must know), when he realized the need for a shorthand term to represent the suite of technologies he was proposing to a client (who, we are assured, was not in the shower with him).

On the other hand, the first use of the term at all, may have been nearly 3000 years earlier, by Homer, who wrote about Ajax the Great (and also Ajax the Lesser) in the Iliad (Book 7, 181–312). Ajax the Great was the tallest and strongest of the Achaeans, and second only to Achilles in skill as a warrior. It isn't clear if the tale of AJAX-The-Technology will be told 3,000 years from today (or even 3,000 days); though we're pretty certain there *is* a parallel between the Trojan War and the desktop wars, but that is for another book.

According to Garret, "AJAX...is really several technologies, each flourishing in its own right, coming together in powerful new ways." AJAX incorporates:

- *Standards-based presentation* using XHTML and CSS; with dynamic display and interaction using the *Document Object Model* (DOM). This allows AJAX, through JavaScript code, to directly manipulate any element on the page.
- Data interchange and manipulation using *XML* and *XSLT*, a non-proprietary and platform independent way of working with data, allowing AJAX to work on any platform using industry standard technology.
- Asynchronous data requests and retrieval using the *XMLHttpRequest* object to request units of information comprising less than an entire page. This has two very important benefits: much less information needs to be sent "through the wire," and the browser can continue working with other portions of a page while waiting for a response from the server.
- Heavy emphasis on client-side processing, to eliminate as many round trips as possible and to greatly improve the performance of the application.
- JavaScript binds everything together. Ajax takes advantage of the industry standard scripting language that is implemented by virtually every browser on every desktop.

They did so by combining the power, speed, and flexibility of AJAX with the drag and drop simplicity of ASP.NET. They created a library of AJAX controls that are as easy to use as the server-side ASP.NET controls we've been using since the Middle Ages. Even more important, they made it relatively easy to create your own drag and drop AJAX controls.

This means you can get started using Microsoft's AJAX controls without first learning how to program in JavaScript or how to write DHTML. That lowers the usability bar enough that there really is no reason not to integrate AJAX into all your ASP.NET applications immediately.

 Don't panic if you *like* JavaScript and you *want* to write your own AJAX controls; you are still free to do so. Just as with custom controls, you can always extend, or even invent if you are so moved.

Now, you can eat your cake and have it too. You can continue to create ASP.NET applications using the same IDE, but add client side script with asynchronous postbacks (especially asynchronous data retrieval!), and you can do so with a library of tested, ready to use controls that fully encapsulate all the JavaScript for you.

The key point, however, is that asynchronous updates improve both the performance of your application and the user's perception of that performance. This is because the page is not posted back to the server, but instead data is retrieved independently of the page being recreated, thus there is no flicker, and data retrieval is far faster.

ScriptManager

Microsoft realized that the job of integrating the standard ASP.NET controls and pages with AJAX controls (that encapsulate JavaScript and DHTML) would be difficult, tedious and repetitious. So they did it for you with the `ScriptManager` control, ensuring that you have access to a fully tested, reliable control that manages the "grunt" work. Adding a `ScriptManager` control to your page (which the IDE does automatically when you create an AJAX-enabled project) solves the problem, and having one on the page that you don't need comes at virtually no cost. Here is the declaration that must appear in every page, and which is put there for you by the IDE:

CODE▶
```
<asp:ScriptManager ID="ScriptManager1" runat="server" />
```

The `ScriptManager` control will also be visible in Design view, as shown in Figure 3-1, but will not be visible when the web site is run.

Implementing partial-page updates is surprisingly easy using ASP.NET AJAX—you just leave the `ScriptManager`'s `EnablePartialRendering` property set to its default value of `True`.

Having done the hard work of *not* changing that property, you can then drag one or more `UpdatePanel` controls onto your page. Each `UpdatePanel` is updated individually and asynchronously, without affecting one another or anything else on the page.

That's it. Instant and unmistakable performance enhancement with almost no programmer effort.

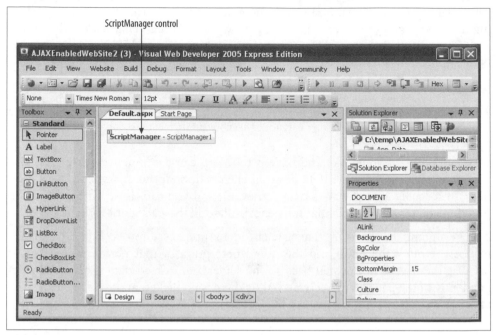

Figure 3-1. The ScriptManager control is visible on the page in Design view, but you won't see it in the browser.

To see this dramatic effect, you will modify the AdventureWorks project from the previous chapter, using update panels to improve performance. Recall in that example (shown in Figure 2-9), a pair of radio buttons was created (but never enabled) to control the visibility of a Panel control whose purpose was to collect personal information. You'll enable that feature now.

Normally, clicking on the radio buttons would cause a postback, which would cause the page to flicker as it was redrawn. With an AJAX UpdatePanel, however, the update will be done asynchronously, and there will be no page flicker.

Begin by making a copy of the AdventureWorks Order Form. Call it Adventure-WorksRevisited. Run it to ensure that it works as expected.

 See Appendix A for instructions on copying a web site.

Remove all the controls below the pnlPersonalInfo panel (everything below that Panel down to—but not including—the closing form tag).

You will also need to delete the no-longer relevant event handlers from the code-behind. (You can easily tell which code-behind methods are no longer relevant by trying to run the web page and looking at the build errors.) As it turns out, this includes all the event handlers from the previous example.

Now add an AJAX UpdatePanel to surround the radio buttons. The finished application is shown in Figure 3-2, which shows the panel both visible and hidden.

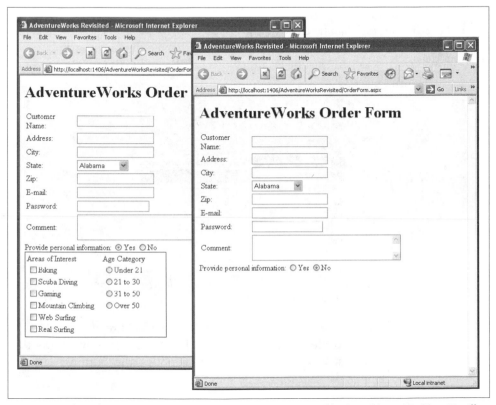

Figure 3-2. The AdventureWorksRevisited web site with the Panel both visible and hidden. You'll see that the AJAX version works much more smoothly than the version from Chapter 2.

Let's give the Yes and No RadioButtons something to do. Select each of the RadioButton controls and take a look at the Properties window. First, be sure the Text property is set correctly for each button—Yes or No. Next, set the AutoPostBack property for each RadioButton to true. As we mentioned in Chapter 2, when AutoPostBack is set to true, the RadioButton immediately initiates a postback to the server when it is clicked, executing any action that should happen.

As you saw in Chapter 2, you indicate what action should be taken with event handlers. In Design view, set the event handler for the Yes button by clicking on the rbYes radio button. In the Properties window, click on the lightning bolt button to switch from properties to events. You will see that one of the events is CheckedChanged.

In the space to the right of the event name, enter the text YesNoEventHandler. Press tab (or Enter) to open the code-behind file, with the cursor positioned in the skeleton of the new event handler, ready for you to enter your custom code. Before you fill in the code for the event handler, though, return to the Design view and click on the rbNo radio button. Again, click in the space next to the same CheckedChanged event handler. This time a down arrow will appear. Clicking that arrow will give you the opportunity to select an existing event handler, as shown in Figure 3-3.

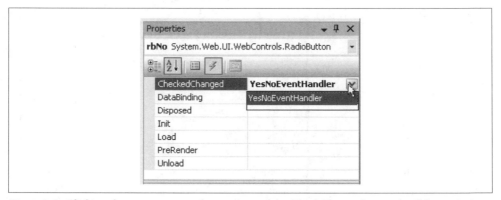

Figure 3-3. Clicking the arrow next to the property of the CheckChanged control will let you wire the control to an event handler that's already created.

Select YesNoEventHandler. Once again, the IDE will take you directly to the event handler in the code-behind file. Notice that the Handles statement now shows that this event handler handles the CheckChanged event for both radio buttons. Add the text shown highlighted in the following code snippet:

```
Protected Sub YesNoEventHandler( _
    ByVal sender As Object, _
    ByVal e As System.EventArgs) _
    Handles rbYes.CheckedChanged, rbNo.CheckedChanged
    pnlPersonalInfo.Visible = rbYes.Checked
End Sub
```

Run the program, and click the Yes and No radio buttons in turn. You should see that the panel is displayed when the Yes button is checked, and hidden when the No button is checked. As you saw in the previous chapter, the Visible attribute specifies whether the panel is rendered, and now you've tied it to the value of the rbYes control.

As you click each button, however, you will probably notice a distinct flicker, or jiggle in the display, as the entire page is redrawn. There may even be a detectable delay. This is because each time you click the button, the entire page is sent back to the server for processing, the event handler is run, and the entire page is sent back to the browser and redrawn.

AJAX solves this problem by asynchronously updating only portions of a page. By updating segments "in the background" you avoid reposting and redrawing the entire page.

In the AdventureWorks example as it is currently written, this postback also causes the user's position on the page to be lost. When the page is rendered from scratch, the browser effectively scrolls back to the top of the page, which can be very annoying.

You can rectify this by setting the MaintainScrollPositionOnPostback property of the Page directive to true. To do so, open the markup file in Source view and edit the Page directive at the top of the file, adding the following highlighted code:

CODE▶

```
<%@ Page Language="VB" AutoEventWireup="true"
    CodeFile="OrderForm.aspx.vb" Inherits="_Default"
    MaintainScrollPositionOnPostback="true"%>
```

Select the ScriptManager control in Design view and look at the Properties window. If the Properties window is not visible, right-click on the control and select Properties. Verify that the EnablePartialRendering property is set to True.

Your goal is to update only the Panel pnlPersonalInfo when the user clicks one of the radio buttons. To do that, you need to *wrap* the Panel and the radio buttons inside an UpdatePanel control, which you'll find in the AJAX Extensions section in your Toolbox.

Make sure you are in Design view, open the AJAX Extensions tab of the Toolbox, and drag an UpdatePanel onto the form (you can do the same in Source view, of course). Now highlight the prompt, the radio buttons, and the pnlPersonalInfo Panel, and drag them all onto that UpdatePanel. That's all there is to it.

Doing this in Source view is very similar: drag the UpdatePanel from the Toolbox onto the window then move the relevant markup inside the UpdatePanel.

Run the program again, and then click the radio buttons, to see the difference This time, there should be no flicker as only the panel reloads. Feel free to say "wow!"

Extending Controls with the Control Toolkit

The AJAX Control Toolkit provides a number of additional AJAX-enabled controls you can use to enhance the functionality of your web application. Some of the more useful controls in the Control Toolkit are listed in Table 3-1.

Table 3-1. A Sample of the AJAX Toolkit Controls

Toolkit Control	Description
Accordion	A control that provides multiple panes, only one of which is visible at a time
AlwaysVisibleControlExtender	Keeps a control visible as the user scrolls the page
AnimationExtender	Helps you animate a panel or other control on your page
CascadingDropDown	The user's selection from one drop down control determines the choices available in the next drop down
CollapsiblePanelExtender	Allows any Panel to collapse and expand
ConfirmButtonExtender	When the user clicks a button, a dialog box pops up to confirm the choice
DragPanelExtender	Lets the user drag a panel around on the page
FilteredTextBoxExtender	Ensures that only "valid" text may be entered into a text box
HoverMenuExtender	Pops up a menu when the mouse hovers over a control
MutuallyExclusive-CheckBoxExtender	Pick none or one of several checkboxes. This provides functionality similar to radio buttons, but with the ability to uncheck all the checkboxes
NoBot	A control which attempts to prevent spam or robot interaction with a web site
NumericUpDownExtender	Adds up/down functionality to a TextBox control; can cycle through numeric values or from a list of provided values
PagingBulletedListExtender	Extends a BulletedList control to provide client-side sorted paging
PasswordStrength	Helps the user pick a good password
Rating	Quick rating, allowing a user to pick the number of stars out of a maximum number (you could use this, for example, to set up a 4-star [or 5-star, or 10-star] rating system for restaurant or movie reviews)
ReorderList	Lets the user reorder the members of a list by dragging them into place
TextBoxWaterMarkExtender	Displays helpful text in a textbox until you start to type
UpdatePanelAnimationExtender	Quick animation of a panel; move, resize, fade
ValidatorCalloutExtender	Extends ASP.NET validation controls by displaying a warning with an image if the field isn't valid

TextBoxWaterMarkExtender

Many of the Toolkit controls are "extenders"—that is, rather than acting alone, they extend the behavior of one of the standard controls. For example, the TextBoxWaterMarkExtender works with a TextBox to add the watermark effect. The extender has properties to identify which TextBox it will modify, what text will be used as the watermark, and what style should be applied to the watermark text itself. Figures 3-4 and 3-5 demonstrate watermarks in action.

| Customer Name: | Your name |
| Address: | Home address |

Figure 3-4. This is what the watermarked control looks like before the user enters any data. The watermark serves as a reminder of what the user should enter, and makes it clear that the field is currently empty.

| Customer Name: | **Jesse Liberty|** |
| Address: | Home address |

Figure 3-5. When the user types in the TextBox, the unwatermarked style is applied, which shows an obvious change from the watermarked style.

To demonstrate the watermark effect, copy the previous example, AdventureWorks-Revisited, to a new web site called AdventureWorksWaterMarks.

Before modifying the page, you need to create a style sheet that will specify the styles for the watermarked and unwatermarked text.

 Styles and style sheets are explained fully in Chapter 6, so we will only show the bare basics here.

To create a style sheet, click Website → Add New Item…. In the Add New Item dialog box, select Style Sheet, accept the default name of *StyleSheet.css*, and then click the Add button, as shown in Figure 3-6.

This will open a style sheet in the editor with an empty body element. Add the highlighted code from Example 3-1 to this style sheet.

Example 3-1. StyleSheet.css for watermarks

```
body {
}
.watermarked {
    padding:2px 0 0 2px;
    border:1px solid #BEBEBE;
    background-color:#F0F8FF;
    color:Gray;
    font-family:Verdana;
    font-weight:lighter;
}
.unwatermarked {
    height:18px;
    width:148px;
    font-weight:bold;
}
```

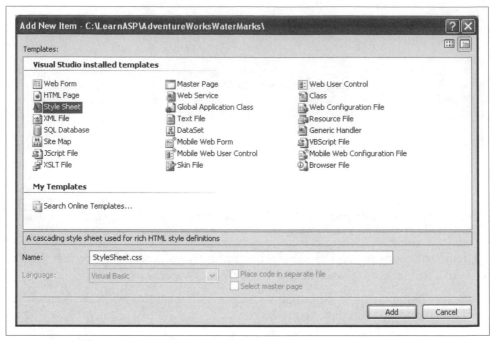

Figure 3-6. To add a style sheet to the web site, use the Add New Item dialog box.

In this code, you're adding two style classes, watermarked and unwatermarked, that will be applied to the text in the example.

Next, in Design view, go to *OrderForm.aspx*. Select the Customer Name Text Box, txtName, and in the Properties window, set the CssClass property to unwatermarked. (The style class names are case sensitive.) Do the same for txtAddress. This sets the style class that will apply to the text the user types into these text boxes, as illustrated in Figure 3-5.

Open the AJAX Control Toolkit section of the Toolbox, and drag a TextBoxWatermarkExtender control into the same table cell as txtName. Change the ID property of the control to CustomerNameWatermark and TargetControlID property to txtName. The ID property is the same as the ID properties for all the other controls you've seen so far, but the TargetControlID property specifies the control that you want the watermark effect to apply to—in this case, it's the TextBox control, txtName. The screen should look something like Figure 3-7. (Note that we've ordered the properties window alphabetically.)

There are two other properties you need to set for this control: WatermarkCssClass and WatermarkText. Unfortunately, these properties are not accessible through the Properties window, so you need to switch to Source view to manually type them in. Before you do that, though, drag another TextBoxWatermarkExtender control into the table cell that contains txtAddress, and set its ID to CustomerAddressWatermark and its TargetControlID property to txtAddress.

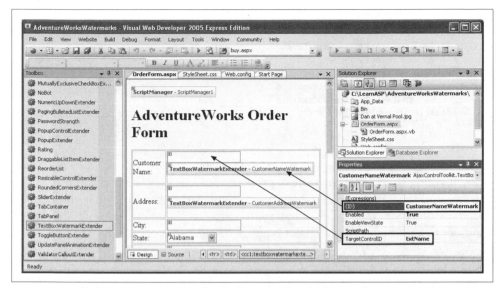

Figure 3-7. Add the TextBoxWatermarkExtender control to the form and set its ID and TargetControlID properties.

Now switch to Source view and add the `WatermarkCssClass` and `WatermarkText` attributes. Add those two lines of code to each control, so that the result looks like Example 3-2.

Example 3-2. TextBoxWatermarkExtender markup

```
<tr>
    <td style="width: 100px">
        Customer Name:
    </td>
    <td style="width: 150px">
        <asp:TextBox ID="txtName" runat="server"
            CssClass="unwatermarked" >
        </asp:TextBox>
        <cc1:TextBoxWatermarkExtender
            ID="CustomerNameWatermark"
            runat="server"
            TargetControlID="txtName"
            WatermarkCssClass="watermarked"
            WatermarkText="Your name" >
        </cc1:TextBoxWatermarkExtender>
    </td>
</tr>
<tr>
    <td style="width: 100px">
        Address:</td>
    <td style="width: 150px">
        <asp:TextBox ID="txtAddress" runat="server"
            CssClass="unwatermarked" >
        </asp:TextBox>
```

Example 3-2. TextBoxWatermarkExtender markup (continued)

```
        <cc1:TextBoxWatermarkExtender
            ID="CustomerAddressWaterMark"
            runat="server"
            TargetControlID="txtAddress"
            WatermarkCssClass="watermarked"
            WatermarkText="Home address" >
        </cc1:TextBoxWatermarkExtender>
    </td>
</tr>
```

This is the code that adds the watermark itself to the TextBox control, before the user types anything in. The WatermarkText property sets the text that will appear in the TextBox, and the WatermarkCssClass property applies the style class that you defined earlier in the style sheet. The result is that the TextBox fields have nicely styled reminder text in them before the user types anything, as you saw in Figure 3-4.

One final step is to add the following line of HTML to the markup file, inside the <head> element in order to make the style sheet visible to the page. Without this line, none of the style classes you created earlier will apply to the page:

CODE▶

```
        <style type="text/css">@import url(StyleSheet.css);</style>
```

Now run the page. The Customer Name and Address fields will look like Figure 3-4. When you type in the text box, the change is noticeable and removes any potential confusion, as shown in Figure 3-5.

PopupControlExtender

Screen real estate on a web page is often at a premium, so the PopupControlExtender is a very useful tool for presenting the maximum information in a minimum of space. You attach a PopupControlExtender to a control. When the user clicks the control a pop-up window appears with additional content. If you put an UpdatePanel into the pop up, it can display data retrieved asynchronously from the server—a very powerful effect.

To see how you can make this feature work for you, you'll modify the previous example, replacing the RadioButtonList used for selecting an age category with a TextBox. You'll add a PopupControlExtender and attach it to the TextBox. The PopupControlExtender will use an UpdatePanel to present the RadioButtonList as a pop up.

Figure 3-8 shows the TextBox waiting to be clicked on. To prompt the user to click inside the TextBox, there's also a TextBoxWatermarkExtender.

Figure 3-9 shows what happens when the user clicks in the TextBox. The watermark disappears, and the pop-up window appears, containing the RadioButtonList showing the categories the user may pick from. Because the list is inside an UpdatePanel, there is no postback to the server (and thus no screen flicker); everything happens on the client side.

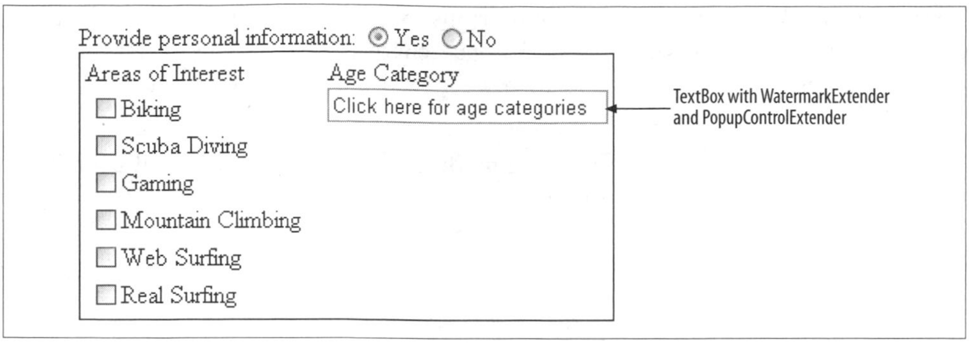

Figure 3-8. The TextBox has a PopupControlExtender attached to it, and also a TextBoxWatermarkExtender to invite users to click it.

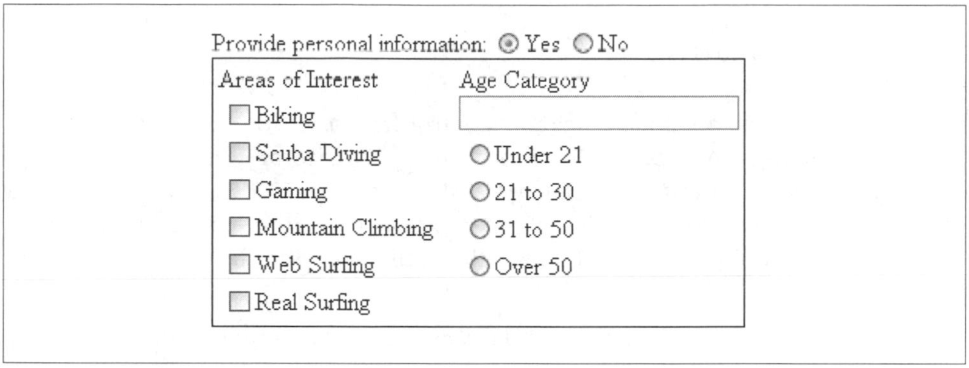

Figure 3-9. When the user clicks on the TextBox with the PopupControlExtender, the pop-up panel opens, showing the radio buttons.

When the user chooses a radio button, the choice is "posted back," but again, using an UpdatePanel, so the rest of the page is unaffected. The panel closes and the choice is displayed in the TextBox, as shown in Figure 3-10.

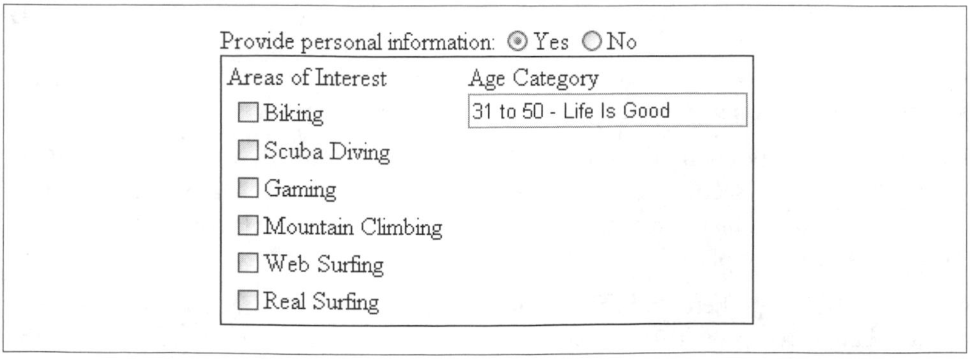

Figure 3-10. After the user makes a selection, the UpdatePanel is closed and the TextBox is updated.

To implement this example, copy the previous example, AdventureWorksWatermarks, to a new web site, called AdventureWorksPopupControl. First we will do all the dragging and dropping and coding, and then we'll follow with an explanation of how it all works.

The previous example had the following markup for the layout table cell containing the Age Category caption and radio buttons:

```
<td style="width: 1024px">
    Age Category
    <br />
    <asp:RadioButtonList ID="rblAge" runat="server"
                    AutoPostBack="True" Width="125px">
        <asp:ListItem>Under 21</asp:ListItem>
        <asp:ListItem>21 to 30</asp:ListItem>
        <asp:ListItem>31 to 50</asp:ListItem>
        <asp:ListItem>Over 50</asp:ListItem>
    </asp:RadioButtonList>
</td>
```

In Design view, drag a standard TextBox control from the Toolbox to the cell that currently contains rblAge. Set its ID property to txtAgeCategory, and its Width property to 175px. Next, from the AJAX Control Toolkit section of the Toolbox, drag a TextBoxWatermarkExtender and a PopupControlExtender into the same table cell. Also, drag a standard Panel control into the cell and set its ID property to pnlAgeCategories.

Set the TargetControlID property of the TextBoxWatermarkExtender to txtAgeCategory (the ID of new TextBox). You also want to set its WatermarkText property to "Click here for age categories" (you will need to switch to Source view because that property is not visible in Design view). You could also set the WatermarkCssClass property, as we did in the previous section, but we will not bother to do so here.

While still in Source view (again, not all the properties are visible in Design view), set the properties of the PopupControlExtender. Set the TargetControlID to the ID of the TextBox (txtAgeCategory). This will cause the pop up to appear when txtAgeCategory is clicked. Set PopupControlID to pnlAgeCategories. This is the control that will pop up when the TextBox is clicked (you will populate that Panel in a moment). Finally, set the Position property of the PopupControlExtender to Bottom.

Now you need to populate the Panel. Switch back to Design view, and then from the AJAX Extensions section of the Toolbox, drag an UpdatePanel control into pnlAgeCategories. Next, drag the pre-existing RadioButtonList (rblAge) inside the UpdatePanel you just placed.

You could stop right here and this would work as is, but edit the RadioButtonList to add explicit Value properties to each of the items. Click on the Smart Tag of the RadioButtonList, then Edit Items to bring up the ListItem Collection Editor, as shown in Figure 3-11.

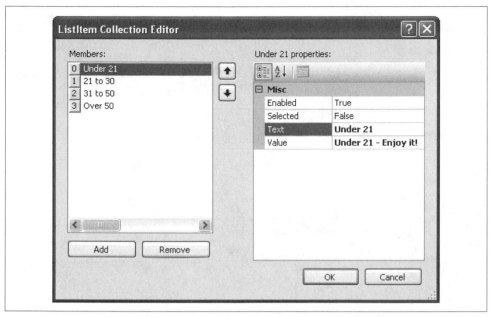

Figure 3-11. After clicking the Smart Tag of the RadioButtonList, you get this ListItem Collection Editor for editing the items in the list.

Click on each of the Members in turn, and change the Value properties as follows:

Text	Value
Under 21	Under 21 - Enjoy it!
21 to 30	21 to 30 - Livin' Large
31 to 50	31 to 50 - Life Is Good
Over 50	Over 50 - Golden Years

When you have modified all the values, the Design view should look something like that shown in Figure 3-12.

 Take a moment to switch back to Source view and look at the mark up that was generated by the IDE. You are of course, free to create this directly in Source view, but note that you will need to place a <contentTemplate> within the <updatePanel>. This is done for you automatically when you use drag and drop in Design view.

The final step is to create an event handler for the RadioButtonList control (rblAge) to handle a selection change. You can do this easily, as you've seen before—double-click on rblAge in Design view. This will open up the code-behind file, create a

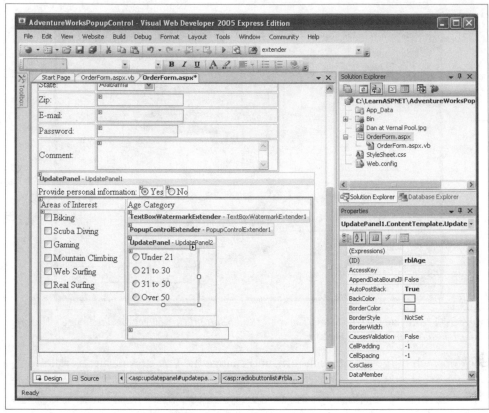

Figure 3-12. The Design view of your form with the PopupControlExtender in place. Notice the UpdatePanel with the RadioButtonList inside it.

skeleton event handler called rblAge_SelectedIndexChanged, and then place the cursor inside that method, ready for typing. Enter the following line of code:

```
PopupControlExtender1.Commit(rblAge.SelectedValue.ToString())
```

This line of code will be executed each time the user changes the selection within the RadioButtonList. The value the user selected is converted to a string (with ToString()) and the Commit method is called to tell the PopupControlExtender to force the page to automatically update itself.

> The ToString() method is a special method that converts text values to a string so that they can be displayed in a label or another appropriate control.

Looking at the Source view, the table cell containing the Age Category components should now look like the code in Example 3-3.

Example 3-3. PopupControlExtender control

```
<td style="width: 1024px">
    Age Category <br />
    <asp:TextBox ID="txtAgeCategory" runat="server" Width="175px">
    </asp:TextBox>

    <cc1:TextBoxWatermarkExtender ID="TextBoxWatermarkExtender1"
        runat="server"
        TargetControlID="txtAgeCategory"
        WatermarkText="Click here for age categories">
    </cc1:TextBoxWatermarkExtender>

    <cc1:PopupControlExtender ID="PopupControlExtender1"
        runat="server"
        TargetControlID="txtAgeCategory"
        PopupControlID="pnlAgeCategories"
        Position="Bottom">
    </cc1:PopupControlExtender>

    <asp:Panel ID="pnlAgeCategories" runat="server" Height="50px"
        Width="125px">
        <asp:UpdatePanel ID="UpdatePanel2" runat="server">
            <ContentTemplate>
                <asp:RadioButtonList ID="rblAge" runat="server"
                    AutoPostBack="True" Width="125px"
                    OnSelectedIndexChanged="rblAge_SelectedIndexChanged">
                    <asp:ListItem Value="Under 21 - Enjoy it!">
                        Under 21</asp:ListItem>
                    <asp:ListItem Value="21 to 30 - Livin' Large">
                        21 to 30
                        </asp:ListItem>
                    <asp:ListItem Value="31 to 50 - Life Is Good">
                        31 to 50
                        </asp:ListItem>
                    <asp:ListItem Value="Over 50 - Golden Years">
                        Over 50
                        </asp:ListItem>
                </asp:RadioButtonList>
            </ContentTemplate>
        </asp:UpdatePanel>
    </asp:Panel>
</td>
```

Don't Panic! While this looks complicated, it breaks down very simply.

All you have is a TextBox control (with an ID of txtAgeCategory), two extenders, and a Panel control. The first extender is a TextBoxWaterMarkExtender, and the second is a PopupControlExtender (their relative order is incidental). Both extenders have a TargetControlID attribute and they are both set to the ID of the TextBox (txtAgeCategory), which makes perfect sense. The PopupControlExtender and the TextBoxWaterMarkExtender are each "extending" the behavior of the TextBox named txtAgeCategory, so they both have txtAgeCategory as a common target.

The `TextBoxWaterMarkExtender` stands on its own, but the `PopupControlExtender` needs a bit of help. It not only needs to know its target (who is it popping up for) but it also needs to know the `ID` of its `PopupControl`—that is, the control it will pop up when it is time to go "Pop!"

In this case, the control it is popping up is `pnlAgeCategories`, which is an ASP.NET `Panel` control, and which serves to "hold" other controls within it. The first control held within this `Panel` is an `UpdatePanel` named `UpdatePanel2`. As you know, anything within an `UpdatePanel` is updated asynchronously, so you place the `RadioButtonList` right into the `UpdatePanel`.

The `RadioButtonList` itself consists of a series of `ListItems`. A `ListItem` may have two very important properties (and in this case, it does)—the text to display (placed between the opening and closing brackets) and a `Value` property. The `Value` property can come in handy—it gives the programmer a way to say "what value is attached to the selected radio button" and not necessarily get back only the text that was displayed.

You also added an event handler for the `SelectedIndexChanged` event of the `RadioButtonList`. Each time the user picks a radio button, the method that you designate (in this case `rblAge_SelectedIndexChanged`) will be called, allowing the control to react to the change. The way to react in this case is to get the value stashed away with the button, and display it in the text box. The way you do this is to call the `Commit` method of the `PopupControlExtender`.

The `Position` property of the `PopupControlExtender` is set to `Bottom`, which places the pop-up window below the target control. The options available for the `Position` property are `Bottom`, `Center`, `Left`, `Right`, and `Top`.

CollapsiblePanelExtender

The `CollapsiblePanelExtender` control extends the standard `Panel` control, allowing it to collapse and expand. This allows you to add regions to the page which the user can collapse and expand at will. A typical use for the collapsible extender would be a product detail sheet that the user can display if interested.

In our case, we'll fill the panel with text and a photo of one of the authors so that his kids will believe he really contributed to this book, however little.

 Lorem Ipsum has been the printing industry's standard placeholder text for over 600 years, and it is typically called *greeking* by typographers. The text is designed to allow the reader to ignore the words and focus on the layout, though it does have its roots in Cicero's finibus bonorum et malorum (The Purpose of Good and Evil).

You can hide or expand the panel at will. When the `CollapsiblePanelExtender` is collapsed, the page will look something like Figure 3-13. When it is expanded, it will look like Figure 3-14.

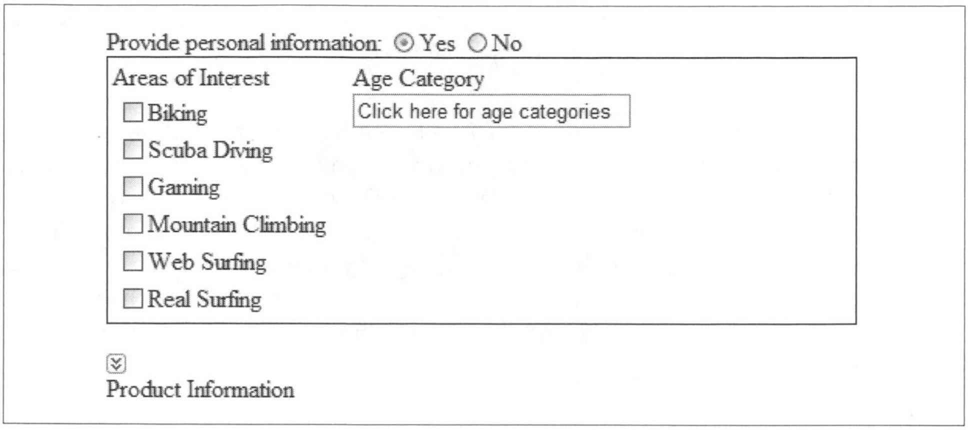

Figure 3-13. When the CollapsiblePanelExtender is collapsed, it hides out of the way, with only the arrow indicating it's there.

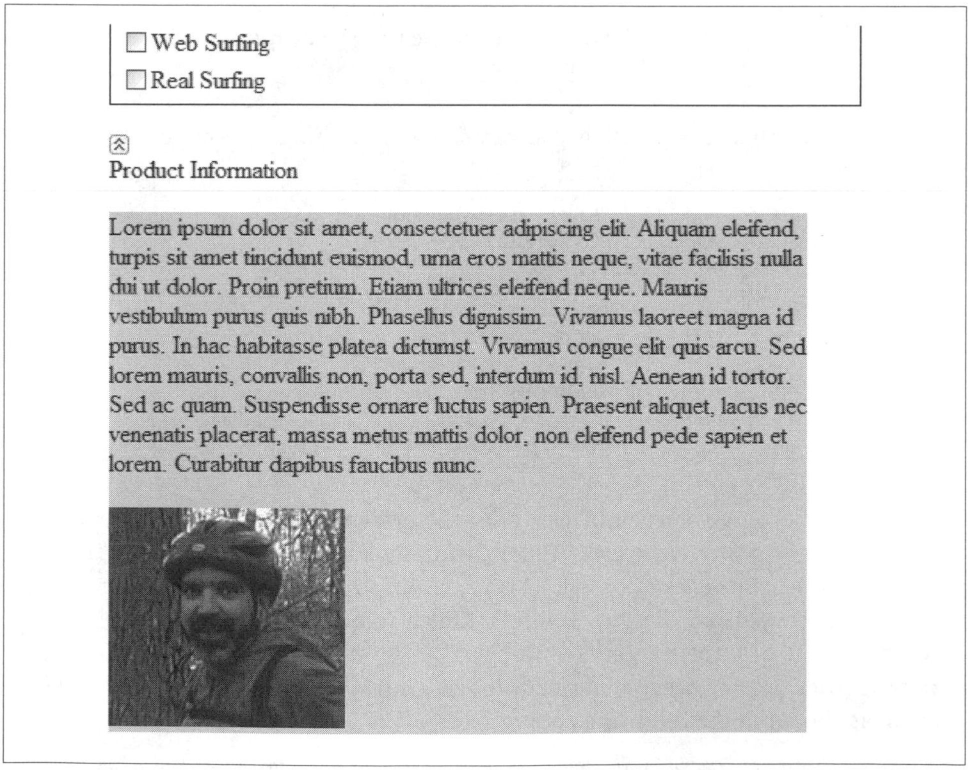

Figure 3-14. When the user clicks the arrow, the CollapsiblePanelExtender is expanded, showing the text and images.

To create this example, copy the previous web site, AdventureWorksPopupControl, to a new web site called AdventureWorksCollapsiblePanelExtender. See Appendix A for instructions on copying web sites.

In Design view, drag a standard ASP.NET Panel control (not an AJAX UpdatePanel) from the Standard section of the Toolbox onto your page, below the other controls already on the page. Set the ID of that Panel to pnlProductInfoHeader. Within the Panel, you need the image for the collapse button and the text to tell the user what is inside the collapsed panel. For the graphic, drag a standard Image control into the Panel, then use the Properties window to set its ID to imgProductInfo_ToggleImage and its ImageUrl property to collapse.jpg. Type the text "Product Information" directly into the Panel.

 The arrow graphics seen above the words "Product Information" in Figures 3-13 and 3-14, are called *collapse.jpg* and *expand.jpg* respectively. Both images are available with the downloadable code. In order to select these, or any image files directly from the Properties window, you must first add the image files to the web site by using the Website → Add Existing Item... menu item.

The markup for this Panel, which you can see by switching to Source view, should look something like this:

```
<asp:Panel ID="pnlProductInfoHeader" runat="server" >
    <asp:Image ID="imgProductInfo_ToggleImage"
        runat="server" ImageUrl="~/collapse.jpg" />
    Product Information
</asp:Panel>
```

 It doesn't much matter in this Image declaration if you set the ImageUrl to *expand.jpg* or *collapse.jpg*, because the CollapsiblePanelExtender control will actually be controlling which image is displayed.

Below that panel, drag a second Panel onto the design surface. This panel will contain the contents of the "expanded" Panel. Using the Properties window, set the ID to pnlProductInfo, set its BackColor to LightGray (from the Web tab of the color picker), and set its Width to 450. From the Toolbox, drag a standard Label control and a standard Image control into this Panel. In either Design or Source view, set the ID and Text properties of the Label, along with the ID and ImageUrl properties of the Image control, as shown in the following code snippet:

```
<asp:Panel ID="pnlProductInfo" runat="server" BackColor="lightgray" Width="450px">
    <br />
    <asp:Label ID="myLabel" runat="server" Text="
Lorem ipsum dolor sit amet, consectetuer adipiscing elit.
Aliquam eleifend, turpis sit amet tincidunt euismod, urna eros mattis
neque, vitae facilisis nulla dui ut dolor. Proin pretium. Etiam ultrices
eleifend neque. Mauris vestibulum purus quis nibh. Phasellus dignissim.
```

```
Vivamus laoreet magna id purus. In hac habitasse platea dictumst. Vivamus
congue elit quis arcu. Sed lorem mauris, convallis non, porta sed, interdum
id, nisl. Aenean id tortor. Sed ac quam. Suspendisse ornare luctus sapien.
Praesent aliquet, lacus nec venenatis placerat, massa metus mattis dolor,
non eleifend pede sapien et lorem. Curabitur dapibus faucibus nunc." />
        <br />
        <br />
        <asp:Image ID="Image1" runat="server"
            ImageUrl="Dan at Vernal Pool.jpg" /><br />
    </asp:Panel>
```

With the collapsed and expanded Panels in place, you can now add the AJAX control—the CollapsiblePanelExtender—and set its attributes. Drag a CollapsiblePanel-
Extender from the AJAX Control Toolkit section of the Toolbox onto the page below
all the existing code. Set its ID to cpeProductInfo then set all the other properties to
match the following control declaration:

CODE▶

```
<cc1:collapsiblepanelextender
id="cpeProductInfo" runat="server"
CollapseControlID="pnlProductInfoHeader"
Collapsed="true"
CollapsedImage="expand.jpg"
CollapsedText="Product Information (Show Details...)"
ExpandControlID="pnlProductInfoHeader"
ExpandedImage="collapse.jpg"
ExpandedText="Product Information (Hide Details...)"
ImageControlID="imgProductInfo_ToggleImage"
SuppressPostBack="true"
TargetControlID="pnlProductInfo" />
```

Here again, you must use Source view as this is another of the properties that are not
accessible in Design view.

The Design view of the web site will look something that shown in Figure 3-15.

The meaning of these properties is as follows:

CollapseControlID / ExpandControlID

>   The controls that will expand or collapse the panel on a click, respectively. If
>   these values are the same, as they are in this example, the panel will toggle its
>   state with each click. Set both of these to pnlProductInfoHeader.

Collapsed

>   Indicates the initial state of the collapsible Panel. For this example, set to true, it
>   will start out in the collapsed state; if this is set to false, it will start out open.
>   You would usually want the panel to start out collapsed.

ImageControlID

>   The ID of an Image control into which an icon indicating the status (collapsed
>   or expanded) of the Panelwill be placed. The extender will replace the source
>   of this Image with the CollapsedImage and ExpandedImage URLs as appropriate.
>   If the ExpandedText or CollapsedText properties are set, they are used as the

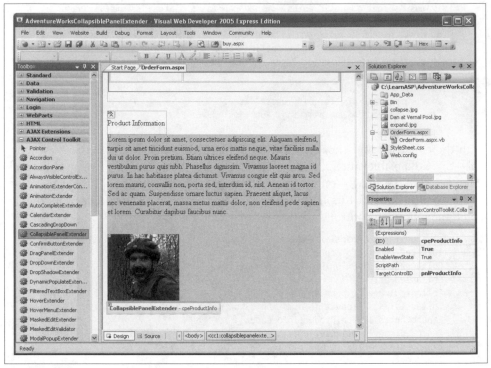

Figure 3-15. Design view of the AdventureWorksCollapsiblePanelExtender web site showing the Panel control to be extended and the CollapsiblePanelExtender control that does the extending.

alternate text for the image, also displaying as a tool tip. Set this to imgProductInfo_ToggleImage.

CollapsedImage

The path to an image used by ImageControlID when the Panel is collapsed. If the Panel is collapsed, you want readers to see an icon indicating that they can expand it. Therefore, set this property to expand.jpg.

CollapsedText

The text to show in the control specified by CollapseControlID when the Panel is collapsed. This text is used as the alternate text of the image if ImageControlID is set, also displaying as a tool tip. Set this to "Product Information (Show Details...)."

ExpandDirection

This property can be set to Vertical or Horizontal to determine whether the Panel expands top-to-bottom or left-to-right. For this exercise, set it to Vertical.

ExpandedImage

The path to an image used by ImageControlID when the Panel is expanded. If the Panel is expanded, you want readers to see an icon indicating that they can collapse it. Therefore, set this to collapse.jpg.

ExpandedText

> The text to show in the control specified by `ExpandControlID` when the `Panel` is expanded. This text is used as the alternate text of the image if `ImageControlID` is set, also displaying as a tool tip. Set this text to "Product Information (Hide Details...)."

SuppressPostBack

> If set to `true`, ensures that the control does not cause a post back when the control is expanded or contracted. That's what you want, so set this property to true.

TargetControlID

> The control that will be expanded or collapsed, in this case the `pnlProductInfo`. The key thing to realize here is that the `CollapsiblePanelExtender` does not itself expand or collapse, it is used to expand and collapse a *different* control and this attribute (`TargetControlID`) identifies the panel it will extend.

Run the web site and you will initially see the `Panel` collapsed, as shown back in Figure 3-13. Click on the icon above Product Information and the Panel expands, displaying its information, as shown in Figure 3-14.

Source Code Listing

The complete source code for the example in this chapter is shown in Example 3-4.

Example 3-4. OrderForm.aspx

```
<%@ Page Language="VB" AutoEventWireup="true" CodeFile="OrderForm.aspx.vb"
Inherits="_Default" %>

<%@ Register Assembly="AjaxControlToolkit" Namespace="AjaxControlToolkit"
TagPrefix="cc1" %>

<!DOCTYPE html PUBLIC "-//W3C//DTD XHTML 1.1//EN"
"http://www.w3.org/TR/xhtml11/DTD/xhtml11.dtd">
<html xmlns="http://www.w3.org/1999/xhtml">
<head runat="server">
    <style type="text/css">@import url(StyleSheet.css);</style>
    <title>AdventureWorks CollapsiblePanelExtender</title>
</head>
<body>
    <form id="form1" runat="server">
        <asp:ScriptManager ID="ScriptManager1" runat="server" />
        <div>
        <h1>AdventureWorks Order Form</h1>
            <table>
                <tr>
                    <td style="width: 100px">
                        Customer Name:</td>
                    <td style="width: 100px">
```

Example 3-4. OrderForm.aspx (continued)

```
                        <asp:TextBox ID="txtName" runat="server"
                            CssClass="unwatermarked">
                        </asp:TextBox>
                        <cc1:TextBoxWatermarkExtender runat="server"
                            ID="CustomerNameWatermark"
                            TargetControlID="txtName"
                            WatermarkCssClass="watermarked"
                            WatermarkText="Your name">
                        </cc1:TextBoxWatermarkExtender>
                    </td>
                </tr>
                <tr>
                    <td style="width: 100px">
                        Address:</td>
                    <td style="width: 100px">
                        <asp:TextBox ID="txtAddress" runat="server"
                            CssClass="unwatermarked"></asp:TextBox>
                        <cc1:TextBoxWatermarkExtender runat="server"
                                ID="CustomerAddressWatermark"
                                TargetControlID="txtAddress"
                                WatermarkCssClass="watermarked"
                                WatermarkText="Home address">
                        </cc1:TextBoxWatermarkExtender>
                    </td>
                </tr>
                <tr>
                    <td style="width: 100px">
                        City:</td>
                    <td style="width: 100px">
                        <asp:TextBox ID="txtCity" runat="server"></asp:TextBox>
                    </td>
                </tr>
                <tr>
                    <td style="width: 100px">
                        State:</td>
                    <td style="width: 100px">
                        <asp:DropDownList ID="ddlState" runat="server">
                            <asp:ListItem Value="AL">Alabama</asp:ListItem>
                            <asp:ListItem Value="AK">Alaska</asp:ListItem>
                            <asp:ListItem Value="CA">California</asp:ListItem>
                            <asp:ListItem Value="CT">Connecticut</asp:ListItem>
                            <asp:ListItem Value="FL">Florida</asp:ListItem>
                            <asp:ListItem Value="PA">Pennsylvania</asp:ListItem>
                            <asp:ListItem Value="TX">Texas</asp:ListItem>
                            <asp:ListItem></asp:ListItem>
                        </asp:DropDownList>
                    </td>
                </tr>
                <tr>
                    <td style="width: 100px">
                        Zip:</td>
```

Example 3-4. OrderForm.aspx (continued)

```
                <td style="width: 100px">
                    <asp:TextBox ID="txtZip" runat="server"></asp:TextBox>
                </td>
        </tr>
        <tr>
                <td style="width: 100px">
                    E-mail:</td>
                <td style="width: 100px">
                    <asp:TextBox ID="txtEmail" runat="server"></asp:TextBox>
                </td>
        </tr>
        <tr>
                <td style="width: 100px">
                    Password:</td>
                <td style="width: 100px">
                    <asp:TextBox ID="txtPassword" runat="server"
                        TextMode="Password"></asp:TextBox></td>
        </tr>
        <tr>
                <td style="width: 100px">
                    Comment:</td>
                <td style="width: 100px">
                    <asp:TextBox ID="txtComment" runat="server" Rows="3"
                        TextMode="MultiLine" Width="300px"></asp:TextBox>
                </td>
        </tr>
    </table>
</div>
<asp:UpdatePanel ID="UpdatePanel1" runat="server">
    <ContentTemplate>
Provide personal information:
<asp:RadioButton ID="rbYes" runat="server" AutoPostBack="True"
    Checked="True"
    GroupName="grpPersonalInfo"
    Text="Yes" ToolTip="Do gather personal info" />
<asp:RadioButton ID="rbNo" runat="server" AutoPostBack="True"
    GroupName="grpPersonalInfo"
    Text="No" ToolTip="Do not gather personal info" /><br />
<asp:Panel ID="pnlPersonalInfo" runat="server"  BorderWidth="1px">
    <table>
        <tr valign="top">
            <td >
                Areas of Interest<br />
                <asp:CheckBoxList ID="cblAreas" runat="server"
                        AutoPostBack="True" Width="150px">
                    <asp:ListItem>Biking</asp:ListItem>
                    <asp:ListItem>Scuba Diving</asp:ListItem>
                    <asp:ListItem>Gaming</asp:ListItem>
                    <asp:ListItem>Mountain Climbing</asp:ListItem>
                    <asp:ListItem>Web Surfing</asp:ListItem>
                    <asp:ListItem>Real Surfing</asp:ListItem>
                </asp:CheckBoxList></td>
```

Example 3-4. OrderForm.aspx (continued)

```
                <td style="width: 121px">
                    Age Category<br />
                    <asp:TextBox ID="txtAgeCategory" runat="server"
                        Width="175px">
                    </asp:TextBox><br />

                    <cc1:TextBoxWatermarkExtender
                        ID="TextBoxWatermarkExtender1" runat="server"
                        TargetControlID="txtAgeCategory"
                        WatermarkText="Click here for age categories">
                    </cc1:TextBoxWatermarkExtender>
                    <cc1:PopupControlExtender ID="PopupControlExtender1"
                        runat="server"
                        TargetControlID="txtAgeCategory"
                        PopupControlID="pnlAgeCategories"
                        Position="Bottom">
                    </cc1:PopupControlExtender>
                    <asp:Panel ID="pnlAgeCategories" runat="server"
                        Height="50px" Width="125px">
                        <asp:UpdatePanel ID="UpdatePanel2" runat="server">
                            <ContentTemplate>
                    <asp:RadioButtonList ID="rblAge" runat="server"
                            AutoPostBack="True" Width="150px"
                        OnSelectedIndexChanged="rblAge_SelectedIndexChanged">
                            <asp:ListItem Value="Under 21 - Enjoy it!">Under 21
                                </asp:ListItem>
                            <asp:ListItem Value="21 to 30 - Livin' Large">21 to 30
                                </asp:ListItem>
                            <asp:ListItem Value="31 to 50 - Life Is Good">31 to 50
                                </asp:ListItem>
                            <asp:ListItem Value="Over 50 - Golden Years">Over 50
                                </asp:ListItem>
                    </asp:RadioButtonList>
                            </ContentTemplate>
                        </asp:UpdatePanel>
                    </asp:Panel>
                </td>
            </tr>
        </table>
</asp:Panel>
    </ContentTemplate>
</asp:UpdatePanel>
<br />
<asp:Panel ID="pnlProductInfoHeader" runat="server"
                Height="50px" Width="125px">
    <asp:Image ID="imgProductInfo_ToggleImage" runat="server"
        ImageUrl="collapse.jpg" /><br />
    Product Information</asp:Panel>
<asp:Panel ID="pnlProductInfo" runat="server" BackColor="LightGray"
    Width="450px">
    <asp:Label ID="myLabel" runat="server" Text=
```

Example 3-4. OrderForm.aspx (continued)

```
                "Lorem ipsum dolor sit amet, consectetuer adipiscing elit.
        Aliquam eleifend, turpis sit amet tincidunt euismod, urna eros mattis
        neque, vitae facilisis nulla dui ut dolor. Proin pretium. Etiam ultrices
        eleifend neque. Mauris vestibulum purus quis nibh. Phasellus dignissim.
        Vivamus laoreet magna id purus. In hac habitasse platea dictumst. Vivamus
        congue elit quis arcu. Sed lorem mauris, convallis non, porta sed, interdum
        id, nisl. Aenean id tortor. Sed ac quam. Suspendisse ornare luctus sapien.
        Praesent aliquet, lacus nec venenatis placerat, massa metus mattis dolor,
        non eleifend pede sapien et lorem. Curabitur dapibus faucibus nunc.">
                </asp:Label>
                <br />
                <br />
                <asp:Image ID="Image1" runat="server"
                            ImageUrl="Dan at Vernal Pool.jpg" />
        </asp:Panel>
        <cc1:CollapsiblePanelExtender ID="cpeProductInfo" runat="server"
                CollapseControlID="pnlProductInfoHeader"
                Collapsed="true"
                CollapsedImage="expand.jpg"
                CollapsedText="Product Information (Show Details...)"
                ExpandControlID="pnlProductInfoHeader"
                ExpandedImage="collapse.jpg"
                ExpandedText="Product  Information (Hide Details...)"
                ImageControlID="imgProductInfo_ToggleImage"
                SuppressPostBack="true"
                TargetControlID="pnlProductInfo">
        </cc1:CollapsiblePanelExtender>

    </form>
</body>
</html>
```

The code-behind for this page is contained in Example 3-5.

Example 3-5. OrderForm.aspx.vb

```
Partial Class _Default
    Inherits System.Web.UI.Page

    Protected Sub YesNoEventHandler(ByVal sender As Object, _
      ByVal e As System.EventArgs) _
      Handles rbNo.CheckedChanged, rbYes.CheckedChanged

        pnlPersonalInfo.Visible = rbYes.Checked
    End Sub

    Protected Sub rblAge_SelectedIndexChanged(ByVal sender As Object, _
      ByVal e As System.EventArgs)
        PopupControlExtender1.Commit(rblAge.SelectedValue.ToString())
    End Sub
End Class
```

Summary

- AJAX is a technique for processing code on the server, and on the user's browser, which dramatically increases performance, both actual and perceived.

- The ASP.NET AJAX control library contain a number of controls that can be used just as easily as standard ASP.NET controls, meaning you don't need to know the JavaScript behind how the controls work.

- The ScriptManager control is the key control that makes ASP.NET AJAX possible by managing the JavaScript for you. The control is placed on every AJAX-enabled page by default, and its EnablePartialRendering property is set to True, so you don't need to do anything yourself.

- Placing controls inside an UpdatePanel control enables you to update those controls without posting back to the server.

- The AJAX Control Toolkit, which is a separate download, has a number of controls called extenders that enhance existing controls, rather than being separate controls themselves. Extender controls have a TargetControlID property that you use to set the existing control that the extender is extending.

- The TextBoxWaterMarkExtender adds a watermark effect to an existing textbox, providing a prompt for the reader to enter data.

- TextBoxWaterMarkExtender can apply a separate style to a text box, if you have a style sheet defined for the project, or it can just add the text you specify.

- The PopupControlExtender can help you make efficient use of the space on your page, by hiding some content until the user clicks on a control.

- You can apply the CollapsiblePanelExtender to a regular Panel control, causing it to hide most of its content until the user clicks on it. The Panel then expands, displaying its content, until the user collapses it.

Now you have a good handle on the basic controls, and you've also seen how to use some of the AJAX extenders to apply some really clever effects to them. The AdventureWorks order form you've been progressively building is looking pretty sophisticated by now. As we've mentioned, though, it doesn't connect to anything behind the scenes, so users can't see the AdventureWorks products, and can't yet place their orders. To do that, you need to learn how to interact with a database. ASP.NET provides a number of controls for retrieving data from a database and displaying it in a number of different ways. With AJAX, they get even better. You'll learn all about them in the next chapter.

Quiz

1. What do you need to do to use a ScriptManager control?
2. Which property of the ScriptManager control enables asynchronous postback?
3. What control do you need to place on your page to enable asynchronous updates?
4. Can you make a page that contains only an extender control?
5. What property is common to all the AJAX extender controls?
6. What view do you use to set the WatermarkText property?
7. Can you use the TextBoxWatermarkExtender without style sheets?
8. What's the advantage of using the PopupControlExtender?
9. What method of the PopupControlExtender do you need to call to display the results?
10. What standard control does the CollapsiblePanelExtender work with?

Exercises

Exercise 3-1. We'll start things off simply. Suppose you have a store that ships only to certain states in the Northeastern United States. In your order form, you want to restrict users to only those states as their shipping destination, so you want to use a drop-down list. You also want to save space on your form, though, so you want to hide that delivery list in a Panel with a PopupControlExtender. For this exercise, you'll only produce the part of the form where users would enter the shipping State. The finished form should look like Figure 3-16.

The drop-down list should contain just the six states shown in Figure 3-16. When the user chooses one of the states, the state's two-letter postal abbreviation should appear in the text box.

Exercise 3-2. Most of the AJAX control extenders that we've shown you in this chapter just do one thing, although they do it very well. There are, however, many more extenders that we haven't shown you, and more are being added all the time. Each one is different, and covering them all in detail would require more space than we have—or would be out of date almost immediately. The best way to learn about the AJAX control extenders is to go to the ASP.NET AJAX Control Toolkit page at *http://ajax.asp.net/ajaxtoolkit/*. There you'll find the latest extenders with examples of how to use them. Many of the extenders are fairly simple, and have properties you can set easily. In this exercise, you'll need to use that documentation as you try out a new extender.

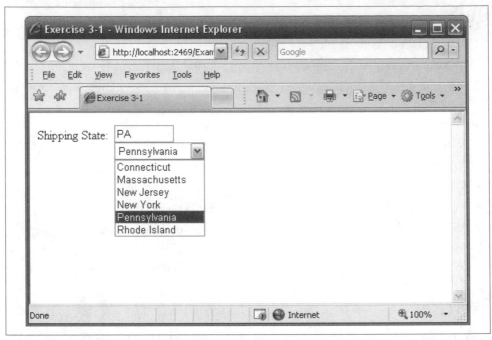

Figure 3-16. Your goal for Exercise 3-1.

For this exercise, you'll use the RoundedCorners extender. Create a new page that includes a Panel with the dimensions 150 pixels by 100 pixels, colored light gray. The Panel should contain a Label, 50 pixels wide, colored dark gray, with text that's white and bold (feel free to use livelier colors; we're choosing ones here that will show up in the book). The Panel should have only its top corners rounded to a radius of 8. The Label should have all its corners rounded to a radius of 2. You'll need the documentation to tell you how to do all that. The result should look like Figure 3-17.

Exercise 3-3. The SliderExtender is another interesting extender, but slightly more complicated than it looks. Create a new page that uses the slider extender to simulate a volume control. The slider should be set horizontally, and should have a range from 0 to 10. The results should look like Figure 3-18. (Hint: The documentation is somewhat unclear. You'll need two textboxes—the slider prevents one from displaying, so you need to use a second textbox, called a *bound control*, to see the value the slider is set to.)

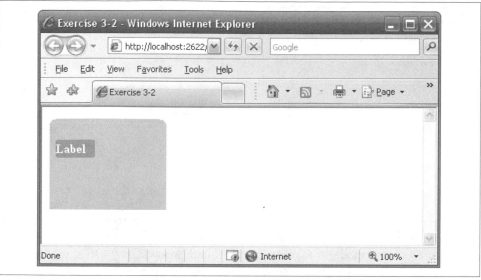

Figure 3-17. Your goal for Exercise 3-2.

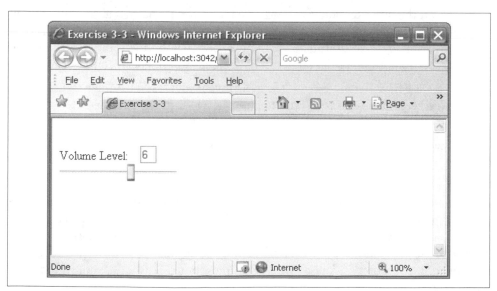

Figure 3-18. Your goal for Exercise 3-3.

CHAPTER 4
Saving and Retrieving Data

So far, you've seen how to make good-looking web pages with clever and useful controls. You know how to change the appearance of the page in response to user selections, and how to use AJAX to enhance the performance of your application. But the applications you've made so far have been limited in what they can actually *do*. In this chapter we add the most frequently sought after functionality: the ability to retrieve, change and store data.

Think about the web sites you visit most often, and you'll find that almost all of them have one thing in common—they interact with persistent data. Persistent data is data that survives a single session; data that you expect will be there the next time you visit. In fact, it may even be data that can have significant financial consequences.

Shopping sites have databases to track their inventories and customer transactions. News sites keep databases with articles and photos in them, perhaps referenced by topic and date. Search engines use unimaginably large (and wicked-fast) databases.

Nearly every real-world commercial web application must be able to perform the four essential "CRUD" interactions with a database: Create, Read, Update, and Delete.

Fortunately, ASP.NET provides controls that make it easy and fast to perform these essential activities. We will demonstrate these interactions with SQL Server Express (or its big brother, SQL Server) but they work equally well—or nearly so—with Microsoft Access and most commercial databases. In theory, you can interact with virtually any collection of data or with XML files, but that is an advanced topic we won't go into here.

Along the way we'll show you enough about database interactions that even if you've never used a relational database, such as SQL Express, you'll have little trouble working with one through your web application.

Getting Data from a Database

To see how to interact with a database, you'll begin by creating a web application that can be used to display information about the AdventureWorks database. You'll start out by simply retrieving and displaying a subset of data. These exercises will teach you how to connect your controls to a database to retrieve, filter, and sort the data and then use the myriad options for presenting it attractively.

As you may remember, AdventureWorks is a free database from Microsoft that represents a fictional company that sells outdoor and extreme sports gear. The database tracks products, inventory, customers, transactions, and suppliers.

 See Chapter 1 for instructions on installing this sample database if you have not already done so.

ASP.NET includes a number of controls specifically designed for displaying data. We'll focus on the `GridView` control, but other data controls include the `DataList`, `Repeater`, `DetailsView`, and `FormView`.

The `GridView` control displays columns and rows of data and allows sorting and paging. It is by far the most popular data display control and is ideal for understanding how data display controls interact with data-retrieval controls and code. The `GridView` control allows the user to click on a column header to sort the data. `GridViews` also let you present just a small subset of the data at one time, called a page, with links for easy access to other pages—this process is called "paging" through data. You can do these, and for numerous other data manipulations, with very little programming. A `GridView` with data from the AdventureWorks database is shown in Figure 4-1.

Binding Data Controls

Database information is stored in memory as tables (just as it is retrieved from a relational database). Tables consist of rows and columns that match nicely to the `GridView` control.

You could write code to pick out each piece of data you want and write it into the appropriate row or column of the data control, but that's time-consuming and error-prone. It is more efficient and safer to *bind* the control directly to the underlying data.

 In the early days of Graphical User Interface (GUI) programming, binding was a bit of a "trick"—great for simple programs, but useless for commercial applications because the minute you wanted to do anything out of the ordinary, the binding would become a straitjacket. Microsoft has solved that with ASP.NET by exposing events on the Data Control that allow you to insert custom code at every stage of the retrieval and binding of the data to the control.

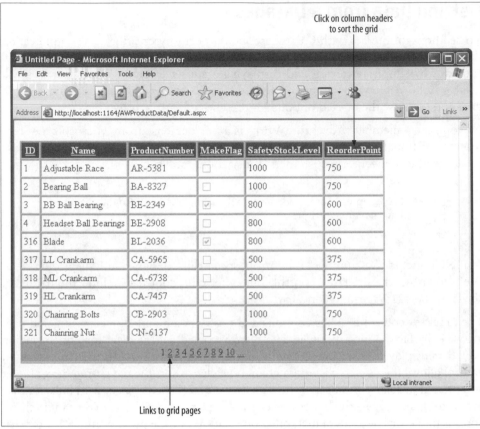

Figure 4-1. This GridView control displays data from the AdventureWorks database in a table format that makes it easier to read, and allows users to click the column headings to sort the data.

Binding is most often used with the larger data controls such as GridView, but you can also bind many other controls, such as DropDownList, ListBox, CheckBoxList, and RadioButtonList. All of these controls have a DataSource property that identifies the source to which the control is bound. For example, you might keep a list of all your customers' names in a database. Binding that data to a ListBox can be a convenient way to allow a customer service representative to quickly pick a customer rather than typing in a name that might otherwise be difficult to spell.

To see how all this works, you'll build the GridView from Figure 4-1. Once you have it up and running, you'll add some features to it, including the ability to use the grid to update the database with new data!

Create a Sample Web Page

To begin, create a new ASP.NET AJAX-enabled web site named *AWProductData*.

The IDE automatically places the all-important `ScriptManager` control onto your page. Open your toolbox and click the Data tab. You'll find two types of objects: display controls, which are designed to present data, and `DataSource` controls, which are designed to help you manage interacting with data sources, as shown in Figure 4-2.

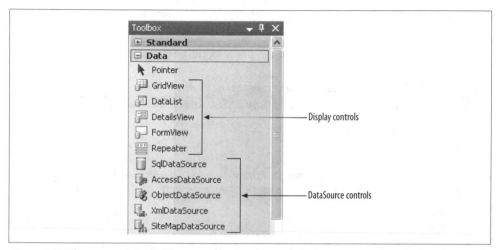

Figure 4-2. The Data tab in the Toolbox contains the controls that you'll need to display data, and to interact with data sources.

Using a DataSource Control

By default, the Data controls are arranged so the display controls are on top, and the `DataSource` controls are below (You can drag them into any order you like or arrange them alphabetically by right-clicking on any control and selecting Sort Items Alphabetically.) There is a `DataSource` control for use with Microsoft SQL Server or SQL Server Express, one for Microsoft Access, one for any type of Object, one for use with SiteMaps (for binding to menu controls—more on this in Chapter 6), and one for XML documents as a data source.

Since the AdventureWorks database is a SQL Server database, you'll use the `SqlDataSource` control whether you are using SQL Server or SQL Server Express. This control will allow you to access the AdventureWorks database, but first you need to direct the control where to find it.

Switch to Design view and drag the `SqlDataSource` control from the Toolbox directly onto the design surface. A Smart Tag will open, as seen in Figure 4-3.

Figure 4-3. A Smart Tag opens when you drag the SqlDataSource control onto your page allowing you to configure the data source.

When you click on Configure Data Source, you invoke a wizard that will walk you through the steps of configuring your data source—hooking up the control to the underlying data table(s).

The first step is to create (or choose) a data connection as seen in Figure 4-4.

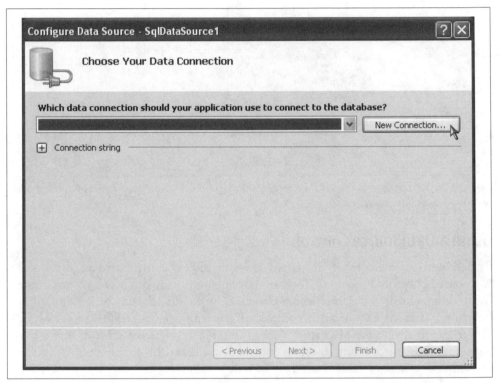

Figure 4-4. To configure your DataSource control, you need to provide it with a data connection. You can choose a preexisting connection from the list (if you have previously created any for this web site), or create a new data connection by clicking the New Connection button.

Previous data connections in this web site will be listed in the drop-down menu. To make a new connection, click the New Connection... button to get the Add Connection dialog shown in Figure 4-5.

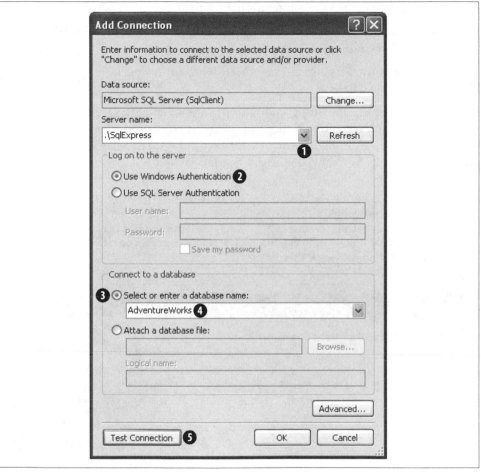

Figure 4-5. The Add Connection dialog is where you specify a new connection for your data source. Select the server, the logon credentials, and finally the database you want to use.

Following the steps in Figure 4-5, prepare your connection to the database:

1. Select your server from the Server Name drop-down menu. If it is not there, type the name of the server. Typically, if you are using SQLExpress, the name will be ".\SqlExpress" (dot-slash then SqlExpress) and if you are using SQL Server it will be the name of your computer, or it will be (local)—including the parentheses.

2. Leave the radio button set to "Use Windows Authentication."

 If Windows Authentication does not work, you may need to use SQL Server authentication. If so, your database administrator will tell you what credentials to enter. They may or may not be the same as your Windows login credentials.

3. Select the option, "Select or enter a database name:".

4. Choose the AdventureWorks database in the database name drop-down.

5. Click the Test Connection button to verify that it all works.

This dialog box constructs a *connection string*, which provides the information necessary to connect to a database on a server.

Click OK to complete the string and return to the Configure Data Source Wizard. Click the plus mark next to "Connection string" to see the connection string you've just created, as shown in Figure 4-6. The segment `Integrated Security=True` was created when you chose Windows Authentication rather than SQL Server Authentication.

 In Figure 4-6, the Wizard displays an expanded data connection in the drop-down menu, consisting of the name of the server (in this case the local machine, `virtdell380`, concatenated with `sqlexpress`, followed by the name of the database and database owner). You don't need to enter this information yourself.

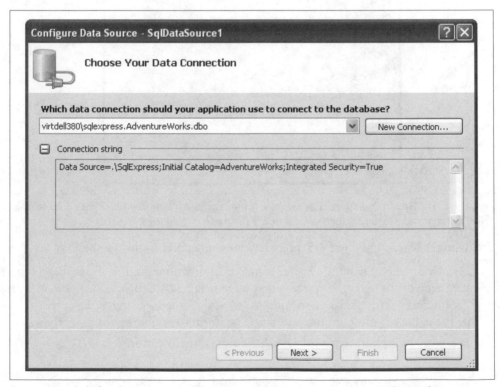

Figure 4-6. Click the plus sign to view the connection string you just created. This is what gives your control access to the database.

When you click Next, the Wizard will ask if you'd like to save this Connection string in the "application configuration file." In an ASP.NET program, the application configuration file is *web.config*, and saving the connection string there is an excellent idea, so be sure to check the checkbox and give the string a name you can easily remember. The Wizard will make a suggestion for the name of the connection string, as shown in Figure 4-7.

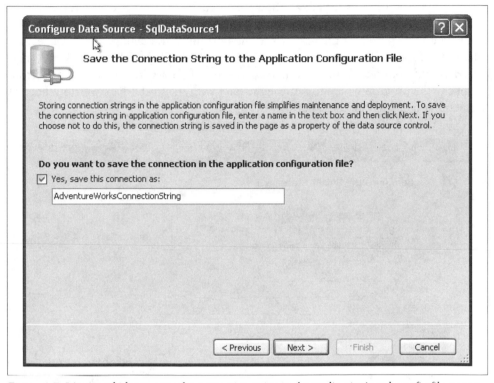

Figure 4-7. It's a good idea to save the connection string in the application's web.config file, so you can use it again with other controls.

This will cause the following lines to be written to *web.config*:

```
<connectionStrings>
    <add name="AdventureWorksConnectionString"
        connectionString="Data Source=.\SqlExpress;
            Initial Catalog=AdventureWorks;Integrated Security=True"
        providerName="System.Data.SqlClient"/>
</connectionStrings>
```

The Wizard next prompts you to configure the SELECT statement. The SELECT statement is the SQL code the control uses to retrieve the exact subset of data you are looking for from the database. Fortunately, if you are not fluent in SQL (most often pronounced "see-quill"), the Wizard will help you build the statement.

Starting with the radio buttons at the top of the dialog box, select "Specify columns from a table or view." (You would select the other button if you had a custom SQL statement prepared, as you'll see shortly.)

Selecting the button, displays the table drop-down menu. Here, you are presented with the various table options that represent the different sets of data in the database. For this exercise, choose the Product table. The various columns from the Product table will be displayed, as shown in Figure 4-8. Simply check the columns you want retrieved, and they'll be added to the SELECT statement. The choices you make will be displayed in the text box at the bottom of the dialog. For this exercise, select the ProductID, Name, ProductNumber, MakeFlag, SafetyStockLevel, and ReorderPoint columns. You could narrow the set of data with the WHERE button, or specify the order in which to retrieve the data with the ORDER BY button. For the moment, you can ignore them both.

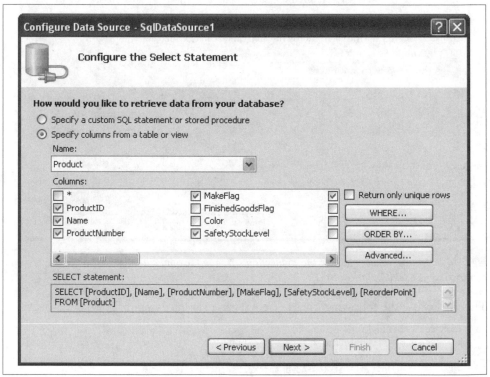

Figure 4-8. To configure the SELECT statement, specify the table and columns within it you want to retrieve, and the Wizard builds the proper SQL statement for you…more or less.

"Pay No Attention to That Man Behind the Curtain"

When you've completed the table setup, click Next, to move to the last page of the Wizard, and then click the Test Query button. The test fails, as shown in Figure 4-9.

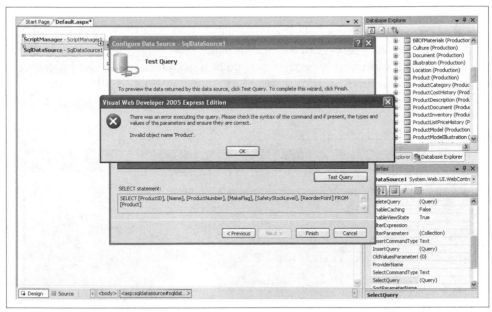

Figure 4-9. The Wizard let you down; the Query Test failed and you're looking at this error message because this database requires a schema name in front of the table names.

In this instance, the Wizard falls on its face. It turns out that the AdventureWorks database prefixes a *schema* name in front of each table name and the Wizard is unprepared for that. It generates a SELECT statement without schema names, as you saw back in Figure 4-8.

Schema in this context refers to an optional name used for organizing the tables in a large database. For example, in the AdventureWorks database, all the tables relating to the HR department have the schema name HumanResources prefixed to every table name, separated by a period, such as HumanResources.EmployeeAddress. Other schemas in the AdventureWorks database include Person, Production, Purchasing, and Sales.

As mentioned, a schema name is optional in SQL. In fact, in our experience, they are rarely used, and the Wizard is unaware of them. However, since the Adventure-Works database (which ships as part of Microsoft SQL Server) does use them, the Wizard becomes confused and flies off to Kansas leaving you on your own.

The square brackets surrounding each field and table name in the generated SELECT statement are not required, but are used to guarantee that there will be no problems if the name includes any space characters (usually a very bad idea in any case). We often remove them from the finished statement to enhance readability.

Think of this as proof that people are not yet entirely replaceable by automation. Hit the Previous button to go back one step and fix the SELECT statement manually. Click the radio button captioned "Specify a custom SQL statement or stored procedure," and then click Next. In the SQL Statement box, shown in Figure 4-10, type in:

```
SELECT ProductID, Name, ProductNumber, MakeFlag, SafetyStockLevel, ReorderPoint
FROM Production.Product
```

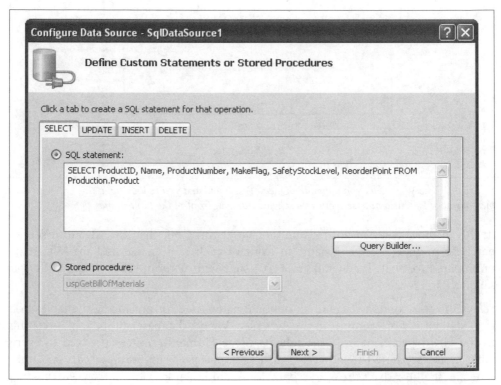

Figure 4-10. The SQL statement editing dialog, after adding the schema name to the table name, and removing all the extraneous square brackets.

As you can see, this is nearly the same SELECT statement that you built with the Wizard in Figure 4-8, except the Product table now has the required schema (Production) in front of it. We've also left out the square brackets on the columns, as mentioned in the note above.

Click Next to proceed to the next page of the Wizard, and then click Test Query. This time, you should get the results shown in Figure 4-11.

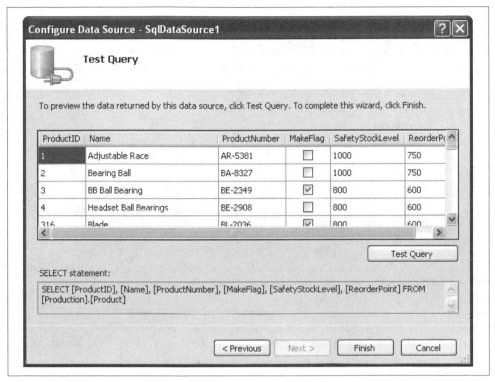

Figure 4-11. *When you test the SELECT statement this time, you'll see the results you were looking for.*

Behold—the triumph of 3 billion years of random mutation and natural selection over 50 years of automation!

Click Finish to save your work. It may not look like much, but you've just enabled your application to access the AdventureWorks database, meaning all that data is now at your control.

Using the GridView Control

Now that the DataSource control is providing the data you want, you need a way to display it. From the Data section of the Toolbox, drag a GridView control onto the page. The GridView control recognizes that a SqlDataSource is on the page and does not create its own.

If you had dragged the GridView onto the page first, it would have given you the opportunity to create a SqlDataSource rather than assuming you'd like to use one already in existence. It pretty much amounts to the same thing.

Click on the GridView's Smart Tag (if it is not already open). Click the drop-down menu next to "Choose Data Source" and select the DataSource control you just created, as shown in Figure 4-12.

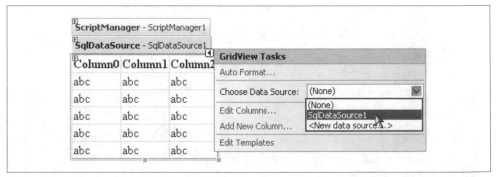

Figure 4-12. The Smart Tag of the GridView control lets you select the data source you want to use.

Once the data source is set, the data grid is redrawn, with a column for each field returned by the data source. The column headers are filled in for you based on the column names in the table that the data source represents.

 You'll have an opportunity to make the grid look much prettier, in just a short while.

Open the Smart Tag again and check "Enable Paging," which allows the grid to show a limited number of entries on each page and provide links to the other pages providing access to all the data. Also check "Enable Sorting," which allows the user to sort the grid by clicking on a column header.

Set the page to be the start page for the application (right-click the page in the Solution Explorer and select "Set As Start Page") and then run the application. Figure 4-13 demonstrates how the screen should appear.

Notice that the MakeFlag column (which is a Boolean value of some obscure use to the AdventureWorks business model) is shown as a checkbox. Also note that each of the column headers are shown as links. Click on one of them now—you see that the grid is sorted by that column. Also notice that at the bottom of the grid are links to page through more data, 10 rows at a time. Click on some of those too, to see the various pages.

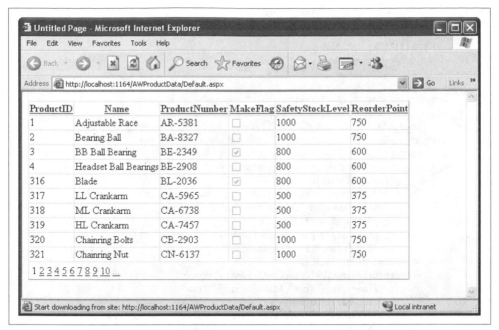

Figure 4-13. With the GridView in place and connected to the data source, you can see the data you asked for. Notice the clickable headings and the paging links.

Each time you click on one of the columns or one of the page numbers the entire page is posted back to the server, and you'll encounter a noticeable delay and flicker. You know how to fix that!

Close the browser and return to Design view. Drag an `UpdatePanel` control onto the page from the AJAX Extensions section of the Toolbox. Drag both the `SqlDataSource` and `GridView` controls already on the page into the `UpdatePanel`.

Run the application again. Notice there are no visible postbacks when you page or sort, and consequently, no flicker.

Auto-Generated Code

Switch to Source view and look at the markup code that was generated for the `GridView`. It should appear as highlighted in Example 4-1.

Example 4-1. GridView auto-generated control source code

```
<%@ Page Language="VB" AutoEventWireup="true" CodeFile="Default.aspx.vb"
Inherits="_Default" %>

<!DOCTYPE html PUBLIC "-//W3C//DTD XHTML 1.1//EN"
"http://www.w3.org/TR/xhtml11/DTD/xhtml11.dtd">
<html xmlns="http://www.w3.org/1999/xhtml">
```

Example 4-1. GridView auto-generated control source code (continued)

```
<head runat="server">
    <title>Untitled Page</title>
</head>
<body>
    <form id="form1" runat="server">
        <asp:ScriptManager ID="ScriptManager1" runat="server" />
        <div>
             </div>
        <asp:UpdatePanel ID="UpdatePanel1" runat="server">
            <ContentTemplate>
                <asp:SqlDataSource ID="SqlDataSource1" runat="server"
                    ConnectionString=
                      "<%$ ConnectionStrings:AdventureWorksConnectionString %>"
                    SelectCommand="SELECT [ProductID], [Name],
                    [ProductNumber],
                    [MakeFlag], [SafetyStockLevel], [ReorderPoint]
                    FROM [Production].[Product]" >
                </asp:SqlDataSource>
                <asp:GridView ID="GridView1" runat="server"
                    AllowPaging="True" AllowSorting="True"
                    AutoGenerateColumns="False"
                    DataKeyNames="ProductID" DataSourceID="SqlDataSource1">
                    <Columns>
                        <asp:BoundField DataField="ProductID"
                                HeaderText="ProductID" InsertVisible="False"
                                ReadOnly="True"
                                SortExpression="ProductID" />
                        <asp:BoundField DataField="Name" HeaderText="Name"
                                SortExpression="Name" />
                        <asp:BoundField DataField="ProductNumber"
                                HeaderText="ProductNumber"
                                SortExpression="ProductNumber" />
                        <asp:CheckBoxField DataField="MakeFlag"
                                HeaderText="MakeFlag"
                                SortExpression="MakeFlag" />
                        <asp:BoundField DataField="SafetyStockLevel"
                                HeaderText="SafetyStockLevel"
                                SortExpression="SafetyStockLevel" />
                        <asp:BoundField DataField="ReorderPoint"
                                HeaderText="ReorderPoint"
                                SortExpression="ReorderPoint" />
                    </Columns>
                </asp:GridView>
            </ContentTemplate>
        </asp:UpdatePanel>
    </form>
</body>
</html>
```

The IDE has done a lot of work for you. It has examined the data source and created a BoundField for each column in the data. Further, it has set the HeaderText to the name of the column in the database, represented by the DataField attribute. It has set the `AllowPaging` and `AllowSorting` properties to true. In addition, it has also set the `SortExpression` to the name of the field. Finally, you'll notice on the declaration of the `GridView` that it has set `AutoGenerateColumns` to `False`.

If you were creating the `GridView` by hand, and if you want to let the grid create all the columns directly from the retrieved data, you could simplify the code by setting `AutoGenerateColumns` to `True`. (If `AutoGenerateColumns` is set to `True`, and you also include explicitly bound columns, then you will display duplicate data.) To see this at work, create a second `GridView` by dragging another `GridView` control from the Toolbox inside the `UpdatePanel`, below the first.

In the Smart Tag, set the Data Source to the same source as that of the first, `SqlDataSource1`. Click on the "Enable Paging" and "Enable Sorting" checkboxes.

Now go to Source view. If necessary, delete the `<columns>` collection from the new grid, `GridView2`. Change `AutoGenerateColumns` to the default value: `True`. The declaration for this second `GridView` should look something like the following:

CODE►
```
<asp:GridView ID="GridView2" runat="server"
        AllowPaging="True" AllowSorting="True"
        DataSourceID="SqlDataSource1" >
</asp:GridView>
```

Run the page. Both grids behave identically and are visually indistinguishable. So why does the IDE create the more complex version? By turning off `AutoGenerateColumns`, the IDE gives you much greater control over the presentation of your data. For example, you can set the headings on the columns (such as changing `ProductNumber` to `Product No.`). You can change the order of the columns or remove columns you don't need, and you can add new columns with controls for manipulating the rows.

You can make these changes by manually coding the HTML in the Source view, or by switching to Design View and clicking the Smart Tag for the `GridView` and choosing Edit Columns. Do that now for GridView1 and you'll see the Fields dialog box, as shown in Figure 4-14.

This dialog box is divided into three main areas: the list of available fields, the list of selected fields (with buttons to remove fields or reorder the list), and the BoundField properties window on the right. When you click on a selected field (such as `ProductID`), you can set the way that field will be displayed in the data grid (such as changing the header to `ID`).

While you're examining what you can do with the `GridView`, let's make it look a little nicer. First, delete or comment out the second (simpler) grid (`GridView2`) you just created a few moments ago. Second, open the Smart Tag on the original grid. Click AutoFormat and choose one of the formatting options. Of course, you can format it by hand, but why work so hard for a simple example? We'll choose "Brown Sugar" because it shows up well in the printed book. Run the application. The output should appear as in Figure 4-15.

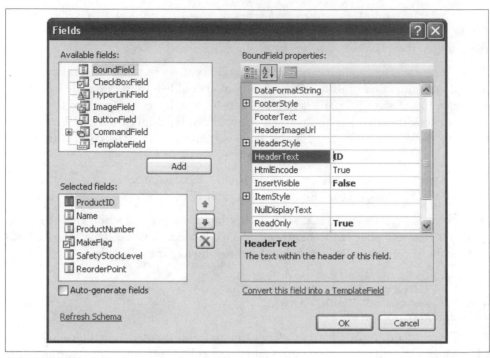

Figure 4-14. The field editor dialog lets you change the properties of your data columns, without having to do it in Source view.

Adding Insert, Update, and Delete Statements

At this point, the SqlDataSource you've created has only a SELECT statement to extract data from the database:

```
SelectCommand="SELECT ProductID, Name, ProductNumber,
    MakeFlag, SafetyStockLevel, ReorderPoint
    FROM Production.Product" >
```

That's fine, if all you want to do is display the data in the database. For a functional site, though, you probably want to be able to add new data, edit existing data, and even delete data. You can do all that just as easily as you did the SELECT statement, by asking your data source control to generate the remaining Create, Retrieve, Update, and Delete statements (fondly known as CRUD statements), using a wizard to make your work easier. To see this in action, switch to Design view, click on the SqlDataSource's Smart Tag, and choose Configure Data Source. The Configure Data Source Wizard opens, displaying your current connection string. Click Next and the Configure Select Statement dialog box is displayed, as shown earlier in Figure 4-8.

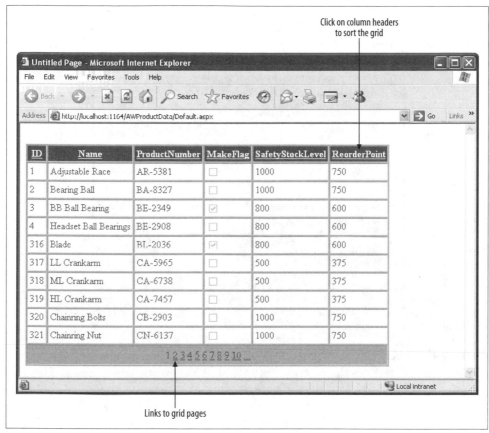

Figure 4-15. The AutoFormat option in the GridView's Smart Tag lets you choose the formatting option that best fits your site, and applies it automatically.

Recall the previous the Configure Data Source Wizard—it did not correctly identify the table in the autogenerated SELECT statement, omitting the schema name. You worked around that by specifying your own SQL statement. Since the SELECT statement you needed was relatively simple to type in, that was not a problem.

However, there is a *lot* of typing involved for all the CRUD statements. So for the rest of these statements, you will use the Wizard to generate the SQL code, and then just fix the table names.

Make sure the "Specify columns from a table or view" radio button is selected, and the Product table is selected. Check the columns you want returned by the SELECT statement (ProductID, Name, ProductNumber, MakeFlag, SafetyStockLevel, ReorderPoint). This will create a new SELECT statement.

Click the Advanced button to open the Advanced SQL Generation Options dialog box. Select the "Generate INSERT, UPDATE, and DELETE statements" checkbox, as shown in Figure 4-16.

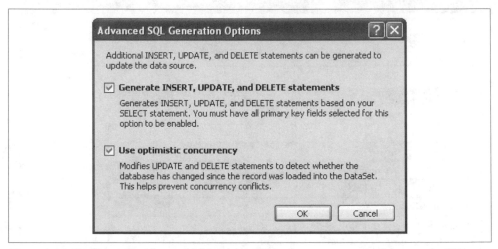

Figure 4-16. You'll use the Advanced SQL Options dialog box to automatically create the SQL statements to add, edit, and delete data from your data source.

Clicking this checkbox instructs the Wizard to create the remaining CRUD statements, and also enables the second checkbox, Use optimistic concurrency. This is a feature that safeguards your data in case another user makes a change to the database at the same time you do. Select this option as well, and Click OK. When you return to the Wizard, click Next then Finish. You may be asked to update your grid, which unfortunately will wipe out all your customization, but the good news is that you are now bound to a data source control that provides all four CRUD methods.

 This Wizard breaks down if any of the fields in the grid can have null values. When a database table is created, you must specify if a column must have data or if null values (no data) are allowed. If you include fields in the GridView which are allowed to be null, then you must handcode the SqlDataSource declaration in Source view.

Open the Smart Tag on the GridView control again, and reapply the look and feel you want. Also—and this is important—select the checkboxes "Enable Editing" and "Enable Deleting."

Switch to Source view. The SqlDataSource markup will appear similar to Example 4-2, except the new SQL commands have been added. You still need to modify the table names, or else you'll get the error you saw earlier (see Figure 4-9). Add the schema name [Production] to each of the four statements highlighted in Example 4-2.

The following code does not include concurrency detection.

Example 4-2. SqlDataSource with CRUD statements

```
<asp:SqlDataSource ID="SqlDataSource1" runat="server"
    ConnectionString="<%$ ConnectionStrings:AdventureWorksConnectionString %>"
    SelectCommand=" SELECT [ProductID], [Name], [ProductNumber],
                    [MakeFlag], [SafetyStockLevel], [ReorderPoint]
                    FROM [Production].[Product]"
    DeleteCommand="DELETE FROM [Production].[Product]
                    WHERE [ProductID] = @ProductID"
    InsertCommand="INSERT INTO [Production].[Product] ([Name],
                    [ProductNumber],
                    [MakeFlag], [SafetyStockLevel], [ReorderPoint])
                    VALUES (@Name, @ProductNumber, @MakeFlag,
                    @SafetyStockLevel,
                    @ReorderPoint)"
    UpdateCommand="UPDATE [Production].[Product] SET [Name] = @Name,
                    [ProductNumber] = @ProductNumber,
                    [MakeFlag] = @MakeFlag,
                    [SafetyStockLevel] = @SafetyStockLevel,
                    [ReorderPoint] = @ReorderPoint
                    WHERE [ProductID] = @ProductID" >
    <DeleteParameters>
        <asp:Parameter Name="ProductID" Type="Int32" />
    </DeleteParameters>
    <UpdateParameters>
        <asp:Parameter Name="Name" Type="String" />
        <asp:Parameter Name="ProductNumber" Type="String" />
        <asp:Parameter Name="MakeFlag" Type="Boolean" />
        <asp:Parameter Name="SafetyStockLevel" Type="Int16" />
        <asp:Parameter Name="ReorderPoint" Type="Int16" />
        <asp:Parameter Name="ProductID" Type="Int32" />
    </UpdateParameters>
    <InsertParameters>
        <asp:Parameter Name="Name" Type="String" />
        <asp:Parameter Name="ProductNumber" Type="String" />
        <asp:Parameter Name="MakeFlag" Type="Boolean" />
        <asp:Parameter Name="SafetyStockLevel" Type="Int16" />
        <asp:Parameter Name="ReorderPoint" Type="Int16" />
    </InsertParameters>
</asp:SqlDataSource>
```

Switch back to Design view and notice the Edit and Delete buttons on each row. They are the result of checking the Enable Editing and Enable Deleting checkboxes.

Taking apart the code in Example 4-2, on the first line is the declaration for the SqlDataSource (and its corresponding closing tag at the bottom). After the ID, the obligatory runat="server", and the ConnectionString attribute, you see four attributes: the SelectCommand (which was there previously) and the new DeleteCommand, InsertCommand, and UpdateCommand.

The DeleteCommand takes a single parameter (@ProductID), which is specified in the DeleteParameters element:

```
<DeleteParameters>
    <asp:Parameter Name="ProductID" Type="Int32" />
</DeleteParameters>
```

—SQL CHEAT SHEET—
Parameters

A parameter to a SQL statement allows for parts of the statement to be replaced when it is actually run. SQL parameters are always preceded with the @ symbol. So, in the following SQL statement:

```
delete from Products where ReorderPoint > @ReorderPoint
```

all the records with a value of ReorderPoint greater than some specified value will be deleted from the Products table. One time the statement is run, that value may be 100, the next time it may be 5.

The UpdateCommand control requires more parameters, one for each column you'll be updating, as well as a parameter for ProductID (to make sure the correct record is updated). Similarly, the InsertCommand takes parameters for each column for the new record. All of these parameters are within the definition of the SqlDataSource.

Displaying and Updating the Data

Now that your SqlDataSource object is ready to go, you only have to set up your GridView control. In Design view, click on the GridView Smart Tag and choose "Edit Columns." Verify that the checkboxes to enable editing and deleting are selected, as shown in Figure 4-17.

If you prefer to have buttons for Edit and Delete, rather than links, click on the Smart Tag and select "Edit Columns...." When the Fields dialog box opens, click the Command Field entry in the Selected Fields area (lower-left corner). This brings up the Command Field Properties in the right-hand window. In the Appearance section of the Fields editor, choose ButtonType and then change Link to Button in the drop-down menu next to ButtonType, as shown in Figure 4-18.

The result is that the commands (Edit and Delete) are shown as buttons, as shown in Figure 4-19.

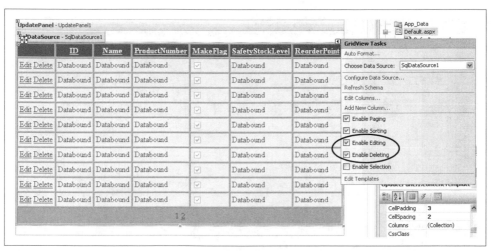

Figure 4-17. Select the Smart Tag on the GridView, and check the boxes to enable editing and deleting.

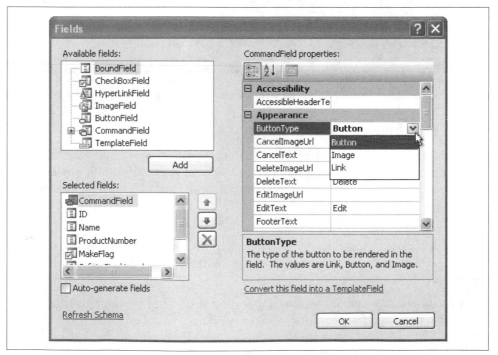

Figure 4-18. Click the Smart Tag of the GridView, then click Edit Columns to get this Fields dialog box where you can select and edit the columns in the GridView. Here, the CommandField button type is being changed.

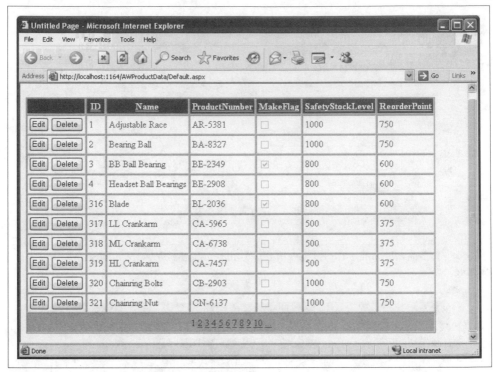

Figure 4-19. You can change the Edit and Delete links in the GridView to buttons, if you prefer.

Take It for a Spin

Start the application. The product database information is loaded into your `GridView`. When you click the Edit button, the data grid automatically enters edit mode. You'll notice that the editable text fields change to text boxes and checkboxes, as appropriate, and the command buttons change from Edit and Delete to Update and Cancel. Make a small change to one field, as shown in Figure 4-20.

When you click the Update button for that row, the grid and the database are both updated, which you can confirm by opening the table in the database, as shown in Figure 4-21.

To open the database table, stop the application first. Then on the right side of the IDE, click the Database Explorer tab (in VWD; it is called Server Explorer in VS2005). Expand the AdventureWorks folder, and then expand the Tables folder. Scroll down until you find the `Product` (`Production`) table (in the IDE, the schema name is displayed in parenthesis *after* the table name—go figure), then right-click it, and select "Show Table Data." This will show you the contents of the table from within the IDE.

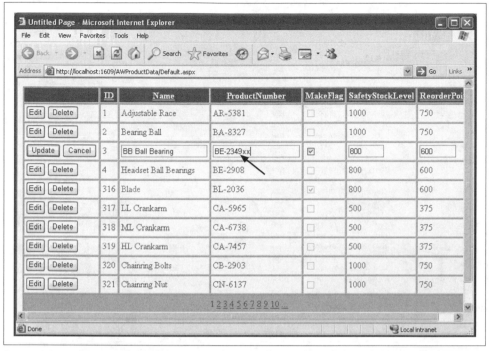

Figure 4-20. When you click Edit on a row, that row enters edit mode. Any fields that can be edited change to text boxes and checkboxes.

Modifying the Grid Based on Events

Suppose you would like you to modify the grid so the contents of the Name column are red when the MakeFlag column is checked, that is, when its value is True. In addition, you want all the ProductNumbers that begin with the letters CA to display in green. You can do this by handling the RowDataBound event. As the GridView is populated with data, each row of data is bound to the GridView individually, and the RowDataBound event is fired once for each row.

To modify the GridView, switch to Design view, click the GridView, click the lightning bolt in the Properties window, and double-click in the method name column (currently blank) to the right of the RowDataBound event. The IDE will create an event handler named GridView1_RowDataBound( ) and then place you in the code-behind file within the skeleton of that method, ready for you to start typing code.

The second argument to this method is of type GridViewRowEventArgs. This object has useful information about the row that is databound, which is accessible through the Row property of the event argument.

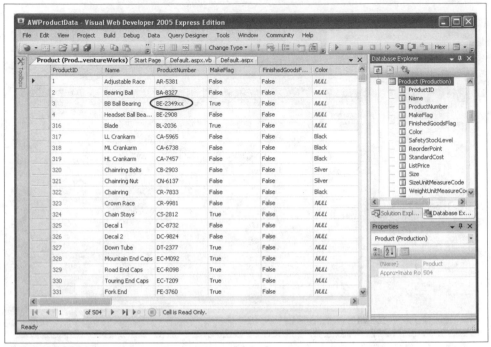

Figure 4-21. If you view the table in the database after editing it in the GridView, you'll see that the changes have been saved.

Enter the code shown in Example 4-3.

Example 4-3. Handling theRowDataBound event

```
Protected Sub GridView1_RowDataBound(ByVal sender As Object, _
            ByVal e As System.Web.UI.WebControls.GridViewRowEventArgs)
   If e.Row.RowType = DataControlRowType.DataRow Then
       Dim cellProductNumber As TableCell = e.Row.Cells(3)  ' ProductNumber column
       If cellProductNumber.Text.Substring(0, 2) = "CA" Then
           cellProductNumber.ForeColor = Drawing.Color.Green
       End If

       Dim cellMakeFlag As TableCell = e.Row.Cells(4)  ' MakeFlag column
       Dim cb As CheckBox = CType(cellMakeFlag.Controls(0), CheckBox)
       If cb.Checked Then
           e.Row.Cells(2).ForeColor = Drawing.Color.Red
       End If
   End If
End Sub
```

The first `If` statement (highlighted in Example 4-3) tests if the type of `Row` passed in as a parameter—in other words, the row that was bound and triggered this event—is a `DataRow` (rather than a header, footer, or something else).

—VB CHEAT SHEET—
If-Then Statements

When you're working with data, you usually don't know what the data will be when you're writing your code. You might want to take different actions depending on the value of a variable. That's what the If-Then statement is for. You've seen how the Checked value of a checkbox or radio button can affect the behavior of other controls. With the If-Then statement, you can be even more flexible:

```
If chkMyCheckBox.Checked = true Then
    txtMyTextBox.Text = "It's true!"
End If
```

The condition you want to evaluate comes after the If, but before the Then. In this case, you want to determine if the checkbox is checked, so the condition is chkMyCheckBox.Checked = true.

If it's true, the statement after the Then is executed, setting txtMyTextBox.Text to "It's true!" You can execute any number of statements in the Then section.

If the condition is false, nothing happens.

You must insert the statement End If at the end of the Then block so that your code knows where the Then block ends and can continue executing as normal from that point.

The Else statement comes into play when you want to take one of two actions. With just an If-Then statement, if the condition you're evaluating is false, nothing happens. However, you might want to take one action if the condition is true, and another if it's false, like this:

```
If chkMyCheckBox.Checked = true Then
    txtMyTextBox.Text = "It's true!"
Else
    txtMyTextBox.Text = "Not true!"
End If
```

This code sends one message to txtMyTextBox if the condition is true, and a different message if it's false.

You have lots of different options when you specify conditions, which are based on a set of "operators" that you're probably already familiar with. For example, instead of testing to see if one part of your condition is equal (=) to another, you could use one of these other operators:

- <> not equal to
- < less than
- > greater than
- <= less than or equal to
- >= greater than or equal to

In short, you can test for any condition that evaluates to true or false—in other words, a Boolean. In fact, the Checked property of a textbox is a Boolean all by itself, so you could have used this for the condition:

```
If chkMyCheckBox.Checked Then
```

Once you know you are dealing with a DataRow, you can extract the cell(s) you want to examine from that row. Here, we will look at two cells: the ProductNumber cell is the fourth cell in the row, at offset (index) 3, and the MakeFlag cell is the fifth cell in, at offset 4. (Remember, all indices are zero-based.)

To access the ProductNumber cell, you define a new variable, cellProductNumber, defined as a TableCell with the As keyword, and set it equal to the cell at offset 3 in the row, like this:

```
Dim cellProductNumber As TableCell = e.Row.Cells(3)
```

Once you have the cell as a variable, you want to get the text contained in the cell to compare to your known value. You do that by accessing the Text property of cellProductNumber, and then using the Substring() function.

The Substring() function, as you might guess from its name, extracts a smaller string from a larger one. This is a pretty simple function to work with. First, you call the function on a string, and you give it two numbers as parameters: the index of the start of the substring, and the length of the substring. As with all other indices, the first character in the string is position zero. You want the first two characters from the Text string, so the starting index is 0, and the length of the substring is 2. Therefore, to get the first two characters from your string, you use the function Substring(0,2). Once you have that substring, you can use a simple If statement to compare it to the string you want to match, "CA":

```
If cellProductNumber.Text.Substring(0, 2) = "CA" Then
```

It there is a match, you want to set the ForeColor property of the cell to green, which you can do using the Drawing.Color.Green property:

```
cellProductNumber.ForeColor = Drawing.Color.Green
```

In the case of the MakeFlag, it is somewhat more complicated. It's easy enough to isolate the cell that contains the checkbox—it's at index 4—and then assign that value to a new variable called cellMakeFlag:

```
Dim cellMakeFlag As TableCell = e.Row.Cells(4)
```

This is the same technique you used to isolate the ProductNumber cell. In this case, though, the Text property of this cell will always be empty. However, it does contain a CheckBox control, which is the only control in the cell. Instead of reading the *text* in the cell, you want to read the *value* of the Checked property of that CheckBox control. Each cell has a collection of all the controls contained in the cell, called Controls, which has a zero-based index. Since the checkbox you want is the only control in the collection, you know it's at cellMakeFlag.Controls(0). Next you define a new variable, cb, which you define as a CheckBox. Then you use the CType function on the control you just isolated, to convert the control to a CheckBox. This works because we know it is a CheckBox:

```
Dim cb As CheckBox = CType(cellMakeFlag.Controls(0), CheckBox)
```

CType converts its first argument into an object of a new type as specified by its second argument. In the case shown here, it is converting a control to a CheckBox. If the object you pass is not of the appropriate type, CType generates an error. Read this statement:

```
Dim cb As CheckBox = CType(cellMakeFlag.Controls(0), CheckBox)
```

as follows: "Find the first item in the Controls collection in cellMakeFlag and convert it to type CheckBox." The result will be an object of type CheckBox or an exception will be thrown. If no exception is thrown, assign the result to the variable cb, which is of type CheckBox.

If you want to be extra careful, you can wrap the CType conversion in a try/catch block, discussed in Chapter 8, but that isn't really necessary here as you know it is a checkbox.

Then you test the Checked property of the CheckBox:

```
If cb.Checked Then
```

If the box is checked, cb.Checked will evaluate to true. If it is checked, you want to set the ForeColor property of the third cell in the row (offset 2), the ProductName column:

```
e.Row.Cells(2).ForeColor = Drawing.Color.Red
```

You set the color of the cell the same way you did for ProductNumber, but notice this time you're not changing the color of the checkbox cell itself—you're changing a different cell in the table.

Run the web site. It will look identical to Figure 4-19, except the product names for which the MakeFlag field is checked will display in red, and some of the product numbers will display in green. (Neither of these changes will be obvious in the printed book, so we will forego a figure showing the color changes.)

Selecting Data from the GridView

Often you need to select a row from the grid and extract data from that row. This is easy to do using the SelectedIndexChanged event of the GridView.

To see how this works, drag a Label control from the Standard section of the Toolbox onto the Design view, below the grid but within the UpdatePanel control. Change the Text property of this Label to Name. Then drag a TextBox control next to the Label. Change its ID property to txtName and set its ReadOnly property to True. You now have a place to display the name of the selected item from the grid.

Click on the Smart Tag of the GridView and check the "Enable Selection" checkbox. This will cause a Select button to display in the first column of the grid, next to the Edit and Delete buttons already there, as shown in Figure 4-22.

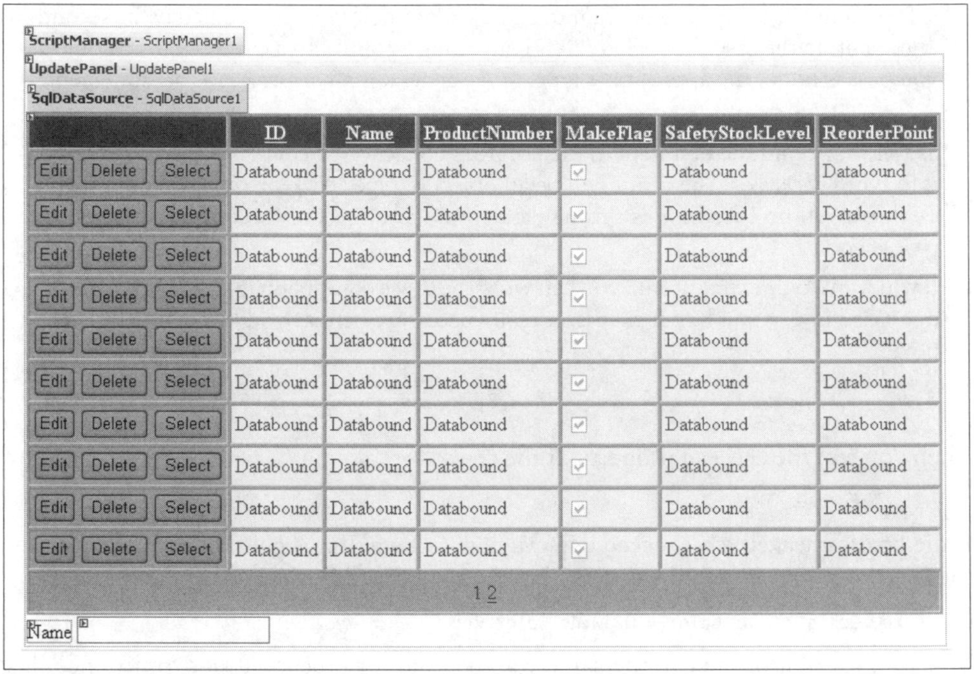

Figure 4-22. Clicking Enable Selection in the Smart Tag causes Select buttons to appear in a GridView.

Now all you need to do is set up the event handler to respond to the Select buttons. Double-click on the Select button in the first row of the grid. This will open up the code-behind file with the skeleton of the SelectedIndexChanged already created for you, ready to accept your custom code. Enter the highlighted code from the following snippet:

```
Protected Sub GridView1_SelectedIndexChanged(ByVal sender As Object, _
    ByVal e As System.EventArgs)
    If GridView1.SelectedRow.RowType = DataControlRowType.DataRow Then
        Dim cellName As TableCell = GridView1.SelectedRow.Cells(2)   ' Name column
        txtName.Text = cellName.Text
    End If
End Sub
```

This code first tests to determine if the selected row is a DataRow (as opposed to a HeaderRow or a FooterRow). If it is a DataRow, it creates a variable of type TableCell, which is assigned to the third cell in the selected row (because of zero-based indexing, the third item will have an index value of 2). Then the Text property of the Text-Box is set equal to the Text property of that cell.

Run the app and click on one of the Select buttons. The name from the selected row appears in the TextBox.

Passing Parameters to the SELECT Query

Sometimes you do not want to display all the records in a table. For example, you might want to have users select a product from your grid and display the order details for it in a second grid on the current page. To do this, you'll need a way to select a product as well as a way to pass the ID of the selected product to the second grid. The Select buttons are already in place from the previous example, so all you need to do now is pass the ID of the selected product to the second grid.

To keep the downloadable source code clear, copy the previous example, AWProductData to a new web site, AWProductDataOrderDetails.

 See Appendix A for details about how to copy a web site.

You need to create a second GridView, which will be used to display the order details. From the Toolbox, drag the second GridView onto the page below the first, and then drag the Label and TextBox inside the UpdatePanel. Open the Smart Tag for the UpdatePanel. As you did earlier in the chapter, create a new data source (name it AdventureWorksOrderDetails), but use the existing connection string. Choose the SalesOrderDetail table, select the desired columns (for this example, SalesOrderID, CarrierTrackingNumber, OrderQty, UnitPrice, UnitPriceDiscount, and LineTotal), and then click the Where button, as shown in Figure 4-23.

A WHERE clause is a SQL language keyword used to narrow the set of data returned by the SELECT statement. In other words, you're saying, "Get me all the records from this table, where this condition is true." The condition could be defined any number of ways—where the amount in inventory is less than 10, where the customer name is "Smith," or where the copyright date is after 1985. It all depends on the types of information you have stored in your columns.

When you click the WHERE button, the Add WHERE Clause dialog opens, which you can see in Figure 4-24. First, you pick the column you want to match on, in this case ProductID. Next, pick the appropriate operator for your condition statement. Your choices include among others, equal to, less than/greater than, like, and contains. For this exercise, use the default (=).

The third drop-down lets you pick the source for the ProductID—that is, where you will get the term you want to match on. You can pick from any one of several objects in the menu or choose None if you'll be providing a source manually. In this case, you'll obtain the source of the ProductID from the first GridView, so choose Control.

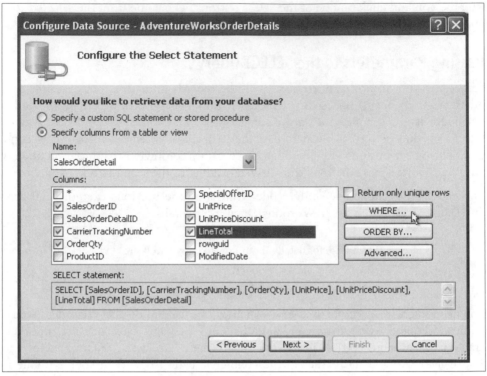

Figure 4-23. Configuring the SalesOrderDetail table SELECT statement is similar to the way you set up the first DataSource, but this time, you'll add a WHERE clause.

When you choose Control, the Parameter properties panel of the dialog wakes up. You are asked to provide the ID of the Control containing the target parameter. Select GridView1. Once you've made all your choices, the screen will resemble Figure 4-24.

Click Add. When you do, the upper portion of the dialog returns to its initial (blank) state and the WHERE clause is added to the WHERE Clause window. You could add additional WHERE clauses at this point, to further restrict the data, but we won't for this example.

Click OK to return to the Configure Select Statement dialog box. While you are at it, sort the results by the SalesOrderID column by clicking on the Order By button. The Add ORDER BY Clause dialog with the SalesOrderID column selected is shown in Figure 4-25. The ORDER BY clause is another SQL keyword, and this one does just what its name implies—it sorts the results using the selected field for sort order.

Click OK until the Configure Data Source Wizard is finished.

Switch to Source view and again fix the name of the tables in the SQL statements that were auto-generated. The markup for the second GridView and its associated SqlDataSource is shown in Example 4-4, with the corrected table names highlighted.

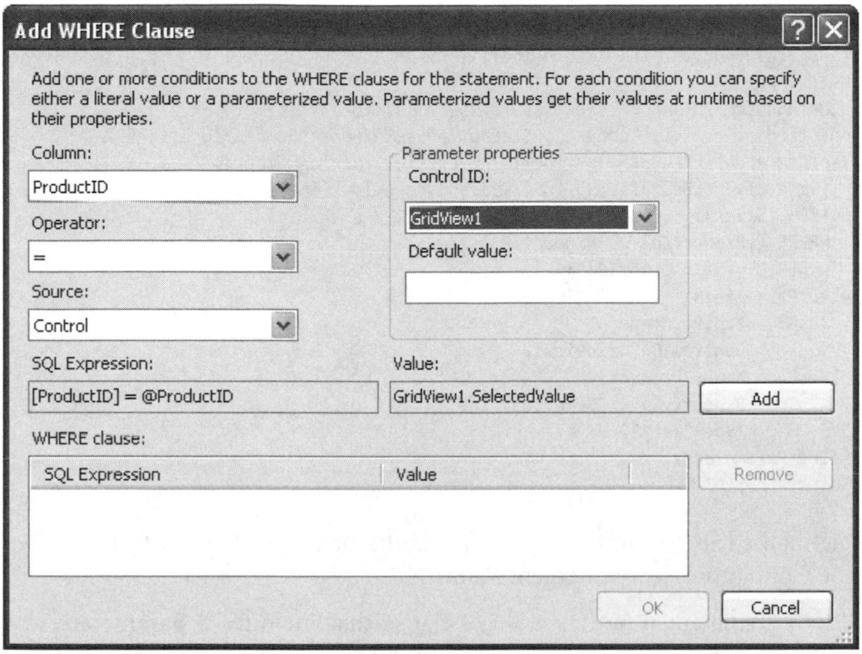

Figure 4-24. Add a Where clause to your SELECT statement with the Add WHERE Clause dialog. You select the column, the operator, and the source here.

Figure 4-25. Add an ORDER BY clause to sort the results of your SELECT statement.

Example 4-4. Order detail grid withSqlDataSource

```
<asp:GridView ID="GridView2" runat="server"
    DataSourceID="AdventureWorksOrderDetails">
</asp:GridView>
<asp:SqlDataSource ID="AdventureWorksOrderDetails" runat="server"
    ConnectionString="<%$ ConnectionStrings:AdventureWorksConnectionString %>"
    SelectCommand="SELECT [SalesOrderID], [CarrierTrackingNumber],
        [OrderQty], [UnitPrice], [UnitPriceDiscount], [LineTotal]
        FROM [Sales].[SalesOrderDetail]
        WHERE ([ProductID] = @ProductID)
        ORDER BY [SalesOrderID]">
    <SelectParameters>
        <asp:ControlParameter
                ControlID="GridView1"
                Name="ProductID"
                PropertyName="SelectedValue"
                Type="Int32" />
    </SelectParameters>
</asp:SqlDataSource>
```

Also highlighted in Example 4-4 are the results of the WHERE and ORDER BY buttons from the Configure Select Statement Wizard.

The SELECT statement now has a WHERE clause that includes a parameterized value (@ProductID). In addition, within the definition of the SqlDataSource control is a definition of the SelectParameters. This includes one parameter of type asp:ControlParameter, which is a parameter that knows how to get its value from a control (in our example, GridView1). In addition, a second property, PropertyName, tells it which property in the GridView to check. A third property, Type, tells it that the type of the value it is getting is of type Int32, so it can properly pass that parameter to the SELECT statement.

You may now reformat your grid and edit the columns as you did for the first grid, and then try out your new page, which should look something like Figure 4-26.

 The AdventureWorks database has no order details for any of the entries with ProductIDs below 707. The first entry with details is on page 22 of the grid, so be sure to move to page 22 (or later) to see product details. If you select a product that does not have any order details, the second grid will *not* appear.

Source Code Listings

The complete markup for the *Default.aspx* file in the AWProductData site is shown in Example 4-5, with the code-behind shown directly after in Example 4-6.

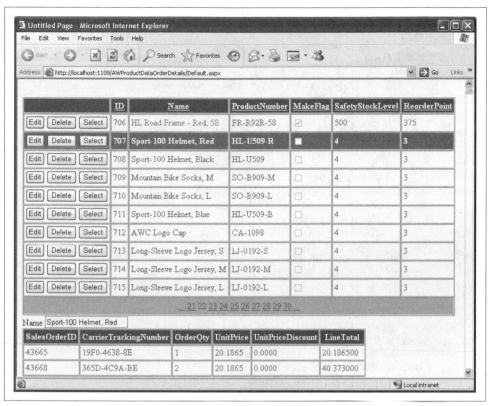

Figure 4-26. When you selected a product in the first grid, the order details appear below in the second grid.

Example 4-5. Default.aspx for AWProductData

```
<%@ Page Language="VB" AutoEventWireup="true" CodeFile="Default.aspx.vb"
    Inherits="_Default" %>

<!DOCTYPE html PUBLIC "-//W3C//DTD XHTML 1.1//EN"
"http://www.w3.org/TR/xhtml11/DTD/xhtml11.dtd">
<html xmlns="http://www.w3.org/1999/xhtml">
<head runat="server">
    <title>Untitled Page</title>
</head>
<body>
    <form id="form1" runat="server">
        <asp:ScriptManager ID="ScriptManager1" runat="server" />
          
        <asp:UpdatePanel ID="UpdatePanel1" runat="server">
            <ContentTemplate>
        <asp:SqlDataSource ID="SqlDataSource1" runat="server"
            ConnectionString=
                "<%$ ConnectionStrings:AdventureWorksConnectionString %>"
```

Example 4-5. Default.aspx for AWProductData (continued)

```
            SelectCommand="SELECT [ProductID], [Name], [ProductNumber], [MakeFlag],
                [SafetyStockLevel], [ReorderPoint] FROM [Production].[Product]"
            DeleteCommand="DELETE FROM [Production].[Product]
                WHERE [ProductID] = @original_ProductID AND [Name] = @original_Name
                    AND [ProductNumber] = @original_ProductNumber
                    AND [MakeFlag] = @original_MakeFlag
                    AND [SafetyStockLevel] = @original_SafetyStockLevel
                    AND [ReorderPoint] = @original_ReorderPoint"
            InsertCommand="INSERT INTO [Production].[Product] ([Name],
                [ProductNumber], [MakeFlag], [SafetyStockLevel], [ReorderPoint])
                VALUES (@Name, @ProductNumber, @MakeFlag, @SafetyStockLevel,
                    @ReorderPoint)"
            UpdateCommand="UPDATE [Production].[Product]
                    SET [Name] = @Name, [ProductNumber] = @ProductNumber,
                     [MakeFlag] = @MakeFlag,
                     [SafetyStockLevel] = @SafetyStockLevel,
                     [ReorderPoint] = @ReorderPoint
                WHERE [ProductID] = @original_ProductID
                    AND [Name] = @original_Name
                    AND [ProductNumber] = @original_ProductNumber
                    AND [MakeFlag] = @original_MakeFlag
                    AND [SafetyStockLevel] = @original_SafetyStockLevel
                    AND [ReorderPoint] = @original_ReorderPoint"
            ConflictDetection="CompareAllValues"
            OldValuesParameterFormatString="original_{0}" >
            <DeleteParameters>
                <asp:Parameter Name="original_ProductID" Type="Int32" />
                <asp:Parameter Name="original_Name" Type="String" />
                <asp:Parameter Name="original_ProductNumber" Type="String" />
                <asp:Parameter Name="original_MakeFlag" Type="Boolean" />
                <asp:Parameter Name="original_SafetyStockLevel" Type="Int16" />
                <asp:Parameter Name="original_ReorderPoint" Type="Int16" />
            </DeleteParameters>
            <UpdateParameters>
                <asp:Parameter Name="Name" Type="String" />
                <asp:Parameter Name="ProductNumber" Type="String" />
                <asp:Parameter Name="MakeFlag" Type="Boolean" />
                <asp:Parameter Name="SafetyStockLevel" Type="Int16" />
                <asp:Parameter Name="ReorderPoint" Type="Int16" />
                <asp:Parameter Name="original_ProductID" Type="Int32" />
                <asp:Parameter Name="original_Name" Type="String" />
                <asp:Parameter Name="original_ProductNumber" Type="String" />
                <asp:Parameter Name="original_MakeFlag" Type="Boolean" />
                <asp:Parameter Name="original_SafetyStockLevel" Type="Int16" />
                <asp:Parameter Name="original_ReorderPoint" Type="Int16" />
            </UpdateParameters>
            <InsertParameters>
                <asp:Parameter Name="Name" Type="String" />
                <asp:Parameter Name="ProductNumber" Type="String" />
                <asp:Parameter Name="MakeFlag" Type="Boolean" />
                <asp:Parameter Name="SafetyStockLevel" Type="Int16" />
                <asp:Parameter Name="ReorderPoint" Type="Int16" />
            </InsertParameters>
```

Example 4-5. Default.aspx for AWProductData (continued)

```
        </asp:SqlDataSource>
                <asp:GridView ID="GridView1" runat="server"
                    AllowPaging="True" AllowSorting="True"
                    AutoGenerateColumns="False"
                    DataKeyNames="ProductID" DataSourceID="SqlDataSource1"
                    BackColor="#DEBA84" BorderColor="#DEBA84" BorderStyle="None"
                    BorderWidth="1px" CellPadding="3" CellSpacing="2"
                    OnRowDataBound="GridView1_RowDataBound"
                    OnSelectedIndexChanged="GridView1_SelectedIndexChanged">
                    <Columns>
                        <asp:CommandField ButtonType="Button"
                                ShowDeleteButton="True" ShowEditButton="True" />
                        <asp:BoundField DataField="ProductID" HeaderText="ID"
                                InsertVisible="False"
                                ReadOnly="True" SortExpression="ProductID" />
                        <asp:BoundField DataField="Name" HeaderText="Name"
                                SortExpression="Name" />
                        <asp:BoundField DataField="ProductNumber"
                                HeaderText="ProductNumber"
                                SortExpression="ProductNumber" />
                        <asp:CheckBoxField DataField="MakeFlag"
                            HeaderText="MakeFlag" SortExpression="MakeFlag" />
                        <asp:BoundField DataField="SafetyStockLevel"
                            HeaderText="SafetyStockLevel"
                            SortExpression="SafetyStockLevel" />
                        <asp:BoundField DataField="ReorderPoint"
                            HeaderText="ReorderPoint"
                            SortExpression="ReorderPoint" />
                    </Columns>
                    <FooterStyle BackColor="#F7DFB5" ForeColor="#8C4510" />
                    <RowStyle BackColor="#FFF7E7" ForeColor="#8C4510" />
                    <SelectedRowStyle BackColor="#738A9C" Font-Bold="True"
                            ForeColor="White" />
                    <PagerStyle ForeColor="#8C4510" HorizontalAlign="Center" />
                    <HeaderStyle BackColor="#A55129" Font-Bold="True"
                            ForeColor="White" />
                </asp:GridView>
                <asp:Label ID="Label1" runat="server" Text="Name"></asp:Label>
                <asp:TextBox ID="txtName" runat="server"></asp:TextBox>
            </ContentTemplate>
        </asp:UpdatePanel>
    </form>
</body>
</html>
```

Example 4-6. Default.aspx.vb for AWProductData

```
Partial Class _Default
    Inherits System.Web.UI.Page

    Protected Sub GridView1_RowDataBound(ByVal sender As Object, _
                ByVal e As System.Web.UI.WebControls.GridViewRowEventArgs)
```

Example 4-6. Default.aspx.vb for AWProductData (continued)

```
        If e.Row.RowType = DataControlRowType.DataRow Then
            Dim cellProductNumber As TableCell = e.Row.Cells(3)  ' ProductNumber
            If cellProductNumber.Text.Substring(0, 2) = "CA" Then
                cellProductNumber.ForeColor = Drawing.Color.Green
            End If

            Dim cellMakeFlag As TableCell = e.Row.Cells(4)  ' MakeFlag column
            Dim cb As CheckBox = CType(cellMakeFlag.Controls(0), CheckBox)
            If cb.Checked Then
                e.Row.Cells(2).ForeColor = Drawing.Color.Red
            End If
        End If
    End Sub

    Protected Sub GridView1_SelectedIndexChanged(ByVal sender As Object, _
            ByVal e As System.EventArgs)
        If GridView1.SelectedRow.RowType = DataControlRowType.DataRow Then
            Dim cellName As TableCell = GridView1.SelectedRow.Cells(2) ' Name
            txtName.Text = cellName.Text
        End If
    End Sub
End Class
```

The complete markup for the *Default.aspx* file in the AWProductDataOrderDetails site is shown in Example 4-7, and the code-behind is shown in Example 4-8.

Example 4-7. Default.aspx for AWProductDataOrderDetails

```
<%@ Page Language="VB" AutoEventWireup="true" CodeFile="Default.aspx.vb"
    Inherits="_Default" %>

<!DOCTYPE html PUBLIC "-//W3C//DTD XHTML 1.1//EN"
"http://www.w3.org/TR/xhtml11/DTD/xhtml11.dtd">
<html xmlns="http://www.w3.org/1999/xhtml">
<head runat="server">
    <title>Untitled Page</title>
</head>
<body>
    <form id="form1" runat="server">
        <asp:ScriptManager ID="ScriptManager1" runat="server" />
          
        <asp:UpdatePanel ID="UpdatePanel1" runat="server">
            <ContentTemplate>
        <asp:SqlDataSource ID="SqlDataSource1" runat="server"
            ConnectionString=
                "<%$ ConnectionStrings:AdventureWorksConnectionString %>"
            SelectCommand="SELECT [ProductID], [Name], [ProductNumber], [MakeFlag],
                [SafetyStockLevel], [ReorderPoint] FROM [Production].[Product]"
            DeleteCommand="DELETE FROM [Production].[Product]
                WHERE [ProductID] = @original_ProductID
                    AND [Name] = @original_Name
                    AND [ProductNumber] = @original_ProductNumber
```

Example 4-7. Default.aspx for AWProductDataOrderDetails (continued)

```
                    AND [MakeFlag] = @original_MakeFlag
                    AND [SafetyStockLevel] = @original_SafetyStockLevel
                    AND [ReorderPoint] = @original_ReorderPoint"
        InsertCommand="INSERT INTO [Production].[Product] ([Name],
            [ProductNumber], [MakeFlag], [SafetyStockLevel], [ReorderPoint])
            VALUES (@Name, @ProductNumber, @MakeFlag, @SafetyStockLevel,
            @ReorderPoint)"
        UpdateCommand="UPDATE [Production].[Product]
            SET [Name] = @Name, [ProductNumber] = @ProductNumber,
                [MakeFlag] = @MakeFlag,
                [SafetyStockLevel] = @SafetyStockLevel,
                [ReorderPoint] = @ReorderPoint
            WHERE [ProductID] = @original_ProductID
                AND [Name] = @original_Name
                AND [ProductNumber] = @original_ProductNumber
                AND [MakeFlag] = @original_MakeFlag
                AND [SafetyStockLevel] = @original_SafetyStockLevel
                AND [ReorderPoint] = @original_ReorderPoint"
        ConflictDetection="CompareAllValues"
        OldValuesParameterFormatString="original_{0}" >
    <DeleteParameters>
        <asp:Parameter Name="original_ProductID" Type="Int32" />
        <asp:Parameter Name="original_Name" Type="String" />
        <asp:Parameter Name="original_ProductNumber" Type="String" />
        <asp:Parameter Name="original_MakeFlag" Type="Boolean" />
        <asp:Parameter Name="original_SafetyStockLevel" Type="Int16" />
        <asp:Parameter Name="original_ReorderPoint" Type="Int16" />
    </DeleteParameters>
    <UpdateParameters>
        <asp:Parameter Name="Name" Type="String" />
        <asp:Parameter Name="ProductNumber" Type="String" />
        <asp:Parameter Name="MakeFlag" Type="Boolean" />
        <asp:Parameter Name="SafetyStockLevel" Type="Int16" />
        <asp:Parameter Name="ReorderPoint" Type="Int16" />
        <asp:Parameter Name="original_ProductID" Type="Int32" />
        <asp:Parameter Name="original_Name" Type="String" />
        <asp:Parameter Name="original_ProductNumber" Type="String" />
        <asp:Parameter Name="original_MakeFlag" Type="Boolean" />
        <asp:Parameter Name="original_SafetyStockLevel" Type="Int16" />
        <asp:Parameter Name="original_ReorderPoint" Type="Int16" />
    </UpdateParameters>
    <InsertParameters>
        <asp:Parameter Name="Name" Type="String" />
        <asp:Parameter Name="ProductNumber" Type="String" />
        <asp:Parameter Name="MakeFlag" Type="Boolean" />
        <asp:Parameter Name="SafetyStockLevel" Type="Int16" />
        <asp:Parameter Name="ReorderPoint" Type="Int16" />
    </InsertParameters>
</asp:SqlDataSource>
        <asp:GridView ID="GridView1" runat="server"
            AllowPaging="True" AllowSorting="True"
            AutoGenerateColumns="False"
```

Example 4-7. Default.aspx for AWProductDataOrderDetails (continued)

```
                    DataKeyNames="ProductID" DataSourceID="SqlDataSource1"
                    BackColor="#DEBA84" BorderColor="#DEBA84" BorderStyle="None"
                    BorderWidth="1px" CellPadding="3" CellSpacing="2"
                    OnRowDataBound="GridView1_RowDataBound"
                    OnSelectedIndexChanged="GridView1_SelectedIndexChanged">
                    <Columns>
                        <asp:CommandField ButtonType="Button"
                            ShowDeleteButton="True"
                            ShowEditButton="True"
                            ShowSelectButton="True" />
                        <asp:BoundField DataField="ProductID" HeaderText="ID"
                            InsertVisible="False"
                            ReadOnly="True"
                            SortExpression="ProductID" />
                        <asp:BoundField DataField="Name" HeaderText="Name"
                            SortExpression="Name" />
                        <asp:BoundField DataField="ProductNumber"
                            HeaderText="ProductNumber"
                            SortExpression="ProductNumber" />
                        <asp:CheckBoxField DataField="MakeFlag"
                            HeaderText="MakeFlag" SortExpression="MakeFlag" />
                        <asp:BoundField DataField="SafetyStockLevel"
                            HeaderText="SafetyStockLevel"
                            SortExpression="SafetyStockLevel" />
                        <asp:BoundField DataField="ReorderPoint"
                            HeaderText="ReorderPoint"
                            SortExpression="ReorderPoint" />
                    </Columns>
                    <FooterStyle BackColor="#F7DFB5" ForeColor="#8C4510" />
                    <RowStyle BackColor="#FFF7E7" ForeColor="#8C4510" />
                    <SelectedRowStyle BackColor="#738A9C" Font-Bold="True"
                            ForeColor="White" />
                    <PagerStyle ForeColor="#8C4510" HorizontalAlign="Center" />
                    <HeaderStyle BackColor="#A55129" Font-Bold="True"
                            ForeColor="White" />
                </asp:GridView>
                <asp:Label ID="Label1" runat="server" Text="Name"></asp:Label>
                <asp:TextBox ID="txtName" runat="server" ReadOnly="True">
                        </asp:TextBox>
                <br />
                <asp:GridView ID="GridView2" runat="server"
                    DataSourceID="AdventureWorksOrderDetails"
                    BackColor="#DEBA84" BorderColor="#DEBA84" BorderStyle="None"
                            BorderWidth="1px"
                    CellPadding="3" CellSpacing="2">
                    <FooterStyle BackColor="#F7DFB5" ForeColor="#8C4510" />
                    <RowStyle BackColor="#FFF7E7" ForeColor="#8C4510" />
                    <SelectedRowStyle BackColor="#738A9C" Font-Bold="True"
                            ForeColor="White" />
                    <PagerStyle ForeColor="#8C4510" HorizontalAlign="Center" />
                    <HeaderStyle BackColor="#A55129" Font-Bold="True"
                            ForeColor="White" />
                </asp:GridView>
```

Example 4-7. Default.aspx for AWProductDataOrderDetails (continued)

```
                  <asp:SqlDataSource ID="AdventureWorksOrderDetails" runat="server"
                     ConnectionString=
                         "<%$ ConnectionStrings:AdventureWorksConnectionString %>"
                     SelectCommand="SELECT [SalesOrderID], [CarrierTrackingNumber],
                         [OrderQty], [UnitPrice], [UnitPriceDiscount], [LineTotal]
                         FROM [Sales].[SalesOrderDetail]
                         WHERE ([ProductID] = @ProductID)
                         ORDER BY [SalesOrderID]">
                     <SelectParameters>
                         <asp:ControlParameter
                             ControlID="GridView1"
                             Name="ProductID"
                             PropertyName="SelectedValue"
                             Type="Int32" />
                     </SelectParameters>
                  </asp:SqlDataSource>
              </ContentTemplate>
           </asp:UpdatePanel>

      </form>
   </body>
</html>
```

Example 4-8. Default.aspx.vb for AWProductDataOrderDetails

```
Partial Class _Default
    Inherits System.Web.UI.Page

    Protected Sub GridView1_RowDataBound(ByVal sender As Object, _
                ByVal e As System.Web.UI.WebControls.GridViewRowEventArgs)
        If e.Row.RowType = DataControlRowType.DataRow Then
            Dim cellProductNumber As TableCell = e.Row.Cells(3)  ' ProductNumber
            If cellProductNumber.Text.Substring(0, 2) = "CA" Then
                cellProductNumber.ForeColor = Drawing.Color.Green
            End If

            Dim cellMakeFlag As TableCell = e.Row.Cells(4)  ' MakeFlag column
            Dim cb As CheckBox = CType(cellMakeFlag.Controls(0), CheckBox)
            If cb.Checked Then
                e.Row.Cells(2).ForeColor = Drawing.Color.Red
            End If
        End If
    End Sub

    Protected Sub GridView1_SelectedIndexChanged(ByVal sender As Object, _
            ByVal e As System.EventArgs)
        If GridView1.SelectedRow.RowType = DataControlRowType.DataRow Then
            Dim cellName As TableCell = GridView1.SelectedRow.Cells(2) ' Name
            txtName.Text = cellName.Text
        End If
    End Sub
End Class
```

Summary

- Most useful web sites make use of a database. ASP.NET provides controls that make it easy to connect to a database, and retrieve and edit data.

- The `GridView` is the most commonly used control for displaying data, although there are others. The `GridView` can sort data, and present it in pages, for easy reading.

- Data controls need to be bound to a data source to display data. To do that, you provide a `DataSource` control, which connects to the database and retrieves the data.

- You configure a `DataSource` control with a wizard that allows you to set a connection string, and then helps you construct a SQL query for retrieving data, or you can enter your own custom query.

- You create a new connection with the Add Connection dialog, and then you can save it in your *web.config* file for future use.

- The SQL `SELECT` statement allows you to specify which columns of data you want to retrieve, and from which table. The Wizard can configure this statement for you automatically.

- The SQL `INSERT`, `UPDATE`, and `DELETE` statements allow you to add, edit, and remove data, respectively. The Wizard can also generate these statements for you automatically, and you can easily add buttons to perform these functions in your `GridView`.

- Optimistic concurrency is a technique that protects your data by only changing the database if no one else has changed it since you read the data. Again, the Wizard can enable optimistic concurrency for you.

- The `WHERE` SQL clause filters the data you retrieve by specifying a condition for the data. A row will only be retrieved if that condition is true.

- You can create event handlers for the `GridView`, which enables you to take action on rows as they're bound, and also allows you to take action on rows as they're selected.

- You can provide parameters to the `SELECT` query, which enables you to display data in a `GridView` based on the value of another control, even another `GridView`.

Adding the ability to access a database is arguably the most powerful improvement you can make to your site. It's easy see how accessing a database would make the Order Form site from previous chapters that much more useful. Even the best order form, though, can't retrieve the right data if users don't give it valid input—if they enter a four-digit zip code, for example, or an improperly formatted credit card number. The whole thing would work much more smoothly if there was a way to check that the user's responses are valid before you spend the time to access the database. The good news is that ASP.NET provides such a way, called *validation*, and that's what you'll learn about in the next chapter.

Quiz

1. What type of control do you need to retrieve data from the database?

2. What is the name of the process for allowing a control, such as a GridView, to extract data from the retrieved tables and format it properly?

3. What is a connection string?

4. What are the four elements of CRUD?

5. How do you attach a data source to a GridView?

6. If your table has many rows, what should you do in the GridView to make it easier to read?

7. What does optimistic concurrency do?

8. How can you enable users to change the contents of the database from your GridView?

9. How can you take an action based on the data in a row, as the table is loaded?

10. How do you filter the amount of data returned from a SELECT query?

Exercises

Exercise 4-1. We'll start out easy, letting you create your own GridView. Create a new web site called Exercise 4-1. Add to it a GridView control that shows records from the Product table with a Weight greater than 100. The GridView should list the Product ID, Product Name, Product Number, Color, and List Price. The user should be able to update and delete records, sort by rows, and page through the content. Use the Professional formatting scheme to give it some style. The result should look like Figure 4-27.

Exercise 4-2. This one is a little trickier, but it lets you see how users could interact with the data in a GridView. Copy the web site from Exercise 4-1 to a new web site, called Exercise 4-2. Add the ability to select rows in your GridView. Add two labels and two read-only textboxes below the GridView to show the selected item's Product Name and color. The result should look like Figure 4-28.

Exercise 4-3. Now it's time to combine what you've learned from previous chapters with the new stuff, and throw a little AJAX into the mix as well. Create a new AJAX-enabled web site called Exercise 4-3. This site should have a radio button that gives readers the opportunity to select whether they want to see data from the Employee table, or the Customer table. The Employee panel should have a GridView showing the EmployeeID, ManagerID, and Title. The Customer panel should have a GridView showing the Customer ID, Account Number, and Customer Type. The table that the

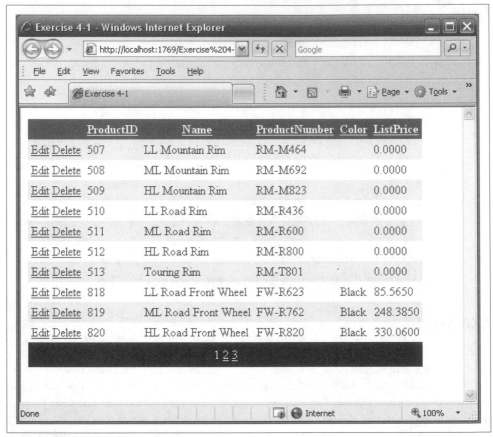

Figure 4-27. Your goal for Exercise 4-1.

reader chooses should appear dynamically in a new panel; the other one should be invisible. The result should look like Figure 4-29.

Exercise 4-4. Ready for a bit of a challenge? Sure you are. You're going to see how to retrieve data based on multiple customer selections—like you would in a shopping site. Create a new web site called Exercise 4-4. This site should have three drop-down menus:

- A Category menu that lists the product categories from the ProductCategory table

- A Subcategory menu that lists the subcategories of the Category listed in the first drop-down, by using the ProductSubcategory table

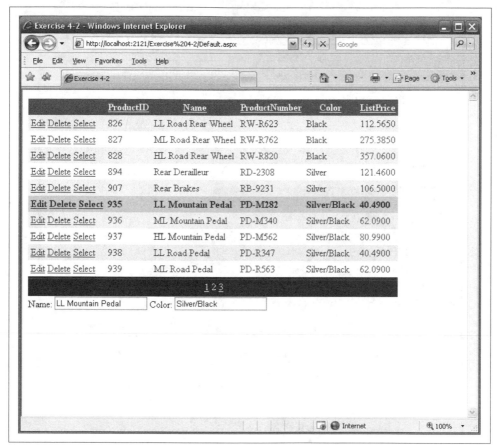

Figure 4-28. Your goal for Exercise 4-2.

- A Color menu that lists the available product colors from the Product menu

In addition, there should be a Submit button that users click. Below all of this is a GridView that displays the Products (from the Product table) that match the chosen subcategory and color. (You don't need to match the category—all that control does is dictate the contents of the Subcategory table.) The GridView should display the ProductID, Name, Product number, and the color, just so you can tell it's working. (Hint: You can use the DISTINCT SQL statement to avoid duplication in your table.) It should look like Figure 4-30.

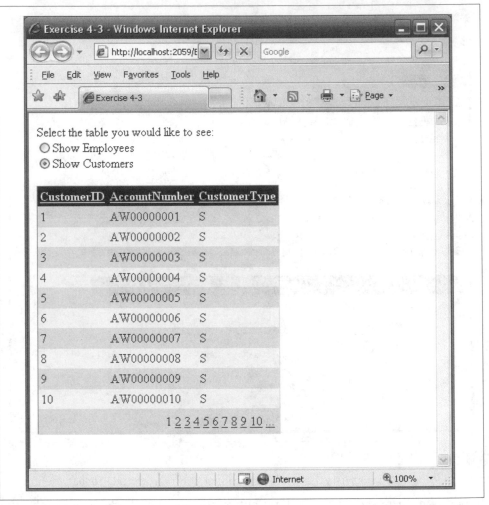

Figure 4-29. Your goal for Exercise 4-3.

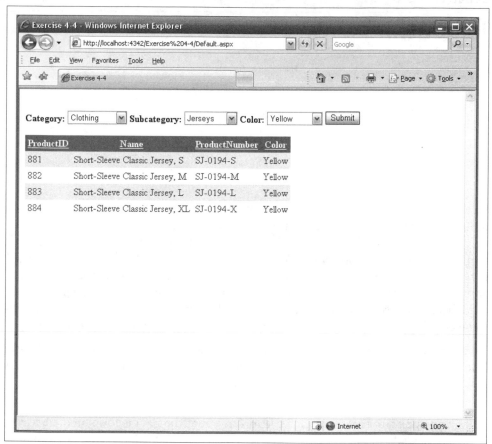

Figure 4-30. Your goal for Exercise 4-4.

CHAPTER 5
Validation

As you have seen in the preceding chapters, many web applications involve user input. The sad fact is, however, that users make mistakes: they skip required fields, they put in six-digit phone numbers, and they return all manner of incorrectly formatted data to your application. Your database routines can choke on corrupted data, and orders can be lost. An incorrectly entered credit card number or omitted address may result in a missed sales opportunity. Fortunately, you can write code that checks the user's input before it gets anywhere near your database code, or anything else dangerous. The process of verifying the user's input is called *validation*.

Traditionally, it takes a great deal of time and effort to write reliable validation code. You need to check each field and create routines for ensuring data integrity. If bad data is found, you need to display an error message so the user knows there is a problem and how to correct it.

In a given application, you may choose to verify that the data is formatted correctly, or the values fall within a given range, or that certain fields have a value at all. For example, if you're processing an order, you may need to ensure that the user has input an address and phone number, that the phone number has the right number of digits (and no letters), and that the Social Security number entered is in the appropriate form of nine digits separated by hyphens.

Some applications require more complex validation, in which you validate that one field is within a range established by two other fields. For example, you might ask in one field what date the customer wishes to arrive at your hotel, and in a second field you might ask for the departure date. When the user books a dinner reservation, you'll want to ensure that the date the user chooses is between the arrival and departure dates.

There is no limit to the complexity of the validation routines you may need to write. Credit cards have checksums built into their values, as do ISBN numbers. Zip and postal codes follow complex patterns, as do international phone numbers. You may need to validate passwords, membership numbers, dollar amounts, dates, runway choices, and launch codes.

In addition, you usually want all of this validation to happen client side so you can avoid the delay of repeated round trips (postbacks) to the server while the user is tinkering with his input. In the past, this was solved by writing client-side JavaScript to validate the input, and then writing server-side script to handle input from browsers that don't support client-side programming. In addition, as a security check, you may want to do server-side validation even though you have validation implemented in the browser, since users can circumvent client-side validation code by creating a malicious page that masquerades as a legitimate page (a tactic known as *spoofing*). Typically, this involved writing your validation code twice, once for the client and once for the server.

As you can see, in traditional Internet programming, validation requires extensive custom programming. The ASP.NET framework simplifies this process by providing rich controls for validating user input. The validation controls allow you to specify how and where error messages will be displayed: either inline with the input controls, aggregated together in a summary report, or both. You can use these controls to validate input for both HTML and ASP.NET server controls. In this chapter, you'll learn how to use all these validation controls, and you'll create a number of pages that you can adapt right away to use on your site.

Validation Controls

You add validation controls to your ASP.NET document as you would add any other control. Within the declaration of the validation control, you specify which other control is being validated. You may freely combine the various validation controls, and you may even write your own custom validation controls, as you'll see later in this chapter.

With current browsers that support DHTML, .NET validation is done on the client side, avoiding the necessity of a round trip to the server. (This client-side validation uses JavaScript but is not part of the AJAX library.) With older browsers, *your* code is unchanged, but the code sent to the client ensures validation at the server.

Sometimes you don't want any validation to occur, such as when a Cancel button is clicked. To prevent validation in these circumstances, many postback controls—such as Button, ImageButton, LinkButton, ListControl, and TextBox—have a CausesValidation property, which you can set to dictate whether validation is performed on the page when the control's default event is raised.

If CausesValidation is set to true, the default value—the postback—will *not* occur if any control on the page fails validation. If CausesValidation is set to false, however, no validation will occur when that button is used to post the page.

ASP.NET supports the following validation controls:

RequiredFieldValidator

> Ensures the user does not leave the field blank and skip over your input control. A RequiredFieldValidator can be tied to a text box, which means that the page will only pass validation if the user enters something into the text box. With selection controls, such as a drop-down or radio buttons, the RequiredFieldValidator ensures the user makes a selection other than the default value you specify. The RequiredFieldValidator does not examine the validity of the data but only ensures that some data is entered or chosen.

RangeValidator

> Ensures that the value entered is within a specified lower and upper boundary. You can specify the range to be within a pair of numbers (greater than 10 and less than 100), a pair of characters (greater than D and less than K), or a pair of dates (after 1/1/08 and before 2/28/08).

CompareValidator

> Compares the user's entry against another value. It can compare against a constant you specify at design time, or against a property value of another control. It can also compare against a database value.

RegularExpressionValidator

> One of the most powerful validators, it compares the user's entry with a regular expression you provide (we'll briefly discuss regular expressions later in the chapter). You can use this validator to check for valid Social Security numbers, phone numbers, passwords, and so forth.

CustomValidator

> If none of these controls meets your needs, you can create your own using the CustomValidator. This checks the user's entry against whatever algorithm you provide in a custom method.

In the remainder of this chapter, we'll examine how to use each of these controls to validate data in ASP.NET applications.

The RequiredFieldValidator

The RequiredFieldValidator ensures the user provides a value for your control, or in the case of drop drop-down lists, that the user picks something other than the default value.

To get started, create a new web site called RequiredFieldValidator. In this section, you're going create the shipping selection web page shown in Design view in Figure 5-1. This is a pretty standard shipping form, as you can see on any number of web sites. You can imagine how you'd incorporate such a page into your own site.

This new web site can use the normal ASP.NET Web Site template rather than the ASP.NET AJAX-Enabled Web Site template. Although ASP.NET validation controls do much of their work client-side using JavaScript, they neither use nor depend on the AJAX libraries.

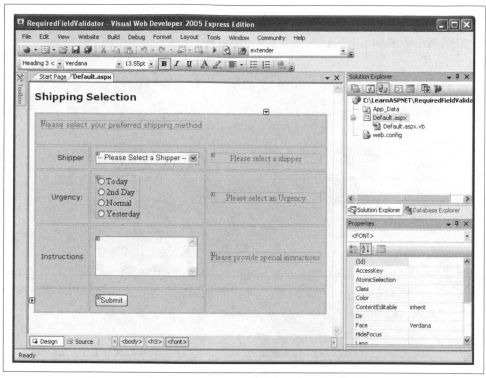

Figure 5-1. This shipping selection page incorporates RequiredFieldValidator controls to ensure that users make selections in each field.

When the user clicks the Submit button, the page is validated to ensure that each field has been modified. If not, the offending field is marked with an error message in red, as shown in Figure 5-2.

You'll use a 3-column, 5-row HTML table to create the page layout, into which you'll place the necessary controls. Using what you've learned from the previous chapters, you can create the table fairly easily, either directly in Source view, or using the Table Wizard, so we won't go over that here. Adding the controls to the form is also pretty easy.

The first row of the table will be a single cell spanning all three columns (using the HTML colspan attribute) containing a Label for displaying any messages. Set the ID of that Label to lblMsg, and set the Text property to an empty string (text = "").

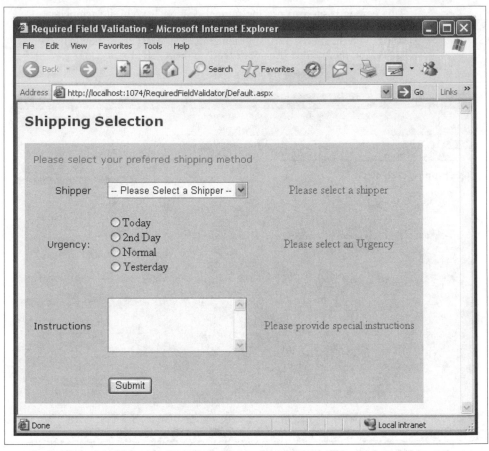

Figure 5-2. The user of this page didn't provide any shipping information before clicking Submit, so the RequiredFieldValidator controls return errors, which you can see in the column on the right.

The first column of the table contains some descriptive captions for the input fields, with the middle column containing the controls to be validated (a DropDownList, a set of RadioButtonList, and a TextBox). Use the ListItem Collection Editor to set the values for the DropDownList to the following:

-- Please Select a Shipper --
US Postal Service
Overnight Express
United Shipping Service
WHL
Pony Express
Starship Transporter

The first item is particularly important, as you'll see in a minute.

For each field that you want validated, you'll add a RequiredFieldValidator control, which is a control like any other. Open the Validation section of the Toolbox, and drag a RequiredFieldValidator into the third cell of the three middle rows, as shown in Figure 5-1. (The code-behind for this example is listed in Example 5-1 and the complete markup is listed in Example 5-2.)

The RequiredFieldValidator control has its own ID, and it also asks for the ID of the control you wish to validate. Therefore, set the ID of the first RequiredFieldValidator you added to reqFieldShipper, and set its ControlToValidate property to ddlShipper (the drop-down list that you are validating). Also be sure to include the text between the opening and closing tags—"– Please select a shipper –". (This text could also be set using the Text property.) All this is shown in the following snippet:

CODE ▶
```
<asp:RequiredFieldValidator
    id="reqFieldShipper"
    ControlToValidate="ddlShipper"
    Display="Static"
    InitialValue="-- Please Select a Shipper --"
    Width="100%" runat=server>
        Please select a shipper
</asp:RequiredFieldValidator>
```

Make sure the Display attribute is set to Static (the default), which tells ASP.NET to allocate room on the page for the validator whether or not there is a message to display. If you set this to Dynamic, space will not be allocated until (and unless) an error message is displayed. Dynamic allocation is powerful, but it can cause your controls to bounce around on the page when the message is displayed. We'll show you how this looks in a minute.

The RequiredFieldValidator has an additional attribute, InitialValue, which you should set to the initial value of the control being validated, in this case a drop-down box. If the user clicks Submit, this initial value will be compared with the value of the drop-down, and if they are the same, the error message will be displayed. This forces the user to change the initial value. In this case, you set the InitialValue to a bit of text asking the user to make a choice. That isn't a valid selection, so you need to make sure that the user chooses something else. You don't want to use InitialValue if you have a default shipper, for example, because that would prevent the reader from selecting the default.

Give the second RequiredFieldValidator an ID of reqFieldUrgency, and set its ControlToValidate property to rblUrgency, to ensure that one of the radio buttons in rblUrgency is selected. Also change the Text property to "Please select an Urgency":

CODE ▶
```
<td align=center rowspan=1>
    <asp:RequiredFieldValidator
        id="reqFieldUrgency"
        ControlToValidate="rblUrgency"
        Display="Static"
        InitialValue=""
```

```
        Width="100%" runat=server>
            Please select an Urgency
    </asp:RequiredFieldValidator>
  </td>
```

You do not need to indicate an initial value this time. Since the control is a radio button list, the validator knows the user is required to pick one of the buttons; if any button is chosen, the validation will be satisfied.

Finally, to complete the example, you'll add a text box and require the user to enter some text in it. The validator is straightforward; set the text box as the ControlToValidate, and enter the error message "Please provide special instructions" into the Text property for display if the box is left empty:

```
<!-- Validator for the text box-->
<td style="HEIGHT: 97px">
   <asp:RequiredFieldValidator
      id="reqFieldBug"
      ControlToValidate="txtInstructions"
      Display="Static"
      Width="100%" runat="server">
      Please provide special instructions
   </asp:RequiredFieldValidator>
 </td>
</tr>
```

The only code required in the code-behind file is the event handler for the Submit button. Double-click on the button in Design view, and you'll be taken to the Click event handler, as usual. Enter the highlighted code from Example 5-1.

Example 5-1. Button Click event handler for RequiredFieldValidator

```
Protected Sub btnSubmit_Click(ByVal sender As Object, _
    ByVal e As System.EventArgs) _
    Handles btnSubmit.Click
    If Page.IsValid Then
        lblMsg.Text = "Page is valid!"
    Else
        ' this code never reached
        lblMsg.Text = "Some of the required fields are empty."
    End If
End Sub
```

When the Submit button is clicked, the validation for each control is checked, and if every control is valid, the IsValid property of the page will return true.

Now go back and set all the validation controls to Dynamic. Run the application and see what happens. No space is allocated for the validation controls, and the browser will consider your table to be only two columns wide rather than three. That is, the table will not allocate any space for the validation messages and will recognize only one column for the prompt and the other for the controls. When you validate the controls (by clicking the Submit button), the table will widen, which can be either disconcerting or attractive, depending on how you manage the display. In this case, you can see the controls jump around when you click Submit, which probably isn't what you want, so after you've played with it a bit, go back and changed the controls to Static.

Take a look back at Example 5-1. Notice the comment that says the else clause will never be reached. Recall that the validation occurs client-side. If the page is not valid, it is never even posted to the server and the server-side code does not run (unless, of course, you set the CausesValidation property to false, as described at the beginning of this chapter).

You can make your pages a bit friendlier for your users by placing the focus on the first control that fails validation. To do so, add the SetFocusOnError property to each validation control and set it to true (the default is false):

```
<asp:RequiredFieldValidator runat=server
    id="reqFieldInstructions"
    ControlToValidate="txtInstructions"
    Display="Static"
    SetFocusOnError="true"
    Width="100%" >
    Please provide special instructions
</asp:RequiredFieldValidator>
```

Run your application again, and click Submit without adding special instructions. After validation, you not only get the message asking you to provide them, but the focus is on the TextBox control, ready for you to enter text. If you set SetFocusOnError on more than one control, and if the page is invalid, the focus will be set to the first control that fails validation and has this property set to true.

The complete source code for the markup file, *default.aspx*, for this example is listed in Example 5-2.

Example 5-2. Default.aspx forRequiredFieldValidator

```
<%@ Page Language="VB" AutoEventWireup="false" CodeFile="Default.aspx.vb"
    Inherits="_Default" %>

<!DOCTYPE html PUBLIC "-//W3C//DTD XHTML 1.0 Transitional//EN"
"http://www.w3.org/TR/xhtml1/DTD/xhtml1-transitional.dtd">

<html xmlns="http://www.w3.org/1999/xhtml" >
<head runat="server">
    <title>Required Field Validation</title>
</head>
<body>
    <h3>
        <font face="Verdana">Shipping Selection</font>
    </h3>
    <form runat="server" ID="frmBugs">
        <div>
         <table bgcolor=gainsboro cellpadding=10>
            <tr valign="top">
```

Example 5-2. Default.aspx forRequiredFieldValidator (continued)

```
            <td colspan=3>
                <!-- Display error messages -->
                <asp:Label ID="lblMsg"
                Text="Please select your preferred shipping method"
                ForeColor="red" Font-Names="Verdana"
                Font-Size="10" runat=server />
                <br>
            </td>
        </tr>
        <tr>
            <td align=right>
                <font face=Verdana size=2>Shipper</font>
            </td>
            <td>
            <!-- Drop down list with the Shippers (must pick one) -->
                <asp:DropDownList id=ddlShipper runat=server>
                    <asp:ListItem>-- Please Select a Shipper --</asp:ListItem>
                    <asp:ListItem>US Postal Service</asp:ListItem>
                    <asp:ListItem>Overnight Express</asp:ListItem>
                    <asp:ListItem>United Shipping Service</asp:ListItem>
                    <asp:ListItem>WHL</asp:ListItem>
                    <asp:ListItem>Pony Express</asp:ListItem>
                    <asp:ListItem>Starship Transporter</asp:ListItem>
                </aspDropDownList>
            </td>
            <!-- Validator for the drop down -->
            <td align=center >
                <asp:RequiredFieldValidator
                    id="reqFieldShipper"
                    ControlToValidate="ddlShipper"
                    Display="Static"
                    InitialValue="-- Please Select a Shipper --"
                    Width="100%" runat=server>
                        Please select a shipper
                </asp:RequiredFieldValidator>
            </td>
        </tr>
        <tr>
            <td align=right>
            <!-- Radio buttons for the urgency -->
                <font face=Verdana size=2>Urgency:</font>
            </td>
            <td>
                <ASP:RadioButtonList id=rblUrgency
                    RepeatLayout="Flow" runat=server>
                    <asp:ListItem>Today</asp:ListItem>
                    <asp:ListItem>2nd Day</asp:ListItem>
                    <asp:ListItem>Normal</asp:ListItem>
                    <asp:ListItem>Yesterday</asp:ListItem>
                </ASP:RadioButtonList>
            </td>
```

Example 5-2. Default.aspx forRequiredFieldValidator (continued)

```
                <!-- Validator for urgency -->
                <td align=center rowspan=1>
                   <asp:RequiredFieldValidator
                        id="reqFieldUrgency"
                        ControlToValidate="rblUrgency"
                        Display="Static"
                        InitialValue=""
                        Width="100%" runat=server>
                            Please select an Urgency
                   </asp:RequiredFieldValidator>
                </td>
            </tr>
            <tr>
                <td align=right style="HEIGHT: 97px">
                   <font face=Verdana size=2>Instructions</font>
                </td>
                <!-- Multi-line text for special instructions -->
                <td style="HEIGHT: 97px">
                   <ASP:TextBox id=txtInstructions runat=server width="183px"
                   textmode="MultiLine" height="68px"/>
                </td>
                <!-- Validator for the text box-->
                <td style="HEIGHT: 97px">
                   <asp:RequiredFieldValidator
                   id="reqFieldInstructions"
                   ControlToValidate="txtInstructions"
                   Display="Static"
                   Width="100%" runat=server>
                       Please provide special instructions
                   </asp:RequiredFieldValidator>
                </td>
            </tr>
            <tr>
                <td>
                </td>
                <td>
                   <ASP:Button id=btnSubmit
                   text="Submit" runat=server />
                </td>
                <td>
                </td>
            </tr>
        </table>
    </div>
    </form>
</body>
</html>
```

The Summary Control

As you saw in the previous example, putting your validation feedback next to each control can be useful, but leads to some possible layout problems. Fortunately, ASP. NET lets you decide how you want to report validation errors. For example, rather than putting error messages alongside the control, you can summarize all the validation failures with a ValidationSummary control. This control can place a summary of the errors in a bulleted list, a simple list, or a paragraph that appears elsewhere on the web page or in a pop-up message box.

To see how this works, create a copy of the RequiredFieldValidator web application, called RequiredFieldValidatorSummary. Switch to Source view. From the Validation section of the Toolbox, drag a ValidationSummary control onto the bottom of the page, after the </table> tag.

 The steps for copying a web site to a new web site are presented in Appendix A.

Set the attributes of this ValidationSummary control to the values highlighted in the following code snippet (you can do this in the Properties window as well, of course):

CODE▸
```
<asp:ValidationSummary ID="valSummary" runat="server"
        DisplayMode="BulletList"
        HeaderText="The following errors were found:"
        ShowSummary="true" />
```

To make this work, you'll need to add an ErrorMessage attribute to the other validation controls. For example, modify the first validation control for the Shipper drop-down menu as follows:

CODE▸
```
<asp:RequiredFieldValidator
    id="reqFieldShipper"
    ControlToValidate="ddlShipper"
    Display="Static"
    InitialValue="-- Please Select a Shipper --"
    ErrorMessage="You did not select a shipper from the drop-down."
    Width="100%" runat=server>*
</asp:RequiredFieldValidator>
```

If this control reports a validation error the text in the ErrorMessage attribute will be displayed in the summary. You've also modified the validator to display an asterisk rather than the more complete error message. Now that you have a summary, you don't need to put a complete error message by each control, you need only flag the error. Now make similar changes for each of the other RequiredFieldValidator controls (you can use the error text displayed in Figure 5-3, or feel free to improvise).

Run your application, and click Submit without making any choices, so that none of the validation controls pass muster. The results are shown in Figure 5-3.

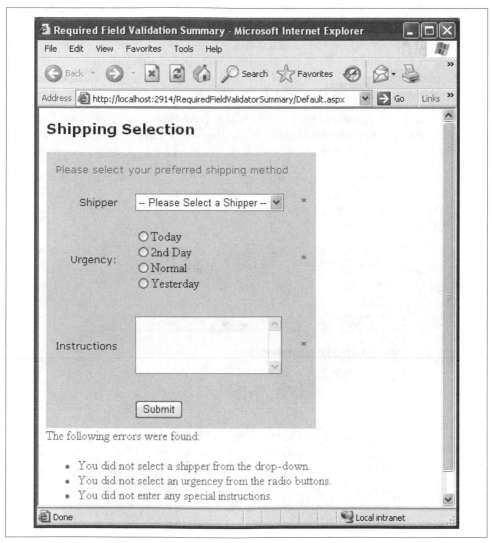

Figure 5-3. When you use a Validation Summary, the controls that didn't pass validation are marked, but more importantly, the summary appears on the page telling the user exactly what's wrong.

In Figure 5-3, the summary of validation errors is presented as a bulleted list. This is the default display mode. Messages can also be displayed as a simple list or a single paragraph, by setting the DisplayMode property of the ValidationSummary to BulletList, List, or SingleParagraph, respectively.

The Compare Validator

While the ability to ensure the user has made some sort of entry is great, you will often want to validate that the entry content is within certain guidelines. A common requirement is to compare the user's input to a constant value, the value of another control, or a database value.

To see this at work, make a new copy of the RequiredValidationSummary web site and name the new web site CompareValidator. In this example, you'll add a new control that asks the user how many packages he expects to receive as part of a shipment.

To do so, just insert a text box (call it txtNumPackages), a required field validator, and a compare validator into a new table row before the row that contains the Submit button. You can do this in either Source view or Design view, although the latter makes it very easy.

Switch to Design view and hover your mouse at the left edge of the table row containing the Submit button. Click on the Smart Tag that appears to select the row, as shown in Figure 5-4.

Figure 5-4. Hovering over the Smart Tag for a table row in Design view allows you to select the row in preparation for inserting a new row above the selected row.

From the IDE menus, click on the Layout → Insert → Row Above. This will insert a blank HTML table row above the selected row. Now drag the relevant controls from the Toolbox into the correct table cells. The table now looks like Figure 5-5 in Design view, with the two validation controls in the last cell circled.

Figure 5-5. A new table row with a TextBox to be validated and the RequiredFieldValidator and CompareValidator validation controls in Design view.

The markup for this is shown in Example 5-3.

Example 5-3. CompareValidator control markup

```
<tr>
    <td>Number of packages:</td>
    <td>
        <ASP:TextBox id="txtNumPackages" runat=server width="50px" />
    </td>
    <td>
        <asp:RequiredFieldValidator runat="server"
            id="RequiredFieldValidatorNumPackages"
            ControlToValidate="txtNumPackages"
            SetFocusOnError=true
```

Example 5-3. CompareValidator control markup (continued)

```
            ErrorMessage ="You did not enter the number of packages"
            Width="100%" >*
        </asp:RequiredFieldValidator>

        <asp:CompareValidator runat="server"
            id="CompareValidatorNumPackages"
            ControlToValidate="txtNumPackages"
            SetFocusOnError=true
            ErrorMessage ="Invalid number of packages"
            Type="Integer"
            Operator="GreaterThan"
            ValueToCompare=0>*</asp:CompareValidator>
    </td>
</tr>
```

Run your application again, and try entering various values into the field. You'll see that if you enter 0, or a negative number, the validation fails. If you enter a positive number, the control passes validation. If you leave it blank, you'll notice that it still fails. Without the RequiredFieldValidator, though, it would have passed.

Both validators are placed into the same cell in the table, and both validators validate the same control: txtNumPackages. The RequiredFieldValidator is needed because the CompareValidator will always return true for null or empty values, as nonintuitive as that sounds.

The CompareValidator's ValueToCompare attribute takes a constant, in this case zero. The Operator attribute determines how the comparison will be made (that is, how the input value must be related to the ValueToCompare).

The possible values for the Operator attribute are Equal, NotEqual, GreaterThan, GreaterThanEqual, LessThan, LessThanEqual, and DataTypeCheck. In this example, to be valid, the input value must be greater than the ValueToCompare constant. Or to put in more relevant terms, the user must send more than zero packages.

You must use the Type attribute to tell the control what type of value it is using. The Type attribute takes one of the ValidationDataType enumerated values: Currency, Date, Double (a Double is VB-speak for a noninteger number, i.e., a decimal number), Integer, or String. In the example, the values are compared as integers, and thus, entering (for example) a character will cause the validation to fail.

Checking the Input Type

Rather than checking that the number of packages is greater than zero, you might want to check that it is a number at all (rather than a letter or date). To do this, you make a minor change to the CompareValidator.

Remove the ValueToCompare attribute and change the Operator attribute from GreaterThan to DataTypeCheck. Because the Type attribute is Integer, the control will report any integer value as valid. Use the following code to replace that for the CompareValidator you added in the last section:

```
<asp:CompareValidator runat="server"
    id="CompareValidatorNumPackages"
    SetFocusOnError=true
    ControlToValidate-" txtNumPackages"
    ErrorMessage ="Invalid number of packages"
    Type="Integer"
    Operator="DataTypeCheck">*
</asp:CompareValidator>
```

Now run the application again, and try entering random data in the text box. You'll see that numbers, even zero or negative numbers, pass validation, while anything else fails. You can imagine how this sort of validation would be useful for order numbers, credit card numbers, or anyplace where the type of data is important.

Comparing to Another Control

You can compare a value in one control to the value in another control, rather than to a constant. A classic use of this might be to ask the user to enter his password twice and then validate that both entries are identical.

The common scenario is that you've asked the user to pick a new password. For security, when the password is entered, the text is disguised with asterisks. Because this will be the password the user will need to log in, you must validate the user entered the password as intended, without errors. The typical solution is to ask the user to enter the password a second time, and then check that the same password was entered each time. The CompareValidator is perfect for this.

To demonstrate this, you'll need to add two table rows to your page, each with a TextBox for use as a password field. The first of these password fields will have a RequiredFieldValidator control; the second will have both a RequiredFieldValidator and a CompareValidator. You can add these rows and controls as you just did in Design view, or directly in Source view. Either way, the markup will look something like that listed in Example 5-4. Be sure to set the correct ControlToValidate attributes of all these new validation controls, as well as the other attributes.

Example 5-4. Password validation usingCompareValidator control

```
<!-- Text fields for passwords -->
<tr>
    <td>Enter your password:</td>
    <td>
    <asp:TextBox id="txtPasswd1" runat="server"
        TextMode="Password"
        Width="80"></asp:TextBox>
    </td>
```

Example 5-4. Password validation usingCompareValidator control (continued)

```
    <td>
    <!-- required to enter the password -->
    <asp:RequiredFieldValidator runat="server"
        id="ReqFieldTxtPassword1"
        ControlToValidate="txtPasswd1"
        ErrorMessage ="Please enter your password"
        Width="100%" >*
    </asp:RequiredFieldValidator>
    </td>
</tr>

<!-- Second password for comparison -->
<tr>
    <td>Re-enter your password:</td>
    <td>
    <asp:TextBox id="txtPasswd2" runat="server"
        TextMode="Password"
        Width="80"></asp:TextBox>
    </td>

    <td>
    <!-- Second password is required -->
    <asp:RequiredFieldValidator runat="server"
        id="ReqFieldTxtPassword2"
        ControlToValidate="txtPasswd2"
        SetFocusOnError="true"
        ErrorMessage ="Please re-enter your password"
        Width="100%" >*
    </asp:RequiredFieldValidator>

    <!-- Second password must match the first -->
    <asp:CompareValidator runat=server
        id="CompValPasswords"
        ControlToValidate="txtPasswd2"
        ErrorMessage ="Passwords do not match"
        SetFocusOnError="true"
        Type="String"
        Operator="Equal"
        ControlToCompare="txtPasswd1">*
    </asp:CompareValidator>
    </td>
</tr>
```

Go ahead and test it out. If the strings you enter don't match, the control will fail validation.

The first table row contains the TextBox control with its TextMode attribute set to "Password". It also contains a RequiredFieldValidator to ensure the user doesn't leave the field blank.

The second row contains a second password text box and a second RequiredFieldValidator (again, the user cannot leave the field blank), but it uses a CompareValidator to check the value of its associated TextBox (txtPasswd2) against that of the first TextBox (txtPasswd1) to verify they both have the same content. The Operator property is set to Equal and the Type property is set to String, so the two strings must match. Notice the two properties set:

```
ControlToValidate="txtPasswd2"
ControlToCompare="txtPasswd1"
```

Both text boxes must have a RequiredField validator. If the CompareValidator compares a string against a null or empty string value, it will pass validation.

Range Checking

At times, you'll want to validate that a user's entry falls within a specific range. That range can be within a pair of numbers, characters, or dates. In addition, you can express the boundaries for the range by using constants or by comparing its value with values found in other controls.

In this example, you'll prompt the user for a number between 10 and 20, and then validate the answer to ensure it was entered properly. To do so, create a new AJAX-enabled web site named RangeValidator. You'll create this exercise entirely in Design mode. To begin, drag four controls onto your page: a label, a text box, a button, and of course, a RangeValidator control, as shown in Figure 5-6.

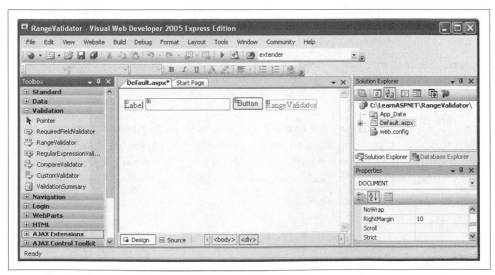

Figure 5-6. Create the RangeValidator page in Design mode. Notice how the RangeValidator control shows up.

Click on the Label and set its Text property to "Enter a number between 10 and 20:". Click on the TextBox, set its ID to txtValue. Click the button and set its Text to Submit. Finally, click on the RangeValidator, and in the Properties window click Type. Choose Integer from the drop-down list. Set the MinimumValue property to 10 and the MaximumValue property to 20. Next, click on the ControlToValidate property, pick the text box, and set the Text property to "Between 10 and 20 please."

Run your application. Enter a value and click Submit. The text "Between 10 and 20 please" will be displayed if the value is not within the range of values specified by the MinimumValue and MaximumValue attributes. The Type attribute designates how the value should be evaluated and may be any of the following types: Currency, Date, Double, Integer, or String.

If there are no validation errors, the page can be submitted; otherwise, the range checking error message is displayed.

If the user leaves the field blank, the validation will pass and the page will be submitted. You'll want to ensure *some* value is entered, so add a RequiredFieldValidator in addition to the RangeValidator.

Regular Expressions

Often, a simple value or range check is insufficient; you must check that the *form* of the data entered is correct. For example, you may need to ensure that a zip code is five digits with the option to accept an extra four digits, an email address is in the form *name@place.com*, credit card information matches the right format, and so forth.

A regular expression validator allows you to verify that a text field matches a *regular expression*. Regular expressions are a language for describing and manipulating text.

 For complete coverage of regular expressions, see *Mastering Regular Expressions*, by Jeffrey Friedl (O'Reilly).

A regular expression consists of two types of characters: literals and metacharacters. A *literal* is a character you wish to match in the target string. A *metacharacter* is a special symbol that acts as a command to the regular expression parser. (The parser is the engine responsible for understanding the regular expression.)

Consider this regular expression:

```
^\d{5}$
```

This will match any string that has exactly five numerals. The initial metacharacter, ^, indicates the beginning of the string. The second metacharacter, \d, indicates a digit. The third metacharacter, {5}, indicates five of the digits, and the final metacharacter, $, indicates the end of the string. Thus, this regular expression matches five digits between the beginning and end of the line and nothing else.

When you use a `RegularExpressionValidator` control with client-side validation, the regular expressions are matched using Jscript, the Microsoft version of JavaScript. This may differ in small details from the regular expression checking done on the server.

A more sophisticated algorithm might accept a five-digit zip code or a nine-digit zip code in the format of 12345-1234 by using the | metacharacter which represents the "or" operator. Rather than using the \d metacharacter, you could designate the range of acceptable values:

CODE▶

```
[0-9]{5}|[0-9]{5}-[0-9]{4}
```

To see how this works, make a copy of the `RangeValidator` example you just created, and name it `RegularExpressionValidator`. Replace the `RangeValidator` control with a `RegularExpressionValidator` control.

Use the Properties window to set the `ControlToValidate` to txtValue and set the text to "Please enter a valid U.S. zip code." Click on the property for Validation Expression, and click on the ellipsis. A Regular Expression Editor pops up with a few common regular expressions, or you can enter your own. Scroll down and choose U.S. ZIP code, as shown in Figure 5-7.

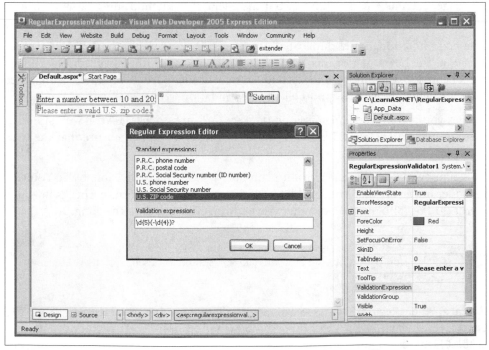

Figure 5-7. The Regular Expression Editor makes it a snap to use the RegularExpressionValidator. Just select the ValidationExpression in the Properties window, and then click the ellipsis button to open the editor.

Run the program, and test out the field by entering some responses. You will see that either a standard five digit zip code or a "Zip+4" will pass validation, but anything else will fail.

 If you choose "Custom," the Validation expression box will be blank, allowing you to enter any expression you choose. For help with creating custom regular expressions, we recommend the program *RegEx Buddy* (*http://www.RegExBuddy.com*).

Custom Validation

There are times when the validation of your data is so specific to your application that you will need to write your own validation method. The CustomValidator is designed to provide all the infrastructure support you need. You point to your validation method and have it return a Boolean value: true or false. The CustomValidator control takes care of all the rest of the work.

Because validation can be performed on both the client (depending on the browser) and the server, the CustomValidator has attributes for specifying a server-side and a client-side method for validation. The server-side method can be written in any .NET language, such as C# or VB.NET, but the client-side method must be written in a scripting language understood by the browser, such as VBScript or JavaScript.

The code functionality is duplicated on the server for two reasons. First, as mentioned at the beginning of this chapter, it prevents a malicious user from bypassing the client-side validation, and second, it makes the page compatible with older browsers which may not support client-side validation.

To get you started, once again copy the RegularExpressionValidator web site to a new site named CustomValidator. In this example, you want to ensure that the user enters an even number.

This time, you'll report an error if the number is not evenly divisible by 2. You can imagine, however, that you could use this technique to perform a checksum on a credit card or ISBN number or otherwise perform complex data checking.

 Most of these checks can be done more easily with a Regular Expression Validator; the custom validator should be used only as a last resort.

Replace the RegularExpressionValidator with a CustomValidator. Set the ControlToValidate field to the ID of the appropriate TextBox, and set EnableClientScript to true (the default). Set the Text property to "Please enter an even number."

CustomValidators have an additional property that can save you a lot of special coding: ValidateEmptyText.

ValidateEmptyText=false

By setting this property to false (the default), the text field will be considered invalid if it is empty, avoiding the need for the RequireFieldValidator that you needed in the previous examples.

The key to making your custom validator work is in setting the client-side validator, which you do in the ClientValidationFunction property. Set this property to ClientValidator, which is the name of a JavaScript function you are going to write momentarily. Also, click the Events lightning bolt button and set the ServerValidate event handler to ServerValidator, a method in the code-behind you are also going to write in just a bit.

To create the JavaScript function, add the following code directly to the markup file in Source view, between the closing </head> element and the opening <body> element:

```
<script language="javascript" type="text/javascript" >
   function ClientValidator(source, args)
   {
      if (args.Value % 2 == 0)
         args.IsValid=true;
      else
         args.IsValid=false;
      return;
   }
</script>
```

This function examines the value passed to the script by the validator; if it is an even number, it will return true. Otherwise, it will return false.

> The standard test for determining if an integer is even or odd is to divide by 2, and check the remainder. If the remainder is 0, the integer is even. If it's 1, the integer is odd.
>
> The function for determining the remainder is called the modulus. In JavaScript (as in most programming languages), the % operator represents the modulus. In other words, if your integer is stored in the variable value, then value % 2 is equal to 0 if value is even.
>
> In VB.NET, the modulus is represented by the Mod operator, not the % operator.

You'll implement the server-side method in the code behind file, *default.aspx.vb*. Copy the highlighted code from Example 5-5 to the code skeleton for ServerValidator you created above.

Example 5-5. Server-side custom validation code

```
Protected Sub ServerValidator(ByVal source As Object, _
    ByVal args As System.Web.UI.WebControls.ServerValidateEventArgs) _
    Handles CustomValidator1.ServerValidate

    args.IsValid = False
    Dim evenNumber As Integer = Int32.Parse(args.Value)
    If evenNumber Mod 2 = 0 Then
        args.IsValid = True
    End If

End Sub
```

This method does the same thing as the client-side validator, only in VB rather than in JavaScript. There are a few things to notice about these methods. First, the value that the CustomValidator is examining is passed to your routine as the Value property of the ServerValidateEventArgs event argument. You convert that string to an int using the Base Class Library Int32 object's static Parse method, as shown.

The declaration for the CustomValidator in the content file sets the client-side method and the server-side method you've designated.

CODE▶
```
<asp:CustomValidator runat="server"
    ID="CustomValidator1"
    ControlToValidate="txtValue"
    ValidateEmptyText=false
    ClientValidationFunction="ClientValidator"
    OnServerValidate="ServerValidator">
    Please enter an even number
</asp:CustomValidator>
```

If you run this program in a current browser and enter an odd number, the page will never be posted back to the server; the JavaScript handles the validation on the browser. If you enter an even number, however, the client-side script *and* the server-side script will run (to protect against spoofing from the client).

Summary

- Users will enter improperly formatted data into your forms, but validation can allow the controls to check that data before it's accepted by your server.

- ASP.NET provides validation controls that can check for a number of common user errors.

- Current browsers can validate input on the client side, eliminating a round trip to the server.

- The RequiredFieldValidator simply checks that the user has made a choice in the specified control. On TextBoxes and DropDownLists, this validator can also make certain that the user has selected an item other than the initial value.

- If you set the `SetFocusOnError` property to `true`, the focus is automatically placed on the control that fails validation, making it easier for the user to find.

- You can use the `ValidationSummary` control to provide detailed feedback to the user in a single spot on your page. You can still mark the individual controls that failed validation, but you don't need to put a lengthy error message next to the control.

- With the `CompareValidator` control, you can check the user's input against a constant value, a database value, or the value of another control. You can check if the input is greater than, less than, or equal to the specified value, or you can simply check that the input is of the desired data type.

- The `RangeValidator` control checks to see if the user's input falls within an appropriate range. You can specify the maximum and minimum values of the range.

- Regular expressions are a language that uses literals and metacharacters to describe and search text strings.

- With the `RegularExpressionValidator`, you can check that the user's input meets the expected pattern for data such as a phone number, a zip code, an email address, or other variations. The Regular Expression Editor provides some common regular expressions, or you can provide your own.

- If none of the existing controls provides the validation you need, you can use a `CustomValidator` to add custom JavaScript code to evaluate the user's input. Your custom code can do anything you like, but it can only return `true` or `false`.

You've created a lot of pages so far, and most of them have had familiar elements that you see as you browse the web every day—form controls, database access, and postbacks, among others. What you have not done so far, though, is create a page that looks like something you'd see on the Web. For that, you need style, and we don't just mean good fashion sense. In the next chapter, you'll learn how to provide a uniform, professional look to all your pages, and how to include special touches, such as navigation tools, that separate a quality web site from just a collection of controls.

Quiz

1. What is the reason for validation?

2. What do you do if you want a button to post the page without checking validation?

3. What is the best type of validator to use for a radio button list?

4. What's the difference between the Static and Dynamic values of the Display property?

5. Suppose the first item in your drop-down list is "Choose a payment method." How do you make sure users choose one?

6. What's the benefit of using the ValidationSummary control?

7. What control should you use to make sure the user can't order more of a single item than you actually have in stock?

8. Suppose you run a hotel that requires at least two guests stay in a double room, but no more than five guests. What control should you use on the "Number of guests" field?

9. How do you check that the user has entered a valid email address?

10. Suppose your theme park offers discounts to customers between the ages of 6 and 12, and also customers over 65. What kind of control would you use to validate the customer is eligible for a discount, while still using a single age field?

Exercises

Exercise 5-1. In the exercises in this chapter, you're going to create a form that users can fill out if they want to participate in a friendly phone survey (I'm told some people like to get survey calls in the middle of dinner). To begin, create a page with a table with three columns: label, control, and validator. Then add text boxes for the user's name, address, city, state, and zip code. Be sure to add the appropriate validators for each field—don't worry about the format of the input right now; you just want to make sure that something is filled in. Finally, add a Submit button. It doesn't matter too much what this form looks like, but it could look something like Figure 5-8.

Exercise 5-2. Let's make things a little more interesting this time. For starters, remove the text from the individual validators to error messages, and add a summary control at the bottom of the form, above the Submit button. Next, you don't want anyone participating in the survey if they're under 18, so add another label and field asking for the user's age. Add appropriate validators to make sure the user isn't too young. Because you're polite, you'll ask for a date when you should call the user, but your survey is only going on in July 2007. Add another table row with a label and a field asking for a date, and add the appropriate validators to make sure the date is sometime in July 2007. Your form should look something like Figure 5-9.

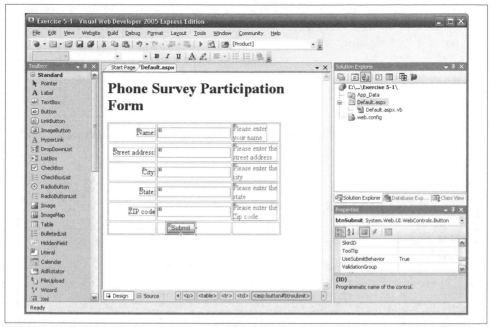

Figure 5-8. Your goal for Exercise 5-1.

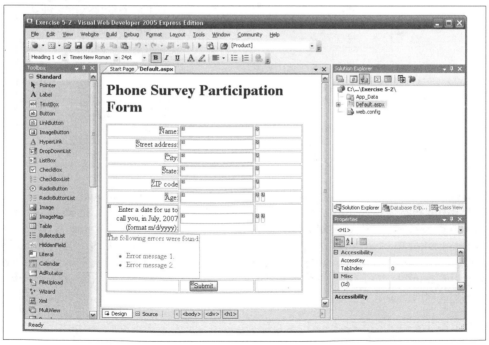

Figure 5-9. Your goal for Exercise 5-2.

Exercise 5-3. If the user doesn't mind being called at home, you might as well make a follow-up call to ask additional survey questions. This call still has to take place in July, but if it's a follow-up call, it would have to be *later* than the first call. Add a row to the table with a label and textbox where users can enter a date for the follow-up call, and add appropriate validators to make sure the follow-up call comes after the initial call. The result should look something like Figure 5-10.

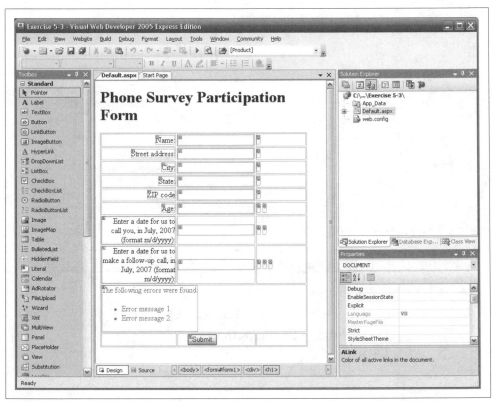

Figure 5-10. Your goal for Exercise 5-3.

Exercise 5-4. If you're going to call the user at home, you'll need a phone number to call. If the user is willing to give out his phone number, you might as well get his email address as well. After all, you never know when you'll need it. But if the user forgets a digit, or leaves off the ".com" from his email address, it'll do you no good. Add two more rows to the table, with labels and text fields where the user can enter a phone number and email address. Then add the appropriate validators to make sure that the input is in the correct form. The form should look something like Figure 5-11.

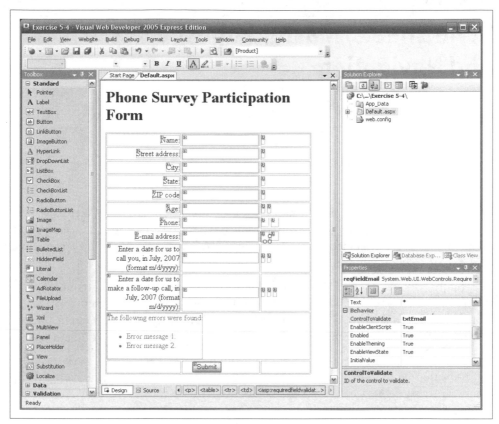

Figure 5-11. Your goal for Exercise 5-4.

CHAPTER 6

Style Sheets, Master Pages, and Navigation

Back in the early mists of time, when the Earth was young and the Web was new (Circa 1994) we created web pages in HTML (HyperText Markup Language). After many eons (or so it seemed), we were able to add styles to the HTML elements, allowing us to take greater control over the presentation of web pages.

Eventually content (the HTML) was divided from presentation and layout through the use of styles, and that was good. In fact, it came to pass that presentation information was given its own file—a style sheet—to allow for reuse, a consistent presentation across many pages, and easier maintenance, and that was very good indeed.

Styles and style sheets are a significant, but often overlooked tool for web developers, too often ignored by "programmers" who disparage style sheets as being in the realm of "designers"—leading to the creation of web applications that are terribly difficult to maintain.

A new innovation for creating sites with a common look and feel across all of the pages are *Master Pages*, covered later in this chapter. Master Pages can easily contain menus and other navigational aids such as site maps and bread crumbs, and these too will be covered in this chapter.

Styles and Style Sheets

A *style* specifies how an object will be rendered to an output device, typically a browser. Styles can be used to manipulate the layout and appearance of controls and text, detailing every aspect from border color to font size.

Web applications use styles to ensure attractive and reasonable display on a wide variety of devices, including desktop and laptop computers, tablet PCs, mobile PCs, telephones, PDAs, televisions, printers, audio devices and media not yet imagined.

Both HTML and ASP.NET controls apply styles through the use of properties and attributes. There are three ways to apply styles to an element on a web page:

Inline
> The style is implemented as an attribute of a specific element.

Document
> A set of styles are declared on and for a single HTML page.

External
> A style sheet is created and "included" in one or more HTML pages.

Cascading Style Sheets

External style sheets are called *cascading style sheets* (CSS), because the style specifications cascade down from the most general (the external style sheet), to the more specific (document level styles), to the most specific (styles applied to particular elements).

If your style sheet says that text boxes should have a white background, but one particular page says that its textboxes will have gray backgrounds, and on that page the seventh text box has its own style calling for a yellow background, the rules will cascade—style sheet, to document, to element. All other pages in your web site will have text boxes whose background color is controlled by the style sheet. Your one document will have text boxes with gray backgrounds, except for the seventh text box, which will have...you guessed it! A yellow background.

 For a complete discussion of CSS, see the following books: *HTML & XHTML: The Definitive Guide*, by Chuck Musciano and Bill Kennedy, or *CSS: The Definitive Guide*, by Eric Meyer, both published by O'Reilly.

Inline Styles

You can apply styles to a specific element using the inline `style` attribute, as shown in the following snippet:

```
<input type="text" value="Sample text" style="color:Red;font-family:Arial;
    font-weight:bold;width:150px;" />
```

The `style` attribute contains one or more style properties, each consisting of a property name and value separated by a colon. Each property-value pair is separated from the next pair by a semicolon.

When you're using ASP.NET controls, you may set inline styles either in the markup or as properties in design view.

Create a new web site called `AspNetInlineStyles`. Switch to Design view and drag a `TextBox` control from the Standard section of the Toolbox onto the page. In the Properties window, set the following properties (you'll need to expand the Font group to set the first two properties):

Property	Value
Font-Bold	True
Font-Name	Arial
ForeColor	Red
Text	Sample Text
Width	150px

The resulting Design view should look something like Figure 6-1.

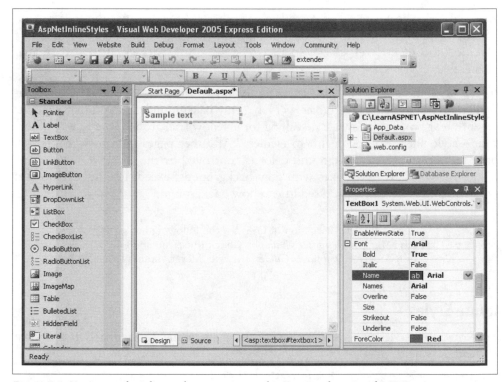

Figure 6-1. You've set the inline style properties on this TextBox by using the IDE.

 When you set the Font Name property, the IDE automatically fills in the Names property for you.

Run the application. When the page comes up in the browser, view the source by clicking on the View → Source menu item in IE6 or Page → View Source in IE7.

Notice how this ASP.NET TextBox is rendered to the page:

```
<input name="TextBox1" type="text" value="Sample text" id="TextBox1"
    style="color:Red;font-family:Arial;font-weight:bold;width:150px;" />
```

It is the same as if you had coded HTML with inline styles, which is, in fact what ASP.NET sends to the browser based on the ASP.NET controls and their properties.

You can also set or change style properties programmatically (as you can any control property).

To see this, close the browser, then drag a Button control from the Standard section of the Toolbox onto the page. Using an If-Then-Else statement, change its Text property to toggle between two colors.

Double-click the Button in Design view to open up the event handler for the Click event. Enter the highlighted code from Example 6-1.

Example 6-1. ButtonClick Event handler

```
Protected Sub Button1_Click(ByVal sender As Object, _
        ByVal e As System.EventArgs) Handles Button1.Click
    If TextBox1.ForeColor = Drawing.Color.Red Then
        TextBox1.ForeColor = Drawing.Color.Green
    Else
        TextBox1.ForeColor = Drawing.Color.Red
    End If
End Sub
```

Run the application. Each time you click the button, the ForeColor property will toggle between Red and Green.

Pros and cons

Inline properties are excellent for overriding the styles in your style sheet for a particular control. Unfortunately, they are very easy to use instead of style sheets, and programmers are often seduced into using inline styles to excess, creating markup that is very difficult to maintain.

Document-Level Styles

Just as you can use inline styles to override a style sheet for a single control, you can also add styles to a single document to override a particular setting for that one page. This is an error-prone technique for any multipage web site (that is, for virtually any serious web site), so we will be brief in our presentation of how to use them.

Document level styles are added to a page with a <style> element in the <head> section of the page as shown in Example 6-2. In this web site, called AspNetDocumentLevel-Styles, the style for the top-level heading, <h1>, will be overridden to display in red, bold, italicized text. Also, a new style will be defined, called GreenText.

Example 6-2. Default.aspx for AspNetDocumentLevelStyles

```
<%@ Page Language="VB" AutoEventWireup="false" CodeFile="Default.aspx.vb" Inherits="_
Default" %>

<!DOCTYPE html PUBLIC "-//W3C//DTD XHTML 1.0 Transitional//EN"
"http://www.w3.org/TR/xhtml1/DTD/xhtml1-transitional.dtd">

<html xmlns="http://www.w3.org/1999/xhtml" >
<head runat="server">
    <title> Special Page </title>
    <style type="text/css">
        <!--
        h1 {color: red; font-style:italic; font-weight:bold;}
        .GreenText {color:green;}
        -->
    </style>
</head>
<body>
    <form id="form1" runat="server">
    <div>
        <h1>A Sample Heading</h1>
        <div class="GreenText">some green text</div>
        <asp:Label ID="Label1" runat="server"
         Text="Green text in an ASP.NET Label control."
         CssClass="GreenText"></asp:Label>
    </div>
    </form>
</body>
</html>
```

Note the period in front of the GreenText style name; it is required.

Also, notice that the style definitions are embedded between HTML comment characters. This is for the benefit of very old browsers that may not recognize styles; they will ignore the styles enclosed in comments.

Figure 6-2 displays the results of this style change.

Pros and cons

It is tempting to use a document-level style either to set the styles for that page or to override the general styles for the entire site. This can be effective, but tends to be hard to maintain.

Experience shows that collecting styles into a set of external style sheets, even if some styles are targeted at a subset of pages (where that subset could be as small as a single page) tends to be far easier to maintain in the long term.

Figure 6-2. The result of using document-level styles. It looks perfectly fine for this one page, but across a whole site, using document-level styles is tough to maintain.

External Style Sheets

The net result is that in most applications, styles are defined in an external file, called (somewhat confusingly) a *style sheet* (or, as already mentioned, a "Cascading Style Sheet," or even an "External Style Sheet.") This style sheet is "imported" into each page by a directive at the top of the *.aspx* page.

To complicate things further, you are not limited to a single style sheet for your entire application. In fact, you are free to create separate style sheets for different sections of your application, or for rendering to different devices.

You first saw the use of a CSS style sheet back in Chapter 3, where you used styles to differentiate the watermarked and unwatermarked text boxes. Look at the CSS Style sheet created for that application, reproduced here in Example 6-3.

Example 6-3. StyleSheet.cssfor AdventureWorksWatermarks web site

```
body {
}
.watermarked {
    padding:2px 0 0 2px;
    border:1px solid #BEBEBE;
    background-color:#F0F8FF;
    color:gray;
    font-family:Verdana;
    font-weight:lighter;
}
```

Example 6-3. StyleSheet.cssfor AdventureWorksWatermarks web site (continued)

```
.unwatermarked {
    height:18px;
    width:148px;
    font-weight:bold;
}
```

There are two *style classes* in this style sheet: watermarked and unwatermarked.

Style classes are defined with a leading period, followed by the name of the class, and then the definition of the style class enclosed in braces. To use a style class, the element must specifically identify the class it wants to use, such as:

```
<asp:TextBox  CssClass="watermarked"...
```

Your style sheet can also define styles for "selectors", and these styles will automatically be applied to matching elements. For example, if you define a selector for the <p> (paragraph) element, all paragraph elements would have that style applied.

The application of styles to both classes and selectors can become complex once you begin nesting, which is why we strongly recommend reading a solid book on CSS syntax (such as those mentioned in the note above). The names used for style classes are case sensitive. If your style sheet has a class called watermarked and you assign the class name Watermarked (with a capital W) it will be ignored, with no error message, leading to many happy hours of debugging.

To see style sheets at work, create a new web site called AspNetExternalStyles.

Click on the Website → Add New Item... menu item and add a style sheet. You could use the default name of *StyleSheet.css*, since we will only be using a single style sheet in this web site, but let's call it *MyStyleSheet.css*.

The default style sheet template looks like the following, with an empty *selector* for the body element:

```
body {
}
```

Add the highlighted code from Example 6-4 to your style sheet to define three style classes for different headings, plus an overridden selector for all paragraph elements. As you type, IntelliSense will show all possible style attributes and provide hints for valid values.

Example 6-4. MyStyleSheet.css

```
body {
}
p {color:blue}
.MyHeading1
{
```

Example 6-4. MyStyleSheet.css (continued)

```
    font-family:Arial Black, Sans-Serif;
    font-style:normal;
    font-weight:bold;
    font-size:xx-large;
    background-color:Aqua;
    color:Red;
    padding-left:.5in;
    padding-right:.5in;
    line-height:1.5in;
}
.MyHeading2
{
    font-family:Arial Black, Sans-Serif;
    font-style:normal;
    font-weight:bold;
    font-size:x-large;
    background-color:Aqua;
    color:Blue;
    padding-left:.1in;
    padding-right:.1in;
    line-height:.75in;
}
.MyHeading3
{
    font-family:Arial Black, Sans-Serif;
    font-style:normal;
    font-weight:bold;
    font-size:large;
    color:Black;
}
.BodyText
{
    font-family:Times New Roman, Serif;
    font-style:normal;
    font-weight:bolder;
    font-size:medium;
}
```

There are a number of possible units of measurement you can use for attributes that require absolute values, such as padding and line-height, In addition, *Relative* units, which are relative to the other content on the page, are also available. Table 6-1 lists both.

Table 6-1. Style length units

Unit	Abbreviation	Type
Width of lowercase "M"	em	Relative
Height of letter "x"	ex	Relative
Pixels	px	Absolute
Inches	In	Absolute

Table 6-1. Style length units (continued)

Unit	Abbreviation	Type
Centimeters	cm	Absolute
Millimeters	mm	Absolute
Points (1/72 inch)	pt	Absolute
Picas (equal to 12 points or 1/6 inch)	pc	Absolute
Percentage	%	Percentage

Any length property can be prefixed with either a plus (+) or minus (−) sign to indicate that the value is to be added or subtracted from the current value of the property.

Open the *default.aspx* file in the IDE. Switch to Design view, and drag a Label control onto the page. Set the Text property to Heading 1. Set the CssClass property to MyHeading1.

Type in some text on the page, select it, and apply the paragraph style to it.

Now drag a second Label control onto the page. Set its Text property to Heading 2 and the CssClass property to MyHeading2. Type some more text on the page after the label.

Drag a third label on the page. Set the Text property to Heading 3 and the CssClass property to MyHeading3. Type some more text on the page.

Add two more Label controls with the CssClass set to MyHeading2 and MyHeading3, along with some text.

To format the text under both MyHeading3 headings, switch to Source view and insert some <div> or <span> elements so that you can apply the BodyText style.

In order to apply a style to an ASP.NET control, you use the CssClass property. However, to apply a style to an HTML control, you use the class property.

And, just as a bit of HTML refresher, both <div> and <span> elements are used primarily to apply style to some content. The difference is that a <div> element incorporates a line break before and after, while a <span> element does not, displaying its content inline with its container. It is convenient to think of a <div> as creating a block, while a <span> delineates a series of characters.

Before the styles will take effect, you need to import the style sheet to the page. Insert the following highlighted line of markup between the opening and closing head tags:

CODE ▶
```
<head runat="server">
    <style type="text/css">@import url(MyStyleSheet.css);</style>
    <title>Untitled Page</title>
</head>
```

The Design view will now look something like Figure 6-3.

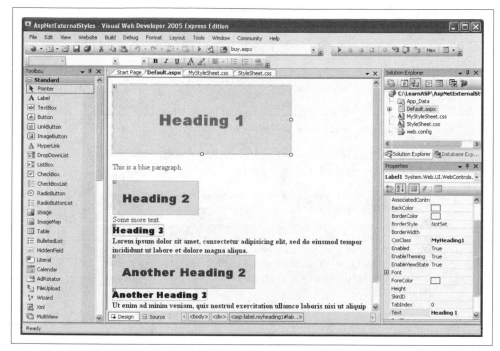

Figure 6-3. *Your AspNetExternalStyles page, in Design view, where you can see all the styles applied.*

Example 6-5 presents the Source view for *Default.aspx*.

Example 6-5. Default.aspx for AspNetExternalStyles

```
<%@ Page Language="VB" AutoEventWireup="false" CodeFile="Default.aspx.vb"
    Inherits="_Default" %>

<!DOCTYPE html PUBLIC "-//W3C//DTD XHTML 1.0 Transitional//EN"
    "http://www.w3.org/TR/xhtml1/DTD/xhtml1-transitional.dtd">

<html xmlns="http://www.w3.org/1999/xhtml" >
<head runat="server">
    <style type="text/css">@import url(MyStyleSheet.css);</style>
    <title>Untitled Page</title>
</head>
<body>
    <form id="form1" runat="server">
    <div>
        <asp:Label ID="Label1" runat="server" CssClass="MyHeading1"
            Text="Heading 1"></asp:Label>
        <p>
        This is a blue paragraph.
        </p>
```

Example 6-5. Default.aspx for AspNetExternalStyles (continued)

```
        <asp:Label ID="Label2" runat="server" CssClass="MyHeading2"
            Text="Heading 2"></asp:Label>
        <br />
        Some more text.
        <br />
        <asp:Label ID="Label3" runat="server" CssClass="MyHeading3"
            Text="Heading 3"></asp:Label>
        <div class="BodyText">
            Lorem ipsum dolor sit amet, consectetur adipisicing elit, sed do
            eiusmod tempor incididunt ut labore et dolore magna aliqua.
        </div>
        <asp:Label ID="Label4" runat="server" CssClass="MyHeading2"
            Text="Another Heading 2"></asp:Label>
        <br />
        <asp:Label ID="Label5" runat="server" CssClass="MyHeading3"
            Text="Another Heading 3"></asp:Label>
        <br />
        <span class="BodyText">
            Ut enim ad minim veniam, quis nostrud exercitation ullamco laboris
            nisi ut aliquip ex ea commodo consequat. Duis aute irure dolor in
            reprehenderit in voluptate velit esse cillum dolore eu fugiat
            nulla pariatur.
        </span>
    </div>
    </form>
</body>
</html>
```

The highlighted line uses the `@import` command to import the style sheet specified in the URL. In this case, a relative URL is provided, which refers to our style sheet in the current directory. Because it is a URL, it can be either relative or absolute. For example, you could provide an absolute URL such as *http://CorporateWebSite.com/stylesheets/handhelds.css*.

 The `@import` command must appear in the `<head>` element, and before any conventional style rules are specified. Otherwise, the imported style sheet will be ignored. This allows the browser to properly cascade styles from the external style sheet down to the element-level styles.

The resulting page is shown in Figure 6-4.

Master Pages

A *master page* acts as a shell or frame shared by all the other pages (or some of the other pages) on your site. It is common to put a logo and perhaps a menu into the master page so that these elements appear at the same location on every page without your having to recode them.

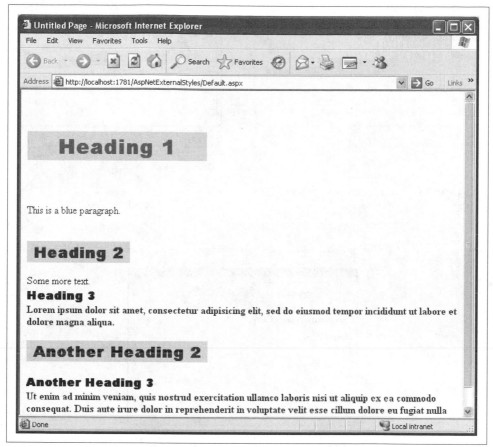

Figure 6-4. This is what the AspNetExternalStyles page looks like in your browser. You need to include the @import statement in your page so that the styles are loaded along with the page content.

Within the master page, you place one or more content placeholder areas, which will be filled with the contents of each of the child pages. This is shown in Figure 6-5.

Unlike cascading style sheets (CSS), which help ensure that similar controls have similar appearances (see the previous section), master pages ensure that all the pages on your site have common elements such as logos, headings, footers, or navigation aids.

To use master pages, follow these steps:

1. Create a new web site.
2. Add a master page to the site.
3. Add content pages based on the master page.

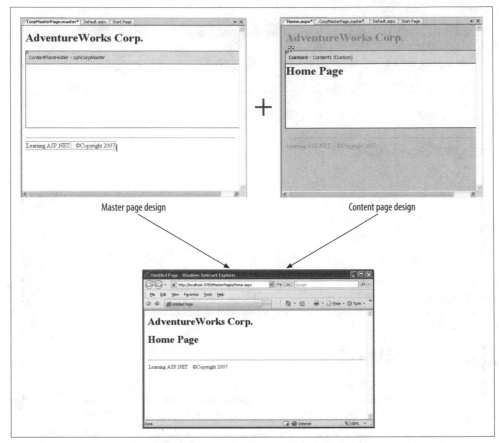

Figure 6-5. *The master page defines the content that should appear on every page of your site, and has placeholders for the content of the individual child pages. When you put them together, you get a web site with a uniform appearance.*

Creating a Master Page

To begin, create a new web site and call it *MasterPages*. Once the new site opens click on Website → Add New Item.... Select Master Page in the dialog box and give it the name, *CorpMasterPage.master*, as shown in Figure 6-6. Be sure to check the "Place code in separate file" checkbox, as indicated in the figure. This causes the code-behind file to be created automatically.

 Even though we don't actually use any server-side code in the master page in this chapter, it is good practice to segregate all your server-side code in a code-behind file, rather than in a script block in the markup file.

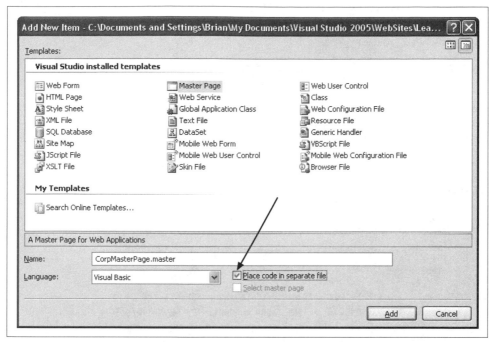

Figure 6-6. *You add a master page from the Website → Add New Item dialog. Be sure to check the "Place code in separate file" checkbox.*

 All master pages *must* have the extension *.master*.

Your new master page has been created with an `<asp:contentplaceholder>` control declaration already in place. Switch to Source view and change the ID of the placeholder to something more meaningful, such as cphCorpMaster, as in the following code:

CODE▶

```
<asp:contentplaceholder id="cphCorpMaster" runat="server">
</asp:contentplaceholder>
```

The placeholder will be filled by the contents of the child page, which in turn will be surrounded by whatever else you place on the Master Page. Within the master page, you may add anything you like surrounding the `<asp:contentplaceholder>`. For example, you might add a logo at the top of the page and a copyright notice in the footer. Perhaps you may want navigation controls to appear consistently positioned along the side of your pages. You can even add other content place holders, giving each a unique ID.

For this example, place an `<h1>` header on the page above the ContentPlaceHolder, and an HTML table below as a footer. The Source view should look something like Example 6-6. Add the highlighted code to your page.

Example 6-6. CorpMasterPage.master

```
<%@ Master Language="VB" CodeFile="CorpMasterPage.master.vb"
    Inherits="CorpMasterPage" %>

<!DOCTYPE html PUBLIC "-//W3C//DTD XHTML 1.0 Transitional//EN"
"http://www.w3.org/TR/xhtml1/DTD/xhtml1-transitional.dtd">

<html xmlns="http://www.w3.org/1999/xhtml" >
<head runat="server">
    <title>Untitled Page</title>
</head>
<body>
    <form id="form1" runat="server">
    <div>
        <h1>AdventureWorks Corp.</h1>
        <asp:contentplaceholder id="cphCorpMaster" runat="server">
        </asp:contentplaceholder>
        <br />
        <hr />
        <table>
            <tr>
                <td width="50%" align="left">Learning ASP.NET</td>
                <td width="50%" align="right"> &copy;Copyright 2007</td>
            </tr>
        </table>
    </div>
    </form>
</body>
</html>
```

Switching to Design view, the master page will look something like that shown in Figure 6-7.

Adding Content Pages

The pages you'll add that will use this master page will put all of their content into the ContentPlaceHolder defined in the master page. When combined, the two create a child page.

 You can put more than one ContentPlaceHolder control on a master page (each has its own ID). This gives you tremendous flexibility in laying out your pages, though experience shows that the majority of sites actually use only a single contentPlaceHolder per Master Page.

For this example, you'll add two new *.aspx* pages, *Home.aspx* and *SecondPage.aspx*. There are two ways to do this.

One way is to click on the Website → Add Content Page menu item. However, this will produce a page with a default name, which you will almost certainly want to change, which is more of a nuisance than it is worth.

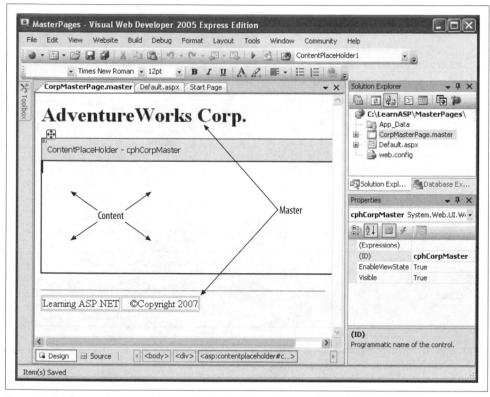

Figure 6-7. This is what your Master page looks like in Design view. The heading at the top and the footer at the bottom will be applied to all your child pages. The content from your child pages will appear in the placeholder.

The better way is to click on Website → Add New Item..., then add a "normal" Web Form. Call the new page *Home.aspx*, and be sure to check both the "Select master page" and "Place code in separate file" checkboxes, as indicated in Figure 6-8.

When you click the Add button, the Select a Master Page dialog will open. Choose *CorpMasterPage.master* (the only master page available at this point), and click OK.

Switch to Design view.

Your new *Home.aspx* page will be shown within the master page. The Content box will allow you to add any content you like, including controls, text, and so forth, but the contents of the master page will be inaccessible.

Add some text and format it as HTML Heading 1 using the Block Format drop-down menu, as indicated in Figure 6-9.

The Design view allows you to see how your new page will look when it is combined with the master page at runtime.

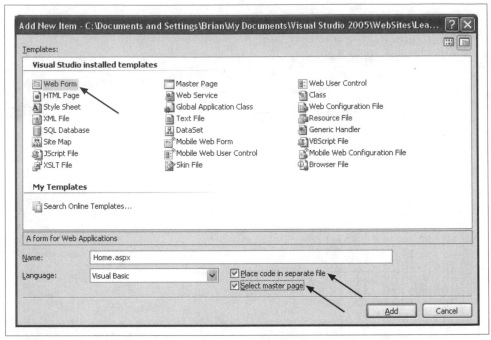

Figure 6-8. The easiest way to add a content page is by adding a new Web Form, and making sure to check the "Place code in separate file" and "Select master page" checkboxes.

The terminology can get a bit confusing, so let's clarify. A master page has an empty `ContentPlaceHolder` control.

You create a separate file called a child page. A child page is a normal *.aspx* file, with a `Page` directive but minus the <html>, <form>, <head>, and <body> tags. Typically, you'll create many child pages for each master.

The contents of each child page are displayed as if they were inserted into the `ContentPlaceHolder` control. In effect, the Master Page is "wrapped around" the child page, allowing all the child pages to share the contents of the master page.

Create the next page, *SecondPage.aspx*, using the same Master page. Using the Master Page ensures that the look and feel of the two pages will be identical.

Take a quick look at the markup generated for the second page:

```
<%@ Page Language="VB"
    MasterPageFile="~/CorpMasterPage.master"
    AutoEventWireup="false"
    CodeFile="SecondPage.aspx.vb"
    Inherits="SecondPage"
    title="Untitled Page" %>
<asp:Content ID="Content1" ContentPlaceHolderID="cphCorpMaster" Runat="Server">
</asp:Content>
```

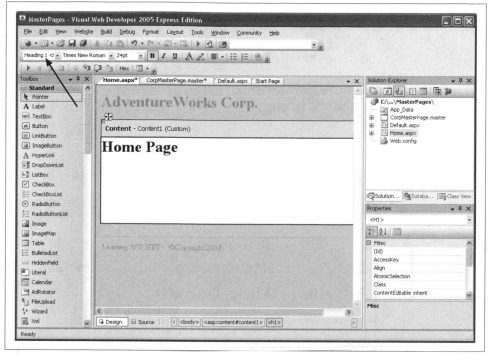

Figure 6-9. When you create a child page, you add content within the placeholder you created before. The contents of the master page are there for you to view, but they're grayed out. In this case, use the Block Format drop-down menu to add some text and format it as a Heading 1.

The Page directive contains a reference to the second page's master page file, as well as some other information necessary to the page. An ASP.NET Content control was added for you automatically.

You can put some simple text in the Content control and then run the two pages, as shown in Figure 6-10.

 This example does not provide any means of navigating from page to page. In order to see these pages, right-click on the page in the Solution Explorer and click on View in Browser. Later in this chapter, we will look at ways to navigate from page to page within a web site.

Using Nested Master Pages

You may want certain stable elements to appear throughout the entire web site, while other elements should be shared only within a specific part of your application. For example, you might have a company-wide header, but need division-specific elements as well. ASP.NET 2.0 lets you create nested master pages. Any given web page can be combined with a nested master page or with the original master, whichever makes more sense for that individual page.

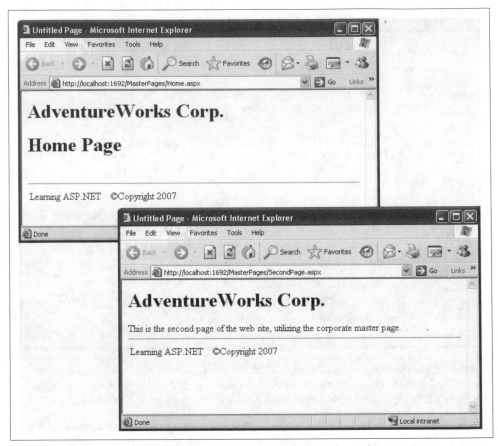

Figure 6-10. This is what your child pages look like when you run the application. As you can see, the header and footer from the master page appear in both.

 In Visual Studio 2005 nested master pages do not display properly. This is fixed in Visual Studio 2008.

Copy the previous example, MasterPages, to a new application, NestedMasterPages.

Add a new master page to the web site, called *SalesMasterPage.master*. As shown back in Figure 6-6, be sure to check the "Place code in separate file" checkbox.

Looking at the Source view, the IDE puts the following boilerplate markup code in *SalesMasterPage.master*:

CODE▶

```
<%@ Master Language="VB" CodeFile="SalesMasterPage.master.vb"
    Inherits="SalesMasterPage" %>

<!DOCTYPE html PUBLIC "-//W3C//DTD XHTML 1.0 Transitional//EN"
    "http://www.w3.org/TR/xhtml1/DTD/xhtml1-transitional.dtd">
```

```
<html xmlns="http://www.w3.org/1999/xhtml" >
<head runat="server">
    <title>Untitled Page</title>
</head>
<body>
    <form id="form1" runat="server">
    <div>
        <asp:contentplaceholder id="ContentPlaceHolder1" runat="server">
        </asp:contentplaceholder>
    </div>
    </form>
</body>
</html>
```

In order to make this a nested master page, delete *all* of this *except* for the Master directive. Then add the highlighted code shown in Example 6-7.

Example 6-7. SalesMasterPage.master

```
<%@ Master Language="VB" CodeFile="SalesMasterPage.master.vb"
    MasterPageFile="~/CorpMasterPage.master"
    Inherits="SalesMasterPage" %>

<asp:Content runat="server" ID="SalesMasterContent"
    ContentPlaceHolderID="cphCorpMaster">
    <table>
        <tr>
            <td>
                <h3>Sales Department Master Page</h3>
                Put information here to display on all the Sales pages.
                <br />
                <br />
            </td>
        </tr>
        <tr>
            <td>
                <asp:ContentPlaceHolder runat="server" ID="cphSalesContent">
                    Default content for Sales
                </asp:ContentPlaceHolder>
            </td>
        </tr>
    </table>
</asp:Content>
```

The Master directive has an additional attribute, MasterPageFile, which points to its master page. This is how ASP.NET knows that this is a nested master page. In this way, master pages can be nested as deep as necessary.

This master page for the Sales department has an ASP.NET Content control, called SalesMasterContent, which contains the content to display on all the Sales pages. In this example, that content consists of an HTML table for layout, along with some additional markup.

Like all Content controls, it has a ContentPlaceHolderID attribute that specifies which ContentPlaceHolder control on *its* master page it will populate—in this case, cphCorpMaster on the *CorpMasterPage.master* master page.

The markup also includes a ContentPlaceHolder control called cphSalesContent. Child pages that use this nested master page will put their content inside this ContentPlaceHolder.

Unfortunately, you cannot use the designer to examine nested pages but you can see the effect once you create a web page that uses this nested master page.

To see the nested master page in action, add two new pages to the web site. Call them *Sales_Orders.aspx* and *Sales_Stores.aspx*. For each, check the "Select master page" checkbox shown in Figure 6-8. Now, when the Select a Master Page dialog comes up, you have two master pages to choose from. Select *SalesMasterPage.master* and click OK, as shown in Figure 6-11.

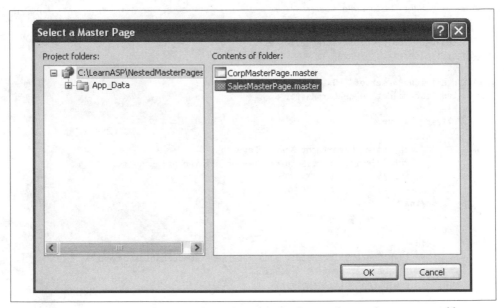

Figure 6-11. When your site uses nested master pages, you have a choice whenever you add a new page.

Add some content to each page to distinguish it. The markup for *Sales_Orders.aspx* is shown in Example 6-8.

Example 6-8. Sales_Orders.aspx

```
<%@ Page Language="VB" MasterPageFile="~/SalesMasterPage.master"
    AutoEventWireup="false" CodeFile="Sales_Orders.aspx.vb"
    Inherits="Sales_Orders" title="Untitled Page" %>
```

Example 6-8. Sales_Orders.aspx (continued)

```
<asp:Content ID="Content1" ContentPlaceHolderID="cphSalesContent"
    Runat="Server">
    <h3>Orders</h3>
    Display Orders information here.
</asp:Content>
```

The results for both pages are shown in Figure 6-12.

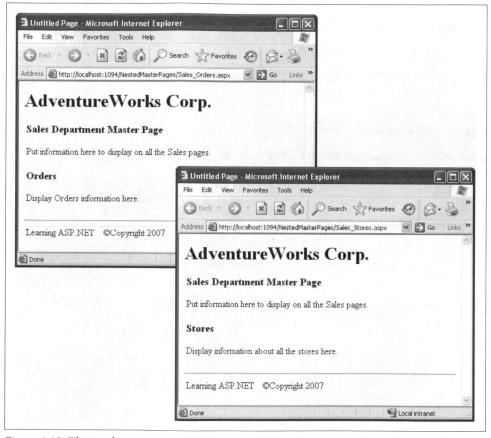

Figure 6-12. This is what your nested child pages look like when you run the application. You can see both the AdventureWorks master page, and the sales department master page, with the child content inside.

Changing the Master Page at Runtime

You may decide that in response to certain events, you'd like to reach up into the master page (from a child page) and change its presentation. To do so, you need to add a public property in the master page that can be accessed by any of the child pages.

To see how this is done, copy the previous example MasterPages to a new web site called ChangingTheMasterPage.

In Source view, open the master page, *CorpMasterPage.master*. From the Standard section of the Toolbox, drag a Label control onto the page between the opening <h1> heading and the existing ContentPlaceHolder control. Change the ID of the Label to lblMessage and remove the Text property. Add an HTML line break and a horizontal rule (<hr />) while you are at it. The Source view of the master page markup will look like Example 6-9, with the new Label control and the additional HTML formatting highlighted.

Example 6-9. CorpMasterPage.master withLabel control added

```
<%@ Master Language="VB" CodeFile="CorpMasterPage.master.vb"
    Inherits="CorpMasterPage" %>

<!DOCTYPE html PUBLIC "-//W3C//DTD XHTML 1.0 Transitional//EN" "http://www.w3.org/TR/
xhtml1/DTD/xhtml1-transitional.dtd">

<html xmlns="http://www.w3.org/1999/xhtml" >
<head runat="server">
    <title>Untitled Page</title>
</head>
<body>
    <form id="form1" runat="server">
    <div>
        <h1>AdventureWorks Corp.</h1>
        <asp:Label ID="lblMessage" runat="server" ></asp:Label>
        <br />
        <hr />
        <asp:contentplaceholder id="cphCorpMaster" runat="server">
        </asp:contentplaceholder>
        <br />
        <hr />
        <table>
            <tr>
                <td width="50%" align="left">Learning ASP.NET</td>
                <td width="50%" align="right">&copy;Copyright 2007</td>
            </tr>
        </table>
    </div>
    </form>
</body>
</html>
```

If you run the web site now, this label will not be visible on any of the child pages because there is no Text property to it.

Open the code-behind for the master page by right-clicking on *CorpMasterPage.master* in the Solution Explorer and selecting View Code. Type in the code highlighted in Example 6-10 to implement the public property.

Notice how IntelliSense helps you complete the code for the property.

Example 6-10. CorpMasterPage.master with public property

```
Partial Class CorpMasterPage
    Inherits System.Web.UI.MasterPage

Private lbl As Label
Public Property MessageLabel() As Label
    Get
        Return lblMessage
    End Get
    Set(ByVal value As Label)
        lbl = value
    End Set
End Property

End Class
```

—VB CHEAT SHEET—
Public and Private Properties

You've seen lots of properties throughout this book. For example, most controls have a Text property. You have also seen the use of local variables in the classes defined in the code-behind files. The declaration for properties and variables include a keyword known as the *access modifier*, which specifies what parts of the program can see that property or variable. The two most common access modifiers are public and private.

If a class member is declared public, then any part of the program that refers to that class can see and use members contained within it (property, variable, or method). On the other hand, if a class member is declared private, then only the code within that class itself can use that member.

To put this into relevant terms, in Example 6-10 the variable lbl is declared as private. Code within the CorpMasterPage class can refer to that variable, but code outside that class cannot. However, the property MessageLabel is declared public. Code outside the class can refer to that property by referring to an instance of the class and the property using dot notation, as will be demonstrated below.

If a member is public, then it will be displayed by IntelliSense where appropriate. If it is private, IntelliSense will never display it.

If you do not declare an access modifier, the default is public, but it is always good practice to explicitly declare it, even if public is what you intend.

Before a child page can use a public property of the master page, it needs to be told the name of the class, or type, that contains the master page. This is done with another directive at the top of the markup of the page. You have already seen Page directives at the top of normal *.aspx* pages, as well as the `Master` directive at the top of the master pages. Now add following `MasterType` directive to the top of *SecondPage.aspx*, after the existing `Page` directive and before any page content:

CODE
```
<%@ MasterType TypeName="CorpMasterPage" %>
```

If you look at the code-behind for the master page *CorpMasterPage.master*, you will see that the name of the class is `CorpMasterPage`. This code, shown in the following snippet, is generated for you automatically by the IDE.

CODE
```
Partial Class CorpMasterPage
    Inherits System.Web.UI.MasterPage
```

Now that the child page has a reference to the class of the master page, it can be referred to in code. To see this, switch *SecondPage.aspx* to Design view. Drag a Button from the Standard section of the Toolbox into the Content section of the page. Change the `ID` of the Button to `btnMessage` and its `Text` property to `Message Master`. Figure 6-13 shows the page in Design view.

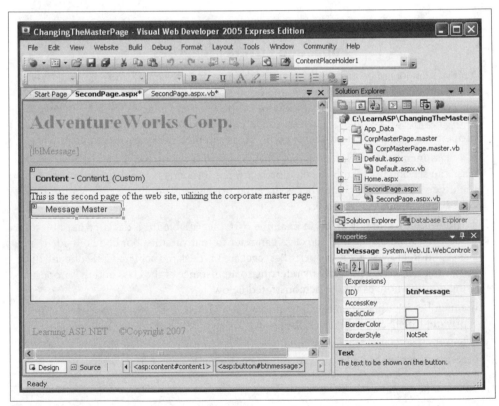

Figure 6-13. You're adding a button to SecondPage.aspx that you're going to use to send a message to the master page.

Double-click on the button to create an event handler for the Click event in the code-behind. Enter the highlighted code from Example 6-11 to this event handler to change the message label on the master page when the button is clicked.

Example 6-11. SecondPage.aspx.vb

```
Partial Class SecondPage
    Inherits System.Web.UI.Page


Protected Sub btnMessage_Click(ByVal sender As Object, _
          ByVal e As System.EventArgs) _
          Handles btnMessage.Click
      Me.Master.MessageLabel.Text = "Button on SecondPage pushed."
End Sub
End Class
```

When *SecondPage.aspx.vb* is run and the button is clicked, it will look similar to Figure 6-14.

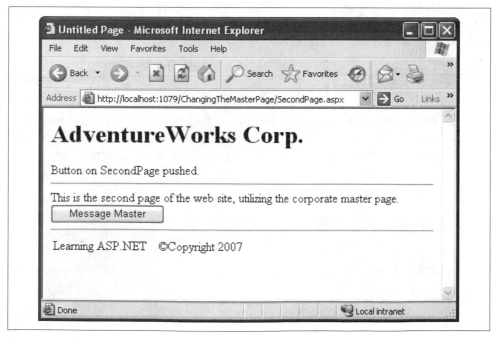

Figure 6-14. When you click the button on Second page, the message is sent to the master page and displayed.

Navigation

Modern commercial web sites can be surprisingly complex, often consisting of dozens, even hundreds of pages. Users will have a more satisfying experience if you provide navigational hints and menus to help them avoid "getting lost," and to enable them to conveniently find all the features of the site.

The ASP.NET toolset includes a number of controls that facilitate this assistance. There are controls for creating both "bread crumbs" (how did I get to this page?) and site maps (how do I find that other page?).

Most of the time you will want these features to be present on every page, and thus master pages are a great asset. If you change the site map or the control, you only need to update the master and all the other pages are "updated" automatically.

Buttons and HyperLinks

The simplest form of navigation is through the use of Buttons, LinkButtons, and Hyperlinks. All three will take the user to a different page. Superficially, LinkButtons and Hyperlinks look the same, while buttons look different (see Figure 6-15). Under the covers, however, LinkButtons and Buttons have much more in common, while Hyperlinks are very different.

Let's clarify. When you click a Hyperlink, you are taken directly to the new page. The first page does not post back to the server. You are immediately transferred to the new page—do not pass Go, do not collect $200.

With a LinkButton (which looks like a Hyperlink) or a Button (which looks like a button), however, the page *is* posted back, and there is an opportunity for you, the developer, to run an event handler *before* control is handed over to the new page.

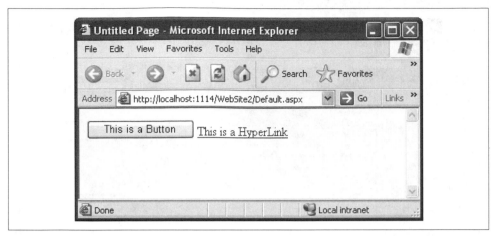

Figure 6-15. A Button control looks like you would expect a button to look, and ditto for the HyperLink control.

Hyperlinks are faster for the user (and simpler for the developer), but they do not give you the opportunity to run code before leaving the page, which is the trade off you'll have to make each time you decide between a Hyperlink and one of the alternatives.

To see how buttons and links can be used for navigation, copy the example from earlier in this chapter, MasterPages, to a new web site called ButtonNavigation.

Open *Home.aspx* in Design view. Drag a Button control onto the page below the header. Change the Text property of the Button to Page 2. It will look something like Figure 6-16.

As previously mentioned, you need to add custom code to make the navigation happen. You'll need to provide some code to handle the Click event, so in Design view, double-click the button and then enter the highlighted lines of code shown in Example 6-12.

Example 6-12. Home.aspx.vb showing theButton Click event handler

```
Partial Class Home
    Inherits System.Web.UI.Page

Protected Sub Button1_Click(ByVal sender As Object, _
        ByVal e As System.EventArgs) Handles Button1.Click
    ' do something here
    Response.Redirect("SecondPage.aspx")
End Sub
End Class
```

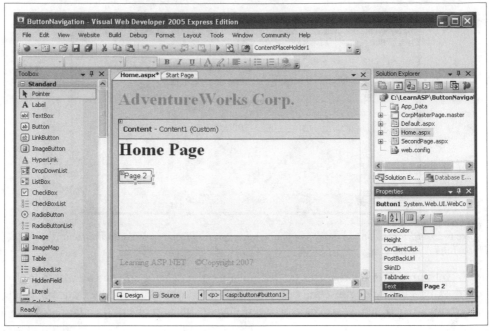

Figure 6-16. You've placed a navigation button on the home page, which will help users find where they're going.

Before the new page is invoked, you can run an event handler. You might do so, for example, to retrieve the status of other controls on the page, interact with a database, perform computations or, most commonly, to stash a value in Session State that will be retrieved by the new page.

 The Button's Click event handler is not the only place where your code is executed during postbacks. You can place code in event handlers for any number of events. By far, the most common is Page Load, where it is routine to place code to process the page. Page Load and other life cycle issues are covered in Chapter 7.

The actual navigation is accomplished with the Redirect method of the HttpResponse class. It is the programmatic equivalent of a hyperlink, immediately transferring to the new page without first posting back to the server. The argument to the method is a string representing the URL of the target page.

The URL can either be relative (as in this example) or absolute. In this example, it refers to a web page in the same directory as the current page. An absolute URL would be completely qualified, irrespective of the current location, such as *http:// LibertyAssociates.com/Samples/SecondPage.aspx*.

Run the page now to see how it works. Clicking on the button posts the page back to the server. If there were a method called Page_Load to handle the Page Load event, it would be executed. Then the code in the Button Click event handler from Example 6-12 would run. The last line in that method would be the Response. Redirect to perform the navigation.

The main attraction to using buttons and links for navigation is that they are very simple and direct. The big problem is that it can be tedious to implement, since you must place every button or link on every page, specify the URL, and handle the Click event for each (for Buttons and LinkButtons). As a case in point, this example so far allows you to navigate from the Home page to the Second page, but not back (without using the browser's Back button). For a web site with many pages and routes, this approach quickly breaks down.

At any rate, add a HyperLink control to *SecondPage.aspx* to allow easy navigation back to the Home page. Go to *SecondPage.aspx* in Design view, hit the Enter key a few times at the end of the line of text already there then drag a HyperLink control on to the page. In the Properties window, set the Text property to Home Page, the ForeColor property to Blue, and the NavigateUrl property to Home.aspx. Figure 6-17 shows the Home page link in Design view.

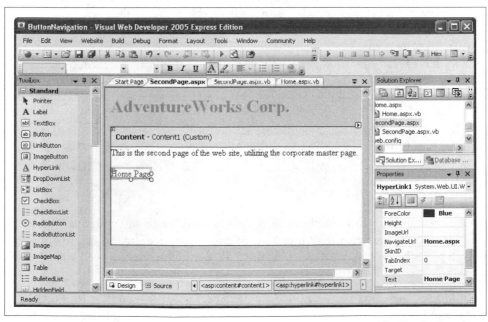

Figure 6-17. A HyperLink in Design view showing the properties set to give it the blue look and a target page to navigate to.

Now if you run the page, there will be hyperlink on the second page to take you back to the Home page. In this example, they behave identically, but if you needed custom code to execute on *SecondPage.aspx*, that would not happen with the HyperLink.

Menus and Bread Crumbs

You've probably seen menus and bread crumbs for navigation on many commercial sites. Menus are familiar from the earliest windowing environments; they offer a set of choices for navigation (they can be pull-down or pop-up selections) and *bread crumbs* take their name from Hansel and Gretel, who left a trail behind them so they could find their way home. In ASP.NET, bread crumbs typically consist of a set of links back through the page hierarchy, making it easy for you to reverse course and take different forks in what otherwise would be a confusing tree of alternative pages.

About Bread Crumbs and Hansel and Gretel

Hansel and Gretel is a short story by the Brothers Grimm (who came by their last name honestly, to judge by the brutality of many of their stories). Written in the late 18th century, the story tells how starving children are abandoned in the forest by their evil stepmother (isn't it always?). They gather white pebbles to find their way home, but she repeats her crime of abandonment and this time the kids have only bread (it is not explained where all the pebbles have gone).

They leave bread crumbs as a trail home, but the forest animals eat them (the bread crumbs, not the kids), and now hopelessly lost, the kids are left to the mercy of a witch who locks Hansel in a cage and makes Gretel her servant, while she fattens them both as potential dinner.

It is from this delightful tale of child abuse and cannibalism that we derive the technical term "bread crumbs" for navigation within ASP.NET

—Source: Wikipedia article "Hansel and Gretel," as of May 30, 2007

To see menus and bread crumbs at work, you'll need a web site with a few pages to simulate a complex web site of hundreds of web pages (feel free to create hundreds of web pages if you like, we'll wait). Figure 6-18 shows how the finished web site will appear.

To build this web site, you will use a single master page, several normal web pages, and a site map to provide information for the menu and the bread crumbs. Later in the chapter you will see how to spiff up the appearance of the menu and the bread crumbs.

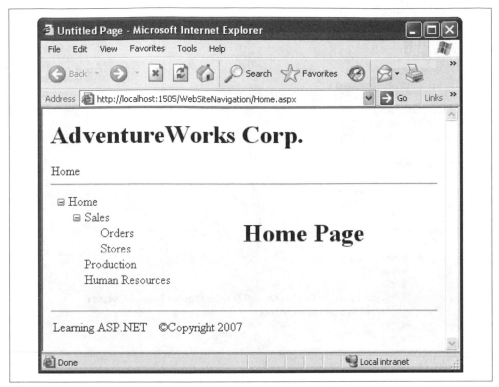

Figure 6-18. When you've completed the web site with menus and bread crumbs, it will look like this.

First you will create the web site with the master page, minus the navigation controls, and all the content pages. Then you will add the site map and the navigation controls.

Create a new web site called WebSiteNavigation. Delete *Default.aspx* by clicking on it in the Solution Explorer and pressing the Delete key. Confirm the deletion by clicking OK.

Add a master page, exactly as you did previously in this chapter. Click on Website → Add New Item.... In the Add New Item dialog box, select Master Page. You can retain the default file name of *MasterPage.master*. Be sure to select the "Place code in separate file" checkbox (see Figure 6-6).

When the master page opens in Source view, the only markup inside the <div> elements is the default ContentPlaceHolder control. Replace that with the highlighted code shown in Example 6-13. This is nearly identical to the *CorpMasterPage.master* from the example shown earlier in the chapter, except the ContentPlaceHolder control is placed inside an HTML table for layout control. Notice that the first cell in the only row in that table is empty at the moment. You will put the menu in that cell shortly.

Example 6-13. MasterPage.master before adding navigation controls

```
<%@ Master Language="VB" CodeFile="MasterPage.master.vb" Inherits="MasterPage" %>

<!DOCTYPE html PUBLIC "-//W3C//DTD XHTML 1.0 Transitional//EN"
"http://www.w3.org/TR/xhtml1/DTD/xhtml1-transitional.dtd">

<html xmlns="http://www.w3.org/1999/xhtml" >
<head runat="server">
    <title>Untitled Page</title>
</head>
<body>
    <form id="form1" runat="server">
    <div>
        <h1>AdventureWorks Corp.</h1>
          <br />
        <hr />
        <table width="100%">
            <tr>
                <td>
                </td>
                <td>
                    <asp:contentplaceholder id="cphCorpMaster" runat="server">
                    </asp:contentplaceholder>
                </td>
            </tr>
        </table>
        <br />
        <hr />
        <table>
            <tr>
                <td width="50%" align="left">Learning ASP.NET</td>
                <td width="50%" align="right">&copy;Copyright 2007</td>
            </tr>
        </table>
    </div>
    </form>
</body>
</html>
```

As you can see from the menu in Figure 6-18, there are six pages in this web site. Add all six of those pages to the web site now. In all cases, be sure to check the "Select master page" checkbox (see Figure 6-8), and to select *MasterPage.master* as the master page (the only choice). The names of the pages to create are:

- *Home.aspx*
- *HR.aspx*
- *Production.aspx*
- *Sales.aspx*
- *Sales_Orders.aspx*
- *Sales_Stores.aspx*

To keep things simple, add only an <h1> heading to the Content area of each page identifying the name of the page.

You are now ready to prepare the site map and add the navigation controls.

Site Maps

Site maps arc used as a data source for navigation controls such `TreeViews`, `Menus`, and `SiteMapPaths` (which provide bread crumbs). Used in conjunction with master pages, these allow for easy and universal navigation without having to place navigation controls on every page of the web site.

Add a site map to the current web site by clicking on Website → Add New Item.... When the Add New Item dialog appears, select Site Map and accept the default name, *Web.sitemap*, as shown in Figure 6-19.

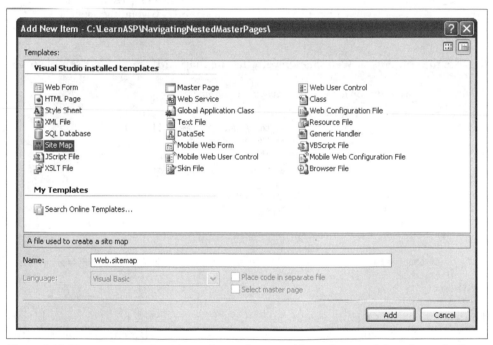

Figure 6-19. To create a new Site Map, select Website → Add New Item, and then choose the Site Map.

When you click Add, the file *Web.sitemap* is added to your web site, and the skeleton of a site map is provided for you, as shown in Example 6-14.

Example 6-14. Web.sitemap skeleton

```
<?xml version="1.0" encoding="utf-8" ?>
<siteMap xmlns="http://schemas.microsoft.com/AspNet/SiteMap-File-1.0" >
    <siteMapNode url="" title=""  description="">
        <siteMapNode url="" title=""  description="" />
        <siteMapNode url="" title=""  description="" />
    </siteMapNode>
</siteMap>
```

The url attribute specifies the page this menu item will link to. The title attribute defines the text that is displayed as the link, and the description attribute is used in the tool tip.

 Neither VWD nor VS2005 provide drag-and-drop support for creating your site map file. You can implement your own SiteMap provider to automate this process or get the site map from another source (such as a database) but this is a very advanced topic, beyond the scope of this book.

Replace the contents of *Web.sitemap* with the site map XML shown in Example 6-15.

Example 6-15. Web.sitemap for WebSiteNavigation example

```
<?xml version="1.0" encoding="utf-8" ?>
<siteMap xmlns="http://schemas.microsoft.com/AspNet/SiteMap-File-1.0" >
    <siteMapNode url="~/Home.aspx" title="Home"  description="Home page">
        <siteMapNode url="~/Sales.aspx" title="Sales"  description="Sales" >
            <siteMapNode url="~/Sales_Orders.aspx" title="Orders"
                description="Orders" />
            <siteMapNode url="~/Sales_Stores.aspx" title="Stores"
                description="Stores" />
        </siteMapNode>
        <siteMapNode url="~/Production.aspx" title="Production"
                description="Production" />
        <siteMapNode url="~/HR.aspx" title="Human Resources" description="HR" />
    </siteMapNode>
</siteMap>
```

The site map is an XML file, as indicated by the first line in the file. The entire hierarchy of the file is contained within a single <sitemap> element that defines the namespace:

```
<siteMap xmlns="http://schemas.microsoft.com/AspNet/SiteMap-File-1.0" >
```

Within the siteMap element is nested exactly one <SiteMapNode> (in this case, Home). Nested within that first <SiteMapNode>, however, is any number of children <SiteMapNode> elements. Each <SiteMapNode> element can in turn have any number of children <SiteMapNode> elements.

In Example 6-15, there are three such children: Sales, Production, and Human Resources. Nested within each of these <SiteMapNode> elements can be more nodes. For example, Sales contains Orders and Stores. You may nest the nodes as deep as you wish.

 ASP.NET is configured to protect files with the extension *.sitemap* so they cannot be seen by a browser.

Once the site map file is in place, you need to identify it to the master page. This is done by dragging a SiteMapDataSource control from the Data section of the Toolbox onto the master page. By default, the SiteMapDataSource control will look for and use the file named *Web.sitemap*.

It doesn't matter where you place this SiteMapDataSource control, as long as it is somewhere between the <form> and </form> tags in Source view. The SiteMapDataSource will be visible in Design view but will not appear when the web site is run.

The Design view should look something like Figure 6-20.

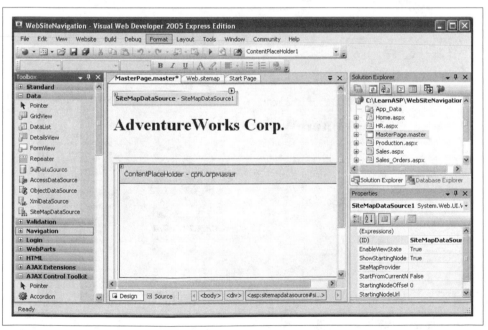

Figure 6-20. Place your SiteMapDataSource control on the master page. It'll show up in Design view, but not in any of the pages that use the master page.

Using Sitemaps

There are two types of controls that can provide site-map menu capability: a TreeView control and a Menu control. To see both at work, you'll first create a TreeView control, then you will comment that out and add a Menu control.

TreeView

The TreeView provides the familiar hierarchical view of items. One very familiar use of a TreeView is the Windows Explorer view of folders and subfolders.

Recall when you created the master page for this example there was an empty table cell in the layout. Switch to Source view, and then, from the Navigation section of the Toolbox, drag a TreeView control into that empty cell. (You can do this in Design view, of course, but we find it easier to use Source view when dragging elements into a cell.)

Switch back to Design view and click on the Smart Tag of the TreeView. Click on the drop-down next to Choose Data Source and select SiteMapDataSource1, the ID of the SiteMapDataSource you just placed on the master page, as shown in Figure 6-21.

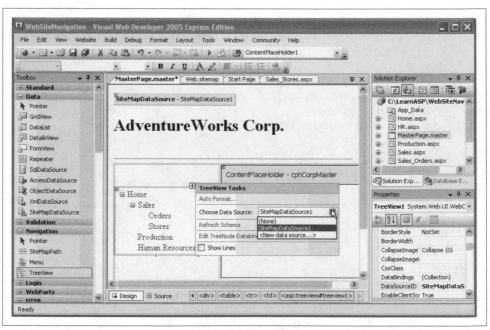

Figure 6-21. Select the data source for the TreeView control from the Smart Tag. In this case, you just have the one SiteMapDataSource control on the master page.

As soon as you select the data source for the TreeView, it will display the nodes from the site map file in Design view.

Set *Home.aspx* as the startup page by right-clicking on it in the Solution Explorer and selecting "Set As Start Page" from the menu.

Run the web site now and see the TreeView menu in action. Click on any of the menu items along the left of the web site and observe how it navigates from page to page. If you click on the Stores menu item, it will look almost exactly like Figure 6-18. The only difference is the bread crumbs are missing because you have not yet placed that control on the page.

Menu items that contain subitems of their own, such as Home and Sales, display a small icon next to them. Clicking on this icon toggles between expanded and collapsed views of these subitems. This structure directly flows from the nesting of SiteMapNodes in the site map file.

Customizing the look and feel of the TreeView

The TreeView control has many properties, methods, and events, which allow you to customize the look and feel of the TreeView.

The easiest way to change the appearance of the TreeView is to view the page in Design view, click the TreeView's Smart Tag, and then click Auto Format..., as shown in Figure 6-22.

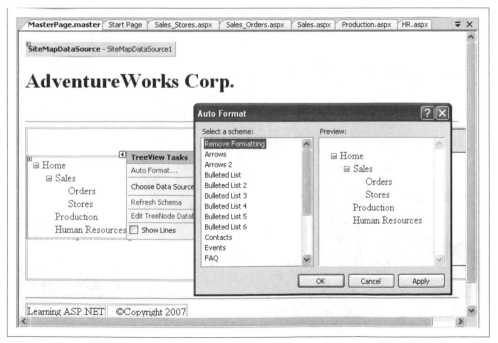

Figure 6-22. The Auto Format options, found in the Smart Tag of the TreeView, provide a number of prebuilt formatting options.

Most of the TreeView's properties have to do with the styles used for the various nodes. There are properties for general nodes, parent nodes, child (leaf) nodes, root nodes, selected nodes, and nodes when the mouse is hovering over them. For each of these node types you can set font attributes, CSS class, fore- and back-colors, spacing and padding, borders, and so on.

Replacing the TreeView with a menu control

Open *MasterPage.master* in Source view and locate the TreeView control. Comment it out and replace it with a Menu control:

```
<!-- <asp:TreeView ID="TreeView1" runat="server"
          DataSourceID="SiteMapDataSource1"
/> -->
 <asp:Menu ID="Menu1" runat="server" DataSourceID="SiteMapDataSource1" />
```

Run the application. Presto! A menu control for navigation. Hover over Home (opening the next level) and then hover over Sales (opening the third level). Finally, click Stores. The results should look like Figure 6-23.

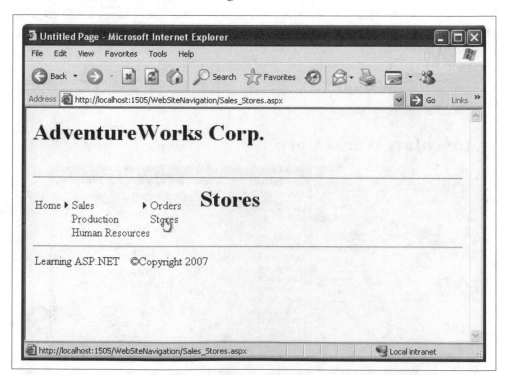

Figure 6-23. You've replaced the TreeView with a menu control, which does all the work for you. When you hover over Stores in the Menu Control, you can navigate to that page.

If the menus start to eat into your content space, you can set their Orientation property to Horizontal (the default is Vertical) and rearrange your layout table to make room for them.

Adjusting the Root Node

If you don't like the way the root node sticks out, you can adjust it. Set the ShowStartingNode property of the SiteMapDataSource control to False, then edit the *Web.sitemap* file so that the original root node is now one level in, and an empty root node takes its place, as in the following:

```
<?xml version="1.0" encoding="utf-8" ?>
<siteMap xmlns="http://schemas.microsoft.com/
AspNet/SiteMap-File-1.0" >
    <siteMapNode title="Root" >
        <siteMapNode url="~/Home.aspx" title="Home"
                     description="Home page">
        <siteMapNode url="~/Sales.aspx" title="Sales"
                     description="Sales" >
            <siteMapNode url="~/Sales_Orders.aspx"
                    title="Orders"
                    description="Orders" />
            <siteMapNode url="~/Sales_Stores.aspx"
                title="Stores"
                description="Stores" />
        </siteMapNode>
        <siteMapNode url="~/Production.aspx"
                title="Production"
                description="Production" />
        <siteMapNode url="~/HR.aspx"
                title="Human Resources"
                description="HR" />
    </siteMapNode>
</siteMap>
```

The only attribute actually required of the root node is the Title.

Accessing site map nodes programmatically

There are times when you may want access to the current node and its subnodes so you can manipulate them programmatically. For example, you may want to log the user's current menu choice to a log file. You can add code to a page to get that information. In the next example, you will display the names of the current node in the *Sales.aspx* page, and its subnodes. First, remove the menu control you added in the previous example, and uncomment the TreeView. Add the highlighted code in Example 6-16 inside the Content tags in *Sales.aspx*, including the <hr/> to provide a bit of a visual break.

Example 6-16. Sales.aspx with addedLabel controls for display of the current and child nodes

```
<%@ Page Language="VB" MasterPageFile="~/MasterPage.master" AutoEventWireup="false"
    CodeFile="Sales.aspx.vb" Inherits="Sales" title="Untitled Page" %>
<asp:Content ID="Content1" ContentPlaceHolderID="cphCorpMaster" Runat="Server">
    <h1>Sales</h1>
    <hr />
    <table>
        <tr>
            <td>
                <b>Current Node:</b>
            </td>
            <td>
                <asp:Label ID="lblCurrentNode" runat="server" />
            </td>
        </tr>
        <tr>
            <td>
                <b>Child Nodes:</b>
            </td>
            <td>
                <asp:Label ID="lblChildNodes" runat="server" />
            </td>
        </tr>
    </table>
</asp:Content>
```

You have added two labels, lblCurrentNode and lblChildNodes, but they have nothing to display yet. For that, you'll need an event handler.

Open the code-behind for this page (click the plus next to *Sales.aspx* in Solution Explorer then double-click *Sales.aspx.vb* that appears below it). Add the highlighted code in Example 6-17 to create an event handler for the Page Load event. You can have the IDE create the skeleton of the event handler for you by selecting (Page Events) from the drop-down at the top left of the editing window and selecting Load from the drop-down menu at the top right of the editing window.

Example 6-17. Sales.aspx.vb showing thePage_Load event handler

```
Partial Class Sales
    Inherits System.Web.UI.Page

    Protected Sub Page_Load(ByVal sender As Object, _
            ByVal e As System.EventArgs) Handles Me.Load
        Try
            Me.lblCurrentNode.Text = SiteMap.CurrentNode.Title

            If SiteMap.CurrentNode.HasChildNodes Then
                For Each node As SiteMapNode In SiteMap.CurrentNode.ChildNodes
                    Me.lblChildNodes.Text += node.Title + "<br />"
                Next
            End If
```

Example 6-17. Sales.aspx.vb showing thePage_Load event handler (continued)

```
        Catch exNull As System.NullReferenceException
            Me.lblCurrentNode.Text = "The XML file is not in the site map!"
        Catch ex As System.Exception
            Me.lblCurrentNode.Text = "Exception! " + ex.Message
        End Try
    End Sub

End Class
```

—VB CHEAT SHEET—
For Each

As you've seen throughout this book, lots of objects contain collections of other objects. Frequently, you'll want to take some action on every object in a collection, but you won't know how many there are. That's where the For Each loop comes in.

In this case, the SiteMap has a collection called ChildNodes, which is a collection of SiteMapNode objects. You want to grab each node in order, extract the Title property, and add it to a label. Here's how the For Each loop breaks down:

```
    For Each node As SiteMapNode In
        SiteMap.CurrentNode.ChildNodes
```

You start with the For Each statement, and then you define a variable, node, which is of type SiteMapNode. Like all variables, node is a placeholder; in this case, you're using node to indicate "the node I'm looking at right now." You use As to indicate that node is of the type SideMapNode, because that's the kind of objects that ChildNodes contains.

Then you use In to indicate where the loop should find the SiteMapNode objects to use, which in this case is inside SiteMap.CurrentNode.ChildNodes. When the loop starts, the first node from the ChildNodes collection gets loaded into node. You take an action on node, in this case extracting the title and adding it to the label:

```
    Me.lblChildNodes.Text += node.Title + "<br />"
```

You could take more than one action, of course, assuming you want that action to be repeated multiple times.

The loop ends with Next. When the loop reaches that point, it dumps the current content of node, and repeats the loop on the next SiteMapNode object from ChildNodes. When the loop has gone through each item in the collection, it stops, and execution of the code continues from after the loop.

In this code, you are setting the Text property of lblCurrentNode to reflect the Title property of the SiteMap's CurrentNode. The SiteMap is an in-memory representation of a site's navigational structure. The SiteMap object itself is created by the site map provider (in this case, by the SiteMapDataSource).

The CurrentNode property returns an object of type SiteMapNode, and the Title property of that SiteMapNode returns the title of that SiteMapNode.

The SiteMapNode's property HasChildNodes returns a Boolean, which is True if there are subnodes to the SiteMapNode. If this is the case, you can iterate through the SiteMapNodeCollection returned by the ChildNodes property. If there are no child nodes, this code does nothing.

When you view this page, the labels display the name of the current node and all its child nodes, as shown in Figure 6-24.

Bread Crumbs

The final thing to add to our example is bread crumbs. Recall from the earlier discussion, bread crumbs are an indicator of where you are in the page hierarchy and how you got there. This is done using the ASP.NET SiteMapPath control.

To see this, go back to *MasterPage.master* in Design view. From the Navigation section of the Toolbox, drag a SiteMapPath control onto the page between the AdventureWorks heading and the horizontal rule, as shown in Figure 6-25.

That's all there is to it!

Run the site and you'll see how the breadcrumbs tell you where you are at all times.

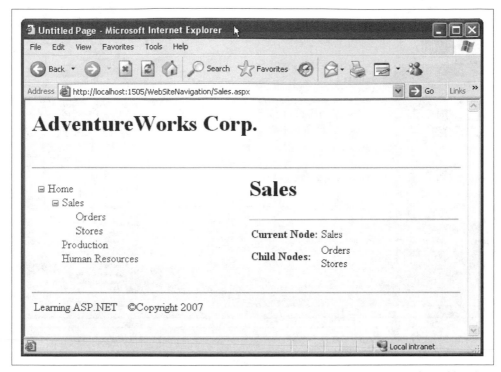

Figure 6-24. *You've added the code that allows you to access the current node, and the child nodes, and list them for the user to see.*

 It is uncommon in production applications to provide both a TreeView and bread crumbs on the same page.

Similar to the TreeView, the SiteMapPath provides many ways to customize the look and feel. Click on the Auto Format item in the Smart Tag shown in Figure 6-25 to see a number of predefined formats. Alternatively, the Properties window provides a similar, if smaller, set of properties, as it did for the TreeView.

In the previous example, the bread crumbs separated the various pages with the greater-than symbol (>). This is easy to change with the PathSeparator property. For example, to use an arrow as the separator symbol, edit the SiteMapPath control in Source view to look like the following:

```
<asp:SiteMapPath ID="SiteMapPath1" runat="server" PathSeparator="->" />
```

The result is shown in Figure 6-26. Compare this with the original bread crumbs shown in Figure 6-18.

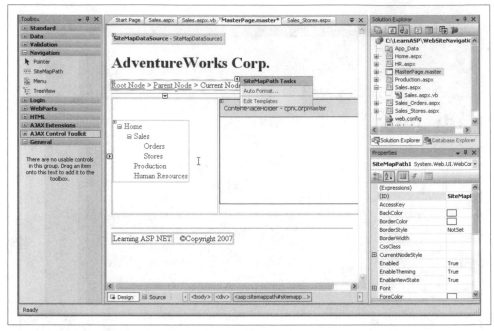

Figure 6-25. Adding navigation with bread crumbs to your site is as simple as placing a SiteMapPath control in Design view.

Summary

- Style sheets hold presentation information for an entire site in a separate file to ensure a consistent look throughout the site.

- A style specifies how a specific element is rendered visually in the browser.

- Style rules are applied in a hierarchical manner, such that more specific styles take precedence over general styles.

- A style property is defined by a property name, followed by a colon, followed by a value. Style properties are separated by semicolons.

- Styles can be applied inline or at the document level, but these methods are error-prone and difficult to maintain. The most effective way to apply styles is with an external file called a style sheet.

- A master page is a template that holds content that you want to appear on all pages of your site. The master page also contains content placeholder areas where you can insert the content of each child page.

- To create a master page, select Website → Add New Item, and choose Master Page from the Add New Item dialog.

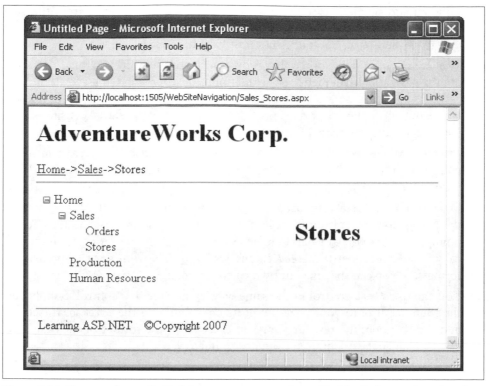

Figure 6-26. You can change the PathSeparator proptery of your SiteMapPath control to alter the look of your bread crumbs; in this case, with an arrow symbol.

- To add content pages that use your master page, select Website → Add New Item, select Web Form from the Add New Item dialog, and be sure to check the "Select master page" checkbox. When you click Add, you'll be asked to choose which master page you want to use. Child pages have a Page directive that indicates their master page.

- You can nest one master page inside another. Create a new master page and delete all the content except for the Master directive. Then insert a MasterPageFile attribute that points to the primary master page. The new submaster page will appear inside the master page, with its own content placeholders.

- You cannot view nested master pages in Design mode in VS2005 or VWD.

- You can change the content of the master page at runtime by implementing a public property on the master page, and adding a MasterType directive to the top of a child page. Once the child page has the class of the master page, the child page can programmatically interact with public properties of the master page.

- ASP.NET provides a number of predefined navigation controls that make it simple to help users move around your site.

- You can add simple `Button` controls that allow users to navigate from the current page to the button's target. The `Response.Redirect` method transfers the user to the new page, but it does not post back to the server first.

- The site map is a data source that provides the information you need to implement a navigation tree, menu, or breadcrumbs on your site. It's an XML file that contains a series of nodes, each representing a page in your site. The IDE doesn't create this file, although it does provide a skeleton if you select Website → Add New Item and choose Site Map.

- After you've created the site map, you can add a `SiteMapDataSource` control to your master page. The `SiteMapDataSource` control uses the file named *Web.sitemap* by default.

- Once you have a `SiteMapDataSource` in place, you can easily add a `TreeView` from the Navigation controls to your site. You set the data source for the `TreeView` to point to the `SiteMapDataSource`, and ASP.NET does the rest for you automatically. You can format the `TreeView` any way you like, from a set of predefined formats, or you can specify your own custom format.

- You can use a `Menu` control in the same way as the `TreeView` control. Simply add the Menu control to your page, point its data source to the `SiteMapDataSource`, and the IDE does the rest for you. You can change the format of the `Menu` control, or change the orientation from horizontal to vertical.

- You can access the nodes in your site map programmatically, using the `CurrentNode` and `ChildNodes` properties.

- Bread crumbs are a tool that indicates the current page, and the preceding pages in the hierarchy. They're more concise and compact than a `TreeView` or a `Menu`. To use bread crumbs, simply place a `SiteMapPath` control on the page with the `SiteMapDataSource`. You don't need to specify the data source; it's done automatically. You can format the bread crumbs as you see fit.

This chapter is one of the first times in this book that you've seen sites that consist of multiple pages. Obviously, most sites in the real world consist of more than one page, and here you've taken your first steps towards more complex sites. You also learned in this chapter how you can make controls in child pages that affect the content of the master page. That's a great technique, but you'll notice that any content you change vanishes as soon as you navigate to another page. If you're going to have sites with multiple pages, you'll need some way of passing data from page to page, or between postbacks. That's called preserving *state*, and you'll learn several ways of doing it in the next chapter.

Quiz

1. What's the most effective way to apply styles on your web page?

2. If a style sheet has rules applying to the text of the whole page, but one specific paragraph has a different style rule applied, which takes precedence?

3. What command do you use to apply a style sheet to your page, and where do you place it?

4. What is the purpose of a master page?

5. How many different master pages can you apply to a particular content page?

6. When you are trying to change the content of a master page at runtime, what does the content page need to affect the master page?

7. What method could you use in a Button Click event handler to navigate to another page?

8. What file do you need for all the navigation controls to work? How is this file generated?

9. What control do you use to enable the navigation controls to access the file?

10. What do you have to do to connect the SiteMapPath control to a data source?

Exercises

Exercise 6-1. In this set of exercises, you'll create a web site for a travel agency called Ajax Travel. First, create a master page containing all the elements that should appear on each page of the site, with the company name at the top, and a copyright notice at the bottom. In addition, Ajax Travel's portfolio of destinations is divided into two categories: Sun and Snow. The home page of the site should offer users a choice between these two categories. Each category should have its own heading, which appears in addition to the company heading. Also, each page in the "Sun" category should carry a message at the bottom reading "Ask about our honeymoon specials!" Each page in the "Snow" category should carry a message at the bottom reading "Ask about our ski vacation packages!" To keep things simple, create just two content pages for each category: the Sun category should have one page for Bermuda, and one for Maui; the Snow category should have one page for Vail, Colorado, and one for St. Moritz, Switzerland. The Maui page should look like Figure 6-27.

The Vail page should look like Figure 6-28.

Exercise 6-2. Add a control to the Home page of the Ajax Travel site asking the user to enter his name. Update the master page of the site so that "Hello <name>!" is displayed at the top of the page. The page should look like Figure 6-29.

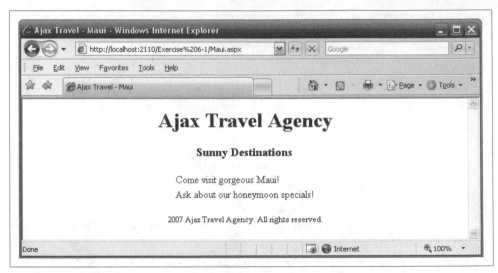

Figure 6-27. Your goal for the "Maui" page of Exercise 6-1.

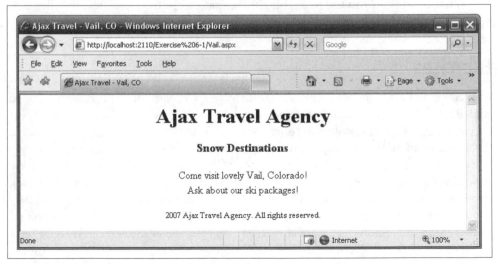

Figure 6-28. Your goal for the "Vail" page of Exercise 6-1.

Exercise 6-3. Remove the user greeting control from the master page. Implement a TreeView and a Menu for site navigation, both on the master page. Let users choose between the two types of navigation control by using a control on the master page, as shown in Figure 6-30.

Exercise 6-4. Add breadcrumbs to your site on the master page, as shown in Figure 6-31.

Figure 6-29. Your goal for Exercise 6-2.

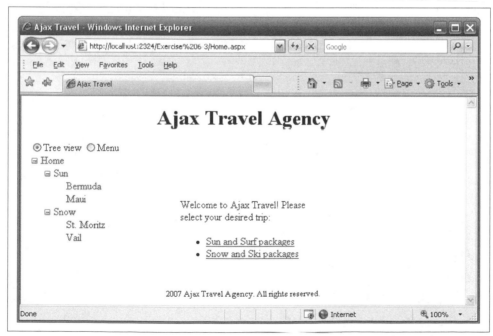

Figure 6-30. Your goal for Exercise 6-3.

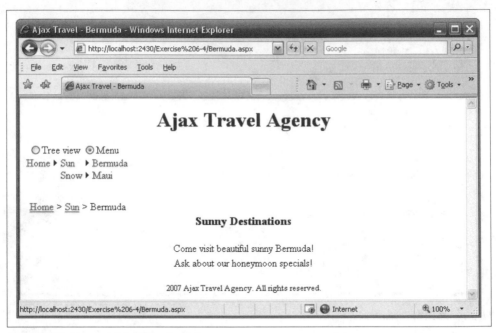

Figure 6-31. Your goal for Exercise 6-4

CHAPTER 7

State and Life Cycle

Most of the web sites you have built in this book have been confined to a single page. In Chapter 6, you learned techniques to provide a single look and feel throughout the site.

When you created the examples in Chapter 6, you may have noticed that any data you entered on a page usually didn't stick around if you went to a different page and came back, or even if you issued a postback on the page you were on. That's because the pages you've built up until now haven't had any way to preserve that kind of information, called *state*.

In each chapter up until now, you've learned about the different kinds of controls and how you use them. We're going to take a slightly different approach in this chapter, and first taking you behind the scenes so you can understand what the page actually does when you click the Submit button. Then you'll find out more about state, and how to hold onto it. By the time you've finished this chapter, you'll have built several sites that can retain state, no matter how much the user clicks around.

Page Life Cycle

A user sits at her browser and types in a URL. A web page appears with text, and images, and buttons, and so forth. She fills in a text box and clicks a button. New data appears in response. How does this work?

Before we begin, it is important to understand a little bit about the "architecture" of the World Wide Web. In the applications you've developed to this point, you've been able to do everything on one computer. But in order for these exercises to work, your single computer is standing in for three or four important pieces of the puzzle, as shown in Figure 7-1.

In the original model of the Web, a browser would send a request for a page, identified by a *Universal Resource Locater* (URL), and then some remote server would return that page. Information would be presented using HTML, a simple markup language that the browser would display. Pages were imagined to be display-only,

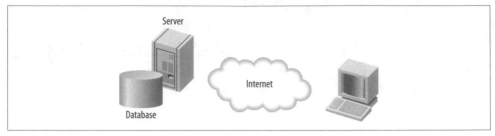

Figure 7-1. When you enter a URL in your browser, your request crosses the Internet to the web server, which may access a database, and then returns the page to your local machine.

with interaction limited to clicking on hyperlinks to move from page to page. Each page was designed to be independent of all the others, and it didn't matter who was looking at a given page, or when.

In a traditional desktop application, on the other hand, you assume that a single user sits down, starts the application, uses it continuously for a while, and then closes the application. This period of time when the user is interacting with the application is called a *session*. If the user enters her name at some point, the application should hold onto that name for the duration of the session in case it needs to be retrieved at some later point. No matter where the user goes in the application, that name is assumed to be the same, and so the application may need to pass that name around to different methods within the code as needed. The user name, along with any other changes she makes, is known as the *state* of the application, and the application needs to preserve that state for at least the duration of the session, and sometimes between sessions.

Desktop applications were always intended to preserve the application state; web pages were not. In fact, the Web was consciously and explicitly designed to be "stateless." This plan worked just fine for a while, but nowadays, web users expect web applications to behave like desktop applications, which means they need a way to preserve state.

To create a session-based interactive application on top of the Web, ASP.NET uses pages that extend traditional HTML pages. These are stored on the web server and combine markup and code to produce HTML for the user's browser.

Some code runs on the server when the page is requested. Some code runs on the server in response to actions taken by the user (pressing a button, for example). Some code is embedded in the page and runs in the browser (AJAX and JavaScript client-side code).

To understand when different bits of code are run, and how the page that is sent to the browser is assembled, you need to understand the "life cycle" of the ASP.NET page.

When an ASP.NET page is requested from the server, the page is loaded into server memory, processed, sent to the user, and unloaded from memory. From the beginning of the life cycle to the end, the goal is to render appropriate HTML to the requesting browser.

At each step, methods and events are available that allow you to override the default behavior or add your own programmatic enhancements. The Page class creates a hierarchical tree of all the controls on the page: the *control tree*.

To see this, you'll create a quick web site called LifeCycle. This site will consist of a single page containing a single Button control. Clicking on the Button will do nothing but cause the page to post back to the server.

In Source view, open *Default.aspx*, and then drag a Button control onto the page between the two <div> tags.

Add the Trace attribute to the Page directive at the top of the file and set its value to true, as shown in Figure 7-2.

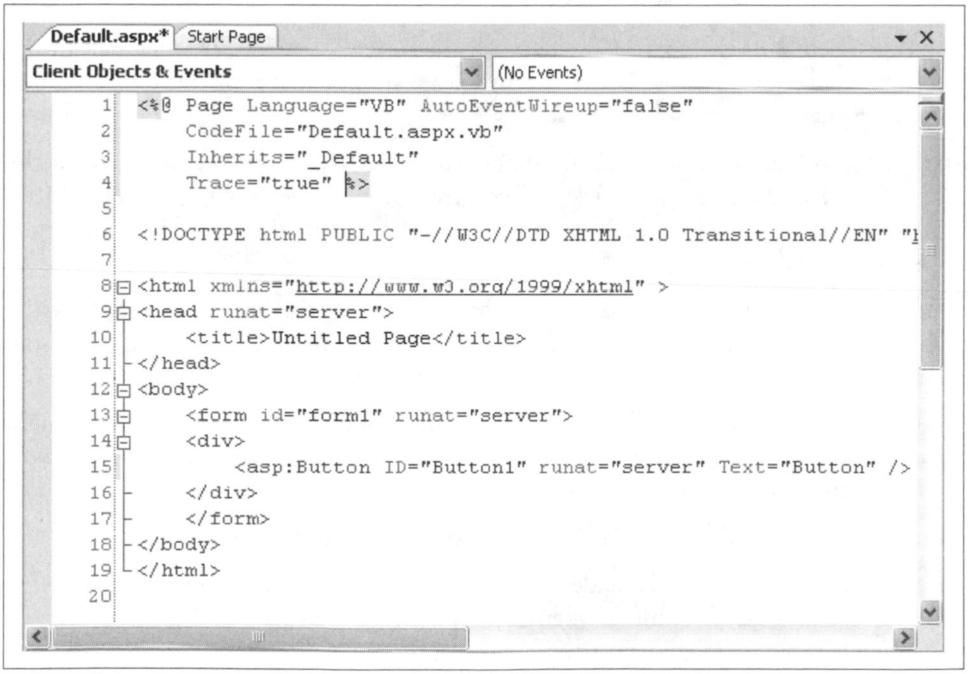

```
Default.aspx*  Start Page                                              ▼ ✕

Client Objects & Events                    ✔   (No Events)              ✔

 1    <%@ Page Language="VB" AutoEventWireup="false"
 2         CodeFile="Default.aspx.vb"
 3         Inherits="_Default"
 4         Trace="true" %>
 5
 6    <!DOCTYPE html PUBLIC "-//W3C//DTD XHTML 1.0 Transitional//EN" "
 7
 8    <html xmlns="http://www.w3.org/1999/xhtml" >
 9    <head runat="server">
10        <title>Untitled Page</title>
11    </head>
12    <body>
13        <form id="form1" runat="server">
14        <div>
15            <asp:Button ID="Button1" runat="server" Text="Button" />
16        </div>
17        </form>
18    </body>
19    </html>
20
```

Figure 7-2. The LifeCycle Default page in Source view shows the single control on the page and the Trace attribute within the Page directive.

We haven't formally introduced the Trace control, but you need it for this exercise. You can see the control tree for any page by adding Trace="true" to the Page directive. We'll cover tracing in detail in Chapter 8.

Run the page. You will see the single button at the top, followed by a ton of information at the bottom. For now, just slide down to the section labeled Control Tree, as shown in Figure 7-3.

Control Tree

Control UniqueID	Type	Render Size Bytes (including children)	ViewState Size Bytes (excluding children)	ControlState Size Bytes (excluding children)
__Page	ASP.default_aspx	714	0	0
ctl02	System.Web.UI.LiteralControl	175	0	0
ctl00	System.Web.UI.HtmlControls.HtmlHead	46	0	0
ctl01	System.Web.UI.HtmlControls.HtmlTitle	33	0	0
ctl03	System.Web.UI.LiteralControl	14	0	0
form1	System.Web.UI.HtmlControls.HtmlForm	459	0	0
ctl04	System.Web.UI.LiteralControl	15	0	0
Button1	System.Web.UI.WebControls.Button	66	0	0
ctl05	System.Web.UI.LiteralControl	18	0	0
ctl06	System.Web.UI.LiteralControl	20	0	0

Figure 7-3. The page Trace contains lots of information about the page, but for now, you're only interested in the Control Tree section, which shows all the controls on the current page.

The Page itself is at the root of the tree. All the named controls are included in the tree, referenced by control ID. In our simple example, there are only two named controls: form1 and Button1.

Static text, including whitespace, newlines, and HTML tags, are represented in the tree as LiteralControls. The order of controls in the tree is strictly hierarchical. Within a given level of the hierarchy, the controls are in the order in which they appear in the markup file.

Web components, including the Page, go through their entire life cycle every time the page is loaded. Events fire first on the Page, then recursively on every object in the control tree.

There are two slightly different sequences in the life cycle: one for the first time a page is loaded, and a second when the page reloads itself in a postback. The life cycle is shown schematically in Figure 7-4.

During the first page load, the life cycle consists of the following steps:

1. A request for the page is made from a browser to the web server. The ASP.NET Framework first determines whether the page already exists in a cache (a section of memory specifically reserved for recently used items). If so, the page is retrieved and returned to the browser and we are done. If not, then the actual page life cycle starts at this point.

2. During the Start phase, the postback mode is determined. If the page was requested by another page, then it was not a postback. If the page was returned to the server for processing and redisplay, then it is a postback. The IsPostBack and PreviousPage properties are set accordingly. The Request and Response properties of the page are also set.

3. The Page Initialization phase contains two events often handled by your code: PreInit and Init. If you do not handle these explicitly yourself, ASP.NET will perform the default behavior on your behalf. During the PreInit event, the target device is determined before the page is initialized, the master page is set, the

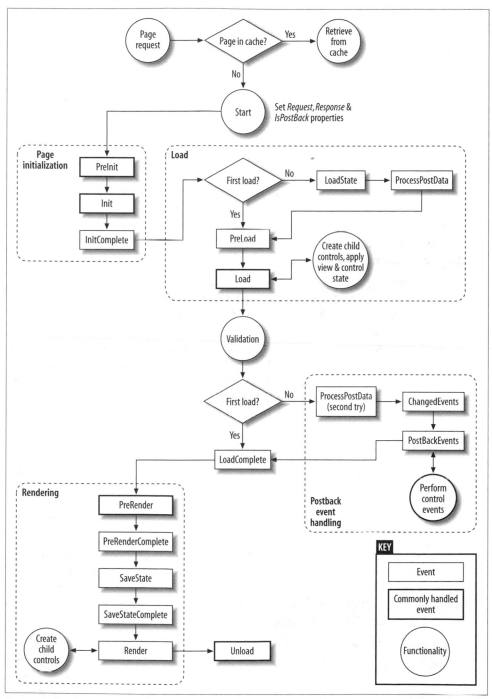

Figure 7-4. Schematic of ASP.NET page life cycle. Events are in rectangles, with commonly handled events in bold rectangles. Areas of functionality are indicated in circles. The dashed round-cornered rectangles delineate the major phases of the cycle.

control tree is built, and the controls are assigned unique IDs, which are made available to your code. Personalization and themes are loaded and applied to the page in this step (these are discussed in Chapter 9).

4. PreInit is the first event in the life cycle that can be trapped and handled. That is, this is the first event that you can write your own code for, to change the default behavior of initializing the page. During the Init event, control properties are read or initialized. If this is a postback it is important to realize that any values stored in view state (described shortly) have not yet been restored to the controls.

5. During the Load event, all the control properties are set. View state information is available and controls in the page's control hierarchy can be accessed. The load phase is routinely modified in a Page_Load method.

6. During the Validation phase, the Validate method is called on all the Validation controls on the page. The IsValid property is set for all those controls and for the page as a whole.

7. During the Rendering phase, personalization, control, and view state is saved. Each control on the page is called in succession to render itself to the browser, that is, to compose itself into HTML that is included in the page's Response property. It is very common to handle the PreRender event with a Page_PreRender method, typically when you must take some action based on the final value of some other control on the page. During the Render event, the HTML is actually generated and sent to the requesting page, although this event is rarely handled unless you are developing custom controls.

8. Unload is the last event of the life cycle. It gives you an opportunity to do any final cleanup, such as close open files and release references to expensive resources, such as database connections.

During postback, the life cycle is the same as during the first load, except for the following:

1. During the Load phase, after initialization is complete, the view and control state is loaded and applied as necessary.

2. After the Validation phase completes, postback data is processed. Control event handlers are now executed. This is important: Control event handlers, such as a Button Click, are not called until after the Page Initialization and Load events are handled. This is important because it is often critical in which order code in the various event handlers is executed.

You can easily see the order in which events are fired on a page by turning on tracing for the page as you did above (setting Trace to true in the Page directive). As shown in Figure 7-5, the Trace Information section of the sample, lists all the page events along with the number of seconds it took for that event to run, both from the start of the life cycle and from the previous event.

Trace Information			
Category	Message	From First(s)	From Last(s)
aspx.page	Begin PreInit		
aspx.page	End PreInit	0.0108170172466054	0.010817
aspx.page	Begin Init	0.0121716586884646	0.001355
aspx.page	End Init	0.022194161548465	0.010023
aspx.page	Begin InitComplete	0.0224251964984377	0.000231
aspx.page	End InitComplete	0.0230518124510238	0.000627
aspx.page	Begin PreLoad	0.0238323585818868	0.000781
aspx.page	End PreLoad	0.0243005745143587	0.000468
aspx.page	Begin Load	0.024392485637141	0.000092
aspx.page	End Load	0.0277314574897089	0.003339
aspx.page	Begin LoadComplete	0.0279613749792222	0.000230
aspx.page	End LoadComplete	0.0284840671090879	0.000523
aspx.page	Begin PreRender	0.0287564480960569	0.000272
aspx.page	End PreRender	0.0430468118154682	0.014290
aspx.page	Begin PreRenderComplete	0.0441089579820899	0.001062
aspx.page	End PreRenderComplete	0.0491176951260565	0.005009
aspx.page	Begin SaveState	0.10967874408619	0.060561
aspx.page	End SaveState	0.213856509696065	0.104178
aspx.page	Begin SaveStateComplete	0.21406575416708	0.000209
aspx.page	End SaveStateComplete	0.216420522720066	0.002355
aspx.page	Begin Render	0.216721957678979	0.000301
aspx.page	End Render	0.390970640123256	0.174249

Figure 7-5. The Trace Information section of the page Trace shows all the page events.

If you click the button to cause a postback, the trace information will include the additional events indicated in Figure 7-4, including ProcessPostData Second Try, ChangedEvents, and PostBackEvent. Often when you're trying to track down why your page is behaving a certain way or why some of your code does not seem to work as you would expect, looking at the life cycle behavior can be very illuminating.

State

State, in the case of a web page, is the current value of all the controls and variables, for the current user, in the current session. The Web is inherently a *stateless* environment, which means that each time a page is posted to the server and then sent back to the browser, the page is created again from scratch. Unless the state of all the controls is explicitly preserved before the page is posted, the state is lost and all the controls will be created with default values. One of the great strengths of ASP.NET is that it automatically maintains state for server controls—both HTML and ASP.NET—so you do not have to write any code to accomplish this. This section will explore how this is done and how you can make use of the ASP.NET state management capabilities.

ASP.NET manages four types of state:

Control state
> Used to provide features such as paging and sorting of GridView controls. Control state cannot be modified, accessed directly, or disabled.

View state
> The state of all the controls on the page. View state only lasts for that one page display, and is updated every time the page is redrawn. It can be disabled for specific controls, the page, or the entire web site.

Session state
> Data specifically saved across page posts, for use by all the pages in a web application.

Application state
> Data available to all the users of a web application, even across multiple sessions.

Table 7-1 compares the kinds of state management (other than Control state, which is not accessible to the developer).

Table 7-1. Comparison of types of state

Feature	View state	Session state	Application state
Uses server resources	No	Yes	Yes
Uses bandwidth	Yes	No	No
Times out	No	Yes	No
Security exposure	Yes	Depends	No
Optimized for nonprimitive types	No	Yes	Yes
Available for arbitrary data	Yes	Yes	Yes
Programmatically accessible	Yes	Yes	Yes
Scope	Page	Session	Application
Survives restart	Yes	Depends on configuration	No

View State

The *view state* is the state of the page and all its controls. The view state is automatically maintained across posts by the ASP.NET Framework. When a page is posted to the server, the view state is read. Just before the page is sent back to the browser, the view state is restored.

The view state is saved in a hidden field on the page. Because the view state is maintained via a form field, this technique works with all browsers. The information saved in the hidden field is Base64 encoded, but not encrypted. As such, any information stored in view state is not immune to prying eyes.

If there is no need to maintain the view state for a given page, you can boost performance by disabling view state for that page. For example, if the page does not post back to itself or if the only control on a page that might need to have its state maintained is populated from a database with every round trip to the server, then there will be no need to maintain the view state for that page. To disable view state for a page, add the EnableViewState attribute with a value of false to the Page directive:

CODE▶
```
<%@ Page Language="VB"  EnableViewState="false" %>
```
The default value for EnableViewState is true.

You can disable the view state for an application by setting the EnableViewState property to false in the <pages> section of the *web.config* configuration file.

You can even maintain or disable the view state for specific controls. This is done with the Control.EnableViewState property, which is a Boolean value with a default of true. Disabling view state for a control, just as for the page, will improve performance. This would be appropriate, for example, in a situation where a GridView is populated from a database every time the page is loaded. In this case, the contents of the control would be overridden by the database query, so there is no point in maintaining view state for that control. If the GridView in question were named gv, the following line of code would disable its view state:

CODE
```
gv.EnableViewState = false;
```

 The simple controls, TextBox, RadioButton, CheckBoxList, and RadioButtonList, ignore the EnableViewState properties, since the current value is always posted back to the server anyway. Complex controls such as the GridView do respect the EnableViewState property. In cases where a DataSource control is used as the data source for a GridView, the data is gathered fresh with every page post. In this case, it is more performant to disable view state.

There are some situations where view state is not the best place to store data. If you need to store a large amount of data, view state is not an efficient mechanism because the data is transferred back and forth to the server with every page post. If you have security concerns about the data, and the data is not being displayed on the page, then including it in view state increases the security exposure. Finally, view state is optimized only for strings, integers, Booleans, arrays, ArrayLists, and hashtables. Other .NET types may be saved in view state but will result in degraded performance and a larger view state footprint.

In some of these instances, session state might be a better alternative; on the other hand, view state does not consume any server resources and does not time out as session state does.

To see view state in action, Create a new web site called ViewState. It does not need to be AJAX-enabled.

This web site will have a TextBox, a Label, and a GridView control. It will also have a Button control to force a postback to the server. In order to better demonstrate view state, you will not use a DataSource control to populate the GridView; rather, we'll use ADO.NET code in the code-behind to gather the data the first time the page loads (don't worry, we'll show you what to do).

The finished Design view of the page will look similar to Figure 7-6.

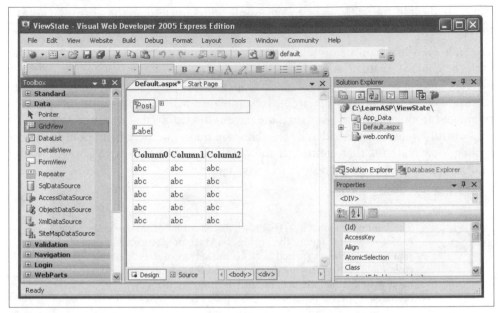

Figure 7-6. You'll create the ViewState page for this example so that it looks like this in Design view.

While in Design view, drag a Button control and a TextBox control onto the page. Change the Text property of the Button to Post, to indicate that it will post back to the server.

Press the Enter key several times then drag a Label control onto the page.

Press the Enter key a few more times. Now drag a GridView control from the Data section of the Toolbox onto the page.

The GridView will be populated from the AdventureWorks database. In preparation for this, add a connection string to the *web.config* file by double-clicking on the file in the Solution Explorer to open the file in the editing window.

Replace this single line (if it exists):

```
<appSettings />
```

with the lines that follow. If the above line of code is not in the file, place the text below anyway (the quoted value should not wrap in your code, as it does on this printed page):

```
<appSettings>
    <add key="AdventureWorks"
        value="Data Source=<server name>;
            Initial Catalog=AdventureWorks;
            Integrated Security=True;" />
</appSettings>
```

Replace the Data Source with the appropriate SQL Server name for your machine. If you are using SQL Express, the Data Source will be something like:

CODE▶
```
Data Source=.\SqlExpress;
```

Open the code-behind for the page by double-clicking on *Default.aspx.vb* in the Solution Explorer. Create an event handler for the Page Load event by selecting (Page Events) in the Class Name drop-down menu at the top left of the editing window, and in the Method Name drop-down at the top right of the editing window, select the Load event. This will insert an empty code skeleton for the Page_Load event handler.

Type the highlighted code inside the Page_Load method from Example 7-1.

Example 7-1. Default.aspx.vb for the ViewState web site

```vb
Imports System.Data
Imports System.Data.SqlClient

Partial Class _Default
    Inherits System.Web.UI.Page

    Protected Sub Page_Load(ByVal sender As Object, _
            ByVal e As System.EventArgs) Handles Me.Load
        If Not IsPostBack Then
            Label1.Text = "Hello World"
            PopulateGrid( )
        End If
    End Sub

    Private Sub PopulateGrid( )
        Dim connectionString As String = _
                ConfigurationManager.AppSettings("AdventureWorks")
        Dim connection As SqlConnection = _
            New SqlConnection(connectionString)
        Dim queryString As String = _
            "select top 1000 AddressLine1, AddressLine2, City, " + _
                "StateProvinceID, PostalCode from Person.Address"
        Dim ds As DataSet = New DataSet( )
        Try
            Dim dataAdapter As SqlDataAdapter = _
                New SqlDataAdapter(queryString, connection)
            dataAdapter.Fill(ds, "Addresses")
            GridView1.DataSource = ds.Tables("Addresses")
            GridView1.DataBind( )
        Catch ex As Exception
            '' Handle exception
        Finally
            connection.Close( )
        End Try
    End Sub

End Class
```

Also from Example 7-1, add the helper method called PopulateGrid, which actually does the work of gathering and binding the data for the GridView. (Again, as with the Trace control earlier, it is not important in this example for you to understand exactly how PopulateGrid works.) In order for PopulateGrid to build properly, you must include the two Imports statements at the top of the code-behind file in Example 7-1.

—VB CHEAT SHEET—
Helper Methods

When your event handler has a lot of code that you might want to use again elsewhere, it's a good idea to separate that code out into another method. You can run that method from various other points in your code, which is known as *calling* the method. To create a helper method, you create a new Sub in the code-behind file. Be careful to place it before the End Class statement and give it a name. The following example shows what this looks like:

```
Private Sub PopulateGrid( )
' Your code goes here.
End Sub
```

To call the method, you simply type the name the function, with the parentheses, at the appropriate point in the code, as in:

```
PopulateGrid( )
```

The execution of the application jumps to the beginning of the method, and then executes the method. When the execution reaches the End Sub statement at the end of the helper method, it returns to the line in the event handler where it left from and continues from there.

If you need to pass values (called parameters) from the calling method into the helper method, you would include them in the parentheses of the method call. This example doesn't pass any parameters.

Run the application. Enter some text in the TextBox and observe the result. Your screen will appear similar to Figure 7-7.

 If you run the page and there is no data visible in the grid after clicking the Post button, you've probably disabled view state for the page (as you are instructed to do below). Make sure the EnableViewState attribute is set to true in the Page directive at the top of the markup file:

```
<%@ Page Language="VB" AutoEventWireup="false"
CodeFile="Default.aspx.vb" EnableViewState="true"
Inherits="_Default" %>
```

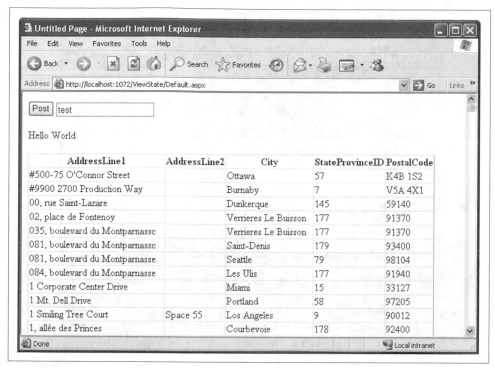

Figure 7-7. After you've entered some text in the TextBox, the ViewState page will look like this. This is the expected result with view state enabled.

Click on the Post button. The page will be posted back to the server, as indicated by the progress indicator in the status line at the bottom of the browser. However, nothing on the page will change.

The contents of the TextBox are preserved by the built-in view state capability of ASP. NET. You have written no code anywhere to do this, it just happens.

Looking at the Page_Load event handler, you can see that the Text property of the Label control is set when the page is first loaded, but not on subsequent post back. Ditto for the GridView—it is populated only the first time the page is loaded. Again, ASP.NET view state is taking care of preserving the data between postbacks.

Now watch what happens when you disable view state for the page. Open *Default. aspx* in Source view. Add the EnableViewState attribute to the Page directive at the top of the file, and set its value to false, as shown highlighted in the following code snippet:

```
<%@ Page Language="VB" AutoEventWireup="false" CodeFile="Default.aspx.vb"
    EnableViewState="false" Inherits="_Default" %>
```

Run the page again. It initially looks the same as Figure 7-7. Click the Post button to post the page back to the server.

The page is very different, as shown in Figure 7-8.

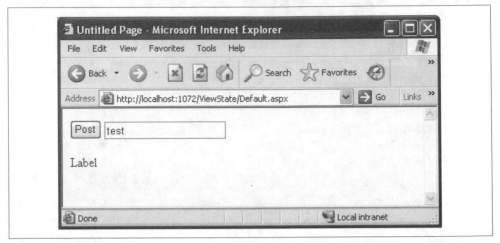

Figure 7-8. When you post the page back with view state disabled, the results are very different.

The TextBox still shows the current value. As mentioned in the note above, simple controls such as TextBox ignore the EnableViewState property and always preserve view state. However, the Label and GridView controls do respect that property. Since they are only populated the first time the page is loaded, they no longer display the current data after the page is posted back to the server. The Label reverts to its default Text property, and the GridView is not even rendered to the browser if there is no data bound to it.

In addition to preserving the values of controls, View state is very handy for something else; you can programmatically stash your own stuff in a data structure known as the *state bag*, using the ViewState keyword. The state bag stores data as attribute/value pairs in a dictionary. The attribute is a string, which is the name of the object stored as the value. The types of objects that can be stored efficiently are the primitive data types, including integers, strings, bytes, and Booleans. You can also store arrays of primitive types. Complex types, such as DataSets and custom objects can be stored as well, but performance will suffer.

The next example demonstrates stashing values in the state bag and then retrieving them. In this example, a counter keeps track of the number of times a button on a page has been clicked. As long as the page is current, the count will be correct. If you move to another page and then return to this page, the count will start over.

Create a new web site called StateBag. On the Default page, drag a Label, called lblCounter, and two buttons. Set the Text property of one button to Increment Counter, and the Text property of the other button to Navigate.

—VB CHEAT SHEET—
Arrays and Dictionaries

You've seen variables in previous chapters, and you've seen collections, like the collection of `ListItems` in a `RadioButtonList`. An array is simply another type of collection, in which you can store a bunch of objects in a single variable, provided they're all of the same type. You declare an array similar to the way you would create a variable:

```
Dim myArray(5) As Integer
```

This code creates an array called `myArray`, which can hold integers. Specifically, the (5) states that the array can hold six integers. Why not five as the code suggests? Because just as with controls, array indexes begin at zero.

To access the third integer in the array, you'd just use this syntax:

```
myArray(2)
```

Use curly braces if you want to initialize the array when you create it:

```
Dim myArray( ) As Integer = {42, 36, 128, 53, 7, 85}
```

Notice you don't have to specify the length of the array; the compiler will automatically set it to a length of six.

Arrays are particularly useful with `ForEach` loops, like this:

```
ForEach i In myArray
  i = i + 1
Next i
```

That little loop increments each element in the array by 1, and you don't need to know what values are in the array, or how many there are.

One drawback to arrays is that if you want to retrieve a value from an array, you either have to know the index of the value you want, or else loop through the array until you find it. The *dictionary* is a specific kind of array (also known as a `Hashtable`) that solves this problem by associating each value with a *key*, instead of an index. For example, you could have a dictionary of U.S. states, using their abbreviations as the key values. Then, to retrieve a state's name, you'd just have to know the abbreviation (the key). The following code snippet creates and partially populates a `Hashtable` to hold the states:

```
Dim States as New Hashtable( )
States.Add("CA", "California")
States.Add("MA", "Massachusetts")
States.Add("PA", "Pennsylvania")
```

To retrieve the name of the dictionary entry with the key value of MA, you would use the following code:

```
Dim strStateName as string = States("MA").ToString( )
```

In the case of the state bag, the attribute names are the keys, and the values of those attributes are stored as the value part of each dictionary pair.

Add another page to the web site by clicking on Website → Add New Item.... Call this new page *AnotherPage.aspx*. Be sure the "Place code in separate file" checkbox is checked. On that page, add a Button control, with its Text property set to Home.

While still in *AnotherPage.aspx*, switch to Design view, and double-click the Home button to open the Click event handler. Add the highlighted code below:

```
Protected Sub Button1_Click(ByVal sender As Object, _
        ByVal e As System.EventArgs) Handles Button1.Click
    Response.Redirect("Default.aspx")
End Sub
```

This button will now navigate back to the Default page.

Open *Default.aspx* in Design view. Double-click the Navigate button to open an event handler for that button, and add the highlighted code in Example 7-2 to the Click event handler.

Right-click on *Default.aspx* in the Solution Explorer and set it as the Start page. Run the web site and verify you can navigate back and forth between the two pages.

Stop the web site then open the code-behind for the Default page, *Default.aspx.vb*. It already has an event handler for the Navigate button. There is no code necessary for the Increment Counter button.

Add an event handler for the Load event for the Default page. Next, add the highlighted code from Example 7-2 to the Page_Load method.

Example 7-2. Default.aspx.vb for StateBag web site

```
Partial Class _Default
    Inherits System.Web.UI.Page

Protected Sub Button2_Click(ByVal sender As Object, _
        ByVal e As System.EventArgs) Handles Button2.Click
    Response.Redirect("AnotherPage.aspx")
End Sub

Protected Sub Page_Load(ByVal sender As Object, _
        ByVal e As System.EventArgs) Handles Me.Load
    ViewState("Counter") += 1
    lblCounter.Text = ViewState("Counter").ToString()
End Sub
End Class
```

Run the site. It will open with something like Figure 7-9. The counter will be initialized to 1.

Click the Increment Counter button. You will see the counter increment in the label. Navigate to the other page and back, however, and the counter will be reset back to 1. Just as in the previous example, the view state is retained through postbacks for controls on the same page, but once you transfer to a different page, that state is abandoned. This is called *scope*—the ViewState data is scoped to the page.

The += operator is VB shorthand for adding the specified amount, and assigning the result to the original variable—in this case, incrementing by 1. The following two statements are equivalent:

```
myVariable = myVariable + 1
myVariable += 1
```

There are also -=, *=, and /= operators.

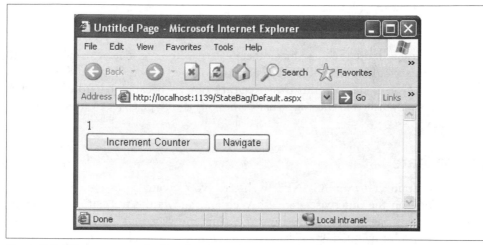

Figure 7-9. When you open the StateBag page, the counter initializes to 1.

In the Page_Load method in Example 7-2, examine the following line:

```
ViewState("Counter") += 1
```

This line creates a ViewState dictionary object if it does not already exist, creates a key in the dictionary called Counter, and associates the value of 1 with Counter. When you click the Increment Counter button, the page posts back, which means that the Load event is raised, and the method is called again. The Counter item already exists in the dictionary, so its value is increased by 1. Note that if the page had a dozen buttons, clicking any of them would increment the counter, since all it takes is a postback to run the code in Page_Load.

 It is interesting to note that if you simply refresh the browser, rather than click a button on the page, the counter will not be incremented.

For this example, that works fine. However, in the general case, it is usually best to first test to see if the object in view state exists before trying to use it.

Consider the case where a string array is put into the state bag in Page_Load with the following lines of code:

```
Dim strArray() As String = New String() {"a", "b", "c"}
ViewState("TestArray") = strArray
```

Then somewhere else in your code, maybe a Button Click event handler, for example, you want to retrieve the contents of that ViewState object and do something with it. You must first verify that the object exists before trying to use it, because if for some reason it does not exist, it will throw an exception and crash your program. You can verify the object's existence with an If...Then block that tests to see if the ViewState object is Nothing, as in the following code snippet:

```
If ViewState("TestArray") IsNot Nothing Then
    Dim strNewArray() As String
    strNewArray = CType(ViewState("TestArray"), String())
End If
```

Then, once you are sure the ViewState object exists, you retrieve it by using the CType function to explicitly convert the object to the desired type. This is necessary no matter what type is stashed into the ViewState object, because regardless of what type of object is stashed in the bag, what comes out is of type Object unless you convert it back.

Session State

When you connect to an ASP.NET web site, you create a *session*. The session imposes state on the otherwise stateless Web and allows the web site to recognize that subsequent page requests are from the same browser that started the session. This allows you to maintain state across pages until you consciously end the session or the session times out. (The default timeout is 20 minutes, which you can change by editing the *web.config* file.)

The scope of a session assumes a single user making many different page requests. The session is not lost until the timeout period goes by with no interaction by the user. If the user goes to lunch and does not click on anything for more than 20 minutes (assuming the default timeout period), the session will terminate. On the other hand, if she clicks once every 19 minutes, the session will be maintained without end.

While an application is running, there will be many sessions, essentially, one for each user interacting with the web site, as indicated in Figure 7-10.

ASP.NET provides session state with the following features:

- Works with browsers that have cookies disabled.
- Identifies if a request is part of an existing session.
- Stores session-scoped data for use across multiple requests.

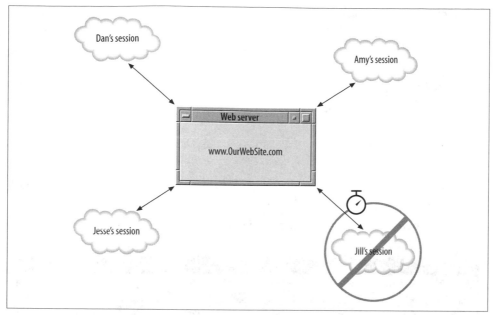

Figure 7-10. A web site can have many simultaneous sessions, one for each user who has not timed out.

- Raises session events such as Session_Start and Session_End, which you can handle in application code.
- Automatically releases session resources if the session ends or times out.

Similar to the ViewState state bag, session data is stored as a collection of attribute/value pair dictionary entries.

You set and retrieve the dictionary objects using the Session keyword, as shown in the next example, which presents a set of radio buttons. Selecting one of the radio buttons sets three session dictionary objects—two strings and a string array. These session dictionary objects are then used to populate a Label control and a DropDownList control.

Create a new web site called SessionState and switch to the Design view for *default. aspx*. Drag onto the page a RadioButtonList control. Set its AutoPostBack property to True, so the effects will occur as soon as you make a selection.

Use the ListItem Collection Editor to create three items, with their Text and Value properties set as follows:

Text	Value
.Net	n
Database	d
Hardware	h

You might also want to set the RepeatDirection property to Horizontal, and set the CellSpacing property to 20, perhaps, to spread things out a bit.

 If this were part of a real application, it might make sense to make this an AJAX-enabled web site and wrap all this in an UpdatePanel to get much snappier performance. For this example, that is neither necessary nor particularly noticeable.

Drag a Label control onto the page and set its ID to lblMessage. Clear its Text property.

Drag a DropDownList control onto the page. Set its ID to ddl and its Visible property to False, so that it will initially be invisible.

The Design view will look something like Figure 7-11.

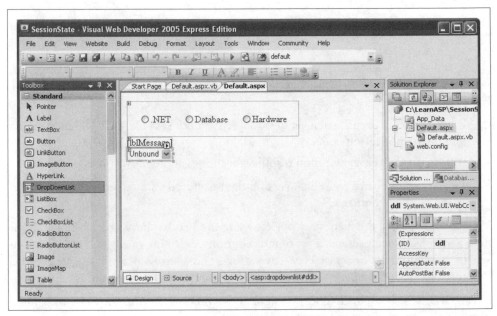

Figure 7-11. This is what the SessionState Default page should look like in Design view once you've created it. However, populating the drop-down list is different than you might expect.

Double-click the RadioButtonList to open the code-behind in an event handler for the default event for that control, SelectedIndexChanged. Enter the code highlighted in Example 7-3. Notice that in addition to the code inside the event handler itself, there is also a helper method called DisplayStuff.

Example 7-3. Default.aspx.vb for SessionState web site

```vb
Partial Class _Default
    Inherits System.Web.UI.Page

Protected Sub RadioButtonList1_SelectedIndexChanged(ByVal sender As Object, _
        ByVal e As System.EventArgs) Handles RadioButtonList1.SelectedIndexChanged
    Dim Books(3) As String

    Session("cattext") = RadioButtonList1.SelectedItem.Text
    Session("catcode") = RadioButtonList1.SelectedItem.Value

    Select Case RadioButtonList1.SelectedItem.Value
        Case "n"
            Books(0) = "Programming Visual Basic 2005"
            Books(1) = "Programming ASP.NET"
            Books(2) = "Programming C#"
        Case "d"
            Books(0) = "Oracle & Open Source"
            Books(1) = "SQL in a Nutshell"
            Books(2) = "Transact SQL Programming"
        Case "h"
            Books(0) = "PC Hardware in a Nutshell"
            Books(1) = "Dictionary of PC Hardware and Data Communications Terms"
            Books(2) = "Linux Device Drivers"
    End Select
    Session("books") = Books
    DisplayStuff()
End Sub

Private Sub DisplayStuff()
    If RadioButtonList1.SelectedIndex = -1 Then
        lblMessage.Text = "You must select a book category"
    Else
        Dim str As String = String.Empty
        str += "You have selected the category "
        str += CType(Session("cattext"), String)
        str += " with code '"
        str += CType(Session("catcode"), String)
        str += "'."
        lblMessage.Text = str

        ddl.Visible = True
        Dim CatBooks() As String = CType(Session("books"), String())

        ' populate the DropDownList
        ddl.Items.Clear()
        For i As Integer = 0 To CatBooks.Length - 1 Step 1
            ddl.Items.Add(New ListItem(CatBooks(i)))
        Next
    End If
End Sub

End Class
```

Run the application and select one of the radio buttons. Then open the drop-down list to see that the items have been populated, as shown in Figure 7-12. Now select one of the other radio buttons. Notice the page posts back immediately, and the content of the drop-down list changes.

The first thing that happens in this code is the Text the user selected is added to the session state and associated with the key "cattext" in the dictionary. Similarly, the Value that goes with that text is stored in Session associated with the key "catcode".

`CODE`

```
Session("cattext") = RadioButtonList1.SelectedItem.Text
Session("catcode") = RadioButtonList1.SelectedItem.Value
```

The Select Case statement is used to populate the drop-down list, depending on the user's selection. In each case, a three-item array called Books is created, but the text for each item varies depending on the Case statement. After Books is populated, it too is saved to Session state:

`CODE`

```
Session("books") = Books
```

Then the DisplayStuff( ) helper method is called. Because cattext, catvalue, and books have all been saved in session state, you don't need to pass their values to the helper method. DisplayStuff( ) can retrieve them directly from the Session dictionary, for example, when it concatenates cattext to the string:

`CODE`

```
str += CType(Session("cattext"), String)
```

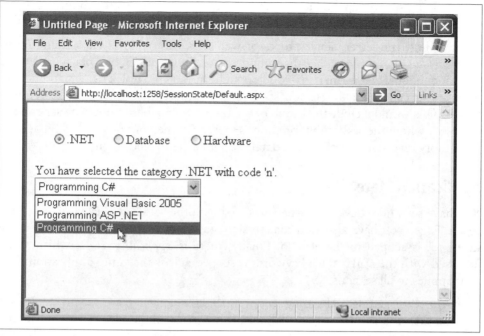

Figure 7-12. When you select one of the radio buttons in the SessionState web site, the content of the drop-down list changes immediately.

Remember, you need to use the `CType` method to convert the value to a string before you can use it.

Similarly, the helper method retrieves the books object, uses `CType` to convert it to an array of strings, and stores it in the new array `CatBooks()`:

```
Dim CatBooks() As String = CType(Session("books"), String())
```

Next, the method uses `CatBooks()` in a loop to populate the drop-down list.

Session state is enabled by default and works right out of the box. To increase performance, you can disable session state on a per-page, per-web site, or per-machine basis.

To disable session state for a page, include the following highlighted attribute in the Page directive at the top of the markup file:

```
<%@ Page Language="VB" AutoEventWireup="false"
    CodeFile="Default.aspx.vb"
    Inherits="_Default"
    EnableSessionState="False" %>
```

Valid values for `EnableSessionState` are `True`, `False`, and `ReadOnly`. `ReadOnly` provides better performance than `True` as long as you do not need to edit the values stored in session. How do the values get into session state if it is set to `ReadOnly`? From another page whose value is `True`.

To configure session state on a per-web site or per-machine basis, you must edit the configuration file, *web.config*, in the web site virtual directory.

For simple single-server, single-processor web sites with relatively low traffic (measured in hits per minute rather than hundreds or thousands of hits per minute), the default configuration is probably good enough. In more complex or demanding scenarios, you can configure Session state to accommodate a wide range of requirements. This would include the length of the timeout, whether or not browser cookies are used, where the session information is stored (in memory on the local machine, in memory on a state server, or in a database somewhere), and so on.

Application State

You have seen how view state, when accessed with the ViewState keyword, is scoped to the Page. You have also seen that session state, when accessed with the Session keyword, is scoped to the Session. Finally, there is *application state*, which when accessed with the Application keyword, is scoped across the entire application; that is, it applies to all sessions.

The syntax for getting and setting values in Application state are exactly analogous to ViewState and Session, so we will not include an example here. There are several things to consider however.

First, because multiple sessions can access the same Application dictionary object, it is possible for two people to change the value simultaneously. This is not an issue for read-only access. However, if the application data is editable by users, it is possible for two (or more) users to overwrite each other's values, resulting in faulty data at best. To prevent this, you can lock the Application object, but that can cause the application to grind to a halt.

Second, unlike view state and specially configured session state, application state always consumes server memory, so do not store too much "stuff" in application state.

Third, data stored in application state will not survive a server restart or crash. If something needs to persist across application halts, you need to store it elsewhere, such as in *web.config* as an AppSetting (but only if it is read-only), or in a database.

And finally, application state is specific to a single processor on a single machine. If your environment includes either multiprocessor servers (web garden) or multiple web servers (web farm), do not use application state. If you need this type of functionality, you will need to create it from scratch, perhaps storing the requisite values in a database.

Summary

- When you issue a request from your browser, that request is sent across the Internet to a remote server, which processes the request, possibly accesses a database, and then returns the HTML to the browser, where the page is rendered.

- A session is the period where a single user interacts with the web application, no matter how many different pages are visited.

- The values of all the controls on the page are referred to as state. The Web was originally intended not to preserve state, but that has evolved over time.

- Each step of the ASP.NET life cycle has events that allow you to change or add to the default behavior for that step.

- The control tree is a hierarchical representation of all the controls on a single page.

- The Trace attribute lets you see a great deal of information about your page, including the control tree.

- The page life cycle differs depending on whether or not the page is loaded as a result of a postback.

- The Start phase determines whether the page was requested by another page, or is a postback.

- The Initialization phase applies personalization and themes to the page, and also reads or initializes control properties.

- The Load phase sets the control properties.

- The Validation phase is where validation methods are checked on all eligible controls on the page.

- The Rendering phase is where each control is called to render itself in the browser.

- The Unload phase is last, and allows you to clean up any resources you need to.

- ASP.NET can automatically maintain state for server controls, avoiding the need to write any custom code.

- View state is the state of the page and any controls on it.

- You can disable the view state, by adding EnableViewState="false" to the Page directive. Simple controls such as text boxes, radio buttons and checkboxes always preserve view state, no matter what you set in the Page directive. More complex controls, however, can have their view state disabled.

- Although the view state is maintained automatically, you can use the state bag of view state to store your own values from page to page, using the ViewState keyword.

- The state bag uses a dictionary structure, with keys and values that you define as needed.

- Session state is not automatically maintained from page to page, but you can specify that objects be preserved in session state.

- Session state also uses a dictionary that you define as needed. You use the `Session` keyword to add items to this dictionary.

- You can disable session state for the page by placing the attribute `EnableSessionState="False"` in the `Page` directive, or for the entire site by editing *web.config*.

- Application state is similar to view state and session state. You can access the dictionary with the `Application` keyword.

By now, you've developed a lot of skills, and created many web pages that look and act professional, both up front and under the hood. When you take your shiny web site with its fancy controls out for a spin in the real world, though, you're going to come up against a tough reality: stuff breaks…a lot. As you may have already discovered from the exercises in this book, a typo in the wrong place, or a misconfigured property, can lead to a site that doesn't work and a lot of time staring at the code trying to figure out where you went wrong. Even when all of your code works perfectly, you can still run into problems with outside data sources, user errors, and other things beyond your control. Errors and bugs are part of programming, and nobody expects you to write perfect code the first time. What you want to learn, though, is how to find and fix bugs in the shortest possible time. The IDE has a host of tools to help you do just that, and that's what we'll discuss next.

Quiz

1. What is a session?

2. What is the state of a page?

3. What attribute can you use to see information about the different stages of the page life cycle?

4. In which life cycle phase does the page determine if it was called as the result of a postback?

5. What event is usually used to take actions during the Load phase?

6. What are the four kinds of state that ASP.NET manages? Which one can you not affect in any way?

7. What does the `EnableViewState="false"` attribute do?

8. Where would you store the value of a counter that is incremented each time the page is loaded?

9. Suppose you wanted to ask the user to enter his or her name on a page, and retain that value the entire time the user is at your site. What's the best mechanism to use?

10. What's the proper syntax for storing that username?

Exercises

Exercise 7-1. You'll start out with a simple exercise that uses your knowledge of the page life cycle. Create a simple page with a label, `lblPostBack`, and a button, `btnPostBack`, with a `Text` property of "Post Back". Write the appropriate code to cause the label to display the message "You're seeing this page for the first time!" when the page initially loads. Whenever the page is loaded as a result of a postback, the label should display the message "Welcome back to the page."

Exercise 7-2. Create a page with a label, `lblMessage`, and a button, `btnPostBack`. The first time you access the page, the label should output a message "Page first accessed at," followed by the date and time. Each time the button is clicked, add a new line to the label with the message "Page posted back at," followed by the date and time. (Hint: If you don't recall how to access the current date and time, see Chapter 3.) Your page should look something like Figure 7-13.

Exercise 7-3. Make the *Default.aspx* page from Exercise 7-2 the home page of the exercise. Add two more pages to the project; call them *SecondPage.aspx* and *ThirdPage.aspx*. Add an `<h1>` to *Default.aspx* to identify it, and then add two navigation buttons to navigate to each of the other two pages.

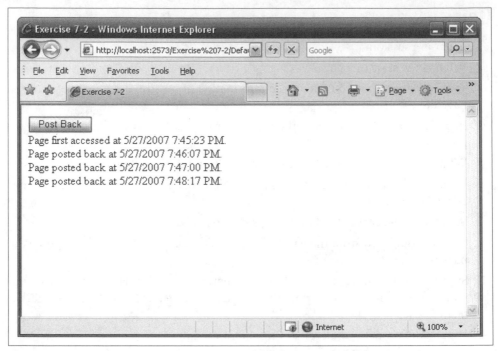

Figure 7-13. Your goal for Exercise 7-2, after clicking the Post Back button a few times.

SecondPage.aspx and *ThirdPage.aspx* should each contain an <h1> to identify them, a button for posting back, two buttons for navigating to each of the other two pages, and a label that displays the string created on the home page. Both of these pages should add a message to the string indicating when they were accessed for the first time, and when they are posted back. After you've navigated around the site for a bit, it should look like Figure 7-14.

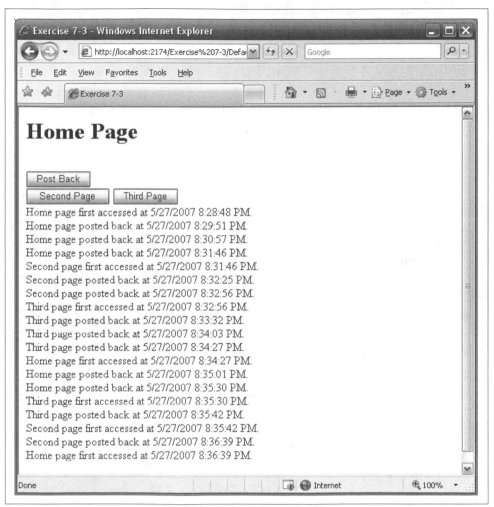

Figure 7-14. Your goal for Exercise 7-3, after clicking around a bit.

CHAPTER 8

Errors, Exceptions, and Bugs, Oh My!

Every computer programmer has run into bugs. It comes with the territory. Many bugs are found during the coding process. Others pop up only when an end user performs a specific and unusual sequence of steps or the program receives unexpected data. You should always try to find bugs early in the development process and avoid having end users find your bugs for you. Countless studies have shown that the earlier you find a bug, the easier and less expensive it is to fix.

If your program does run into a problem, you will want to recover quickly and invisibly, or, at worst, fail gracefully. ASP.NET provides tools and features to help reach these goals:

Tracing
> You can trace program execution at either the page or application level. ASP.NET provides an extensible trace log with program life-cycle information.

Symbolic debugging
> You can step through your program line by line, set breakpoints, examine and modify variables and expressions, and step into and out of classes, even those written in other languages.

Error handling
> You can handle standard or custom errors at the application or page level. You can also show different error pages for different errors.

To get started exploring the ASP.NET debugging tools, you should first create a simple web site to which you will add tracing code. You will then introduce bugs into the program and use the debugger to find and fix the bugs.

Creating the Sample Application

To start, create a new web site and name it DebuggingApp. This will consist of a single web page containing a header label, a DropDownList with a label below it to display the selected item, and a hyperlink.

In Design view, drag a Label control to the top of the page and set its Text property to the following:

```
Tracing, Debugging & Error Handling Demo
```

Change its Font-Name property to Arial Black, its Font-Size property to Large, and its Font-Bold property to True.

Drag a DropDownList control onto the form. Set its ID property to ddlBooks. Change its AutoPostBack property to True.

Add a label below the DropDownList with an ID of lblDdl. Set the Text property so it is empty.

Finally, add a HyperLink control below lblDdl. Set its ID property to hlTest. Change the Text property to "Link To" and change the NavigateUrl property to *TestLink. aspx*. No page with this name exists. This is an intentional error to demonstrate error handling later in the chapter.

The Design view will look something like that shown in Figure 8-1.

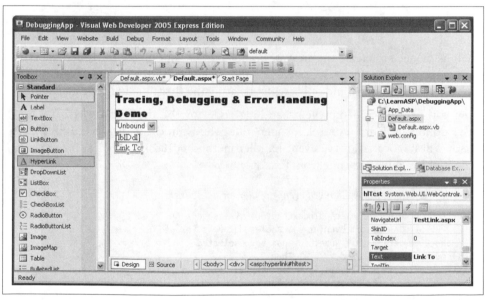

Figure 8-1. Here's what the sample application, DebuggingApp, looks like in Design view.

The DropDownList will be dynamically populated every time the page loads in the Page_Load method. To create this method, double-click *Default.aspx.vb* in the Solution Explorer to open the code-behind file. Click the Class Name drop-down at the upper left of the editing window and select (Page Events). Click the Method Name drop-down on the upper right and select the Load event to create the code skeleton for the Page_Load method. Enter the highlighted code from Example 8-1 into the Page_Load method.

Example 8-1. Page_Load method for the Default page in DebuggingApp

```
Protected Sub Page_Load(ByVal sender As Object, _
        ByVal e As System.EventArgs) Handles Me.Load
    If Not IsPostBack Then
        ' Build 2 dimensional array for the lists
        ' First dimension contains bookname
        ' Second dimension contains ISBN number
        Dim books(,) As String = { _
            {"Programming Silverlight", "0000000001"}, _
            {"Programming .NET 3", "0000000002"}, _
            {"Programming ASP.NET, 4th Edition", "0000000003"}, _
            {"Programming Visual Basic 9", "0000000004"}, _
            {"Programming C#, 5th Edition", "0000000005"}, _
            {"Learning ASP.NET ", "0596513976"} _
        }

        '  Now populate the list
        For i As Integer = 0 To books.GetLength(0) - 1
            '  add both Text and Value
            ddlBooks.Items.Add(New ListItem(books(i, 0), books(i, 1)))
        Next
    End If
End Sub
```

There is no need to create the array of book names and populate the DropDownList on every page load because view state will handle that on postback. Therefore, you test the IsPostBack property and only create the array the first time the page is loaded.

Now you need to add the event-handling code for the drop-down list. In Design view, double-click the control to open the code-behind file, *Default.aspx.vb*. The cursor will be located in the event handler method ddlBooks_SelectedIndexChanged. Type in the highlighted code from Example 8-2.

Example 8-2. SelectedIndexChanged event handler for ddlBooks

```
Protected Sub ddlBooks_SelectedIndexChanged(ByVal sender As Object, _
        ByVal e As System.EventArgs) Handles ddlBooks.SelectedIndexChanged
    ' check to verify that something has been selected
    If ddlBooks.SelectedIndex <> -1 Then
        lblDdl.Text = ddlBooks.SelectedItem.Text + " ---> ISBN: " _
            + ddlBooks.SelectedItem.Value
    End If
End Sub
```

Run the app and select a book title from the DropDownList. You will see something similar to Figure 8-2.

You will use this application through the rest of this chapter to demonstrate various techniques for analyzing and debugging code in ASP.NET and for handling errors in your application.

—VB CHEAT SHEET—
For Loops

You saw the For Each loop back in Chapter 6; the For loop is simply a more general version. The first line of a For loop has three parts: the condition, the beginning, and the end. Usually, you create a loop control variable, often an integer named i, to be the condition. For example, if you wanted a loop that would run ten times, you would start it like this:

```
For i As Integer = 1 To 10
```

Inside the loop, you place whatever code you want to run on each iteration. Then you end the loop with a Next statement. That causes execution to return to the beginning of the loop until the condition reaches the upper limit.

You can also use your control variable within the loop, as it increments. For example, this loop would add the numbers 1 through 10 to myString:

```
For i As Integer = 1 To 10
    myString = myString + i + " "
Next
```

This works because each time through the loop, i will be incremented.

Usually, you don't know exactly how many times you want your loop to run, so you set the upper limit at runtime. In Example 8-1, you want to loop through each item in the books array. Array index start at 0, as we've mentioned, and you use the GetLength( ) method on the array to find out how many items are contained in it. However, the length of the array starts at 1, not 0, so you have to use GetLength( ) - 1 to find the correct upper boundary for the loop:

```
For i As Integer = 0 To books.GetLength(0) - 1
```

Notice that i is also used within the loop, to extract the item with the index of i from books, and add it to the ddlBooks collection of ListItems, also with the same index of i.

Tracing

Tracing is the technique of reporting the value or state of things in your program, as it runs. It is an easy way to determine what is going on in your program. Back in the days of classic ASP, the only way to trace what was happening in your code was to insert Response.Write statements in strategic places. This allowed you to see that you had reached a known point in the code and, perhaps, to display the value of some variables. The big problem with this hand-tracing technique, aside from the amount of work involved, was that you had to laboriously remove or comment out all those statements before the program went into production. ASP.NET provides better and easier ways of gathering the trace information.

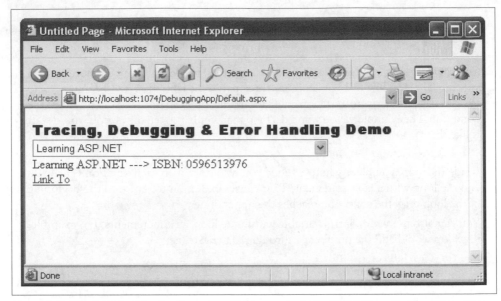

Figure 8-2. Here's DebuggingApp in action. After you select a book title from the DropDownList, its title and ISBN are output in the Label.

Page-Level Tracing

To add page-level tracing, modify the Page directive at the top of the *.aspx* page (in Source view) by adding a Trace attribute and setting its value to true, as follows (remember to close the browser first):

```
<%@ Page Language="VB" AutoEventWireup="false" CodeFile="Default.aspx.vb"
    Inherits="_Default" Trace="true" %>
```

When you view this page, tables will be appended to the bottom of the page that contain a wealth of information about your web application. Select a book from the drop-down list and you will see something like Figure 8-3.

The top section, labeled Request Details, shows basic information, including the SessionID, the Time of Request, Request Type, and Status Code (see Table 8-1). Every time the page is posted to the server, this information is updated. If you change the selection (remember that AutoPostBack is set to true), you will see that the Time of Request is updated, but the SessionID remains constant.

> Every web user has seen at least some of these status codes in their normal browsing, including the ubiquitous "404 - Not Found". For a complete list, go to *http://en.wikipedia.org/wiki/List_of_HTTP_status_ codes*.

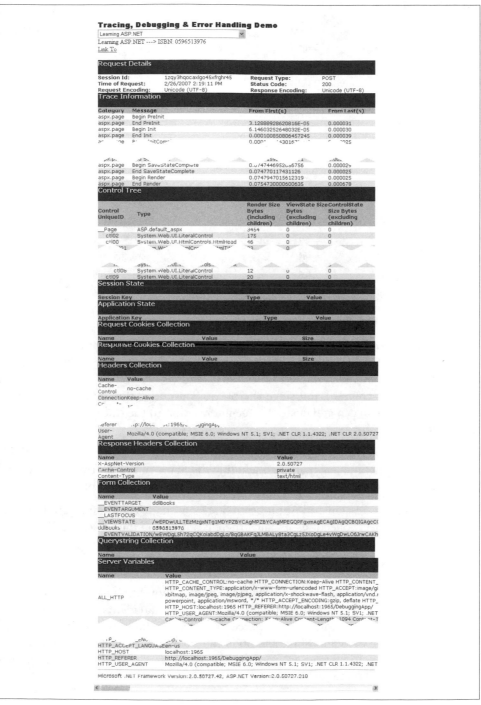

Figure 8-3. When you enable tracing in your file, you get a lot of data as a result.

Table 8-1. Commonly Used HTTP Status Codes

Category	Number	Description
Informational (100–199)	100	Continue
	101	Switching protocols
Successful (200–299)	200	OK
	204	No content
Redirection (300–399)	301	Moved permanently
	305	Use proxy
	307	Temporary redirect
Client Errors (400–499)	400	Bad request
	401	Unauthorized
	402	Payment required
	403	Forbidden
	404	Not found
	408	Request timeout
	417	Expectation failed
Server Error (500–599)	500	Internal Server Error

The next section, labeled "Trace Information," is the *trace log* (this section was shown briefly in Chapter 7 in the discussion of life cycle), which provides life-cycle information. This includes elapsed times, in seconds, since the page was initialized (the From First(s) column) and since the previous event in the life cycle (the From Last(s) column). You can add custom trace information to the trace log, as explained later in the next section.

The next section in the trace, under the heading Control Tree, lists all the controls on the page in a hierarchical manner, including the name of the control, its type, and its size in bytes, on the page, in the ViewState state bag, and in control state.

This is followed by Session and Application State summaries, and itemizations of the Cookies and Headers collections. Finally, there is a list of all the server variables.

Inserting into the Trace Log

You can add custom information to the trace output by writing to the Trace object. This object exposes two methods for putting your own statements into the trace log: Write and Warn. The only difference between the two methods is that Warn writes to the log in red. The Warn and Write methods can take either a single argument, two arguments, or two strings and an exception object (generated by the .NET Framework when using a try/catch block), as the following cases illustrate:

Trace.Warn("Warning Message")
    Inserts a record into the trace log with the message passed in as a string.

```
Trace.Warn("Category","Warning Message")
```
Inserts a record into the trace log with the category and message you pass in.

```
Trace.Warn("Category","Warning Message", excp)
```
Inserts a record into the trace log with a category, warning message, and exception.

To see this in action, add the highlighted code from Example 8-3 to the code-behind file in your sample web site, DebuggingApp.

Example 8-3. Writing to the Trace object

```
Protected Sub Page_Load(ByVal sender As Object, _
        ByVal e As System.EventArgs) Handles Me.Load
    Trace.Write("In Page_Load")
    If Not IsPostBack Then
        Trace.Write("Page_Load", "Not PostBack.")
        ' Build 2 dimensional array for the lists
        ' First dimension contains bookname
        ' Second dimension contains ISBN number
        Dim books(,) As String = { _
            {"Programming Silverlight", "0000000001"}, _
            {"Programming .NET 3", "0000000002"}, _
            {"Programming ASP.NET, 4th Edition", "0000000003"}, _
            {"Programming Visual Basic 9", "0000000004"}, _
            {"Programming C#, 5th Edition", "0000000005"}, _
            {"Learning ASP.NET ", "0596513976"} _
        }

        '  Now populate the list
        For i As Integer = 0 To books.GetLength(0) - 1
            '  add both Text and Value
            ddlBooks.Items.Add(New ListItem(books(i, 0), books(i, 1)))
        Next
    End If
End Sub


Protected Sub ddlBooks_SelectedIndexChanged(ByVal sender As Object, _
        ByVal e As System.EventArgs) Handles ddlBooks.SelectedIndexChanged
    ' force an exception
    Try
        Dim a As Integer = 0
        Dim b As Integer = 5 / a
    Catch ex As Exception
        Trace.Warn("User Action", "Calling b=5/a", ex)
    End Try

    ' check to verify that something has been selected
    If ddlBooks.SelectedIndex <> -1 Then
        lblDdl.Text = ddlBooks.SelectedItem.Text + " ---> ISBN: " _
            + ddlBooks.SelectedItem.Value
    End If
End Sub
```

The first message is added in the Page_Load method to signal that you've entered that method:

```
Trace.Write("In Page_Load")
```

The second message is added if the page is not a postback:

```
If Not IsPostBack Then
    Trace.Write("Page_Load", "Not PostBack.")
```

This second message is categorized as Page_Load; using a category can help you organize the trace output. The effect of these two Write statements is shown in Figure 8-4.

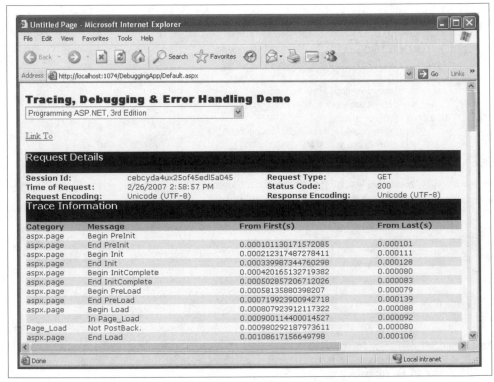

Figure 8-4. You can insert Trace.Write statements in your code to send specific messages to the trace output.

The third message is added to demonstrate the process of inserting an exception into the error log. The ddlBooks_SelectedIndexChanged event handler now contains code to force an exception by dividing by zero. The code catches that exception and logs the exception with a Trace statement, as shown by the following code fragment:

```
Try
    Dim a As Integer = 0
    Dim b As Integer = 5 / a
Catch ex As Exception
    Trace.Warn("User Action", "Calling b=5/a", ex)
End Try
```

The output from this Trace statement is shown in Figure 8-5.

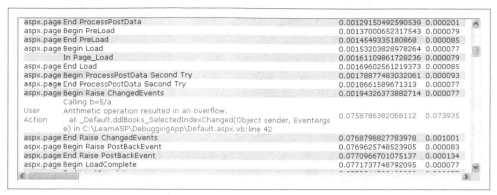

Figure 8-5. When you use Trace.Warn to indicate a caught exception, it looks like this. The Trace.Warn output displays in red.

Because this Trace statement was written by calling the Warn method rather than the Write method, the trace output appears in red onscreen (though not in your printed copy of this book). Notice that string you passed in, Calling b=5/a, is displayed, followed by an error message extracted automatically from the exception object.

Implementing Trace statements is easy, and when it's time to put your page into production, all these statements can remain in place. The only modification you need to make is to change the Trace attribute in the Page directive from true to false.

Debugging

Tracing provides you with a snapshot of the steps your code has taken after the code has run. At times, however, you'd like to monitor your code while it is running. What you want is more of a CAT scan than an autopsy. The code equivalent of a CAT scan is a symbolic debugger.

When you run your code in the debugger, you can watch your code work, step by step. As you walk through the code, you can see the variables change values, and you can watch as objects are created and destroyed.

This section will provide a brief introduction to the most important parts of the debugger that accompanies the VS/VWD IDE. For complete coverage of how to use the debugger, we urge you to spend time with the documentation and to experiment freely. The debugger is one of the most powerful tools at your disposal for learning ASP.NET.

An application can be configured to either enable or disable debugging. This is done through the configuration file, *web.config*. As you've already seen many times, the first time you run a new application, a dialog box will pop up, offering to automatically make the necessary edits to *web.config* to enable debugging.

The debugging configuration information is contained within the <compilation> section, within the <system.web> section, which in turn is contained within the <configuration> section. So, a typical compilation configuration snippet will look something like Example 8-4.

Example 8-4. Debug configuration code snippet from web.config

```
<?xml version="1.0"?>
<configuration>

   <system.web>
.
.
.

    <compilation debug="true" strict="false" explicit="true"/>
 />
```

Setting debug to `false` improves the runtime performance of the application.

The Debug Toolbar

A *Debug toolbar* is available in the IDE. To make it visible, click the View → Toolbars menu commands, and then click Debug, if it is not checked. Table 8-2 shows the icons that appear on the Debug toolbar.

Table 8-2. Debug toolbar icons

Icon	Debug menu equivalent	Keyboard shortcut	Description
			Toolbar handle. Click and drag to move the toolbar to a new location.
	Start/Continue	F5	Starts or continues executing the program.
	Break All	Ctrl-Alt-Break	Stops program execution at the currently executing line.
	Stop Debugging	Shift-F5	Stops debugging.
	Restart	Ctrl-Shift-F5	Stops the run currently being debugged and immediately begins a new run.
			Shows next statement that will be executed.
	Step Into	F11	If the current line contains a call to a method or function, this icon will single-step the debugger into that method or function.
	Step Over	F10	If the current line contains a call to a method or function, this icon will not step into that method or function but will go to the next line after the call.

Table 8-2. Debug toolbar icons (continued)

Icon	Debug menu equivalent	Keyboard shortcut	Description
	Step Out	Shift-F11	If the current line is in a method or function, that method or function will complete and the debugger will stop on the line after the method or function call.
Hex			Hexadecimal display toggle.
	Output		Debug window selector.
			Toolbar options. Offers options for adding and removing buttons from all toolbars (Debug, Text Editor, and so on).

Breakpoints

The crux of the biscuit is the apostrophe.
—Frank Zappa, "Apostrophe (')"

Breakpoints are at the heart of debugging. A breakpoint is an instruction to .NET to run to a specific line in your code and to stop and wait for you to examine the current state of the application. As the execution is paused, you can do the following:

- Examine and modify values of variables and expressions.
- Single-step through the code.
- Move into and out of methods and functions, even stepping into classes written in other .NET languages compliant with the Common Language Runtime.
- Perform any number of other debugging and analysis tasks.

Setting a breakpoint

You can set a breakpoint in any window editing a .NET-compliant language, such as VB or C#, by single-clicking the gray vertical bar along the left margin of the window. A red dot will appear in the left margin and the line of code will be highlighted, as shown in Figure 8-6.

Breakpoint window

You can see all the breakpoints currently set by looking at the *Breakpoint window*.

For some strange reason, the Breakpoint window is available in Visual Studio 2005 but not in Visual Web Developer 2005.

To display the Breakpoint window, perform any one of the following actions:

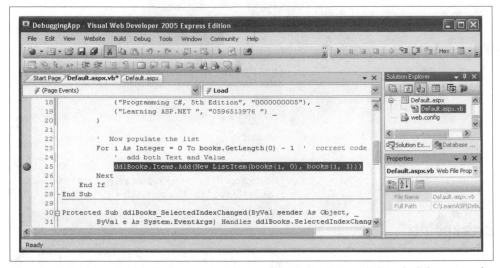

Figure 8-6. *Setting a breakpoint in a code-editing window is simple; just click in the left margin of your code.*

- Press Ctrl-Alt-B.
- Select Breakpoints from the Debug → Windows menu command.
- Click the Windows icon of the Debug toolbar and select Breakpoints.

A Breakpoint window is shown in Figure 8-7.

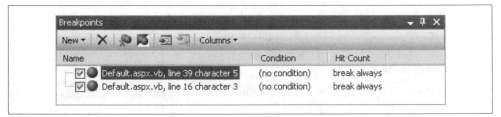

Figure 8-7. *The Breakpoint window shows you all the breakpoints you currently have set. Unfortunately, this window is only available in Visual Studio 2005.*

You can toggle a breakpoint between Enabled and Disabled by clicking the corresponding checkbox in the Breakpoint window.

Breakpoint properties

Sometimes you don't want a breakpoint to stop execution every time the line is reached. VS2005 offers several properties that can be set to modify the behavior of a breakpoint. These properties can be set via the property menu, arrived at in either of two ways:

- Right-click the breakpoint glyph in the left margin.
- Open the Breakpoint window and right-click the desired breakpoint.

 Again, this feature is available only in Visual Studio 2005, not VWD. However, right-clicking the breakpoint glyph in the left margin in VWD will offer the choice of deleting or disabling the breakpoint.

In either case, you will see the context menu shown in Figure 8-8.

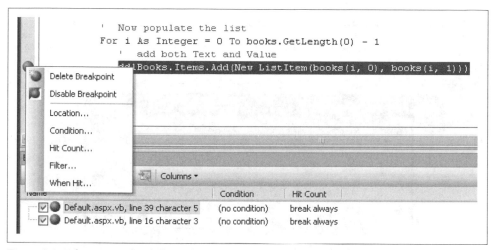

Figure 8-8. When you right-click in a breakpoint, you'll see this properties menu, where you can delete or disable a breakpoint, and also make a number of refinements to the breakpoint's behavior.

The first two items in the breakpoint properties menu allow you to delete or disable the selected breakpoint. The Disable menu item will toggle each time you click it, and when the breakpoint is disabled, the icon will appear as an empty circle.

The following menu items are available:

Location. The Location menu item brings up the dialog box shown in Figure 8-9, which is fairly self-explanatory. Using this dialog box is equivalent to setting a breakpoint in the code window, with a few additional options.

Condition. The Condition button brings up the dialog box shown in Figure 8-10.

You can enter any valid expression in the edit field. This expression is evaluated when program execution reaches the breakpoint. Depending on which radio button is selected and how the Condition expression evaluates, the program execution will either pause or move on. The two radio buttons are labeled as follows:

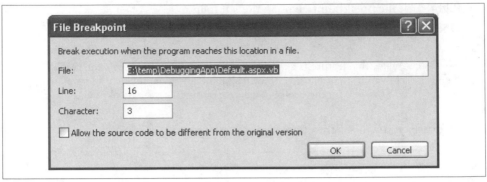

Figure 8-9. You can use the File Breakpoint dialog box to set a breakpoint at a specific spot in your file.

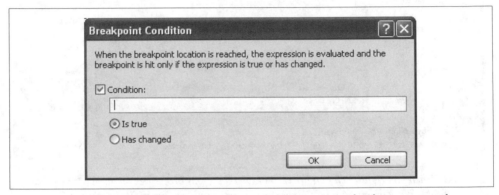

Figure 8-10. You can use the Breakpoint Condition dialog box to specify when you want the breakpoint to stop execution.

Is true

> If the Condition entered evaluates to a Boolean true, the program will pause.

Has changed

> If the Condition entered has changed, then the program will pause. On the first pass through the piece of code being debugged, the breakpoint will never pause execution because there is nothing to compare against. On the second and subsequent passes, the expression will have been initialized and the comparison will take place.

Hit count. Hit count is the number of times that spot in the code has been executed since either the run began or the Reset Hit Count button was pressed. The Hit Count button brings up the dialog box shown in Figure 8-11.

Clicking the drop-down list presents the following options:

- Break always
- Break always when the hit count is equal to

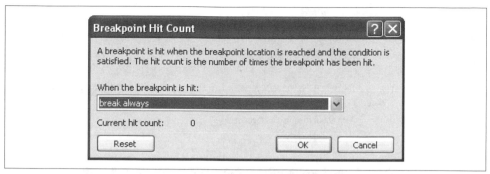

Figure 8-11. You can use the Breakpoint Hit Count dialog box to cause the breakpoint to only activate at set intervals.

- Break always when the hit count is a multiple of
- Break always when the hit count is greater than or equal to

If you click any option other than "break always" (the default), the dialog box will add an edit field for you to enter a target hit count.

Suppose this is a breakpoint set in a loop of some sort. You select "break when the hit count is a multiple of" and enter 5 in the edit field. The program will pause execution every fifth time it runs.

When a hit count is set, the red breakpoint icon in the left margin of the window has a plus sign in the middle of it.

When Hit…. The When Hit menu item brings up the dialog box shown in Figure 8-12. By default, the Print a message checkbox is unchecked. When this box is checked, the red circular breakpoint icon in the left margin of the window changes to a diamond shape.

You can also elect to run one of a large selection of predefined macros, such as Find-Case, SaveView, and SaveBackup.

By default, the Continue execution checkbox is checked.

Breakpoint icons

Each breakpoint symbol, or *glyph*, conveys a different type of breakpoint. These glyphs appear in Table 8-3.

Table 8-3. Breakpoint glyphs

Icon	Type	Description
●	Enabled	A normal, active breakpoint. If breakpoint conditions or hit count settings are met, execution will pause at this line.
○	Disabled	Execution will not pause at this line until the breakpoint is re-enabled.

Table 8-3. Breakpoint glyphs (continued)

Icon	Type	Description
	Error	The location or condition is not valid.
	Warning	The code at this line is not yet loaded, so a breakpoint can't be set. If the code is subsequently loaded, the breakpoint will become enabled.
	Hit Count	A Hit Count condition has been set.

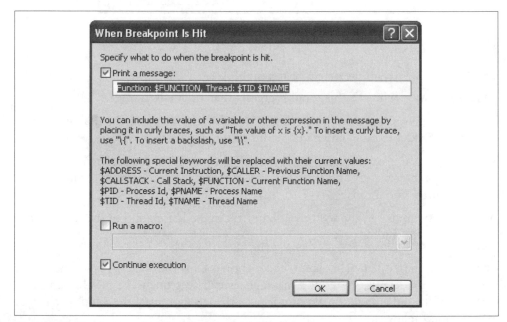

Figure 8-12. You can use the When Breakpoint Is Hit dialog box to output a message or run a macro whenever the breakpoint is reached.

Stepping Through Code

One of the most powerful techniques for debugging an application is to single-step through the code, giving you the opportunity to see the execution flow and to examine the value of variables, properties, objects, and so on. To see this in action, go to the code-behind file in the example. Place a breakpoint on the call to the Add method of the DropDownList control's Items collection, the line in the Page_Load method where the items are added to the DropDownList. Then run the program.

The breakpoint will be hit, and the program will stop execution at the line of code containing the breakpoint, which will turn yellow. The breakpoint glyph in the left margin will have a yellow arrow on top of it. The screen should look like Figure 8-13.

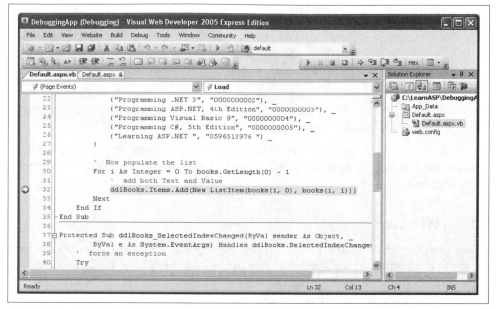

```
DebuggingApp (Debugging) - Visual Web Developer 2005 Express Edition

File   Edit   View   Website   Build   Debug   Tools   Window   Community   Help

Default.aspx.vb   Default.aspx

(Page Events)                          Load

22              ("Programming .NET 3", "0000000002"), _
23              ("Programming ASP.NET, 4th Edition", "0000000003"), _
24              ("Programming Visual Basic 9", "0000000004"), _
25              ("Programming C#, 5th Edition", "0000000005"), _
26              ("Learning ASP.NET ", "0596513976 ") _
27          )
28
29          ' Now populate the list
30          For i As Integer = 0 To books.GetLength(0) - 1
31              ' add both Text and Value
32              ddlBooks.Items.Add(New ListItem(books(i, 0), books(i, 1)))
33          Next
34      End If
35  End Sub
36
37  Protected Sub ddlBooks_SelectedIndexChanged(ByVal sender As Object, _
38          ByVal e As System.EventArgs) Handles ddlBooks.SelectedIndexChange(
39      ' force an exception
40      Try

Ready                                   Ln 32      Col 13      Ch 4      INS
```

Solution Explorer
C:\LearnASP\DebuggingA
  App_Data
  Default.aspx
    Default.aspx.vb
  web.config

Figure 8-13. When a breakpoint is hit, the program's execution stops, and the current line of code is highlighted.

You can now move forward a single statement or line at a time, stepping into any methods or functions as you go, by using one of the following techniques:

- Select the Debug → Step Into menu command.
- Click the Step Into icon (see Table 8-3 for a picture of the icon).
- Press F11.

You can step through the code without going through called functions or methods. That is, you can step over the calls rather than into the calls, using one of the following techniques:

- Select the Debug → Step Over menu item.
- Click the Step Over icon (see Table 8-3 for a picture of the icon).
- Press F10.

Finally, if you are debugging in a called method or function, you can step out of that method or function call, using one of the following techniques:

- Select the Debug → Step Out menu command.
- Click the Step Out icon (see Table 8-3 for a picture of the icon).
- Press Shift-F11.

Examining Variables and Objects

Once the program is stopped, it is incredibly intuitive and easy to examine the value of objects and variables currently in scope. Place the mouse cursor over the top of any variable or object in the code, wait a moment, and then a little pop-up window will appear with its current value.

If the cursor is hovering over a variable, the pop up will contain the type of variable, its value (if relevant), and any other properties it may have.

If the cursor is hovering over some other object, the pop-up window will contain information relevant to its type, including its full namespace, syntax, and a descriptive line of help.

Debug Windows

When the program execution is paused for debugging, a number of windows may appear at the bottom of the IDE, as shown in Figure 8-14. These debug windows are optimized to show program information in a specific way. The following sections describe the most commonly used windows.

All the debug windows can be accessed in one of three ways: with a shortcut key combination, from the Debug → Windows menu command, or from the Windows icon of the Debug toolbar, as indicated in Figure 8-14. Table 8-4 summarizes the debug windows, along with the shortcut keys for accessing each window.

 Visual Studio 2005, but not VWD, includes some additional, more arcane debug windows, including ones for Threads, Modules, Registers, and Memory.

Table 8-4. Debug windows

Window name	Shortcut keys	Description
Immediate	Ctrl-Alt-I	View any variable or expression.
Locals	Ctrl-Alt-V followed by L	View all variables in the current context.
Watch	Ctrl-Alt-W, followed by either 1, 2, 3, or 4	View up to four different sets of variables of your choosing.
Call Stack	Ctrl-Alt-C	View all methods on the call stack.
Script Explorer	Ctrl-Alt-N	Lists script files currently loaded in the program being debugged.

Immediate window

The *Immediate window* allows you to type almost any variable, property, or expression and immediately see its value.

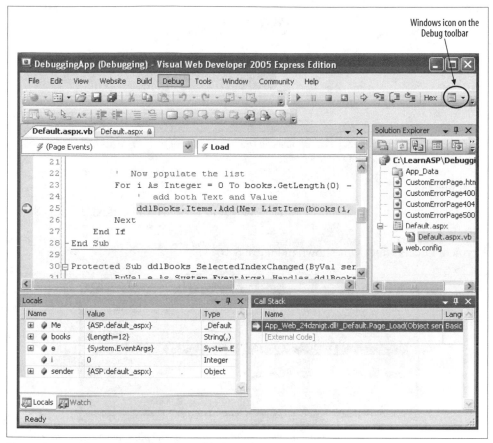

Figure 8-14. Debug windows are accessible from the Debug menu, a shortcut key combination, or by clicking the Windows icon on the Debug toolbar.

To see the value of an expression, prepend it with a question mark. For instance, if the breakpoint is on the line shown in Figure 8-13, you will see the value of the integer i by entering the following line:

```
?i
```

in the Immediate window and pressing Enter. Figure 8-15 shows the result of that exercise; additionally, this figure shows the process of assigning a new value to the variable i and then viewing its value again. If you change the value of a variable in the Immediate window and then continue to run the program, the new value will now be in effect.

You can clear the contents of the Immediate window by right-clicking anywhere in the window and selecting Clear All. Close the window by clicking the X in the upper-right corner. If you close the window and subsequently bring it back up in the same session, it will still have all the previous contents.

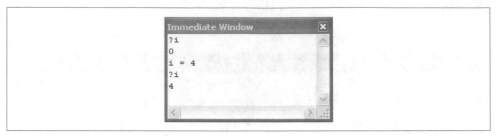

Figure 8-15. The Immediate window allows you to see the value of a variable at the current breakpoint, and also to change that variable.

Locals window

The *Locals window* shows all the variables local to the current context displayed in a hierarchical table.

A typical Locals window is shown in Figure 8-16.

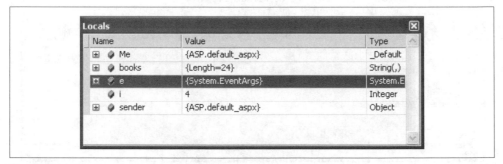

Figure 8-16. The Locals window shows all the current variables at the point where execution stopped.

There are columns for the name of the object, its value, and its type. A plus sign next to an object indicates that it has child objects that are not displayed, while a minus sign indicates that its child objects are visible. Clicking a plus symbol drills down the tree and shows any children, while clicking a minus symbol contracts the tree and displays only the parent.

A very useful feature is that values that change in the current step display in red.

You can select and edit the value of any variable. The value will display as red in the Locals window. Any changes to values take effect immediately.

Watch window

The *Watch window* is the same as the Locals window, except that it shows only variables, properties, or expressions you enter into the Name field in the window or drag from another window. The biggest advantage of using a Watch window is that it allows you to decide exactly which objects you want to watch.

In addition to typing in the name of the object you want to watch, you can also drag and drop variables, properties, or expressions from a code window. Select the object in the code you want to put in the Watch window and then drag it to the Name field in the open Watch window.

You can also drag and drop objects from the Locals windows into the Watch window. To do so, both the source window and the Watch window must be open. Highlight a line in the Locals window and drag it down over the Watch tab. The Watch window will come to the foreground. Continue dragging the object to an empty line in the Watch window.

Call Stack window

The *Call Stack window* displays the names of the methods on the call stack and their parameter types and values. You can control which information is displayed in the Call Stack window by right-clicking anywhere in the window and toggling field names that appear in the lower portion of the pop-up menu.

Error Handling

You can and should avoid bugs, but there are runtime errors that cannot be avoided and should be handled as gracefully as possible. You would like to avoid having the end user see ugly or cryptic error messages, or worse, having the application crash. Errors can arise from any number of causes: user action, such as entering invalidly formatted text into a field, program logic errors, or circumstances entirely out of your control, such as an unavailable file or a downed network.

The simplest bugs to find and fix are syntax errors: violations of the rules of the language. For example, suppose you had the following line of code in your VB program:

CODE ►
```
Dim i as Integr
```

When you compile the program, you will get a compiler error because the keyword to declare an integer is misspelled.

Using the IDE dramatically reduces your syntax errors. Depending on how the IDE is configured, any code element that isn't recognized is underlined. If Auto List Members is turned on (Tools → Options → Text Editor → All Languages), the incidence of syntax errors is further reduced. Check the "Show All Settings" checkbox (and leave it checked) to see these menu options.

If any syntax errors remain or if you are using a different editor, then any syntax errors will be caught by the compiler every time you build the project. It is very difficult for a syntax error to slip by into production code.

When the compiler finds a syntax error, an error message containing the location of the error and a terse explanation will be displayed in the Output window of the IDE. If the error is caused by something such as an unbalanced parenthesis or bracket, or a missing semicolon in C#, then the actual error may not be on the reported line.

More problematic, and often more difficult to catch, are errors in *logic*. The program successfully compiles and may run perfectly well most of the time, yet still contain errors in logic. The very hardest bugs to find are those that occur least often. If you can't reproduce the problem, it is terribly difficult to find it.

While you will try to eliminate all the bugs from your code, you do want your program to react gracefully when a subtle bug or unexpected problem rears its ugly head.

Unhandled Errors

To demonstrate what happens if there is no error handling in place, modify the sample project from this chapter to force some errors.

Go to the code-behind file. Find the For loop that populates the DropDownList in the Page_Load method. Change the test expression to cause an error intentionally at runtime. For example, change the line:

```
For i As Integer = 0 To books.GetLength(0) - 1
```

to:

```
For i As Integer = 0 To books.GetLength(0) + 1
```

When this code runs, it will try to add more items than have been defined in the books array, thus causing a runtime error. This is not a subtle bug, but it serves to demonstrate how the system reacts to runtime errors.

When you run this example in the IDE, execution will stop at the line causing the error, as shown in Figure 8-17, preventing you from seeing the error page. Just press F5 to continue running, or click the Debug → Continue menu item to get to the error page.

Let the program run. As expected, an error is generated immediately, and the generic ASP.NET error page is displayed to the user, as shown in Figure 8-18.

This generic error page is actually fairly useful to the developer or technical support person who will be trying to track down and fix any bugs. It tells you the error type, the line in the code that is the approximate error location, and a stack trace to help in tracking down how that line of code was reached.

You can replace this detailed error page with a custom error page and can control who gets to see what by setting the mode attribute of the CustomErrors element in the configuration file, as will be described next.

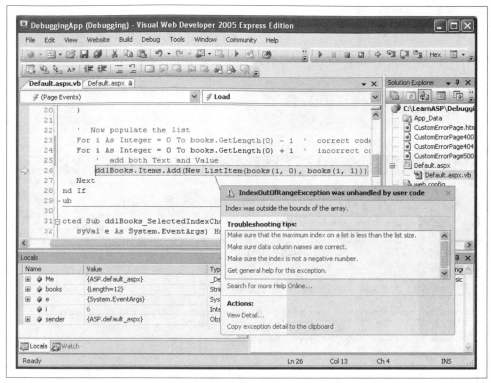

Figure 8-17. When the program encounters a runtime error, the IDE stops execution and points out the problem.

Application-Wide Error Pages

The previous section showed the default error pages presented for unhandled errors. This is fine for a developer, but if the application is in production, it would be much more aesthetically pleasing if the user were presented with an error page that looked less intimidating.

The goal is to intercept the error before it has a chance to send the generic error page to the client. This is done on an application-wide basis by modifying the configuration file, *web.config*.

The error-handling configuration information in *web.config* is contained within the <customErrors> section within the <system.web> section, which is contained within the <configuration> section. A typical <customErrors> section will look like Example 8-5.

Example 8-5. Custom error section from web.config

```
<?xml version="1.0"?>
<configuration>
```

Example 8-5. Custom error section fromweb.config (continued)

```
<system.web>
 .
 .
 .
<customErrors
   defaultRedirect="CustomErrorPage.htm"
   mode="On"
/>
```

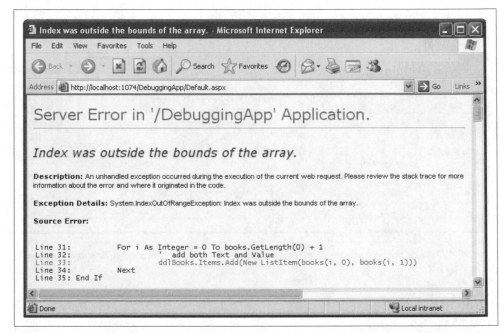

Figure 8-18. When you run an application with a logic error, the application may still compile, but fail at runtime. In that case, you'll see a generic error page like this one.

There are two possible attributes for the `<customErrors>` section: `defaultRedirect` and `mode`.

`defaultRedirect` is an attribute that contains the URL of the page to display in the case of any error not otherwise handled. In Example 8-5, the `defaultRedirect` page is `CustomErrorPage.htm`. This example is a simple HTML page contained in the same folder as the rest of the web site. The contents of this page are shown in Example 8-6.

Example 8-6. CustomErrorPage.htm

```
<html>
   <head>
      <title>Error Page</title>
   </head>
```

Example 8-6. CustomErrorPage.htm (continued)

```
    <body>
        <h1>Sorry - you've got an error.</h1>
    </body>
</html>
```

If the custom error page to be displayed is not in the same folder as the rest of the application, then you need to include either a relative or a fully qualified URL in the `defaultRedirect` attribute.

`mode` is an attribute that enables or disables custom error pages for the application. It can have three possible values:

On

Enables custom errors for the entire application.

Off

Disables custom errors for the entire application.

RemoteOnly

Enables custom errors only for remote clients. Local clients will see the generic error page. In this way, developers can see all the possible error information, but end users will see the custom error page.

Edit your *web.config* file to look like Example 8-5, adding the `customErrors` element inside the `<system.web>` tags; then add a new item to your web site called *Custom-ErrorPage.htm*. The full markup for this web page is listed in Example 8-6. Run the program. Instead of Figure 8-18, you will see something like Figure 8-19.

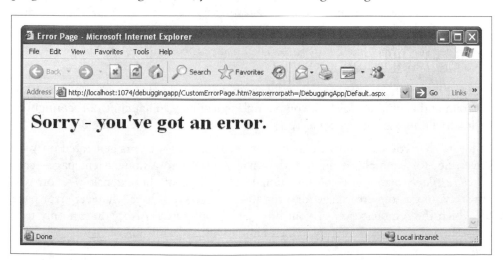

Figure 8-19. CustomErrorPage resulting from unhandled error with custom errors configured in web.config.

Obviously, you'll want to put more information on your custom error page, such as instructions or contact information, but you get the idea. Showing dynamic information about the error on the custom error page is also possible.

You can even use a different custom error page for different errors. To do this, you need to include one or more <error> subtags in the <customErrors> section of *web. config*. For example, modify *web.config* to look like the code snippet in Example 8-7.

Example 8-7. Custom error code snippet with <error> subtags from web.config

```
<?xml version="1.0"?>
<configuration>

   <system.web>
.
.
.
   <customErrors mode="On"
      defaultRedirect="CustomErrorPage.htm">
      <error statusCode="400" redirect="CustomErrorPage400.htm"/>
      <error statusCode="404" redirect="CustomErrorPage404.htm"/>
      <error statusCode="500" redirect="CustomErrorPage500.htm"/>
   </customErrors>
```

Copy *CustomErrorPage.htm* three times and rename the copies to the filenames in the <error> subtags in Example 8-7. Do this by right-clicking *CustomErrorPage.htm* in the Solution Explorer and selecting Copy. Then, right-click the web site root folder and select Paste. Next, right-click the new copy of the file and select Rename. Edit the files so each displays a unique message.

Run the program again with the intentional error in the For loop still in place. You should see something like Figure 8-20. The error number shown will likely be one of the status codes listed back in Table 8-1.

Fix the error in the For loop so the program will at least load correctly. Then run the program and click the hyperlink you put on the test page. That control is configured to link to a nonexistent *.aspx* file. You should see something like Figure 8-21.

Be aware that you can only display custom error pages for errors generated on *your* server. So, for example, if the hyperlink had been set to a nonexistent page—say, *http://TestPage.comx* (note the intentional misspelling of the extension)—you will not see your custom error page for error 404. Instead, you'll see whatever error page for which the remote server or your browser is configured. Also, you can only trap the 404 error if the page you are trying to link to has an extension of *.aspx*.

Page-Specific Error Pages

You can override the application-level error pages for any specific page by modifying the Page directive at the top of the *.aspx* file.

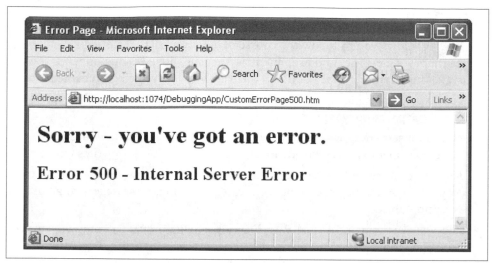

Figure 8-20. Custom error page for Error 500.

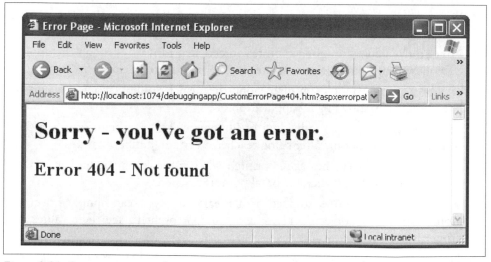

Figure 8-21. Custom error page for Error 404.

Modify the Page directive in *Default.aspx* file of the DebuggingApp so it appears as follows (note the highlighted ErrorPage attribute, which has been added):

```
<%@ Page Language="VB" AutoEventWireup="false" CodeFile="Default.aspx.vb"
    Inherits="_Default" Trace="false"
    ErrorPage="PageSpecificErrorPage.aspx" %>
```

If there is an error on this page, the PageSpecificErrorPage.aspx page will be displayed. If there is an application-level custom error page defined in *web.config*, it will be overridden by the Page directive.

Summary

- Tracing allows you to follow the course of your application through the various stages of its life cycle, and examine its state as it runs. Tracing appends a great deal of information to the bottom of the page for which tracing is enabled.

- To turn on tracing for a specific page, add the `Trace` attribute to the `Page` directive of the page you want to trace, and set it to `True`.

- You can insert your own information into the trace log with the `Trace.Write` and `Trace.Warn` methods. They're identical, except that `Trace.Warn` writes in red.

- The `Trace.Write` and `Trace.Warn` methods can accept a message string, a category string and a message string, or a category string, a message string, and an exception object.

- The Visual Studio and Visual Web Developer IDEs provide a complete suite of debugging tools.

- A breakpoint stops execution of an application at a point that you specify, to allow you to examine the state of the application at that point.

- When the application is paused at a breakpoint, you can inspect and change the current values of variables and expressions.

- After you've paused at a breakpoint, you can step forward through the application one line at a time, or you can step over or into method calls.

- The breakpoint window (available only in Visual Studio) shows you all the breakpoints currently in your application.

- You can specify that an individual breakpoint will stop execution if a specific condition is true, or only after being reached a certain number of times.

- You can specify what message is printed when a breakpoint is hit, or you can specify a macro to run when the breakpoint is reached.

- When the application is stopped at a breakpoint, you can simply hover the mouse cursor over objects and variables at that point to see their values and properties.

- The Immediate debug window allows you to type a variable, property, or expression, and see or modify its current value.

- The Locals window shows the variables in the current context, and their current values.

- The Watch window is a subset of the Locals window, but it shows only those variables that you specify.

- Syntax errors are errors that violate the rules of the programming language. The IDE checks for syntax errors as you write your code, and underlines any code element that doesn't fit. If you attempt to run an application with a syntax error, the application will not run, and the IDE will pop up an informational box at the point of the error.

- Logic errors occur when the code is syntactically correct, but doesn't behave as intended. These errors are more difficult to deal with because the IDE cannot find them for you. You need to write code to handle those errors so they don't stop your application, or at least provide a way for the application to fail with a minimum of surprise to the user.

- ASP.NET provides default error pages that appear when an unexpected error occurs in the application. These pages have useful information for developers, but not so much for users.

- To prevent the user from seeing the default error pages, you can define custom pages to handle errors.

- When you want to use custom error pages, you have to add a `<customErrors>` section to the *web.config* file, and set the `mode` attribute to either `On` or `RemoteOnly`.

- You can create specific error pages for individual types of errors. Create a new `<error>` section within the `<customErrors>` section, and specify the `statusCode` attribute for which you want to create a custom page.

- If you want to specify an error page to be used on one specific page of your site, instead of the entire application, add the `ErrorPage` attribute to the `Page` directive, and specify the location of the custom error page.

You've spent the last couple of chapters behind the scenes, figuring out ways to enhance your site and the user's experience that are totally invisible to the user (or should be, if everything goes well). In the next chapter, it's time to get back to things that the user can see. You'll learn how to change the entire visual appearance of your site with themes and skins, and how to let the user choose his or her preference for viewing your site. Of course, if users are going to customize their experiences, they'll need to identify themselves to you. Or maybe you don't want just anybody coming into your site and changing things around. That means you'll need some security measures, which is the first thing we'll talk about in the next chapter.

Quiz

1. How do I turn on tracing for a specific page?

2. What is the difference between the `Trace.Write` and `Trace.Warn` methods?

3. What are the three possible arguments to the `Trace.Write` and `Trace.Warn` methods?

4. How do you set a breakpoint in your code?

5. How do I determine the current value of a variable when the application is stopped at a breakpoint?

6. How do I modify the value of a variable while the application is running?

7. What information can you find in the Locals window?

8. What is the difference between syntax and logic errors?

9. What setting do you need to specify before you can use a custom error page?

10. How do you specify that a specific page should use its own custom error page instead of the application-wide pages?

Exercises

Exercise 8-1. Download the file Exercise 8-1 from this book's web site. This application is a part of a page for an online men's clothing store. At the moment, this application runs correctly. Enable tracing on this page, and insert a warning into the trace that indicates when the execution is in the event handler for the drop-down list.

Exercise 8-2. Download the file Exercise 8-2 from this book's web site. This application is similar to the first, but it has a problem. Instead of showing the name of the product in the details pane, some other text is showing up instead, as shown in Figure 8-22. Find the problem and resolve it.

Exercise 8-3. Same site, different problem. Download the file Exercise 8-3 from this book's web site. In this case, the product details don't show up at all, as shown in Figure 8-23. Find the problem and resolve it.

Exercise 8-4. Download the file Exercise 8-4 from the book's web site. The product page now has a hyperlink for users to get customer assistance (and it seems like they'll need it). Unfortunately, the customer assistance page hasn't been created yet. Create a custom error page to handle this error, and give the user the option to return to the product page.

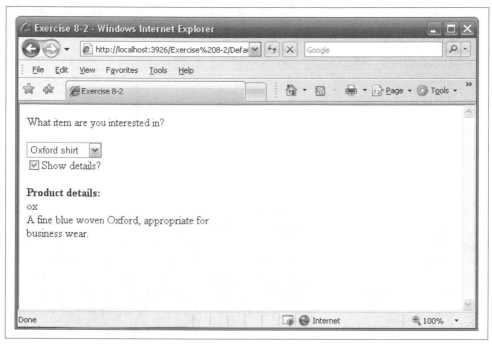

Figure 8-22. The problem in Exercise 8-2.

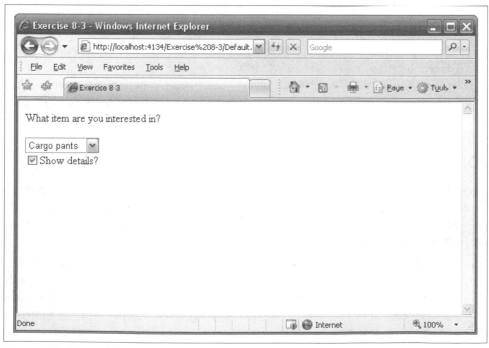

Figure 8-23. The problem in Exercise 8-3.

CHAPTER 9

Security and Personalization

Nearly everything you've learned about so far in this book has been aimed at increasing the interactivity of your web sites—giving the user control over his or her experience with your site. But why should that interactivity just be limited to data? With ASP.NET 2.0, you can allow readers to customize the appearance of your site based on their preferences. You can allow users to identify themselves to your site, so that you can save their preferences and restore them whenever they visit. Of course, having users log in is also useful for security reasons. You can restrict parts of your site to access just by certain users or groups.

In this chapter, you'll build a functional site with multiple pages, some public and some not. You'll use the ASP.NET login controls, and see just how easy they are to use and customize to your needs. You'll then adapt the site to restrict pages to specific roles, and see how to manage your users. You'll enhance your site by letting users enter personal information that you'll store and produce on demand, and you'll learn how to provide content for users who'd rather remain anonymous. Finally, you'll modify the appearance of the controls on your site with themes, and you'll see how you can let users set their own themes, and retain those settings with their other personal information.

Forms-Based Security

Many Internet sites require that users "log in." This allows the site both to restrict access to "members" and also allows the user to *personalize* the site to their individual needs. These include allowing the site to remember the user's preferences, profile information, shopping cart contents, and so forth.

Forms-based security is a common technique for validating that the person who is trying to log in to a web site is who they say they are. It presents the user with a web page, or form, containing fields that the user can fill in and submit. Server-side code processes the credentials submitted, such as the username and password, and determines whether the user can proceed.

Not that long ago, creating the "plumbing" of logging in was a tedious and time-consuming job: You had to create membership tables, create the ability to maintain secure passwords, ensure authorization on each page, assign users to "roles" (such as guest, member, owner, wizard, and more), and so on. You also had to write all the controls to allow the user to log in, to recover passwords, to change passwords, and so forth.

With ASP.NET 2.0 and AJAX, all of that has become wonderfully simplified.

Creating Users with the WAT

Visual Studio 2005 offers a wizard called the Web Site Administrative Tool, abbreviated the WAT. This tremendously powerful tool is hidden under the menu choice Website → ASP.NET Configuration for no apparent reason.

> If the Web Site Administration Tool were a true acronym, it would be WSAT, but that is very hard to say if English is your first language. Interestingly, the name itself reflects Microsoft's apparent ambivalence, (reflected within VS/VWD) of whether web site is one word or two. It is used as one word in the menus, but as two in the WAT. We've tried to use it as two words throughout this book, except when we don't.

To try it out, create a new web site called FormsBasedSecurityWAT and then follow these menu selections. The WAT should open in its own browser window.

Select Website → ASP.NET Configuration. Click the Security tab (or the Security link), as shown in Figure 9-1. (Note: "Web Site" is two words in the heading!)

This screen is used for interactively creating users, roles, and access rules. By default, the authentication type is Windows, which means that all user authentication and password management is handled by Windows using your normal Windows sign-on account. This can be quite handy for an *intranet* web site (a web site used only within a single company).

Because we are concerned with Internet accounts (accounts open to the world), change the authentication type to Forms-based. To do so, click the "Select authentication type" link under the Users heading, indicated in Figure 9-1.

This brings up the screen shown in Figure 9-2. Select the radio button labeled "From the internet," and then click the Done button.

> Please note the schizophrenia of this tool: To get to the WAT, you click "ASP.NET Configuration"; to get forms-based security, you click "From the internet"—you never quite click what you expect, but it does all make sense, sort of.

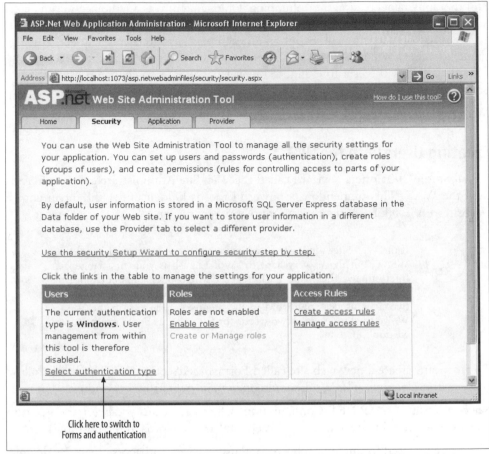

Figure 9-1. *Web Site Administration Tool (WAT) is hidden under the Website menu. On the Security screen, you'll find a link to switch from Windows security to forms-based security.*

After you click the Done button, you return to the previous page, but the display under Users has changed, as shown in Figure 9-3. You can create users, manage existing users, or change the authentication type back to Windows.

Click the Create User link to create your first user, as shown in Figure 9-4. Be sure the Active User checkbox remains checked, or else the user will not be able to log into the web site.

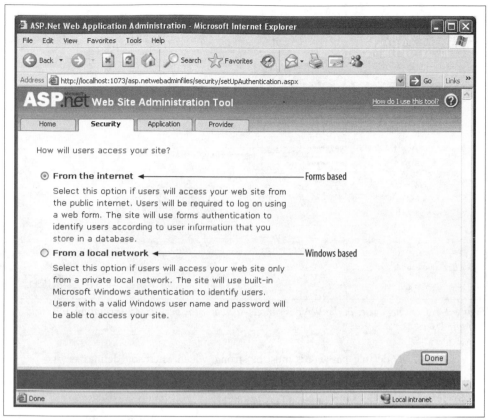

Figure 9-2. Select "From the internet" to change the Authentication type from Windows-based security to forms-based security.

Figure 9-3. After you change the security type to forms-based, you'll see the number of existing users on the Security tab. You can create new users or manage existing ones from here.

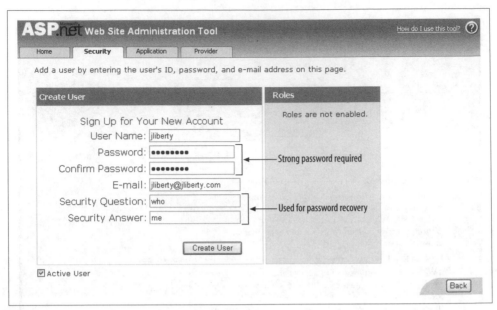

Figure 9-4. Creating a user in the WAT is simple; just enter the pertinent information and click "Create User."

 By default, passwords must be **strong**, which Microsoft defines as: at least seven characters in length and consisting of both alphanumeric and nonalphanumeric characters. So **danh** would not be strong, nor would **danh123**, but **danh123!** would be.

The strong password requirements may differ in other security areas, such as requiring both upper- and lowercase letters, or numbers. For more information, go to *www.msdn.microsoft.com* and search for **strong passwords**.

The CreateUserWizard control, which you will see later in this chapter, has a PasswordRegularExpression property that allows you to substitute your own password requirements. With it, you can dictate how "strong" your passwords need to be.

Creating at least one user through the WAT sets up a Security database with all the tables that ASP.NET's forms-based security system will need to support your use of the forms-based security system.

Your *web.config* file will be modified by the WAT to include the following line under <system.web>:

CODE►
```
<authentication mode="Forms" />
```

In addition, a file-based database will be created in the App_Data directory of your application, named *ASPNETDB.MDF*. To view this, click View → Server Explorer to open the Server Explorer Window. If you're using VWD, click View → Database

Explorer instead. If you don't already see *ASPNETDB.MDF*, then within that window, right-click Data Connections and select "Add Connections...." This will open the Add Connection dialog box, shown in Figure 9-5.

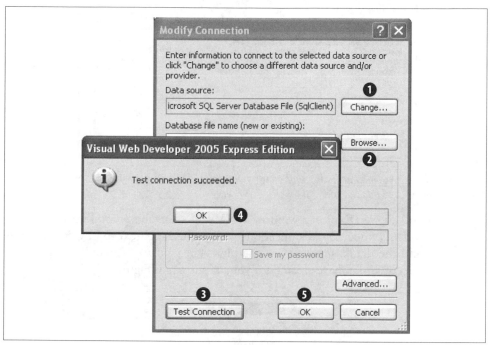

Figure 9-5. In the Add Connection dialog box, click the buttons in the order shown.

I've numbered five of the buttons. Let's take them in order.

First, click the button numbered 1 to change the Data Source to the Data File you just created. This will open a new modal dialog (Change Data Source). From the drop-down, choose Microsoft SQL Server Database File, as shown in Figure 9-6.

Clicking OK will return you to the Add Connection dialog box.

We're up to the button labeled 2. Click the Browse button and navigate to the App_ Data directory for your new application, and then click the *mdf* file that the WAT created for you.

Leave the radio button (hidden in the figure by the Test Connection Succeeded dialog box) set to *Use Windows Authentication*. Don't be confused; you are allowing Windows Authentication to get to the security database only, not to get to the application you are building.

For step 3, click "Test Connection." If all is right, the modal dialog box, unfortunately named "Microsoft Visual Studio," will open saying that your test connection succeeded. Click the OK button (4), which will return you to the Add Connection button, and you can click OK (5).

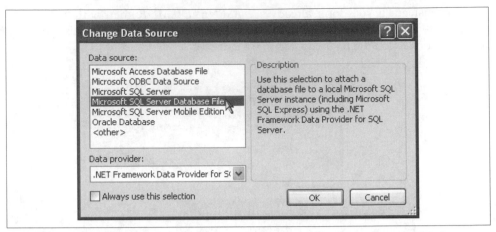

Figure 9-6. The first step in accessing the Security Database is selecting a Microsoft SQL Server Database File as the Data Source.

Visual Studio's Server Explorer window (or VWD's Database Explorer) will now show *aspnetdb.mdf* under DataConnections with a plus sign next to it. Click the plus sign to expand the database, and click the plus sign next to "Tables" to see all the tables in the Security database created for you, as shown in Figure 9-7.

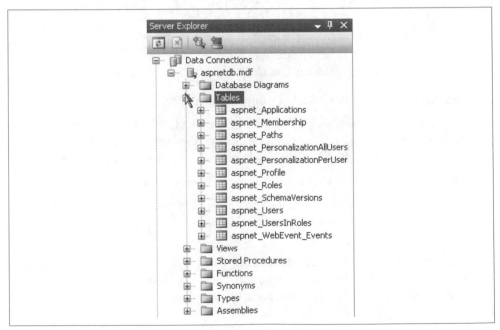

Figure 9-7. Expanding the tables in the Security Database shows all the tables that the Security Database created automatically.

You can look at the data in any of these tables by right-clicking the table name and selecting "Show Table Data."

Managing Users Programmatically

You saw how to create users using the WAT. Now you will add users programmatically, from within your web site. Use the web site created previously in this chapter, FormsBasedSecurityWAT. You will add two new pages: a welcome page that displays different information depending on whether the user is logged in, and a login page that allows a user to log in.

Creating user accounts

In a secured web site, before a user can log in, an account for that user must be created. This can be done in the WAT, as you have seen, but accounts can also be created from within the running program.

Look at the web site created previously in this chapter, FormsBasedSecurityWAT. Delete *Default.aspx* by selecting it in the Solution Explorer and pressing the Delete key.

Add a new page called *CreateAccount.aspx*. Make sure the checkbox for "Place code in separate file" is checked, and the "Select master page" checkbox is not checked.

Switch to Design view and drag a `CreateUserWizard` control from the Login section of the Toolbox onto the page, as shown in Figure 9-8.

The CreateUserWizard control prompts the user for a username, a password (twice), an email address, and a security question and answer. All of this is configurable through the control declaration created in the *.aspx* file for you, through the Properties window, or more commonly, through the Smart Tag, indicated in Figure 9-8.

Click the control and find the `ContinueDestinationPageUrl` property in the Properties window. Click in the cell next to the property, then on the ellipses (...) button that appears in that cell. The Select URL dialog box will appear. Choose *CreateAccount.aspx*—that is, the page itself—so that you will be brought back to the same page after a new user is created.

Set the title of the page by clicking the Design window of the page, finding the Title property in the Properties window, and changing it from `Untitled Page` to `Create User`.

Finally, set the *CreateAccount.aspx* as the startup page by right-clicking the page in the Solution Explorer and selecting Set As Start Page. The resulting page is shown in Figure 9-9.

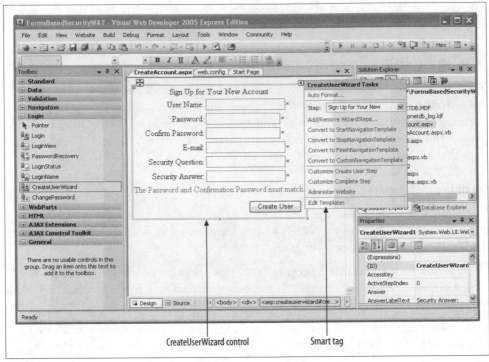

Figure 9-8. *CreateUserWizard control showing the Smart Tag.*

Fill in all the fields (with different values than the user you created before) and click Create User. The new user account will be created and a confirmation screen will be displayed. Click the Continue button on the confirmation screen, which will bring you right back to the CreateAccount page.

Add a few more accounts, and then stop the application. For these examples, we added the following four users:

> dhurwitz
> jliberty
> jmontana
> tbrady

If you would like, examine the database tables to ensure that the new members have been added.

Creating a welcome page

Close the browser if it is open, and then add a new page to the web site called *Welcome.aspx*. Switch to Design view and drag a LoginStatus control from the Login section of the Toolbox onto the form.

Figure 9-9. The CreateAccount.aspx page looks complicated, but it's really just one control that handles everything.

This control looks like a hyperlink with the text Login. The Smart Tag for the control indicates that you are looking at the template for when the user is not logged in, as shown in Figure 9-10. You can use the drop-down in the Smart Tag to see the link and text for Logged In status.

You can use the Properties window to change the properties of the LoginStatus control—for example, to change the displayed text for the logged-in status, LoginText, or the logged-out status, LogoutText.

It would be nice to see who is logged in, or other content, based on whether the current user is logged in or not. To do this, drag a LoginView control from the Login section of the Toolbox onto the page. Notice that this control has two views: AnonymousTemplate and LoggedInTemplate. The template that will be displayed depends on whether the user has logged in—the AnonymousTemplate is presented to users who aren't logged in.

Click the Smart Tag and confirm that the view is set to AnonymousTemplate. Type some text in the box to display when the user is not logged in, as shown in Figure 9-11.

Click the Smart Tag and select the LoggedInTemplate. Drag a LoginName control into the box to display the username of the logged-in user along with some text, as shown in Figure 9-12.

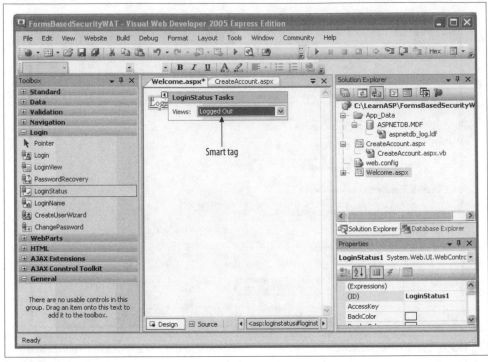

Figure 9-10. The LoginStatus control has a Smart Tag that you can use to customize the messages for logged-in or logged-out users.

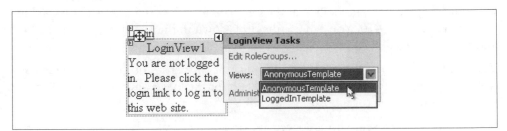

Figure 9-11. The LoginView control also has two separate templates, depending on whether the user is logged in. Here it's showing the Anonymous template, for logged-out users.

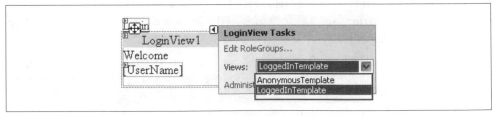

Figure 9-12. Here the LoginView control is showing the Logged In template, and using a LoginName control to greet the user specifically.

Creating a login page

Add a new page to the web site called *Login.aspx*. It must be called exactly that or the other controls will not know which page to call. Switch to Design view and drag a Login control from the Login section of the Toolbox onto the page, as shown in Figure 9-13. The Login control is the primary control your users will use to log in to your site. To make the page look more professional, click the AutoFormat menu item in the Smart Tag, and pick one of the predefined formats.

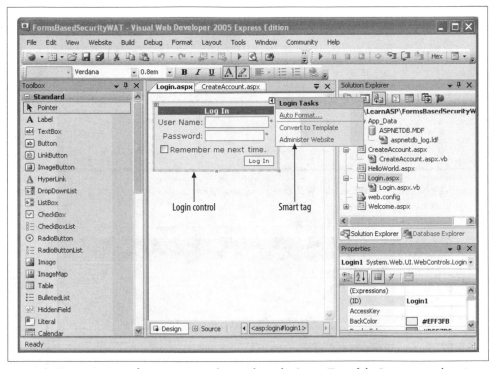

Figure 9-13. You can use the AutoFormat feature from the Smart Tag of the Login control to give your page a more professional appearance.

Make sure that the Welcome page is the Start page and then run the application. The Welcome page will display its "Not Logged In" message, as shown in Figure 9-14.

Click the link to go to the login page. Enter the user name and password of one of the users you created previously. If you enter the credentials correctly, you will see a page similar to that shown in Figure 9-15.

If you enter either of the credentials incorrectly, you will see the page shown in Figure 9-16. You can re-enter the username and password to try again.

You can also use a PasswordRecovery control, which by default invalidates the current password, and sends the user a new one. Using it properly requires you to configure SMTP on your web server, which is slightly too complex for this example.

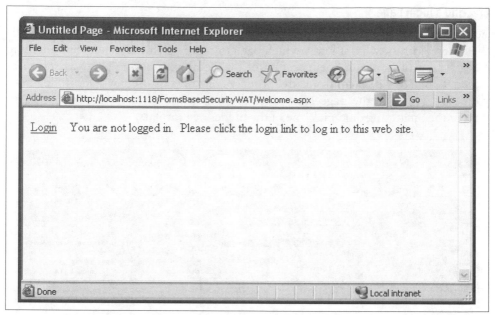

Figure 9-14. When you first see the Welcome page, you're not logged in, so you're greeted the same as any other user.

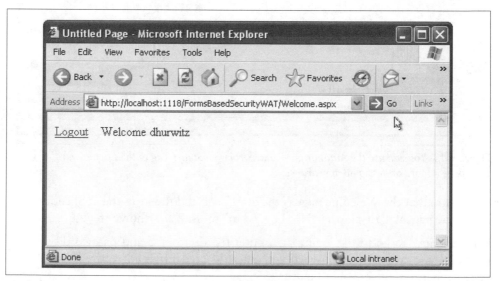

Figure 9-15. Once you log in successfully, the Welcome Page becomes friendlier.

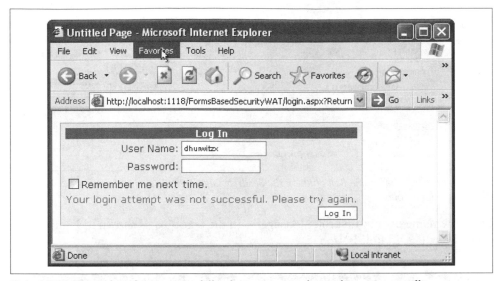

Figure 9-16. If you don't log in successfully, the Login control provides a message telling you so. This message is generated automatically by the control.

Roles

A *role* is a specific set of permissions that has been given a name. Users can be members of one or more roles. For example, a user may be an Administrator, which gives them permission to change data; or a Guest, which does not give them permission to change data. Or a user can be a member of both the Administrator and the User roles, in which case that person will have all the permissions of both roles.

To see this in action, copy the previous example FormBasedSecurityWAT to a new web site—call it SecurityRoles.

Set *Welcome.aspx* as the Start page and run the site to make sure it still works and you can log in.

Use the WAT to enable roles and add the existing users to those roles. Open the WAT by clicking Website → ASP.NET Configuration. When the WAT opens, click the Security tab or link (they are equivalent) to go to the Security page.

There are three management areas across the page, as shown in Figure 9-17. Under the Roles category, there is an "Enable Roles" link, indicated in Figure 9-17. Click this link to enable roles.

The link will change to read "Disable Roles" and the link below, "Create or Manage roles," will become available. Click that link to create some roles.

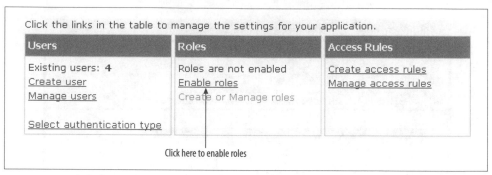

Figure 9-17. Click the Enable Roles link on the Security Page of the Web Site Administration Tool (WAT) to enable roles.

Enter the name of your first role—Manager—in the text box, as shown in Figure 9-18; then click the Add Role button.

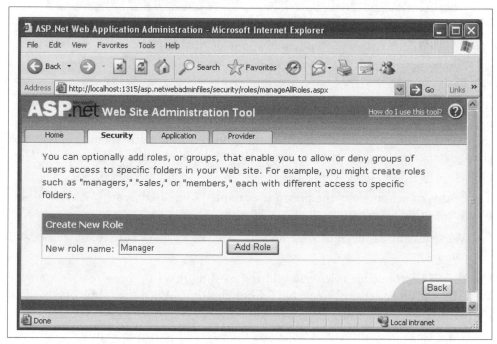

Figure 9-18. Creating a role called Manager in the WAT is simple—just click the Create or Manage Roles link, and create some new roles.

Add two more roles, SalesRep and Customer. The screen will now list all the available roles, as shown in Figure 9-19.

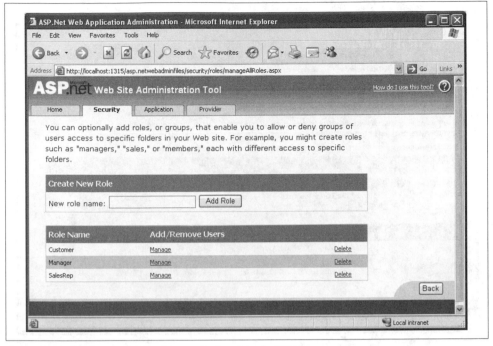

Figure 9-19. All the available roles are displayed in the WAT.

There are links for each role for deleting or otherwise managing the role. The next thing you need to do is add some users to the roles. Under the Add/Remove Users column header, click the Manage link for the Manager role, to bring up a search screen. You can search by username or e-mail address, or, as shown in Figure 9-20, you can click one of the letters to list all the users whose username begins with that letter.

As you can also see in Figure 9-20, we have checked User Is In Role for jliberty to be a member of the Manager role, but jmontana is not a member of that role.

You can also click the Back button at the bottom-right corner of the screen to move back to the Security page and click the Manage Users link under the Users category shown in Figure 9-17, to bring up the user management screen shown in Figure 9-21.

Click the Edit roles link next to the dhurwitz name to get a series of checkboxes for adding dhurwitz to any of the roles. In Figure 9-22, dhurwitz has been added to the Manager and SalesRep roles.

While on this page, also add jmontana and tbrady to the Customer role.

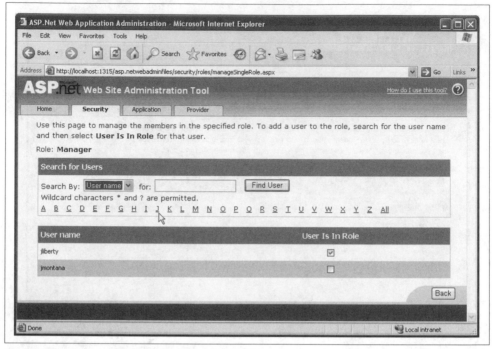

Figure 9-20. You can easily search for users to add to a given role in the Add/Remove Users page.

Restricting Access

Although you have set the startup page of the ongoing example to be *Welcome.aspx*, there is nothing to prevent a user, malicious or otherwise, from entering the URL of a specific page, such as *CreateAccount.aspx*, into the address box of a browser.

To see this, run the current example, with *Welcome.aspx* set as the start page, as you have been doing all along. The browser will open *Welcome.aspx*, with an address similar to the following:

> *http://localhost:1296/SecurityRoles/Welcome.aspx*

You have probably noticed that every time you run a web site from within the IDE, the URL displayed in the browser address box contains localhost and a number separated by a colon. localhost refers to the local machine serving a web page to itself. The number is the *port*, or address into a server. Every time the IDE runs a web site, it chooses at random a different port to use.

Some port numbers are referred to as *well-known ports*, meaning that they have a standardized usage. For example, port 80 is commonly used for HTTP requests (i.e., web sites) and ports 20 and 21 are commonly used for FTP. The port numbers from 1 through 1024 are reserved for well-known ports.

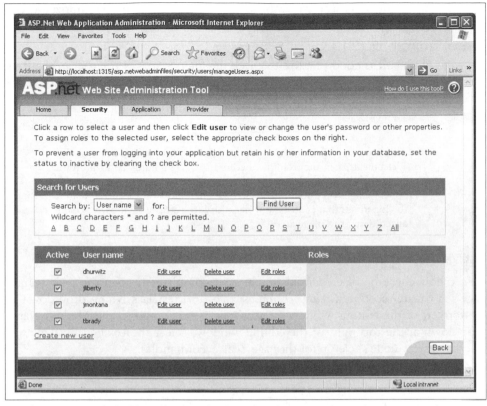

Figure 9-21. Instead of adding users to roles from the roles page, you can use this screen for managing users in the WAT.

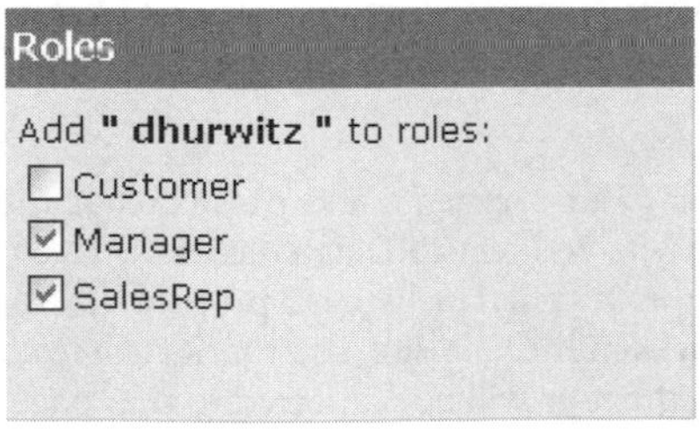

Figure 9-22. When you click the Edit roles link, the page allows you to add a user to roles.

Edit this address to point instead to the CreateAccount page, as follows:

http://localhost:1296/SecurityRoles/CreateAccount.aspx

That page will open, regardless of your credentials (are you logged in; what roles are you in?).

This can lead to obvious security problems, providing access to unauthorized users. It can also cause database corruption or exceptions being thrown when your database code assumes that you will have a valid user id and you have none.

To avoid all this, it is good practice to check the login status of the user in the Page Load event of every page in the web site. If the user is not logged in (or is not in the correct role), you can then redirect the user to the appropriate page (often the login page).

 This security is not necessary in the normal start page of the web site, *Welcome.aspx* in the example, because the LoginStatus control on the page already takes care of this. It may also not be necessary in many "open" pages on public sites where you may not want to force visitors to "log in" until it is absolutely necessary (to retrieve their own personalized data or to place an order).

Testing for login status

To see how checking of credentials might be accomplished, open the code-behind page for CreateAccount, *CreateAccount.aspx.vb*. In the Class Name drop-down at the top left of the editing window, select (Page Events), and in the Method Name drop-down at the top right of the editing window, select the Load event. This will insert an empty code skeleton for the Page_Load event handler.

Type the following code inside the Page_Load method:

```
If User.Identity.IsAuthenticated = False Then
    Response.Redirect("Login.aspx")
End If
```

Now run the application. Before logging in, edit the page address in the browser to go to *CreateAccount.aspx*. Instead of CreateAccount opening, you will be immediately taken to the login page.

 If you enter a valid username and password at this point, the Login control will try to redirect to Default.aspx, a page that does not exist. Instead, set the DestinationPageUrl property of the Login control to one of the pages in the web site, such as *Welcome.aspx*. Then on a successful login, the user will be redirected to that page.

On the other hand, if you run the web site and log in, and then edit the browser address to open CreateAccount, you will in fact go to that page.

Testing for role-based authentication membership

You can also limit access to pages based on the role, or roles, to which the current, logged-in user belongs.

Add another page to the SecurityRoles web site called *ManagersPage.aspx*. As the name implies, this page will be accessible only to managers. To keep the example simple, for now this page will have only an identifying heading and a button to return to the Welcome page, shown in bold in Example 9-1. You can do this in either Source view or Design view.

Example 9-1. The markup for the ManagersPage.aspx

```
<%@ Page Language="VB" AutoEventWireup="false" CodeFile="ManagersPage.aspx.vb"
Inherits="ManagersPage" %>

<!DOCTYPE html PUBLIC "-//W3C//DTD XHTML 1.0 Transitional//EN"
"http://www.w3.org/TR/xhtml1/DTD/xhtml1-transitional.dtd">

<html xmlns="http://www.w3.org/1999/xhtml" >
<head runat="server">
    <title>Untitled Page</title>
</head>
<body>
    <form id="form1" runat="server">
    <div>
        <h1>Manager's Page</h1>
        <asp:Button ID="btnWelcome" runat="server"
            Text="Return to Welcome" />
    </div>
    </form>
</body>
</html>
```

Switch to Design view and double-click the Return to Welcome button to open up an event handler for Click event. Add the following highlighted line of code:

CODE ▶
```
Protected Sub btnWelcome_Click(ByVal sender As Object, _
        ByVal e As System.EventArgs) Handles btnWelcome.Click
    Response.Redirect("Welcome.aspx")
End Sub
```

While you are at it, add a button to the Welcome page for navigating to the Manager's Page, as shown in Figure 9-23. Set the ID of the button to btnManagersPage, because you will be referring to the button in code elsewhere, and set its Enabled property to False. In a moment, you will add some code to the Page_Load event handler to enable or disable the button depending on the login status.

Double-click that button in Design view and add the following highlighted line of code to the Click event handler:

CODE ▶
```
Protected Sub Button1_Click(ByVal sender As Object, _
        ByVal e As System.EventArgs) Handles btnManagersPage.Click
    Response.Redirect("ManagersPage.aspx")
End Sub
```

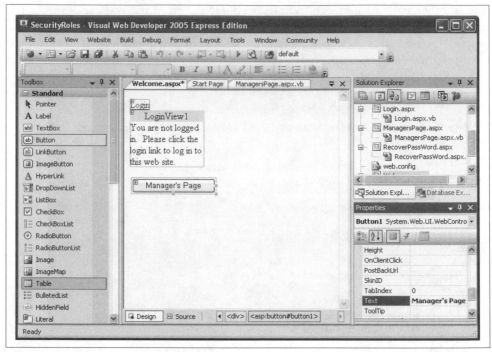

Figure 9-23. Add a button to the Welcome page in Design view, for navigating to the Manager's page.

Next, add an event handler for the Page Load event. Then add the following high-lighted code to run every time the page loads:

```
Protected Sub Page_Load(ByVal sender As Object, _
        ByVal e As System.EventArgs) Handles Me.Load
    If User.Identity.IsAuthenticated = True Then
        btnManagersPage.Enabled = True
    Else
        btnManagersPage.Enabled = False
    End If
End Sub
```

Including both an If and an Else clause ensures that the Enabled state of the button will always be what you want, regardless of the circumstances.

Run the app. The Welcome page opens with the Login link and contents of the AnonymousTemplate displayed, and the Manager's Page button is disabled.

Log in as a user in the managers role, say dhurwitz, and the button will become enabled. Click that button to move to the Manager's Page; then click the button on that page to return to the Welcome page.

There is still a problem with this application, however: If you log in with one of the usernames that are not in the Manager's role, such as tbrady, you still are allowed to go to the Manager's page. Let's fix this.

Go to the code-behind for the Manager's page, *ManagersPage.aspx.vb*. Create an event handler for the Page Load event. Enter the following highlighted code to the event handler:

```
Protected Sub Page_Load(ByVal sender As Object, _
        ByVal e As System.EventArgs) Handles Me.Load
    If User.IsInRole("Manager") = False Then
        Response.Redirect("NoPrivs.aspx")
    End If
End Sub
```

This code will redirect to a page called *NoPrivs.aspx* if the current user is not a member of the Manager role. So, create that page, making it very similar to *ManagersPage.aspx*, with only a heading, some text, and a button to redirect back to the Welcome page, as shown in Figure 9-24.

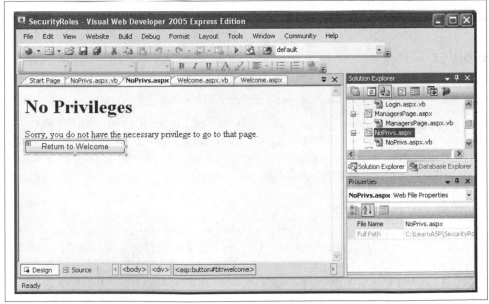

Figure 9-24. The NoPrivs page in Design view. This is the page where users will be redirected if they try to access a page for which they do not have permissions.

Double-click the button to open an event handler for the Click event and enter the following highlighted line of code:

```
Protected Sub btnWelcome_Click(ByVal sender As Object, _
        ByVal e As System.EventArgs) Handles btnWelcome.Click
    Response.Redirect("Welcome.aspx")
End Sub
```

Now when you run the app, if you log in with a username that is a member of the Manager role, you can navigate to the Manager's page. Otherwise, you cannot get to the Manager's page; you are directed instead to NoPrivs.

In a real application, it would make more sense to only enable the Manager's Page button on the Welcome page if the user were a member of the Manager role, not simply logged in. However, then we would not have an easy way to demonstrate how to restrict access to a page based on the role of the current user.

Personalization

Personalization allows the user to modify your site to reflect his or her own tastes. It also allows you to keep track of the user's "progress" through a sequence of steps or selections made on a page from one visit to another. Many sites use personalization to create persistent "wish lists," "shopping carts," and so forth.

This used to be a huge and complicated job—keeping track of a user's set of preferences and the state of a user's personal information. Fortunately, that is all made easier now with ASP.NET 2.0.

Profiles

Copy the previous example, SecurityRoles, to a new web site called SitePersonalization. Set *Welcome.aspx* as the start page and run it to make sure everything still works.

One of the easiest ways to personalize a site is to define profile information that you will maintain for each user. Profile information can include such simple data as the user's real name, address, and telephone numbers, or, as you'll see later, it can include more complex user-defined data.

Simple data types

To use profiles, you have to make some modifications to your *web.config* file for the project. The first step is adding a new section called <profile>, setting the enabled property to true, and specifying defaultProvider as AspNetSqlProfileProvider. The defaultProvider property holds the data for the profiles; AspNetSqlProfileProvider is the built-in provider for ASP.NET.

Then you need to modify *web.config* to indicate which pieces of profile information to save. You add a <properties> section to the <profile> declaration, and then use the <add> attribute to add the names of any profile data you want to save. Add the highlighted lines in Example 9-2 to your *web.config*.

Example 9-2. Modifications to web.config for enabling profiles

```
<?xml version="1.0"?>
<configuration xmlns="http://schemas.microsoft.com/.NetConfiguration/v2.0">
    <appSettings/>
    <connectionStrings/>
    <system.web>
        <roleManager enabled="true" />
```

```
            <compilation debug="true" strict="false" explicit="true"/>
            <profile enabled="true" defaultProvider="AspNetSqlProfileProvider">
                <properties>
                    <add name="lastName" />
                    <add name="firstName" />
                    <add name="phoneNumber" />
                    <add name="birthDate" type="System.DateTime" />
                </properties>
            </profile>
            <pages>
                <!-- stuff omitted for brevity --!>
            </pages>
            <authentication mode="Forms"/>
        </system.web>
    </configuration>
```

 Your *web.config* file may look somewhat different depending on your machine configuration and the databases you have installed. Also, boilerplate comments and lines unrelated to this topic have been removed from Example 9-2.

The configuration shown in Example 9-2 causes ASP.NET to create storage for four pieces of information: first and last name, phone number, and birth date. The default storage type is String. Notice, however, that you are storing the birth date as a DateTime object.

You can gather this personalization information any way you like. For this example, open *Welcome.aspx* and switch to Design view. Click the Smart Tag of the Login-View control and select the LoggedInTemplate view, as shown in Figure 9-25.

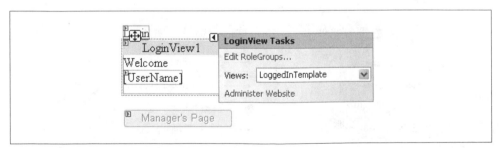

Figure 9-25. Select the LoggedInTemplate view of the LoginView control. You're currently welcoming the user by using the UserName, but you'll change that.

Now drag a HyperLink control from the Toolbox onto the LoginView control. Set its Text property to "Add Profile Info" and the NavigateUrl property to ProfileInfo.aspx (which you will create shortly). The Design view will look something like Figure 9-26.

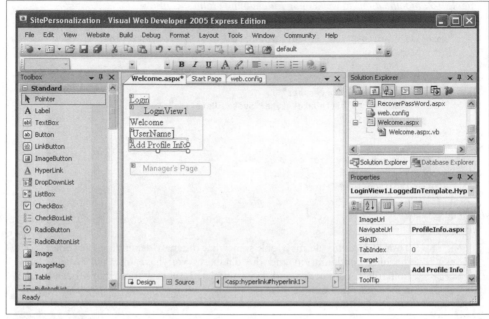

Figure 9-26. *Add the HyperLink control to the LoginView control to link to the page where you'll gather profile information.*

Now create the page for gathering the profile information referred to in the NavigateUrl property of the HyperLink, *ProfileInfo.aspx*. Remember to check the box to place the code in a separate file. Add a table for layout to the page, and within the table, add labels and TextBoxes, as well as a Save button, as shown in Design view in Figure 9-27.

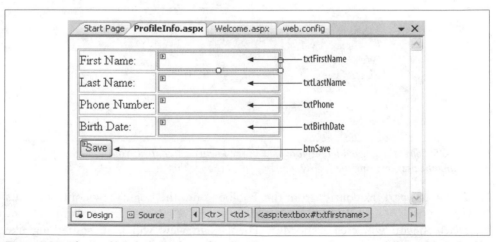

Figure 9-27. *The ProfileInfo page, shown here in Design view, is where users will enter their profile information.*

All that remains to be done is to add an event handler for the Save button. Double-click the Save button in Design view to open up a code skeleton for the Click event handler. Add the following highlighted code:

```
Protected Sub btnSave_Click(ByVal sender As Object, _
        ByVal e As System.EventArgs) Handles btnSave.Click
    If Profile.IsAnonymous = False Then
        Profile.lastName = Me.txtLastName.Text
        Profile.firstName = Me.txtFirstName.Text
        Profile.phoneNumber = Me.txtPhone.Text
        Profile.birthDate = CType(Me.txtBirthDate.Text, System.DateTime)
    End If
    Response.Redirect("Welcome.aspx")
End Sub
```

Until the web site is built for the first time, the IDE will think all these Profile properties are invalid and underline them with the dreaded squiggly line. Either click the Build → Build Web Site menu item or just run the page.

The first line you added uses the IsAnonymous property of the Profile object. You can't set the profile properties if the user isn't logged in, so you need to check that first. The Profile object has properties that correspond to the properties you added in *web.config*. To test that the Profile object has, in fact, stored this data, add a Panel control to the bottom of the Welcome page, as shown in Figure 9-28. Set the ID property of the Panel control to pnlInfo and set its Visible property to False, so that it will not normally display. The Labels within the Panel control should be named lblFullName, lblPhone, and lblBirthDate. You should also set the Text properties of these Labels as shown in Figure 9-28.

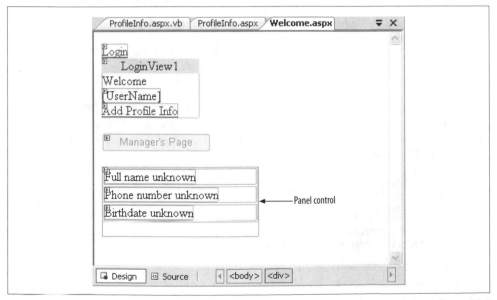

Figure 9-28. WelcomePage in Design view showing the panel for displaying the Profile information.

The panel has a table with three rows, and each row has a Label control that is initialized to say that the value is unknown (this is not normally needed, but is included here to ensure that the data you see is retrieved from the Profile object). When the page is loaded, the event handler checks to see if you have Profile data for this user and, if so, you assign that data to the appropriate controls and set the Visible property of pnlInfo to True.

You'll need to add a bit of code to the code-behind for the Welcome page, *Welcome. aspx.vb*, so that when the page loads, it will check to see if you have a profile, and if so, it will make the panel visible. You have previously created an event handler for the Page Load event for this page and added some code, so add the highlighted code from Example 9-3 to that pre-existing event handler.

Example 9-3. Page_Load for Welcome page showing how Profile information is retrieved and displayed

```
Protected Sub Page_Load(ByVal sender As Object, _
        ByVal e As System.EventArgs) Handles Me.Load
    If User.Identity.IsAuthenticated = True Then
        btnManagersPage.Enabled = True
    Else
        btnManagersPage.Enabled = False
    End If

    If Not IsPostBack And _
            Profile.UserName IsNot Nothing And _
            Profile.IsAnonymous = False Then
        Me.pnlInfo.Visible = True
        Me.lblFullName.Text = Profile.firstName & " " & Profile.lastName
        Me.lblPhone.Text = Profile.phoneNumber
        Me.lblBirthDate.Text = Profile.birthDate.ToShortDateString()
    Else
        Me.pnlInfo.Visible = False
    End If
End Sub
```

When you start the application, you are asked to log in. Once logged in, a new hyperlink appears: Add Profile Info. This was created by the hyperlink you added to the LoggedInTemplate earlier. Clicking that link brings you to your new profile page, as shown in Figure 9-29.

When you click Save and return to the Welcome page, the Page_Load event fires. The Page_Load contains a three-part If statement:

CODE ▶
```
    If Not IsPostBack And _
            Profile.UserName IsNot Nothing And _
            Profile.IsAnonymous = False Then
```

All parts of the If statement evaluate True: This page is not loading as a result of a postback, the UserName value in the profile is not Nothing, and the user is logged in, and thus not anonymous.

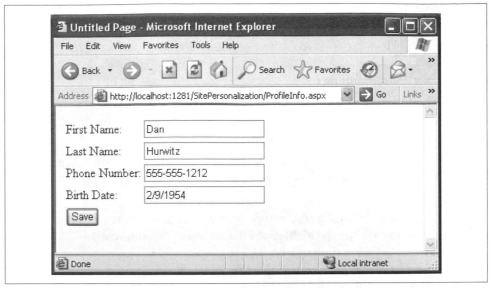

Figure 9-29. ProfileInfo page for gathering profile information.

Your profile information is displayed, as shown in Figure 9-30.

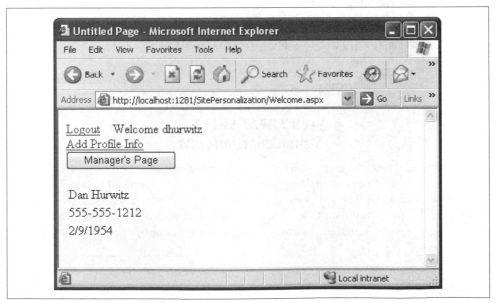

Figure 9-30. Profile information displayed on the Welcome page.

If you are logged in but have not yet entered any profile data, the default values will display, which are a blank string for string values and 01/01/0001 for the date.

Complex data types

The information we've saved so far in the profile has been simple (built-in) data, but of course you may want to save either user-defined types or collections. These are considered "complex data types" and require just a bit of extra work, as you'll see with the *Sports* profile information in the very next example.

Close the browser and copy the previous example, SitePersonalization, to a new web site called SitePersonalizationComplex. Set the Welcome page as the Start page and run the site to verify that everything works.

In this web site, you will add a CheckBoxList control to the ProfileInfo page so users can select their favorite sports and store them in a profile using a StringCollection object.

Add a new property, called Sports, of type StringCollection, to the profile element in *web.config*, as indicated by the highlighted line of code in Example 9-4.

Example 9-4. Profile element of web.config with a complex type added

```
<profile enabled="true" defaultProvider="AspNetSqlProfileProvider">
    <properties>
        <add name="lastName" />
        <add name="firstName" />
        <add name="phoneNumber" />
        <add name="birthDate" type="System.DateTime" />
        <add name="Sports"
            type="System.Collections.Specialized.StringCollection" />
    </properties>
</profile>
```

—VB CHEAT SHEET—
StringCollection Class

The StringCollection class, which is a member of the System.Collections. Specialized namespace, is used to represent a collection of strings. Elements within the collection can be accessed using a zero-based integer index. A number of methods are provided for manipulating the collection, including the ability to add items, find the index of specific items, and remove items either by index or by specifying the string.

Edit the page *ProfileInfo.aspx*. Add a row to the layout table above the Save button and put a CheckBoxList control in that row—name it cblSports. In Design view, click the Smart Tag of the CheckBoxList and click Edit Items.... Add several sports to the ListItem Collection Editor dialog box, as shown in Figure 9-31.

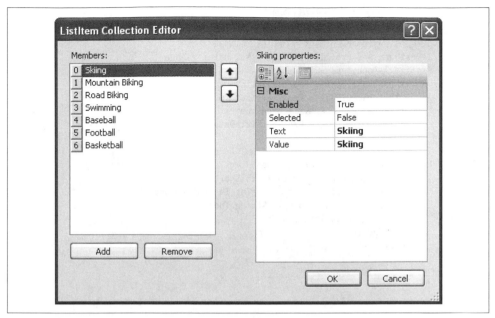

Figure 9-31. Adding items to the CheckBoxList control.

Now you need to enhance the event handler for the Save button to add the selected items to the new Profile property, as shown in the highlighted code in Example 9-5.

Example 9-5. btnSave_Click event handler modified to process complex Profile property

```
Protected Sub btnSave_Click(ByVal sender As Object, _
        ByVal e As System.EventArgs) Handles btnSave.Click
    If Profile.IsAnonymous = False Then
        Profile.lastName = Me.txtLastName.Text
        Profile.firstName = Me.txtFirstName.Text
        Profile.phoneNumber = Me.txtPhone.Text
        Profile.birthDate = CType(Me.txtBirthDate.Text, System.DateTime)

        Profile.Sports = New System.Collections.Specialized.StringCollection( )
        For Each item As ListItem In Me.cblSports.Items
            If item.Selected Then
                Profile.Sports.Add(item.Value.ToString( ))
            End If
        Next

    End If
    Response.Redirect("Welcome.aspx")
End Sub
```

You also need to create an event handler for the Page Load event, so the page will open with the user's up-to-date profile information. Create that event the same way you did earlier, and then add the body of the method, highlighted in Example 9-6.

Example 9-6. Page_Load for ProfileInfo.aspx.vb

```
Protected Sub Page_Load(ByVal sender As Object, _
        ByVal e As System.EventArgs) Handles Me.Load
    If Not IsPostBack And Profile.UserName IsNot Nothing Then
        If Profile.IsAnonymous = False Then
            Me.txtLastName.Text = Profile.lastName
            Me.txtFirstName.Text = Profile.firstName
            Me.txtPhone.Text = Profile.phoneNumber
            Me.txtBirthDate.Text = Profile.birthDate.ToShortDateString()
        End If

        If Profile.Sports IsNot Nothing Then
            For Each item As ListItem In Me.cblSports.Items
                For Each profileString As String In Profile.Sports
                    If item.Text = profileString Then
                        item.Selected = True
                    End If
                Next
            Next
        End If
    End If
End Sub
```

Each time you navigate to the Profile page, the values are updated from the existing profile (if any) in Page_Load and you are free to change them and save the new values, as shown in Figure 9-32.

However, after you save this page and go back to the Welcome page, the sports selections are not displayed. To do so, add a ListBox control, called lbSports, to the already existing Panel control pnlInfo, as shown in Figure 9-33. The selections will be displayed in lbSports.

Modify the pre-existing Page_Load sub in *Welcome.aspx.vb* to bind the contents of the Profile.Sports property to the ListBox, by adding the highlighted code from Example 9-7.

Example 9-7. Page_Load for Welcome.aspx.vb modified to bind the Profile.Sports data to the ListBox

```
Protected Sub Page_Load(ByVal sender As Object, _
        ByVal e As System.EventArgs) Handles Me.Load
    If User.Identity.IsAuthenticated = True Then
        btnManagersPage.Enabled = True
    Else
        btnManagersPage.Enabled = False
    End If

    If Not IsPostBack And _
            Profile.UserName IsNot Nothing And _
            Profile.IsAnonymous = False Then
```

Example 9-7. Page_Load for Welcome.aspx.vb modified to bind the Profile.Sports data to the ListBox (continued)

```
        Me.pnlInfo.Visible = True
        Me.lblFullName.Text = Profile.firstName & " " & Profile.lastName
        Me.lblPhone.Text = Profile.phoneNumber
        Me.lblBirthDate.Text = Profile.birthDate.ToShortDateString()

        If Profile.Sports IsNot Nothing Then
            For Each sport As String In Profile.Sports
                Me.lbSports.Items.Add(sport)
            Next
        End If
    Else
        Me.pnlInfo.Visible = False
    End If

End Sub
```

Figure 9-32. The ProfileInfo page now has a CheckBoxList control showing complex profile properties, and furthermore, the Profile object retains the data, so that it can be reloaded whenever the user returns to this page.

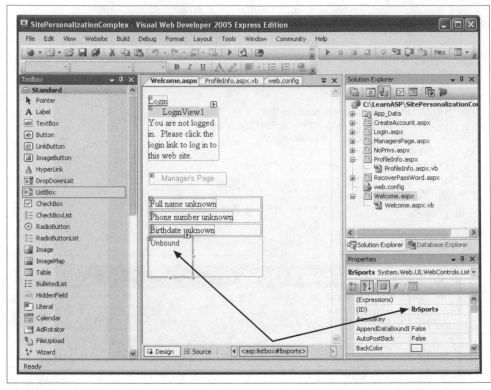

Figure 9-33. Add a ListBox control to the Welcome page to display the complex profile property.

When you click Save in the Profile page and return to the Welcome page, your saved profile information is displayed, as shown in Figure 9-34.

Anonymous Personalization

Often you will want to allow your user to use your site for a while before logging in. Along the way, the user may fill in information that you will want to store in the user's profile once the user is logged in. Imagine, for example, that the user has a shopping cart. Your use model may be that anonymous users (those who are not logged in) may add items to the cart. If they want the cart to persist after they leave, or if they want to buy the items, they must log in; otherwise, you'll toss the cart after their session times out.

You need a way to store their anonymous profile, and, more important, you need a way to merge that anonymous profile with their actual profile once you know who they really are. No problem; ASP.NET provides for that very circumstance.

Copy the previous example, SitePersonalizationComplex, to a new web site called AnonymousPersonalization. Set *Welcome.aspx* as the Start page and run the site to verify that everything is working.

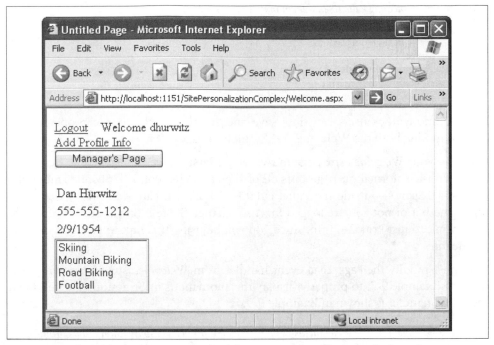

Figure 9-34. The Welcome page now displays the contents of Profile.Sports for logged-in users.

To enable anonymous personalization, add the highlighted lines from Example 9-8 to your *web.config* file. Also highlighted in Example 9-8 is adding the `allowAnonymous` attribute to the Sports profile property.

Example 9-8. web.config edits to enable anonymous personalization

```xml
<?xml version="1.0"?>
<configuration xmlns="http://schemas.microsoft.com/.NetConfiguration/v2.0">
    <appSettings/>
    <connectionStrings/>
    <system.web>
        <anonymousIdentification enabled="true" />
        <roleManager enabled="true" />
        <compilation debug="true" strict="false" explicit="true"/>
        <profile enabled="true" defaultProvider="AspNetSqlProfileProvider">
            <properties>
                <add name="lastName" />
                <add name="firstName" />
                <add name="phoneNumber" />
                <add name="birthDate" type="System.DateTime" />
                <add name="Sports"
                    type="System.Collections.Specialized.StringCollection"
                    allowAnonymous="true" />
            </properties>
        </profile>
```

Example 9-8. web.config edits to enable anonymous personalization (continued)

```
        <pages>
            <!-- stuff omitted for brevity --!>
        </pages>
        <authentication mode="Forms"/>
    </system.web>
</configuration>
```

Because anonymous users can now save and see the Sports profile property, you need to modify both the Welcome and ProfileInfo pages.

Redesign your *Welcome.aspx* page in two ways: First, move the HyperLink that leads to the Profile Information page outside of the LoginView control. Second, move the ListBox (lbSports) outside the Panel pnlInfo. Thus, you can see both of these features whether or not you are logged in. Also, change the text on the Add Profile Info HyperLink to just Profile Info, since you will be using this link to add and edit the profile info.

You must modify the Page_Load event handler from *Welcome.aspx.vb*, shown previously in Example 9-7, to properly display the anonymous information. The modified Page_Load handler is shown in Example 9-9.

Example 9-9. Page_Load in Welcome.aspx.vb modified to properly display anonymous profile properties

```
Protected Sub Page_Load(ByVal sender As Object, _
        ByVal e As System.EventArgs) Handles Me.Load
    If User.Identity.IsAuthenticated = True Then
        btnManagersPage.Enabled = True
    Else
        btnManagersPage.Enabled = False
    End If


    If Not IsPostBack And _
            Profile.UserName IsNot Nothing Then
        If Profile.IsAnonymous = False Then
            Me.pnlInfo.Visible = True
            Me.lblFullName.Text = Profile.firstName & " " & Profile.lastName
            Me.lblPhone.Text = Profile.phoneNumber
            Me.lblBirthDate.Text = Profile.birthDate.ToShortDateString()
        End If

        If Profile.Sports IsNot Nothing Then
            For Each sport As String In Profile.Sports
                Me.lbSports.Items.Add(sport)
            Next
        End If
    Else
        Me.pnlInfo.Visible = False
    End If

End Sub
```

When an anonymous user fills in the profile information, the user will automatically be assigned a Globally Unique Identifier (GUID), and an entry will be made in the database for that ID. However, note that only those properties marked with allowAnonymous may be stored, so you must modify your btnSave_Click event handler in *ProfileInfo.aspx.vb*. Bracket the entries for all the profile elements *except* Sports in an If statement that tests whether the user is currently Anonymous. The new btnSave_Click event handler for *ProfileInfo.aspx.vb* is shown in Example 9-10.

Example 9-10. Save event handler for ProfileInfo.aspx.vb with code for saving Sports property moved outside of test for IsAnonymous

```
Protected Sub btnSave_Click(ByVal sender As Object, _
      ByVal e As System.EventArgs) Handles btnSave.Click
   If Profile.IsAnonymous = False Then
      Profile.lastName = Me.txtLastName.Text
      Profile.firstName = Me.txtFirstName.Text
      Profile.phoneNumber = Me.txtPhone.Text
      Profile.birthDate = CType(Me.txtBirthDate.Text, System.DateTime)
   End If

   Profile.Sports = New System.Collections.Specialized.StringCollection()
   For Each item As ListItem In Me.cblSports.Items
      If item.Selected Then
         Profile.Sports.Add(item.Value.ToString())
      End If
   Next

   Response.Redirect("Welcome.aspx")
End Sub
```

The effect of the new code shown in Example 9-10 is that you check whether the IsAnonymous property is False. If it is, then you are dealing with a logged-in user, and you can get all of the properties; otherwise, you can get only those that are allowed for anonymous users.

Modify the *ProfileInfo* page so that the non-anonymous data is in a panel that will be invisible for users who are not logged in. The simplest way to do this may be to switch to Source view and bracket the non-anonymous code inside a panel (don't forget to end the anonymous table before ending the panel, then inserting another opening table tag), as shown in Example 9-11.

Example 9-11. ProfileInfo.aspx with the addition of a panel for hiding nonanonymous information

```
<%@ Page Language="VB" AutoEventWireup="false" CodeFile="ProfileInfo.aspx.vb"
   Inherits="ProfileInfo" %>

<!DOCTYPE html PUBLIC "-//W3C//DTD XHTML 1.0 Transitional//EN"
   "http://www.w3.org/TR/xhtml1/DTD/xhtml1-transitional.dtd">
```

Example 9-11. ProfileInfo.aspx with the addition of a panel for hiding nonanonymous information (continued)

```
<html xmlns="http://www.w3.org/1999/xhtml" >
<head runat="server">
    <title>Untitled Page</title>
</head>
<body>
    <form id="form1" runat="server">
    <div>
        <asp:Panel ID="pnlNonAnonymousInfo" runat="server" >
            <table>
                <tr>
                    <td>First Name:</td>
                    <td>
                        <asp:TextBox ID="txtFirstName" runat="server" />
                    </td>
                </tr>
                <tr>
                    <td>Last Name:</td>
                    <td>
                        <asp:TextBox ID="txtLastName" runat="server" />
                    </td>
                </tr>
                <tr>
                    <td>Phone Number:</td>
                    <td>
                        <asp:TextBox ID="txtPhone" runat="server" />
                    </td>
                </tr>
                <tr>
                    <td>Birth Date:</td>
                    <td>
                        <asp:TextBox ID="txtBirthDate" runat="server" />
                    </td>
                </tr>
            </table>
        </asp:Panel>
        <table>
            <tr>
                <td colspan="2">
                    <asp:CheckBoxList ID="cblSports" runat="server" >
                        <asp:ListItem>Skiing</asp:ListItem>
                        <asp:ListItem>Mountain Biking</asp:ListItem>
                        <asp:ListItem>Road Biking</asp:ListItem>
                        <asp:ListItem>Swimming</asp:ListItem>
                        <asp:ListItem>Baseball</asp:ListItem>
                        <asp:ListItem>Football</asp:ListItem>
                        <asp:ListItem>Basketball</asp:ListItem>
                    </asp:CheckBoxList>
                </td>
            </tr>
```

Example 9-11. ProfileInfo.aspx with the addition of a panel for hiding nonanonymous information (continued)

```
            <tr>
                <td colspan="2">
                    <asp:Button ID="btnSave" runat="server" Text="Save"/>
                </td>
            </tr>
        </table>

    </div>
    </form>
</body>
</html>
```

In order to hide this panel if the user is anonymous, edit the Page_Load event handler in *ProfileInfo.aspx.vb*, as shown in Example 9-12. This code controls the visibility of pnlNonAnonymousInfo based on whether or not the user is anonymous. Under any circumstances, the Sports preferences will be displayed.

Example 9-12. Page_Load in ProfileInfo.aspx.vb modified to properly display anonymous profile properties

```
Protected Sub Page_Load(ByVal sender As Object, _
        ByVal e As System.EventArgs) Handles Me.Load
    If Not IsPostBack And Profile.UserName IsNot Nothing Then
        If Profile.IsAnonymous = True Then
            Me.pnlNonAnonymousInfo.Visible = False
        Else
            Me.pnlNonAnonymousInfo.Visible = True
            Me.txtLastName.Text = Profile.lastName
            Me.txtFirstName.Text = Profile.firstName
            Me.txtPhone.Text = Profile.phoneNumber
            Me.txtBirthDate.Text = Profile.birthDate.ToShortDateString()
        End If

        If Profile.Sports IsNot Nothing Then
            For Each item As ListItem In Me.cblSports.Items
                For Each profileString As String In Profile.Sports
                    If item.Text = profileString Then
                        item.Selected = True
                    End If
                Next
            Next
        End If ' close for If Profile.Sports IsNot Nothing
    End If ' close for If Not IsPostBack And Profile.UserName IsNot Nothing
End Sub
```

Run the application. Do *not* log in, but do click the Profile Info link. Select a few sports and click Save. When you return to the Welcome page, you are still not logged in, but your selected sports are displayed, as shown in Figure 9-35.

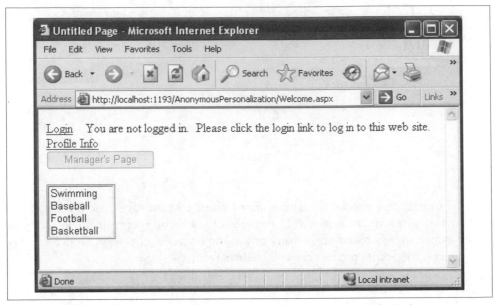

Figure 9-35. *The Profile information for an anonymous user is reflected on the Welcome page, without logging in.*

Migrating anonymous data to an actual user's record

When the user *does* log in, you must migrate the Profile data you've accumulated for the anonymous user to the authenticated user's record (so that, for example, shopping cart items are not lost). You do this by writing a global handler in *global.asax*.

Your project probably does not yet have a *global.asax* file, so click the Website → Add New Item menu item. One of your choices will be Global Application Class, and it will default to the name *global.asax*. Click Add to accept the default name.

When a user logs in to an ASP.NET application, the MigrateAnonymous event is fired automatically. You can handle that event with a method in *global.asax*. The code to do so is listed in Example 9-13.

Example 9-13. MigrateAnonymous event handler in global.asax

```
Sub Profile_MigrateAnonymous(ByVal sender As Object, _
  ByVal e As ProfileMigrateEventArgs)
    Dim anonymousProfile As ProfileCommon = Profile.GetProfile(e.AnonymousID)
    If anonymousProfile IsNot Nothing And _
     anonymousProfile.Sports IsNot Nothing Then
        For Each str As String In anonymousProfile.Sports
            Profile.Sports.Remove(str)    ' remove duplicates
            Profile.Sports.Add(str)
        Next
    End If
End Sub
```

The event argument for `MigrateAnonymous` is of type `ProfileMigrateEventArgs`. This event argument has a property called `AnonymousID`, which contains the ID of the anonymous user (this is all done automatically). The first step, then, in this method is to get the profile that corresponds to the `AnonymousID` of the anonymous user:

```
Dim anonymousProfile As ProfileCommon = Profile.GetProfile(e.AnonymousId)
```

If there is such a profile—that is, if the profile is not `Nothing`—then you know that there is a matching anonymous profile, and that you may choose whatever data you need from that profile. In this case, you copy over the `Sports` collection.

Themes and Skins

Many users like to personalize their favorite web sites by setting the look and feel to meet their own aesthetic preferences. ASP.NET 2.0 supports that requirement with "themes."

A *theme* is a collection of skins. A *skin* describes how a *control* should look. A skin can define style sheet attributes, images, colors, and so forth.

Having multiple themes allows your users to choose how they want your site to look by switching from one set of skins to another at the touch of a button. Combined with personalization, your site can remember the look and feel each user prefers.

There are two types of themes. The first, called *stylesheet themes*, define styles that may be overridden by the page or control. These are, essentially, equivalent to CSS style sheets. The second type, called *customization themes*, cannot be overridden. You set a stylesheet theme by adding the `StyleSheetTheme` attribute to the `Page` directive, and, similarly, you set a customization theme by setting the `Theme` attribute in the `Page` directive.

In any given page, the properties for the controls are set in this order:

- Properties are applied first from a stylesheet theme.
- Properties are then overridden based on properties set in the control.
- Properties are then overridden based on a customization theme.

Thus, the customization theme is guaranteed to have the final word in determining the look and feel of the control.

Skins themselves come in two flavors: *default skins* and *explicitly named skins*. Thus, you might create a Labels skin file called *Labels.skin* with this declaration:

```
<asp:Label runat="server"
    ForeColor="Blue" Font-Size="Large"
    Font-Bold="True" Font-Italic="True" />
```

This is a default skin for all `Label` controls. It looks just like the declaration of an ASP.NET `Label` control (minus the ID attribute), but it is housed in a skin file and, thus, is used to define the look and feel of all Label objects within that skin file's theme.

In addition, however, you might decide that some labels must be red. To accomplish this, create a second skin, but assign this skin a `SkinID` property:

```
<asp:Label runat="server" SkinID="RedLabel"
    ForeColor="Red" Font-Size="Large"
    Font-Bold="True" Font-Italic="True" />
```

Any label that does not have a `SkinID` attribute will get the default skin; any label that sets `SkinID="Red"` will get your named skin.

The steps to providing a personalized web site are as follows:

1. Create the test site.

2. Organize your themes and skins.

3. Enable themes and skins for your site.

4. Specify themes declaratively if you wish.

Create the Test Site

To demonstrate the use of themes and skins, copy the previous example web site, AnonymousPersonalization, to a new web site, called Themes. Set the start page to *Welcome.aspx* and test the application to make sure it still works as expected.

The first thing to do is to add some controls whose look and feel you can set.

Open *Welcome.aspx*, create a table with two rows and four columns for layout underneath `lbSports`, and drag on some new controls, as shown in Figure 9-36.

There are four labels: `lblListBox`, `lblRadioButtonList`, `lblCalendar`, and `lblTextBox`. Each of these labels provides a caption for the neighboring control, a ListBox, a RadioButtonList, a Calendar, and a TextBox, respectively. Use the default properties for all, other than the IDs and Text properties of the Label controls.

You'll also need to click the Smart Tag for both `ListBox1` and `RadioButtonList1`. For each of these, choose Edit the List items. In the ListItem Collection Editor, add four items to `ListBox1` and six items to `RadioButtonList1`, the result of which is shown in Figure 9-36. In this example, the ListItems are named First Item, RadioButton1, and so on. These are not the default names; they are just chosen to make the example clear.

You will use themes to change the look and feel of the new controls.

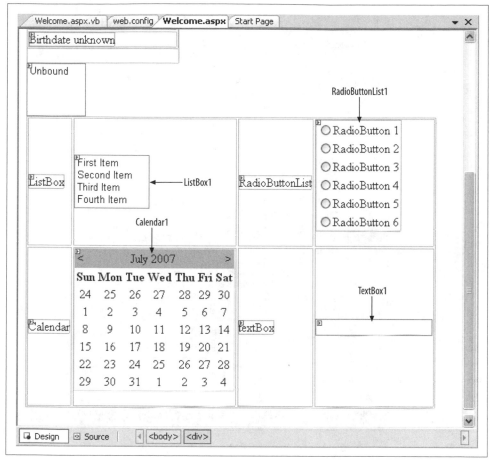

Figure 9-36. Themes test page in Design view showing the four Label controls and the controls they caption.

Organize Site Themes and Skins

Themes are stored in your project in a special folder named App_Themes. To create this folder, go to Solution Explorer, right-click the web site, and choose Add ASP.NET Folder → Theme, as shown in Figure 9-37. Name the new folder *Dark Blue*—the folder *App_Themes* will be created automatically, with a Theme folder named *Dark Blue* immediately under it. Right-click App_Themes in the Solution Explorer and again select Add ASP.NET Folder. Create a second theme folder, named *Psychedelic*.

Right-click the *Dark Blue* theme folder and choose Add New Item. From the template lists, choose Skin File and name it *Button.skin* (to hold all the button skins for your Dark Blue theme), as shown in Figure 9-38.

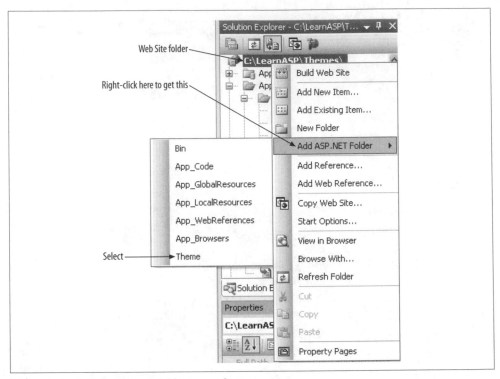

Figure 9-37. Adding a Theme folder to a web site.

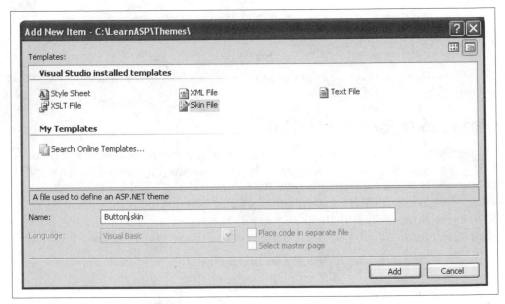

Figure 9-38. Adding a new Skin file.

Each skin file is just a text file that contains a definition for the control type, but with no ID. Thus, your *Button.skin* file for the Dark Blue theme might look like this:

```
<asp:Button runat="server"
    ForeColor="Blue"
    Font-Size="Large" Font-Bold="True" Font-Italic="True" />
```

Create skin files for each of the following types in both themes:

- *Button.skin*
- *Calendar.skin*
- *Label.skin*
- *ListBox.skin*
- *RadioButtonList.skin*
- *TextBox.skin*

 It is not required that the name of the skin file corresponds to the type of control referenced in the file, but it does simplify site maintenance. In fact, it is not even necessary for each control to go into a separate skin file, so you could put them all into a single skin file.

At this point, your Solution Explorer should look more or less like Figure 9-39.

The rest of these skin files are empty right now, so you should create some skins for the purpose of this example. Copy the code from *Button.skin*, and paste it into *Calendar.skin*. Change asp:Button to asp:Calendar, and now the calendar skin file is ready to go. Use the same procedure for all the skin files in the Dark Blue theme. Then do the same for the skin files in the Psychedelic theme, but feel free to change the color and size of the fonts in these files as you see fit.

Enable Themes and Skins

To let your users choose the theme they like and have their preference stored in their profile, you need only to add a single line to the properties element in the profile element of *web.config*:

```
<add name="Theme" />
```

Strictly speaking, adding this line to *web.config* is not necessary to enable themes on a site. It is only necessary to enable saving themes to a user profile.

Save and rebuild your application.

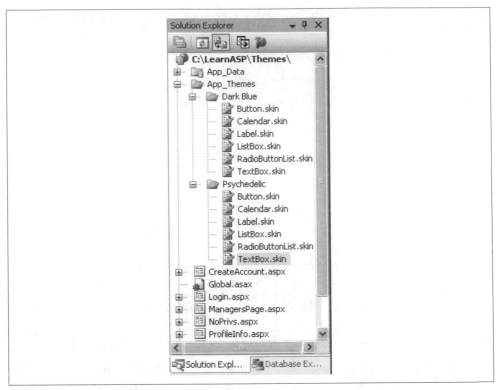

Figure 9-39. Skins in Solution Explorer.

 In order to run an ASP.NET web site, the application must be *built*, or compiled. When you run a web site from within the IDE, it is built automatically, as indicated on the status line at the bottom of the window. It is also possible to build the application without running it by clicking the Build menu item and choosing one of the options: Build Page, Build Web Site, or Rebuild Web Site. Normally, a page or code file is not rebuilt if nothing has changed. The Rebuild menu item forces a rebuild of all components.

Sometimes it is helpful to build the site without running it just to check for syntax and compiler errors. Also, sometimes the IDE gets confused until the app is rebuilt, so everything is known to the system.

That was easy.

Specify Themes for Your Page

You can set the themes on your page either declaratively or programmatically. For example, to set a theme declaratively for *Welcome.aspx*, add the Theme attribute to the Page directive:

```
<%@ Page Language="VB" AutoEventWireup="false" CodeFile="Welcome.aspx.vb"
        Inherits="Welcome" Theme="Dark Blue" %>
```

Set *Welcome.aspx* as the start page. Run the app now and you will see the Dark Blue theme applied, as shown in Figure 9-40. (Obviously the monochromatic printed book will not show the colors in full splendor.)

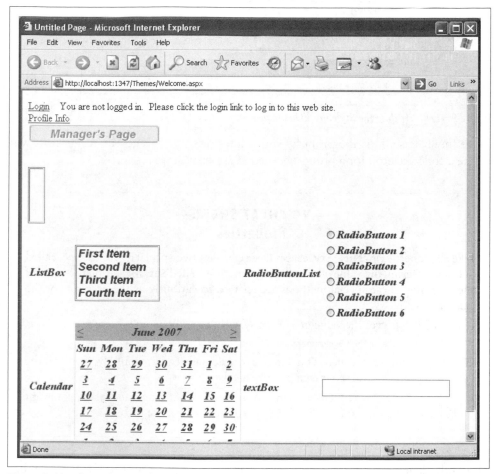

Figure 9-40. *The page is rendered using the Dark Blue theme as a result of adding the Theme attribute to the Page directive.*

You can also set the theme programmatically, either by hardcoding it or (even better) by setting it from the user's profile.

StyleSheet themes are set by overriding the StyleSheetTheme property for the page. IntelliSense will help you with this. Open *Welcome.aspx.vb* and scroll to the bottom of the class. Type the word **overrides** just above the End Class statement and all the overridable members are shown. Start typing *sty* and IntelliSense will scroll to the property you want: StyleSheetTheme, as shown in Figure 9-41.

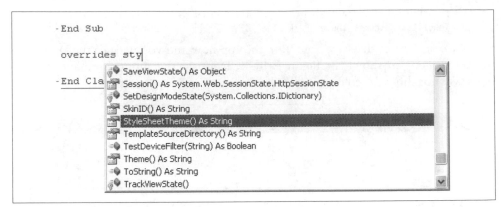

Figure 9-41. Overriding the StyleSheetTheme property.

Once IntelliSense finds the property you want, press the Tab key to accept it. It will create a code skeleton for a property called StyleSheetTheme.

—VB CHEAT SHEET—
Properties

Like all properties in .NET, StyleSheetTheme can have two special methods: one, called Get, for retrieving the value of the property; another, called Set, for setting the value of the property. These special methods are referred to variously as the *accessors* or the *getter* and *setter*.

If your code retrieves the value of a property, as in the following:

```
Dim i as Integer = SomeProperty
```

The getter is implicitly called. You don't have to actually call it. Similarly, if you set the value of a property, the setter is implicitly called.

If a property needs to be read-only, then omit the setter. If for some reason, you want to disallow using the value of the property, you could omit the getter.

This code skeleton includes default code for both the getter and setter. Replace that default code with the highlighted code in Example 9-14.

Example 9-14. Setting the StyleSheetTheme property

```
Public Overrides Property StyleSheetTheme() As String
    Get
        If Profile.IsAnonymous = False _
        And Profile.Theme IsNot Nothing Then
            Return Profile.Theme
        Else
            Return "Dark Blue"
        End If
```

Example 9-14. Setting the StyleSheetTheme property (continued)

```
    End Get
    Set(ByVal value As String)
        Profile.Theme = value
    End Set
End Property
```

If you are going to set a *customization* theme programmatically, however, you must do so from the page's PreInit event handler, because the theme must be set before the controls are created. A Page_PreInit event handler is created the same way a Page_Load event handler is created: Select (Page Events) in the left drop-down and PreInit in the right. Create the PreInit event handler and type in the bolded code from Example 9-15.

Example 9-15. PreInit event handler in Welcome.aspx.vb

```
Protected Sub Page_PreInit(ByVal sender As Object, _
        ByVal e As System.EventArgs) Handles Me.PreInit
    If Profile.IsAnonymous = False Then
        Page.Theme = Profile.Theme
    End If
End Sub
```

Setting the theme in PreInit creates a bit of a difficulty when you want to allow the user to change the theme at runtime. If you create a control that posts the page back with a new theme, the PreInit code runs *before* the event handler for the button that changes the theme (see the discussion of the page life cycle in Chapter 7). So, by the time the theme is changed, the controls have already been drawn.

To overcome this, you must, unfortunately, refresh the page again. This can be done easily enough by calling the Server.Transfer method from the event handler, which also sets the theme.

To see this, add two buttons to *Welcome.aspx*, labeled Psychedelic and Dark Blue with ID's of btnPsychedelic and btnDarkBlue, respectively. You will want both buttons to share the same event handler, Set_Theme, shown in Example 9-16. An easy way to have the IDE set up that event handler for you is to switch to Design view and click one of the buttons. Click the lightning bolt in the Properties window to go to the events, click next to the Click event, and type in the method name Set_Theme. You are now ready to type in the event handler. Once the method exists in your code-behind, you can hook the other button to the method by clicking the button and selecting the method from the drop-down next to the Click event in the Properties window.

You'll cast the sender to the Button type and check its Text property, setting the theme appropriately.

Example 9-16. Set_Theme method Button Click event handler in Welcome.aspx.vb for handling the buttons that set the theme

```
Protected Sub Set_Theme(ByVal sender As Object, _
        ByVal e As System.EventArgs) _
        Handles btnPsychedelic.Click, btnDarkBlue.Click
    Dim btn As Button = CType(sender, Button)
    If btn.Text = "Psychedelic" Then
        Profile.Theme = "Psychedelic"
    Else
        Profile.Theme = "Dark Blue"
    End If

    Server.Transfer(Request.FilePath)
End Sub
```

What's going on here is that you're creating a new Button object called btn. That Button is set to be equivalent to the button that raised the event (sender). If the Text property of the sender is "Psychedelic," you set the Psychedelic theme. If not, the event must have come from the Dark Blue button, and that theme is set instead.

There is one more problem. If you run this page and try to set the theme before you are logged in, an exception will result. The Theme property cannot be set for an anonymous user.

To prevent this from happening, you will hide the two theme buttons unless the user is logged in. To do so, add the following two lines to the Page_Load method of *Welcome.aspx.vb*:

CODE▶
```
btnDarkBlue.Visible = Not Profile.IsAnonymous
btnPsychedelic.Visible = Not Profile.IsAnonymous
```

These lines set the Visible property of the Buttons to the opposite of the IsAnonymous property. If the user is logged in, IsAnonymous is False, so the button's Visible property is set True. Now when the user logs in, the page will look something like that shown in Figure 9-42.

When the user is not logged in, the Welcome page's default theme will be used. Once the user sets a theme, that theme will be used when you return to the Welcome page.

Using Named Skins

You can override the theme for particular controls by using *named skins*. You can set the lblRadioButtonList label to be red even in the Dark Blue theme, by using a named skin. To accomplish this, create two Label skins in the *Label.skin* file within the *Dark Blue* folder:

CODE▶
```
<asp:Label Runat="server"
    ForeColor="Blue" Font-Size="Large"
    Font-Bold="True" Font-Italic="True" />
```

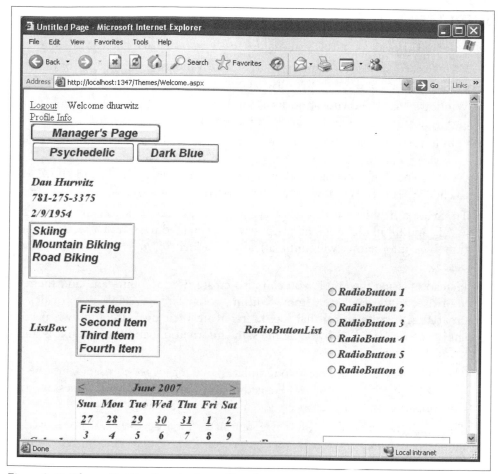

Figure 9-42. ThemesTestPageRunningLoggedIn.gif

```
<asp:Label Runat="server" SkinID="Red"
    ForeColor="Red" Font-Size="Large"
    Font-Bold="True" Font-Italic="True" />
```

The first skin is the default; the second is a named skin, because it has a `SkinID` property set to `Red`. Click the `lblRadioButtonList` control (that is the `Label`, not the `RadioButtonList`) on the Welcome page in Design view and set the `SkinID` property to Red (you may need to switch the Properties window back to properties from events). Or, open the source for *Welcome.aspx* and find the `lblRadioButtonList` and add the attribute `SkinID="Red"`:

```
<asp:Label ID="lblRadioButtonList" Runat="server" Text="Radio Button List"
    SkinID="Red"/>
```

When you log in and set your theme to Dark Blue, you'll find that the label for the `RadioButtonList` is Red.

Summary

- ASP.NET provides controls you can use to allow a user to log in to your site.
- Forms-based authentication is a technique for validating the identity of the user of the web page and is useful for users connecting across the Internet.
- Windows-based authentication lets Windows handle the authentication tasks, and is most useful for users connecting on an intranet.
- Before users can log in to your site, you need to create user accounts for them. One way to do this is administratively, using the Web Site Administrative Tool (WAT). The WAT presents itself in a separate browser window, and allows you to choose between Windows- and forms-based authentication.
- To create a new user with the WAT, you simply need to select the link in the WAT, and fill in the user's name, password, email address, and a security question. The information will automatically be added to your site's security database.
- Instead of using the WAT, you can also create user accounts and add them to your security database from within your site. ASP.NET provides a `CreateUserWizard` control that lets users create their own accounts when your site is running. Users provide all the same information, and the account is automatically created.
- The `LoginStatus` control has two templates: one for logged-in users, and one for users who aren't logged in yet. Logged-in users are greeted with a message you can configure, and other users are given a link so they can log in.
- The `LoginView` control also has two templates for logged-in and not-logged-in (anonymous) users. You can use this control to display customized content based on the user's login status.
- The `Login` control is the control where users enter a username and password to log in to your site.
- The `PasswordRecovery` control automatically resets a user's password and sends them an email notifying them of the change. This requires an SMTP server.
- Another way to determine what users can and can't see on your site is to use Roles. You define a specific role, assign users to that role, and then specify what pages members of the role can or cannot access.
- You can enable roles, create new roles, and add users to roles from the WAT.
- A good practice on sites where security is important is to check the login status of the user in the Page Load event of every page.
- The `User.Identity.IsAuthenticated` property is a Boolean that you can use to take action based on whether the user is logged in.
- To determine if a user is a member of a specific role, you can use the `User.IsInRole` Boolean.

- Personalization allows your users to dictate certain aspects of the site, which persist from one visit to the next. Personalization options can include your site's appearance, personal information, shopping carts, and other choices.

- A simple way to provide personalization is to define a profile for each user, and store their personalization choices there.

- To use profiles in your site, modify *web.config*, create a profile section, and set the enabled property to true. Then create a <properties> section within the profile section, and use the add attribute to add the names of any profile information you want to store.

- The default storage type for a profile property is string, but you can specify a different type with the Type attribute.

- The Profile.IsAnonymous property is a Boolean that lets you take action based on whether the user is logged in or not (using an anonymous profile).

- If you want your user to be able to use your site without logging in, you can enable anonymous personalization. Simply add a line to *web.config* setting <anonymousIdentification enabled = "true" />.

- When the user logs in, if you want to copy the user's profile from the anonymous profile to the user's permanent profile, you need to handle the MigrateAnonymous event, which is automatically raised when the user logs in. The code for your event handler should copy the properties from the anonymous profile to the logged-in profile.

- You can also allow users to customize the visual appearance of your site with themes. A theme is made up of skins, each of which provides the visual appearance of a single control.

- Themes are stored in a folder within your projects named App_Themes. Each subfolder within App_Themes is the name of a specific theme. Within the named theme folders, you store specific skin files, one for each control you want to modify.

- A skin file looks like a control declaration, but it has no ID property, just appearance properties.

- To enable users to set the theme of your site, simply add <add name="Theme" /> to the properties element in the profile section of *web.config*.

- To specify a theme on your page, just add a Theme attribute to the Page directive. To set the theme programmatically, you need to add an Overrides Property StyleSheetTheme( ) method to the class for the page, and set the accessors appropriately.

- To set a customization theme programmatically, you need to add a PreInit event handler, so that the theme is specified before the controls are created.

- To specify the theme for a specific control, use named skins, by setting a SkinID property in the skin file.

You've now tried out just about every section of the ASP.NET toolbox, and you've seen controls ranging from the simple to the complex. You've learned how controls work together, and how to create event handlers for them. You know how to create sites that use master pages, allow users to log in, provide navigation tools, access databases, and do it all while using Ajax to enhance the experience. What's left to do? It's time to put it all together, of course. In the next chapter, you'll find a project that uses everything you've learned so far to build a fully functional web site.

Quiz

1. What are the two methods for creating users for your site?
2. What is the difference between forms-based security and Windows authentication?
3. Where is the user information stored in your site?
4. What control do you need to add to enable users to create their own accounts?
5. What tool do you use to add users to roles?
6. What property do you use to restrict access to a page based on a role?
7. What do you need to do to enable user profiles in your site?
8. How do you retain profile information for a user without logging in?
9. What's the difference between style sheet themes and customization themes?
10. Where do you specify settings for a skin?

Exercises

Exercise 9-1. In this set of exercises, you're going to create a web site that hosts discussion forums for tropical fish enthusiasts. You won't actually write the code for the forums, but you'll build the framework so that users can log in if they wish and customize the site. Start by creating a site that has a front page welcoming users to the site and stating their login status. Add a login page, and a separate page where users can create their own accounts. Create a few users by whatever method you like to test these pages. The page for a logged-in user would look like Figure 9-43.

Exercise 9-2. You've made a good start, making the site available to users, but you currently have no content. Copy the site to a new web site named Exercise 9-2, and add two content pages, which will be placeholders for the forums. One page should be available to all users, for general discussion of fish; call it *fishforum.aspx*. The other page should only be available to site moderators; call it *siteadmin.aspx*. You may want to put moderator-specific content there in the future. Be sure to provide hyperlinks to reach the two content pages from the Home page, and also links to take users from the content pages back to the Home page.

Exercise 9-3. You've made sure that your site is only available to registered users, but now you should take advantage of the user accounts to personalize the users' experience. Copy the site to a new web site named Exercise 9-3. Add a page to the site where users can customize their profiles. Add a label to have users enter their preferred name. Add another label where they can enter how many fish they have. Add a radio button group where users can choose between tropical or freshwater fish. Give them a DropDownList where they can choose their favorite fish type. The Profile page should look something like Figure 9-44 when it's filled in.

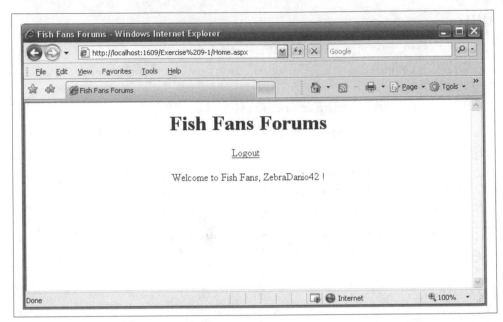

Figure 9-43. Your goal for Exercise 9-1.

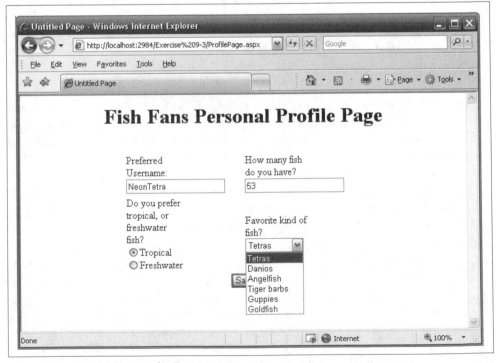

Figure 9-44. The Profile page for Exercise 9-3.

On the home page, provide an opportunity for logged-in users to edit their profile, and also display the contents of the profile on the home page. The home page should look something like Figure 9-45 when the user is logged in.

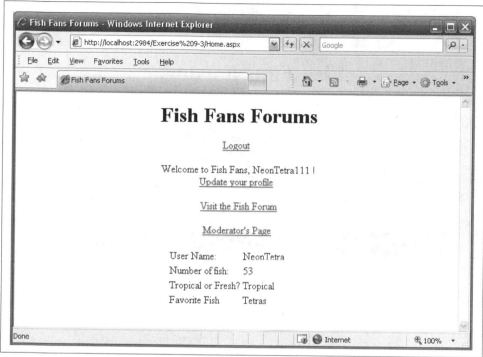

Figure 9-45. The home page for Exercise 9-3.

Exercise 9-4. A page about tropical fish isn't very much fun unless it's colorful, but users probably want to color their pages to match their favorite fish. We'll keep it simple for this exercise: Just create two theme files, with skin files for labels and buttons. Create the two theme files as follows:

- Angelfish theme: For buttons, set the foreground to yellow, the background to black, and the text to large. For labels, set the foreground to white, the background to black, and the text to large.

- Clownfish theme: For both buttons and labels, set the foreground to white, the background to orange, and the text to large.

Add a section to the user profile that lets users pick the theme they want to use, and have it displayed on all the pages of the site. The front page should look like Figure 9-46 for a user who has chosen the Angelfish theme.

Figure 9-46. Your goal for Exercise 9-4.

CHAPTER 10

Putting It All Together

You've now practiced using just about every tool in the ASP.NET toolbox. You've made dozens of sample applications, and you've gotten a feel for just how easy it is to make functional web sites with just a few controls. Now it's time to put those skills to the test. In this chapter, you'll make a fully functional shopping application for the AdventureWorks company. Unlike the order form you made in Chapter 2, this application will use all the skills you've learned. It uses data controls to display the AdventureWorks database and retrieve the content the user wants, done in AJAX to speed things along. It has a shopping cart to store the items the user has purchased. It uses session state to pass that information on to a purchasing page. It incorporates validation controls to make sure the user enters good data. It has master pages that provide a consistent look and feel to the site, and custom error pages in case of problems. Finally, it has login controls to ensure that only registered users can access the pages of the site. In short, it's a fully functional working application.

Getting Started

 Create a new AJAX-enabled web site entitled AllTogether. This is the site that you'll use throughout the example in this chapter. This chapter consists of a single large example. As we build up the example, we will provide code listings and snippets along the way. At the end of the chapter are complete code listings for the entire example so you can see how everything fits together. You can also download the example, as well as all the other examples in this book, from *www.LibertyAssociates.com*.

Add a Master page to the web site, *MasterPage.master*. Be sure that the "Place Code in separate file" checkbox is checked.

Delete the *Default.aspx* file; you won't need it.

Add an Images folder to the web site by right-clicking on the root folder in the Solution Explorer and selecting New Folder. Insert a folder and call it *Images*.

 Create the logo file *AdventureWorksLogo-250x70.gif* using any image-editing tool you like (our logo file is 250 pixels wide by 70 pixels high), or download it from this book's web site. Once the image file is on your machine, it must be added to the project. Right-click on the Images folder and select Add Existing Item. Then navigate to the logo file, whereever it is on your file system, and select it. It will automatically be copied to the Images folder and added to the project.

Adding Styles

You'll be using CSS styles for the various parts of your site, so you need to define the styles first. Add a CSS style sheet to the web site by selecting Website → Add New Item, and selecting Style Sheet. You can keep the default name of *StyleSheet.css*.

Copy in the styles from Example 10-1.

Example 10-1. StyleSheet.css

```
body
{
font-family:Arial;
}
.ButtonSelect
{
font-weight:normal;
font-size:x-small;
background-color:Yellow;
color:Blue;
}
.ButtonText
{
font-weight:bold;
font-size:x-small;
color:Black;
}
.Hyperlink
{
font-weight:normal;
font-size:small;
color:Blue;
text-decoration:underline;
}
.LabelMedium
{
font-weight:bold;
font-size:Medium;
color:Black;
}
```

Example 10-1. StyleSheet.css (continued)

```
.LabelSmall
{
font-weight:bold;
font-size:small;
color:Black;
}
.ListHeading
{
font-weight:bold;
text-decoration:underline;
font-size:x-small;
color:Black;
}
.MenuText
{
font-weight:normal;
font-size:small;
color:Blue;
}
.PageTitle
{
font-weight:bold;
font-size:xx-large;
color:Green;
}
.PageSubTitle
{
font-weight:bold;
font-size:x-large;
color:Blue;
}
.TableCells
{
font-weight:normal;
font-size:small;
color:Black;
text-align:left;
vertical-align:top;
}
.TableColumnHeading
{
font-weight:bold;
text-decoration:underline;
font-size:small;
color:Black;
text-align:left;
}
.TableColumnHeadingRight
{
text-align:right;
}
```

Example 10-1. StyleSheet.css (continued)

```css
.TableNumberDecimal
{
font-weight:normal;
font-size:small;
color:Black;
text-align:right;
}
.TableRowHeading
{
font-weight:bold;
text-decoration:none;
font-size:small;
color:Black;
text-align:left;
}
.TextBold
{
font-weight:bold;
font-style:italic;
font-size:medium;
color:Black;
}
.TextNormal
{
font-weight:normal;
font-size:medium;
color:Black;
}
.TextSmall
{
font-weight:normal;
font-size:small;
color:Black;
}
.TextXSmall
{
font-weight:normal;
font-size:x-small;
color:Black;
}
.ValidationError
{
font-weight:normal;
font-size:small;
}
.Warning
{
font-weight:bold;
font-size:Small;
color:Red;
}
```

Example 10-1. StyleSheet.css (continued)

```css
.WarningRoutine
{
font-weight:normal;
font-size:Small;
color:Red;
}
```

Using Master Pages

Add a new page, *Login.aspx*. Check both checkboxes: "Place code in separate file" and "Select master page." When the Master Page dialog comes up, select *MasterPage. master*.

Add several other new pages: *Home.aspx*, *Products.aspx*, *Cart.aspx*, *Purchase.aspx*, and *Confirm.aspx*. For each of these, select the same master page. Set *Home.aspx* to be the startup page.

Open *MasterPage.master*. Add a style statement to the <head> element to import the style sheet, as in the highlighted line in the following snippet:

CODE
```html
<head runat="server">
    <title>Untitled Page</title>
    <style type="text/css">@import url(StyleSheet.css); </style>
</head>
```

Add an HTML table for layout, inside the <div> element, but before the content placeholder control. You can use the IDE tools or just type it manually in the Source view window. With the help of Intellisense, I find it easier to type it manually.

Add the controls highlighted below:

CODE
```html
<table border="0">
    <tr>
        <td colspan="4">
            <table>
                <tr>
                    <td width="10px"> </td>
                    <td>
                        <asp:ImageButton ID="ibLogo" runat="server"
                            ImageUrl="~/images/AdventureWorksLogo-250x70.gif"
                            AlternateText="AdventureWorks logo"
                            PostBackUrl="~/Home.aspx" />
                    </td>
                    <td width="10px"> </td>
                    <td width="500px" align="right">
                        <span class="PageTitle">Adventure Works</span>
                        <br />
                        <asp:Label ID="lblPageSubTitle" runat="server"
                            CssClass="PageSubTitle" Text="Page SubTitle"/>
                        <br />
```

```
                    <asp:Label id="lblTime" runat="server"
                        CssClass="TextXSmall"/>
                </td>
                <td width="10px"> </td>
            </tr>
            <tr>
                <td colspan="5">
                    <hr />
                </td>
            </tr>
        </table>
    </td>
</tr>
</table>
<asp:contentplaceholder id="ContentPlaceHolder1" runat="server" >
</asp:contentplaceholder>
```

This code defines the table that you're going to use to hold the content of the master page. The first cell contains an ImageButton control to hold the logo for the site; when users click on the logo, it will take them to the *Home.aspx* page. The control uses the logo image you created earlier.

The cell to the right of the logo contains some text for the title, and a pair of labels. Note the use of the <span> element on the page title; this allows you to apply a CSS class to it. The first label will contain the page subtitle, which will change depending on the page the user is on. The other label contains the date and time, just for convenience.

Also note the use of the border="0" in the opening <table> tag. This is a vestige of the development process. Although you might not want borders in the finished site, it is often helpful to make the cell borders visible during development by setting the border thickness to 1 pixel with border="1". Then when you are satisfied with the layout, set the borders back to 0 so they are no longer visible.

You'll need to populate the Label that shows the time, so open *MasterPage.master. vb*, the code-behind for the master page. Create an event handler for the Page_Load event by selecting (PageEvents) from the left drop-down menu and Load from the right drop-down menu. Enter the following line of code:

CODE▶
```
lblTime.Text = DateTime.Now.ToString()
```

Open *Home.aspx*. Edit the Page directive at the top of the file to set the title attribute; also add the trace attribute at this time, but set it to false. You'll need this because you know you are going to want to turn trace on or off during various phases of development.

Add a MasterType directive to the file also. This will enable the content page to access properties declared in the master page:

CODE▶
```
<%@ Page Language="VB" MasterPageFile="~/MasterPage.master" AutoEventWireup="false"
    CodeFile="Home.aspx.vb" Inherits="Home" title="Home Page" Trace="false"%>
```

```
<%@ MasterType TypeName="MasterPage" %>
<asp:Content ID="Content1" ContentPlaceHolderID="ContentPlaceHolder1"
    Runat="Server">
</asp:Content>
```

Run the site now, to see what you've done so far. You should see something like Figure 10-1.

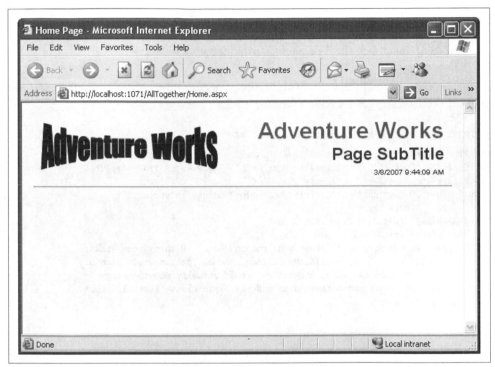

Figure 10-1. Here's how the Home page looks with nothing on it and the page subtitle not yet set.

You want the page subtitle to display the current page; for example, Home or Products. The label is already in place in the master page.

Go to the code-behind file for the master page. Add the following code outside the Page_Load method and inside the class definition to create a public property called PageSubTitle, of type Label:

```
Public Property PageSubTitle() As Label
    Get
        Return lblPageSubTitle
    End Get
    Set(ByVal value As Label)
        lblPageSubTitle = value
    End Set
End Property
```

Then in the code-behind of the Home page, create a Page_Load method with the following highlighted line of code:

CODE ▶

```
Protected Sub Page_Load(ByVal sender As Object, _
        ByVal e As System.EventArgs) Handles Me.Load
    Me.Master.PageSubTitle.Text = "Home"
End Sub
```

 If the IDE draws squiggly lines indicating some sort of problem, try building the web site by clicking on the Build menu item and selecting Build Web Site. The spurious error indicators will go away.

Switch over to the Source view of the Home page and add some content inside the Content control, such as listed in Example 10-2.

Example 10-2. Markup for the Home page - Home.aspx

```
<%@ Page Language="VB" MasterPageFile="~/MasterPage.master" AutoEventWireup="false"
    CodeFile="Home.aspx.vb" Inherits="Home" title="Home Page" Trace="false"%>
<%@ MasterType TypeName="MasterPage" %>
<asp:Content ID="Content1" ContentPlaceHolderID="ContentPlaceHolder1"
        Runat="Server">
    <h2>This Is Your Home Page</h2>
    <div class="TextNormal">
        You can put some stuff about your company here.  Perhaps some links.
        Of course, in a real world application, the navigation would probably
        much more complex. Also, the buttons would actually do something,
        rather than just wave their arms and say <span class="TextBold">Look
        at me!</span>
    </div>
</asp:Content>
```

Running the site now gives Figure 10-2 for the Home page.

Setting Up Roles and Users

Your page has a good foundation, but you should add a measure of security to it to separate the customers from the managers. The next step is to enable security and then create a few users for your site.

Go to the WAT, by selecting Website → ASP Configuration. Click on Security, and then click on Select authentication type under the Users column. Because this site will be available on the Internet, forms-based security is the way to go. Change the Authentication type to Forms by selecting "From the internet." You'll be setting up some roles to group the AdventureWorks users into customers, employees, and managers. Back on the Security page, click on Enable roles. The security page should now look something like Figure 10-3.

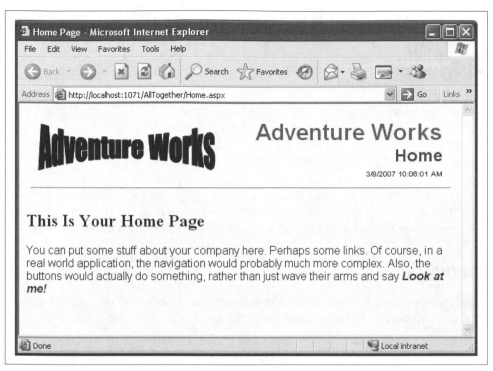

Figure 10-2. The Home page now has the subtitle set and some content added.

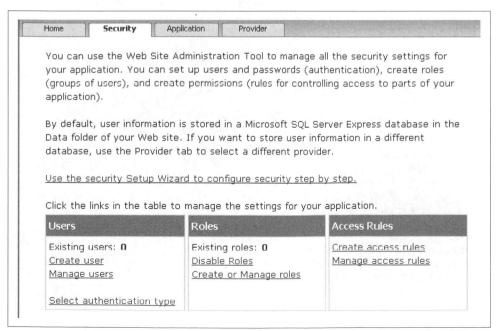

Figure 10-3. You've switched to Forms authentication, and enabled roles for your site, but there aren't any users just yet.

Click on Create or Manage roles, and create three roles: Manager, Employee, and Customer.

Click on the Back button to go back to the Security page. Click on Create user, and create three users, as follows:

User	Password	Role
dhurwitz	dan123!	Employee
jliberty	jesse123!	Customer
rhampster	rich123!	Manager

You must also provide an email address and a security question and answer for each user. We will not be using that information in this example, so it does not matter what you enter. Close the WAT. Now you have three users to work with for this example.

Logging In

Now that you have your users, you need a way for them to log in. Edit the master page markup file to add some login functionality.

Add another table row to the layout table, listed in Example 10-3. Note that the `ContentPlaceHolder` control has been moved to within one of the table cells.

Example 10-3. Code snippet from MasterPage.master containing the login controls

```
<tr>
    <td width="5px"> </td>
    <td width="150px" valign="top">
        <asp:LoginStatus ID="LoginStatus1" runat="server" CssClass="Hyperlink" />
        <br />
        <asp:LoginView ID="LoginView1" runat="server" >
            <LoggedInTemplate>
                <span class="WarningRoutine">Welcome</span>
                <asp:LoginName ID="LoginName1" runat="server"
                    CssClass="WarningRoutine"/>
            </LoggedInTemplate>
            <AnonymousTemplate>
                <span class="WarningRoutine">You are not logged in.
                    Please click the login link to log in to this website.</span>
            </AnonymousTemplate>
        </asp:LoginView>
    </td>
    <td width="5px"> </td>
    <td width="700px" valign="top" bgcolor="yellow">
        <asp:contentplaceholder id="ContentPlaceHolder1" runat="server" >
        </asp:contentplaceholder>
    </td>
</tr>
```

This code adds a new row to the table on the master page. The first cell is just a spacer. The second cell holds a LoginStatus control and a LoginView control to go with it. Notice that the CssClass properties of both controls have been set, so you can apply styles to them. The LoginView control has text added to it to present appropriate messages to logged-in or anonymous users.

The third cell in the row now holds the ContentPlaceHolder control, so be sure to move the ContentPlaceHolder control that was outside the table to this cell.

Edit the *Login.aspx* page that you created earlier. Set the title in the Page directive and add the same MasterType directive that you added to the Home page. Drag a Login control into the Content area. Switch to Design view, click on the Smart Tag of the Login control, and click on Auto Format. Select the "Professional" scheme. Set the DestinationPageUrl property to ~/Home.aspx, so that users will be returned to the Home page after they log in. You will end up with something like Example 10-4 for the markup for the Login page, with the changes highlighted.

Example 10-4. Login.aspx

```
<%@ Page Language="VB" MasterPageFile="~/MasterPage.master" AutoEventWireup="false"
    CodeFile="Login.aspx.vb" Inherits="Login" title="Login" Trace="false" %>
<%@ MasterType TypeName="MasterPage" %>
<asp:Content ID="Content1" ContentPlaceHolderID="ContentPlaceHolder1"
        Runat="Server">
    <asp:Login ID="Login1" runat="server" DestinationPageUrl="~/home.aspx"
            BackColor="#F7F6F3" BorderColor="#E6E2D8" BorderPadding="4"
            BorderStyle="Solid" BorderWidth="1px" Font-Names="Verdana"
            Font-Size="0.8em" ForeColor="#333333">
        <TitleTextStyle BackColor="#5D7B9D" Font-Bold="True"
            Font-Size="0.9em" ForeColor="White" />
        <InstructionTextStyle Font-Italic="True" ForeColor="Black" />
        <TextBoxStyle Font-Size="0.8em" />
        <LoginButtonStyle BackColor="#FFFBFF" BorderColor="#CCCCCC"
            BorderStyle="Solid" BorderWidth="1px"
            Font-Names="Verdana" Font-Size="0.8em" ForeColor="#284775" />
    </asp:Login>
</asp:Content>
```

Open the code-behind of the Login page. Create an event handler for the Page_load event and add the following highlighted line of code:

```
Protected Sub Page_Load(ByVal sender As Object, _
        ByVal e As System.EventArgs) Handles Me.Load
    Me.Master.PageSubTitle.Text = "Login"
End Sub
```

All this does is set the page subtitle in the master page area.

Now run the site. You will see the first screen shown in Figure 10-4.

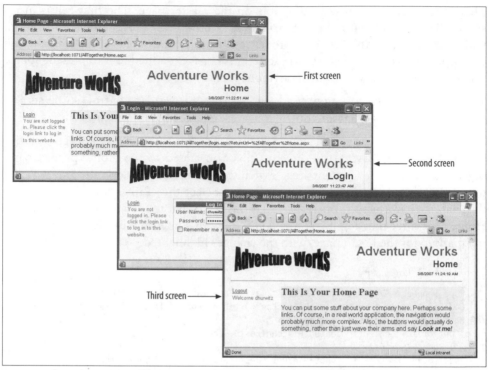

First screen

Second screen

Third screen

Figure 10-4. When you first run the site, you'll see the screen on the left. After you click the Login link, you'll be taken to the second screen, and after you've successfully logged in, you'll be taken back to the Home page, which now looks like the third screen.

Click on the Login link to get the Login page, shown as the second screen in Figure 10-4. Entering the username and password for one of the user accounts you created earlier in this chapter. After you click on the Log In button, you will be brought back to the Home page, shown as the third screen in Figure 10-4.

Earlier, you enabled roles in the WAT and added each user to one of the three roles: Manager, Customer, and Employee. As you saw in Chapter 9, you can use these roles to present customized content to the users who visit the page. You'll add two Panel controls to the Home page that present content depending on the user's role. Edit *Home.aspx* to see this in action. Add two Panel controls, as listed in Example 10-5, to the page, inside the Content control, after the closing <div> for the text that all users see.

Example 10-5. Role-specific content in Home.aspx

```
<asp:Panel ID="pnlEmployee" runat="server" Visible="false" >
    <h3>Employee Information</h3>
    <div class="TextNormal">
        This panel should only be visible to users are a members of the
        <b>Employee</b> role. Turning on the visibility of this Panel occurs in the
        Page_Load event handler.
```

Example 10-5. Role-specific content in Home.aspx (continued)

```
        </div>
</asp:Panel>
<asp:Panel ID="pnlManager" runat="server" Visible="false" >
    <h3>Manager Information</h3>
    <div class="TextNormal">
        This panel should only be visible to users are a members of the
        <b>Manager</b> role. Turning on the visibility of this Panel occurs in the
        Page_Load event handler.
    </div>
</asp:Panel>
```

Switch over to the code-behind for the Home page, *Home.aspx.vb*. Add the highlighted lines of code from Example 10-6 to the Page_Load event handler.

Example 10-6. Controlling visibility based on roles in Home.aspx.vb

```
Protected Sub Page_Load(ByVal sender As Object, _
        ByVal e As System.EventArgs) Handles Me.Load
    Me.Master.PageSubTitle.Text = "Home"

    ' control the visibility of sections restricted to specific roles
    pnlManager.Visible = User.IsInRole("Manager")
    pnlEmployee.Visible = User.IsInRole("Employee")
End Sub
```

The code here is very simple; it sets the visibility of each panel depending on the value of the IsInRole method for the appropriate role.

Before logging in, the Home page will still look like the first screen in Figure 10-4. If you log in as rhampster, who is a member of the Managers role (it's only fitting that the boss is a rodent), you will see Figure 10-5.

Now, log out and log in as user dhurwitz, and you'll see just the content of pnlEmployee. Log in again as user jliberty, and you won't see either panel because customers don't need to see employee-specific information. Of course, if you make a user a member of both the Manager and Employee roles, she would see both panels.

Navigation

The front page of your site is looking pretty good. Users can identify themselves, and see the custom content. The master page is working as planned, and each page identifies itself appropriately. The next thing to do is add some navigation tools so that users can find their way around, which means you have to create a site map. Close the browser if it is open, and select Website → Add New Item, and choose Site Map. Accept the default name of *Web.sitemap*.

As you learned in Chapter 6, the site map is an XML file, and you have to create it manually—the IDE won't do it for you. Open the *web.sitemap* file, and replace the default boilerplate with the highlighted code in Example 10-7.

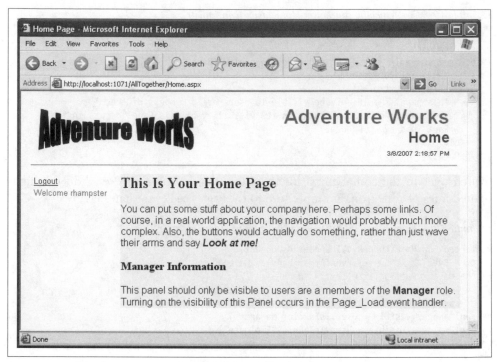

Figure 10-5. If you log in as a member of the Manager role, you'll see the manager-specific information.

Example 10-7. Web.sitemap

```
<?xml version="1.0" encoding="utf-8" ?>
<siteMap xmlns="http://schemas.microsoft.com/AspNet/SiteMap-File-1.0" >
    <siteMapNode title="Root"  >
        <siteMapNode url="~/Home.aspx" title="Home"  description="Home page" />
        <siteMapNode url="~/Products.aspx" title="Products"
            description="Products offered by AdventureWorks" />
        <siteMapNode url="~/Cart.aspx" title="Shopping Cart"
            description="Items selected for purchase" />
        <siteMapNode url="~/Purchase.aspx" title="Purchase"
            description="Purchase your selected items" />
    </siteMapNode>
</siteMap>
```

Now that you have the site map file, you'll add the navigation controls to the master page. Add the following code to *MasterPage.master*, in the same table cell and after the LoginView control:

```
<hr />
<asp:SiteMapDataSource ID="SiteMapDataSource1" runat="server"
    ShowStartingNode="false" />
<asp:Menu ID="Menu1" runat="server" DataSourceID="SiteMapDataSource1"
    CssClass="MenuText" />
```

In this case, you're using a Menu control, rather than a TreeView. Note that the DataSourceID property of the Menu control points to the SiteMapDataSource control that you just created. You've set the control's ShowStartingNode property of the SiteMapDataSource control to false to suppress display of the root node in the menu.

You don't want anonymous users to be able to use the menu, so add the following code to the *MasterPage.master.vb* Page_Load to disable the menu if the user is not logged in:

CODE ▶
```
If Page.User.Identity.IsAuthenticated = False Then
    Menu1.Enabled = False
End If
```

Anonymous users will be able to see the menu; they just won't be able to click anything on it.

At this point, a user could bypass the login by entering the URL of any of the other pages directly into the browser. To prevent this, add the following code to the Page_Load method of every page in the web site except Home and Login (which are already taken care of):

CODE ▶
```
If User.Identity.IsAuthenticated = False Then
    Response.Redirect("login.aspx")
End If
```

Go ahead and try out the site now, to make sure everything is working. When you first see the Home page, you'll see that the navigation menu is disabled. Try entering *cart.aspx* in the address field of your browser. You'll see that you're taken back to the Login page instead.

One other navigation aid that you can add is setting the page subtitle in the master page, to identify to the user where they are. You have already done this for the Home and Login pages. For the rest of the pages, add the MasterType directive to the top of the relevant markup file:

CODE ▶
```
<%@ MasterType TypeName="MasterPage" %>
```

While in each page markup file, also set the title attribute of the Page directive.

Then go to the Page_Load method of each page code-behind file and add a line similar to the following (for the Purchase page), which sets the page subtitle:

CODE ▶
```
Me.Master.PageSubTitle.Text = "Purchase"
```

 Most real-world sites would have a somewhat deeper menu structure and so might benefit from a SiteMapPath control to provide breadcrumbs. This would be especially true if the Home page were truly the root node.

Test out everything to see how it works.

Products Page

The intent of the Products page is to allow the user to select a product category, and then see a grid displaying all the products in that category. The user can select any of these products to see more detail about that product, and if she wants, she can add that item to the shopping cart by clicking on a button.

This page has several data-bound controls: a `RadioButtonList` for selecting the product category, a `GridView` for displaying the products (filtered by category), and a `DetailsView` for displaying details about the currently selected item.

In addition, visibility of some of the controls is turned off, depending on circumstances. Initially, only the `RadioButtonList` is visible. Once the user has selected a category, the `GridView` is made visible. When the user selects a product from the `GridView`, the `DetailsView` and its associated button for adding the item to the cart are made visible.

Open *Products.aspx*. You will start with a data source control that will power all the other controls. Go to Source view, if not there already, and drag a `SqlDataSource` control from the Data section of the Toolbox into the `Content` control on the page. Set the control's ID to `sqlCategories`. Switch to Design view and click on the Smart Tag. Configure it to point to the AdventureWorks database—if you did the examples in Chapter 4, you may still have a data connection set up that refers to Adventure-Works.mdf. If not, you should probably flip back to Chapter 4 and review the section on creating a database connection. In the "Configure the Select Statement" portion of the Wizard, select the "Specify a custom SQL statement" radio button. After you click Next, enter the following custom statement:

CODE▶
```
select Name, ProductCategoryID from Production.ProductCategory order by Name
```

You could have built this statement in the Wizard, but remember from Chapter 4 that the IDE doesn't automatically include the `Production` schema in the Select statement, so this custom statement is easier. Test the query to make sure everything is working, and finish the Wizard.

Drag a `RadioButtonList` control from the Standard section of the Toolbox onto the content section of the page. Set its ID to `rblCategories`. In Design view, click on its Smart Tag and select Choose Data Source. In the Data Source Configuration Wizard, select `sqlCategories` as the data source, `Name` as the data field to display, and `ProductCategoryID` as the data field for the value, as shown in Figure 10-6.

 If none of the fields are visible in the drop-down menus, click on the Refresh Schema link, indicated with the arrow in Figure 10-6.

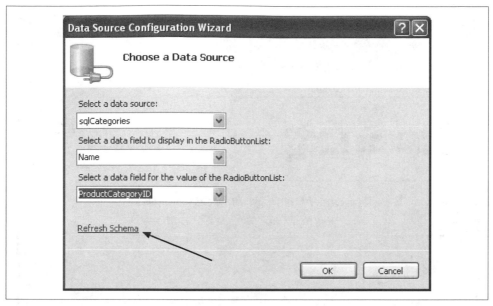

Figure 10-6. If you can't see any of the data fields in the drop-down menu controls, click the "Refresh Schema" link to see them.

Set the RepeatDirection property of rblCategories to Horizontal, and the AutoPostBack property to True, so that the page will post back as soon as a change is made (later you will add AJAX features to avoid the flicker), and the CssClass property to LabelSmall.

Run the web site, log in, and go to the Products page. You will see a set of four radio buttons, as shown in Figure 10-7.

Stop the application, and then drag another SqlDataSource control onto the content area to be the data source for the products grid. Set its ID to sqlProducts. This data source will return all the products of the category specified in the radio buttons, so you need to pass the value of the selected radio button to the data source as a parameter. Unfortunately, the Data Source Configuration Wizard shown in Figure 10-6 does not do parameterized queries, so you need to enter the code directly into Source view, as shown in the following code snippet:

```
<asp:SqlDataSource id="sqlProducts" runat="server"
    ConnectionString=
        "<%$ ConnectionStrings:AdventureWorksConnectionString %>">
    <SelectParameters>
        <asp:ControlParameter ControlID="rblCategories"
            Name="ProductCategoryID"
            PropertyName="SelectedValue" />
    </SelectParameters>
</asp:SqlDataSource>
```

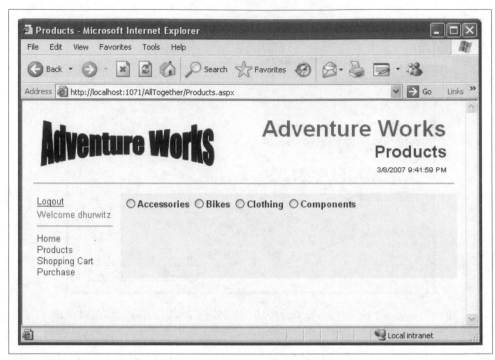

Figure 10-7. Once you've logged in and navigated to the Products page, you'll see the list of product radio buttons.

The `ConnectionString` attribute points to the previously configured connection string. Your connection string may have a different name than that shown here. The `SelectParameters` element specifies that the parameter will be called `ProductCategoryID` and will come from the `SelectedValue` property of the `rblCategories` control.

But where is the SQL Select command, and where is this parameter used? You could declare a `SelectCommand` attribute, as you did for the first `SqlDataSource`, but this query is sort of long and complex, with a subquery as well as the parameter. So you will set the `SelectCommand` property of the control programmatically in the `Page_Load` of the Products page. Open the `Page_Load` method in *Products.aspx.vb*, and add the following code:

```
Dim strCommand As String = String.Empty
strCommand = "select ProductID, Name, ProductNumber, ListPrice from " + _
            "Production.Product "
strCommand += "where ProductSubcategoryID in "
strCommand += "(select ProductSubcategoryID from " + _
            "Production.ProductSubcategory "
strCommand += "where ProductCategoryID = "
strCommand += "@ProductCategoryID)"
sqlProducts.SelectCommand = strCommand
```

The parameter, ProductCategoryID (highlighted in the above code snippet), preceded by the @ character, assumes the value of the selected radio button. When the page first loads and none of the radio buttons are selected, this query returns nothing, so the GridView does not display. But as soon as a value is selected, the query returns rows and they display in the GridView.

To see this, drag a GridView control from the Data section of the Toolbox onto the content area. Set its ID property to gvProducts and its DataKeyNames property to ProductID. In Design view, click on its Smart Tag and set its Data Source to be sqlProducts. While the Smart Tag is open, check the Enable Paging, Enable Sorting, and Enable Selection checkboxes, as shown in Figure 10-8.

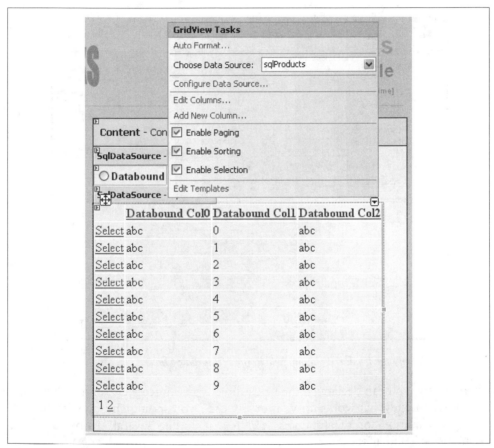

Figure 10-8. After you've selected the data source, and enabled Paging, Sorting, and Selection, the gvProducts GridView will look like this.

Click on the Edit Columns link in the Smart Tag to specify the columns from the SELECT query: ProductID, Name, ProductNumber, and ListPrice. Be sure to uncheck the Auto-generate fields checkbox. Although you want all the fields from the query to display, manually adding the columns to the GridView allows you to fully specify the appearance and behavior of each column.

As you add each field from the query, make sure BoundField is selected in the Available fields list, and then click the Add button. For the first column, set the DataField for this BoundField to ProductID, the SortExpression to ProductID, the HeaderText to ID, and the ItemStyle Width to 50px, as shown in Figure 10-9. Then add each of the other columns in the same way.

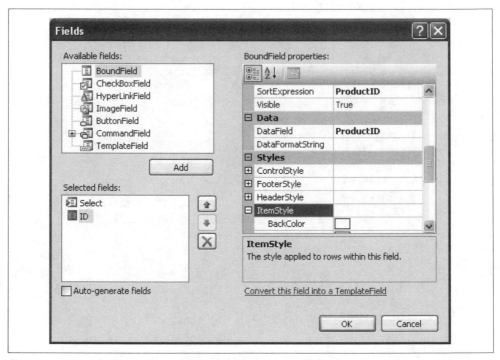

Figure 10-9. Specify the ProductID bound field in the Fields dialog box.

Alternatively, you can declare all the fields directly in Source view, or any combination of techniques that works for you. In any case, you should end up with the following declaration for the products GridView, including several attributes of the GridView itself and all the columns within the <Columns> element:

```
<asp:GridView id="gvProducts" runat="server"
    DataSourceID="sqlProducts" DataKeyNames="ProductID"
    AllowSorting="True" AllowPaging="True"
    AutoGenerateColumns="False"
    HeaderStyle-CssClass="TableColumnHeading"
    RowStyle-CssClass="TableCells">
```

```
<Columns>
    <asp:CommandField ShowSelectButton="True" ItemStyle-Width="50"
        ControlStyle-CssClass="ButtonSelect" />
    <asp:BoundField DataField="ProductID" HeaderText="ID"
        SortExpression="ProductID">
        <ItemStyle Width="50px" />
    </asp:BoundField>
    <asp:BoundField DataField="Name" HeaderText="Name"
        SortExpression="Name">
        <ItemStyle Width="225px" />
    </asp:BoundField>
    <asp:BoundField DataField="ProductNumber"
        HeaderText="Product Number"
        SortExpression="ProductNumber">
        <ItemStyle Width="90px" />
    </asp:BoundField>
    <asp:BoundField DataField="ListPrice" HeaderText="Cost"
        SortExpression="ListPrice"
        ItemStyle-CssClass="TableNumberDecimal"
        HeaderStyle-CssClass="TableColumnHeadingRight">
        <ItemStyle Width="60px" />
    </asp:BoundField>
</Columns>
</asp:GridView>
```

The DataKeyNames attribute is very important. It specifies the name (or names) of the field(s) that make up the primary key for the items displayed. In this example, the primary key is a single field, ProductID.

As you can see, there are many CSS-related attributes, all of which allow you to apply a style to a specific type of element in the grid.

Now run the site, log in, navigate to the Products page, and select a category. You'll see that all the products for that category are listed in the grid.

Now you need to display the item details when the user selects an item from the grid. Drag a Panel control onto the page, inside the Content area but after gvProducts. Set its ID to pnlProduct. Inside the Panel is going to be a layout table with a DetailsView control data bound to another SqlDataSource.

The DetailsView control has not been used previously in this book. It is a databound control, similar to the GridView, but it is used to display or edit a single record at a time. In this example, it displays the details about the single record selected from the GridView.

The contents of the pnlProduct are listed in Example 10-8.

Example 10-8. Panel pnlProduct on Products page

```
<asp:Panel id="pnlProduct" runat="server" Visible="false">
    <table width="100%">
        <tr>
            <td valign="top">
```

Example 10-8. Panel pnlProduct on Products page (continued)

```
            <asp:Button id="btnAddToCart" runat="server"
                Text="Add To Cart" OnClick="btnAddToCart_Click"
                CssClass="ButtonText" />
            <div class="ListHeading">Items In Cart</div>
            <asp:Label ID="lblCart" runat="server" CssClass="TextSmall"
                Width="90"/>
        </td>
        <td valign="top">
            <asp:SqlDataSource id="sqlDetailsView" runat="server"
                ConnectionString=
                    "<%$ ConnectionStrings:AdventureWorksConnectionString %>">
                <SelectParameters>
                    <asp:ControlParameter ControlID="gvProducts"
                        Name="ProductID"
                        PropertyName="SelectedDataKey.Values['ProductID']" />
                </SelectParameters>
            </asp:SqlDataSource>
            <asp:DetailsView id="DetailsView1" runat="server"
                DataSourceID="sqlDetailsView" DataKeyNames="ProductID"
                AutoGenerateRows="false"
                CssClass="TableCells" BorderWidth="0"
                FieldHeaderStyle-CssClass="TableRowHeading"
                CellSpacing="2" CellPadding="2" Width="500px" Height="50px">
                <Fields>
                    <asp:BoundField DataField="ProductID"
                            HeaderText="Product ID:"
                            SortExpression="ProductID" />
                    <asp:BoundField DataField="Name" HeaderText="Name:"
                            SortExpression="Name" />
                    <asp:BoundField DataField="ProductNumber"
                            HeaderText="Product #:"
                            SortExpression="ProductNumber" />
                    <asp:BoundField DataField="ListPrice" HeaderText="Cost:"
                            SortExpression="ListPrice"
                            DataFormatString="{0:C}" HtmlEncode="false"/>
                    <asp:BoundField DataField="Color" HeaderText="Color:"
                            SortExpression="Color" />
                    <asp:BoundField DataField="CategoryName"
                            HeaderText="Category:"
                            SortExpression="CategoryName" />
                    <asp:BoundField DataField="SubcategoryName"
                            HeaderText="SubCategory:"
                            SortExpression="SubcategoryName" />
                    <asp:BoundField DataField="Description"
                            HeaderText="Description:"
                            SortExpression="Description" />
                </Fields>
            </asp:DetailsView>
        </td>
    </tr>
  </table>
</asp:Panel>
```

As with the previous parameterized query, you will set the SelectCommand for the data source, sqlDetailsView, in the Page_Load of the Products page. Add the following code to the Page_Load method, after setting the SelectCommand property of the previous data source:

```
strCommand = String.Empty
strCommand += "select product.*, subcat.ProductSubcategoryID, " + _
        "subcat.Name as SubcategoryName, "
strCommand += "cat.ProductCategoryID, cat.Name as CategoryName, "
strCommand += "model.Name as ModelName, model.CatalogDescription, " + _
        "model.Instructions, "
strCommand += "description.Description "
strCommand += "from Production.Product product "
strCommand += "join Production.ProductSubcategory subcat on " + _
        "product.ProductSubcategoryID = subcat.ProductSubcategoryID "
strCommand += "join Production.ProductCategory cat on subcat.ProductCategoryID = " +_
        "cat.ProductCategoryID "
strCommand += "join Production.ProductModel model on product.ProductModelID = " + _
        "model.ProductModelID "
strCommand += "join Production.ProductModelProductDescriptionCulture culture on " + _
        "model.ProductModelID = culture.ProductModelID "
strCommand += "join Production.ProductDescription description on " + _
        "culture.ProductDescriptionID = description.ProductDescriptionID "
strCommand += "where product.ProductID = @ProductID and culture.CultureID = 'en' "
sqlDetailsView.SelectCommand = strCommand
```

Inside the Panel is also a Button, btnAddToCart. Switch to Design view and double-click the button to open the code-behind in the skeleton of an event handler, ready for you to type. The event handler code is included in Example 10-9. This method retrieves the ProductID of the selected item using the Value of the SelectedDataKey property of the GridView. Then it checks if the Session object exists, and in either case updates it with the currently selected item as a comma-separated string. It also displays the contents of the cart in a Label control. (The space trailing the comma allows the content of the Label control to wrap when many items are listed.)

While you're in the code-behind, add the single line event handler for the SelectedIndexChanged event of the grid gvProducts, also listed in Example 10-9. This displays the details of the selected item.

Also add an event handler to gvProducts for the RowDataBound event. This allows you to apply formatting to the cost display. There is an easier way to set the format in this case, which you will use later in the chapter, but this demonstrates a really powerful technique that comes in handy with almost every project. That technique involves looking at each row as it is bound to the data and applying some formatting on a row-by row basis. It is even possible to make different formatting decisions based on the content of each row.

All of the queries you have seen in this book so far have been simple SELECT statements from a single table. The true strength of a relational database comes from using multiple tables to contain *normalized* data. Data that has been normalized essentially means there is no duplicate data.

Suppose you have a database containing employment information. Each employee has not only a job title but also a job description. Rather than have identical job descriptions in the Employee table for every employee with the same job, it is much better to have the job titles and descriptions in a separate Jobs table, and then refer to that Jobs record in the Employees table. There is said to be a *relationship* between the Employees table the Jobs table.

Now, however, when you want to query the data, you must join the two tables back together in your query statement. This is done with the SQL keyword JOIN.

The JOIN keyword alone, as used in the preceding snippet, is the default join type, known as an *inner join*. This means that any rows in either table that do not match the selection criteria will not be included in the results.

There are many circumstances where you do not want to omit these records, in which case you must use an *outer join*. There are several different types of outer joins, including left, right, cross, and full, depending on which data specifically you want to include and which to omit.

For a complete discussion on SQL queries in general and joins in particular, we highly recommend *Transact-SQL Programming*, by Kevin Kline et al. (O'Reilly). Although this book is a bit dated, only covering up through SQL Server 7.0, the basic syntax has not changed, and this book remains a primary reference for SQL programming.

Finally, add an event handler for the SelectedIndexChanged of the RadioButtonList rblCategories, which hides the detail Panel when a new category is selected. This prevents the details of the previous item remaining displayed.

Example 10-9. Products.aspx.vb event handlers

```
Protected Sub btnAddToCart_Click(ByVal sender As Object, _
      ByVal e As System.EventArgs)
   ' the contents of the cart will be saved in a Session object as
   '    a string of comma-delimited values of ProductID's
   Dim strCart As String = String.Empty
   Dim strProductId As String = gvProducts.SelectedDataKey.Value.ToString()

   If Session("Cart") Is Nothing Then
      strCart = strProductId
   Else
      strCart = Session("Cart").ToString() + ", " + strProductId
   End If
```

Example 10-9. Products.aspx.vb event handlers (continued)

```
    Session("Cart") = strCart
    lblCart.Text = strCart
End Sub

Protected Sub gvProducts_SelectedIndexChanged(ByVal sender As Object, _
        ByVal e As System.EventArgs) _
        Handles gvProducts.SelectedIndexChanged
    pnlProduct.Visible = True
End Sub

Protected Sub gvProducts_RowDataBound(ByVal sender As Object, _
        ByVal e As System.Web.UI.WebControls.GridViewRowEventArgs) _
        Handles gvProducts.RowDataBound
    Dim str As String = String.Empty
    If e.Row.RowType = DataControlRowType.DataRow Then
        Dim cell As TableCell = e.Row.Cells(4)    ' ListPrice cell
        Dim nCost As Decimal
        Try
            nCost = CType(cell.Text, Decimal)
            str = nCost.ToString("##,##0.00", Nothing)
        Catch ex As ApplicationException
            str = "n.a."
        Finally
            cell.Text = str
        End Try
    End If
End Sub

Protected Sub rblCategories_SelectedIndexChanged(ByVal sender As Object, _
        ByVal e As System.EventArgs) _
        Handles rblCategories.SelectedIndexChanged
    pnlProduct.Visible = False
End Sub
```

The finished Products page, with several items added to the cart, is shown in Figure 10-10.

Adding AJAX

It is pathetically easy to spice up the performance of the Products page with a little help from AJAX. All you need to do is wrap the entire contents of the Content control inside an `UpdatePanel` control. You can do this by dragging an `UpdatePanel` control from the AJAX Extensions section of the Toolbox onto the page in Design view, and then dragging all the existing content inside the `UpdatePanel`. Alternatively, go to Source view and add the following highlighted lines of code, wrapping the content of the `Content` control.

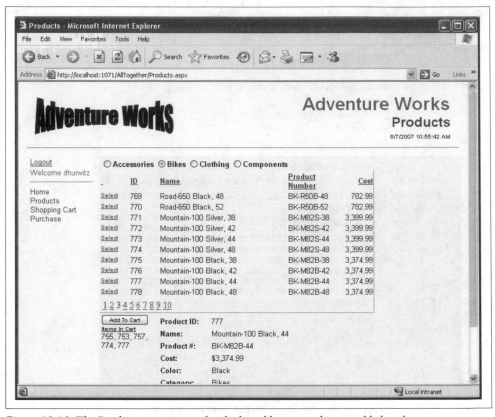

Figure 10-10. The Products page is now finished, and has several items added to the cart.

```
<asp:Content ID="Content1" ContentPlaceHolderID="ContentPlaceHolder1"
        Runat="Server">
    <asp:UpdatePanel id="UpdatePanel1" runat="server">
        <ContentTemplate>

            ... all the content goes here ...

        </ContentTemplate>
    </asp:UpdatePanel>
</asp:Content>
```

The ScriptManager control should be on the master page, so you don't have to add one to every content page. So open *MasterPage.master* and drag a ScriptManager control onto the page, if it is not already there.

> When you put all the content inside the UpdatePanel, the IDE may complain all of a sudden about the validity of ASP.NET controls. Ignore this; it will work fine.
>
> However, this "feature" of the IDE does make it more difficult to develop, because IntelliSense will not work. That is why we waited until the end of developing this page to add the AJAX.

Cart Page

The Cart page displays the contents of the cart and allows you to remove items from the cart. It also provides a button to purchase the items in the cart, which would, of course, take you to the Purchase page.

 Of course, a full-featured cart would provide much more functionality than the simple cart shown here. For example, your fully featured commercial site might uses personalization to remember what was added to the cart in previous sessions and restore that information in a new session. It would almost certainly allow the user to change the quantity ordered of a given item, not to mention things such as size or color.

Open *Cart.aspx*. Drag a SqlDataSource control onto the content area of the page. Set its ID to sqlCart. Configure it similar to the SqlDataSource in Example 10-8. Here is the markup for the control. It looks complex, but really it is a straightforward SELECT statement against the Production.Product table, with five joins:

```
<asp:SqlDataSource ID="sqlCart" runat="server"
    ConnectionString="<%$ ConnectionStrings:AdventureWorksConnectionString %>"
    SelectCommand= "select product.ProductID, product.Name, product.ProductNumber,
        product.Color,
        subcat.Name as SubcategoryName, cat.Name as CategoryName,
        description.Description
        from Production.Product product
        join Production.ProductSubcategory subcat on
            product.ProductSubcategoryID = subcat.ProductSubcategoryID
        join Production.ProductCategory cat on
            subcat.ProductCategoryID = cat.ProductCategoryID
        join Production.ProductModel model on
            product.ProductModelID = model.ProductModelID
        join Production.ProductModelProductDescriptionCulture culture on
            model.ProductModelID = culture.ProductModelID
        join Production.ProductDescription description on
            culture.ProductDescriptionID = description.ProductDescriptionID">
</asp:SqlDataSource>
```

This query needs a WHERE clause. The parameter in the WHERE clause needs to come from the Session object. ASP.NET actually makes this really easy under some circumstances—but not these circumstances, as we will now describe.

You saw previously in Example 10-8 the use of the <SelectParameters> element of the SqlDataSource, reproduced here, with a parameter based on the value of another control on the page:

```
<SelectParameters>
    <asp:ControlParameter ControlID="gvProducts"
        Name="ProductID" PropertyName="SelectedDataKey.Values['ProductID']" />
</SelectParameters>
```

There are other types of SelectParameters controls, including a SessionParameter, which comes from a Session object. The reason that will not work here is due to a "quirk" of the SQL used to construct the query. I'll explain.

The cart is stored in a string as a comma-separated list of ProductIDs, which are stored in the database as integers. The query sent to the database has a where clause using the in keyword, as in:

CODE►
```
where product.ProductID in (753,845,143) and culture.CultureID = 'en'
```

SQL Server knows that ProductID is an integer and is able to parse the contents of the parenthesis as a list of integers. However, when you use the SessionParameter control, it encloses the contents of the parenthesis with quotes, as in:

CODE►
```
where product.ProductID in ("753,845,143") and culture.CultureID = 'en'
```

That makes it a string, and SQL Server cannot parse it as a set of integers. There may be a way to deal with this in SQL, but it is easier, and more instructive, to work around this by hooking in the Selecting event of the SqlDataSource control. This event is raised just before the query is sent to the database, and is a convenient time to modify the query.

Add the code from Example 10-10 to handle this event (as well as events for two controls you will place on the page in just a moment). It retrieves the Session object and constructs the where clause, setting the CommandText subproperty of the event argument's Command property. Because this event is raised before the query is executed, changing the CommandText of the query allows you to modify the query before it is run; using this technique, you can have the WHERE clause refer to a specific ProductID.

Example 10-10. Cart.aspx.vb event handlers

```
Protected Sub sqlCart_Selecting(ByVal sender As Object, _
        ByVal e As System.Web.UI.WebControls.SqlDataSourceSelectingEventArgs) _
        Handles sqlCart.Selecting

    Trace.Warn("sqlCart_Selecting")        ' to aid in debugging

    Dim strCart As String = String.Empty
    If Session("Cart") IsNot Nothing Then
        strCart = Session("Cart").ToString
        e.Command.CommandText &= " where product.ProductID in (" + _
            strCart + _
            ") and culture.CultureID = 'en' "
    Else
        e.Cancel = True
    End If
End Sub


Protected Sub btnPurchase_Click(ByVal sender As Object, _
        ByVal e As System.EventArgs) _
        Handles btnPurchase.Click
```

Example 10-10. Cart.aspx.vb event handlers (continued)

```
        Response.Redirect("Purchase.aspx")
    End Sub


    Protected Sub gvCart_SelectedIndexChanged(ByVal sender As Object, _
            ByVal e As System.EventArgs) _
            Handles gvCart.SelectedIndexChanged
        Dim strProductID As String = gvCart.SelectedRow.Cells(1).Text
        If Session("Cart") IsNot Nothing Then
            ' remove the selected ProductID from the Session string
            ' Retrieve the session string.
            Dim strCart As String = Session("Cart").ToString()
            Dim arIDs As String() = strCart.Split(New [Char]() {","c})

            ' iterate through the ID's comprising the string array
            ' rebuild the cart string, leaving out the matching ID
            strCart = String.Empty
            For Each str As String In arIDs
                ' use Trim to remove leading and trailing spaces
                If str.Trim() <> strProductID.Trim() Then
                    strCart += str + ", "
                End If
            Next

            ' remove the trailing space and comma
            If strCart.Length > 1 Then
                strCart = strCart.Trim()
                strCart = strCart.Substring(0, strCart.Length - 1)
            End If

            ' put it back into Session
            Session("Cart") = strCart

            ' rebind the GridView, which will force the SqlDataSource to requery
            gvCart.DataBind()
        End If          ' close for test for Session
    End Sub
```

Now drag a GridView onto the page, setting its ID to gvCart. Configure it similar to the previous GridView. Here is the markup for gvCart:

```
<asp:GridView ID="gvCart" runat="server"
        DataSourceID="sqlCart"
        AllowPaging="True" AllowSorting="True" Width="100%"
        AutoGenerateColumns="False"
        HeaderStyle-CssClass="TableColumnHeading"
        RowStyle-CssClass="TableCells">
    <Columns>
        <asp:CommandField ShowSelectButton="True" SelectText="Remove"
            ControlStyle-CssClass="ButtonSelect" ItemStyle-Width="50px"
                ItemStyle-HorizontalAlign="Center"/>
        <asp:BoundField DataField="ProductID" HeaderText="ID"
                ItemStyle-Width="50px"/>
```

```
            <asp:BoundField DataField="ProductNumber" HeaderText="Product Number"
                    ItemStyle-Width="90px" />
            <asp:BoundField DataField="Color" HeaderText="Color"
                    ItemStyle-Width="60px" />
            <asp:BoundField DataField="CategoryName" HeaderText="Cat"
                    ItemStyle-Width="75px" />
            <asp:BoundField DataField="SubcategoryName" HeaderText="SubCat"
                    ItemStyle-Width="75px" />
            <asp:BoundField DataField="Description" HeaderText="Description"  />
        </Columns>
    </asp:GridView>
```

Below the `GridView` place an HTML `<br />` element and an ASP.NET Button control
called btnPurchase.

`CODE`
```
<br />
<asp:Button ID="btnPurchase" runat="server" Text="Purchase Items in the Cart"
        CssClass="ButtonText"/>
```

The code to handle the `Click` event of this button is included in Example 10-10. All
this event handler does is redirect readers to the Purchase page, which you'll create
shortly.

The Remove button on each row of the `GridView` is not a normal ASP.NET Button
control, but rather a `SelectButton` with its `SelectText` property set to `Remove`. Clicking a `SelectButton` in a GridView selects that row of the grid. This is handled with
the gvCart_SelectedIndexChanged event handler, included in Example 10-10.

Run through the app, logging in and adding some items to the cart. Then switch to
the Cart page. You will see something similar to Figure 10-11.

Purchase Page

Clicking on the Purchase button on the Cart page brings you to the Purchase page.
This page is used to gather billing and shipping information from the customer. It
has a layout table with a bunch of `TextBox` controls, a couple of `RadioButtonLists`, a
Buy Now button, and a bunch of associated validation controls.

The first row of the layout table is just a heading. The second row collects the Name.
This is a required field, so it has a `RequiredFieldValidator`.

`CODE`
```
<table border="0" class="TableRowHeading">
    <tr>
        <td colspan="4">
            Billing Information
        </td>
    </tr>
    <tr>
        <td>Name</td>
        <td colspan="4">
            <asp:TextBox ID="txtName" runat="server" Width="250" />
```

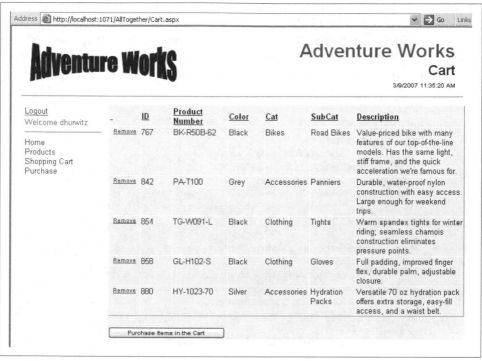

Figure 10-11. Here's what the cart page looks like after you've added some items to the cart.

```
<asp:RequiredFieldValidator ID="rfName" runat="server"
    ControlToValidate="txtName"
    Display="Dynamic" ErrorMessage="Name is a required field."
    CssClass="ValidationError">*</asp:RequiredFieldValidator></td>
    </tr>
```

All the validation controls on this page will use Dynamic Display, so room will only be allocated on the page if it is necessary to display the validation text. For this and all the other validation controls, the validation text is simply an asterisk to display next to the invalid control. A ValidationSummary control at the bottom of the page will gather all the ErrorMessages into a single location.

The next row is the Address, which is very similar to the Name row:

```
<tr>
    <td>Address</td>
    <td colspan="3">
        <asp:TextBox ID="txtAddress" runat="server" Width="250" />
        <asp:RequiredFieldValidator ID="rfAddress" runat="server"
            ControlToValidate="txtAddress"
            Display="Dynamic" ErrorMessage="Address is a required field."
            CssClass="ValidationError">*</asp:RequiredFieldValidator></td>
    </tr>
```

Next is a row for both City and State. City is a straightforward TextBox, just like Name and Address. However, the State control is a DropDownList that is populated from the database. A SqlDataSource is used to populate this DropDownList and another one further down used as part of the shipping address with a list of state names from the database. It is a very simple query; there are no parameters necessary.

CODE▶

```
<tr>
    <td>City</td>
    <td style="width: 181px">
        <asp:TextBox ID="txtCity" runat="server" />
        <asp:RequiredFieldValidator ID="rfCity" runat="server"
            ControlToValidate="txtCity"
            Display="Dynamic" ErrorMessage="City is a required field."
            CssClass="ValidationError">*</asp:RequiredFieldValidator>
    </td>
    <td>
        <asp:SqlDataSource ID="sqlStates" runat="server"
            ConnectionString=
                "<%$ ConnectionStrings:AdventureWorksConnectionString %>"
            SelectCommand="SELECT StateProvinceCode, [Name]
                    FROM Person.StateProvince
                    WHERE CountryRegionCode = 'US' order by [Name]">
        </asp:SqlDataSource>
        <asp:DropDownList ID="ddlStates" runat="server"
            DataSourceID="sqlStates"
            DataTextField="Name" DataValueField="StateProvinceCode" />
    </td>
</tr>
```

The next row gathers the zip code, validated by a RegularExpressionValidator to be a valid U.S. zip code, as well as being required. The regular expression requires either five digits or five digits plus four more separated by a dash.

CODE▶

```
<tr>
    <td>Zip</td>
    <td style="width: 181px">
        <asp:TextBox ID="txtZip" runat="server" />
        <asp:RequiredFieldValidator ID="rfZip" runat="server"
            ControlToValidate="txtZip"
            Display="Dynamic" ErrorMessage="Zip is a required field."
            CssClass="ValidationError">*</asp:RequiredFieldValidator>
        <asp:RegularExpressionValidator ID="reZip" runat="server"
            ErrorMessage="Invalid Zip format"
            ControlToValidate="txtZip"
            Display="Dynamic"
            ValidationExpression="^\d{5}$|^\d{5}-\d{4}$"
            CssClass="ValidationError">*</asp:RegularExpressionValidator>
    </td>
</tr>
```

Next is a row to gather credit card information. A RadioButtonList allows the user a choice of credit card type, and again validates that the user makes a choice.

CODE

```
        <tr>
            <td>Card</td>
            <td colspan="3" >
                <asp:RadioButtonList ID="rblCardType" runat="server"
                        RepeatDirection="Horizontal">
                    <asp:ListItem Value="am" Text="American Express" />
                    <asp:ListItem Value="d" Text="Discover" />
                    <asp:ListItem Value="mc" Text="MasterCard" />
                    <asp:ListItem Value="v" Text="Visa" />
                </asp:RadioButtonList>
                <asp:RequiredFieldValidator ID="rfCreditCard" runat="server"
                    ErrorMessage="Credit Card type is missing."
                    ControlToValidate="rblCardType" Display="Dynamic"
                    InitialValue=""
                    CssClass="ValidationError">*</asp:RequiredFieldValidator>
            </td>
        </tr>
```

The next row gathers the credit card number and security code. Both are required and both use a RegularExpressionValidator to ensure valid formats.

CODE

```
        <tr>
            <td>CC #</td>
            <td style="width: 181px">
                <asp:TextBox ID="txtCCNumber" runat="server" />
                <asp:RequiredFieldValidator ID="rfCCNumber" runat="server"
                    ControlToValidate="txtCCNumber"
                    Display="Dynamic"
                    ErrorMessage="Credit Card Number is a required field."
                    CssClass="ValidationError">*</asp:RequiredFieldValidator>
                <asp:RegularExpressionValidator ID="reCCNumber" runat="server"
                    ErrorMessage="Invalid Credit Card Number"
                    ControlToValidate="txtCCNumber"
                    Display="Dynamic"
                    ValidationExpression=
                        "^(\d{4}-){3}\d{4}$|^(\d{4} ){3}\d{4}$|^\d{16}$"
                    CssClass="ValidationError">*</asp:RegularExpressionValidator>
            </td>
            <td align="right">Security Code</td>
            <td>
                <asp:TextBox ID="txtSecurityCode" runat="server" />
                <asp:RequiredFieldValidator ID="rfSecurityCode" runat="server"
                    ControlToValidate="txtSecurityCode"
                    Display="Dynamic"
                    ErrorMessage="Security Code is a required field."
                    CssClass="ValidationError">*</asp:RequiredFieldValidator>
                <asp:RegularExpressionValidator ID="reSecurityCode" runat="server"
                    ErrorMessage="Invalid Security Code"
                    ControlToValidate="txtSecurityCode"
                    Display="Dynamic"
                    ValidationExpression="^\d{3}$"
                    CssClass="ValidationError">*</asp:RegularExpressionValidator>
            </td>
        </tr>
```

The credit card number formats allowed are any of the following:

```
1234-1234-1234-1234
1234 1234 1234 1234
1234123412341234
```

 It drives me batty when web sites require a credit card number with no spaces or dashes. It is so easy to accept those characters and just remove them before submission, and it would greatly reduce input errors. Long numbers are much easier to enter and read with intervening spaces or dashes.

The security number is simply a three-digit number.

The next row contains a RadioButtonList to give the user the choice of shipping to the billing address or a different shipping address. Depending on the selected value of that control, a Panel control containing a field for the shipping address is either made visible or not. The code for doing this is contained in an event handler for the SelectedIndexChanged event of rblShippingAddress, included in Example 10-11.

```
<tr>
    <td colspan="2">
        Shipping Information
    </td>
    <td colspan="2">
        <asp:RadioButtonList ID="rblShippingAddress" runat="server"
            AutoPostBack="true" RepeatDirection="Horizontal">
            <asp:ListItem Value="billing" Text="Ship to Billing Address"
                    Selected="True" />
            <asp:ListItem Value="different"
                    Text="Ship to Different Address" />
        </asp:RadioButtonList>
    </td>
</tr>
```

AutoPostBack is set to true so that the page will respond immediately when the user changes the selection. If a different address is required, then a Panel contained in the next row is made visible.

```
<tr>
    <td colspan="4">
        <asp:Panel ID="pnlShippingAddress" runat="server" Visible="false" >
            <table border="0">
                <tr>
                    <td>Address</td>
                    <td colspan="3">
                        <asp:TextBox ID="txtShippingAddress" runat="server"
                            Width="250" />
                    </td>
                </tr>
                <tr>
                    <td>City</td>
```

```
            <td>
                <asp:TextBox ID="txtShippingCity" runat="server" />
            </td>
            <td>
                <asp:DropDownList ID="ddlShippingStates"
                    runat="server"
                    DataSourceID="sqlStates"
                    DataTextField="Name"
                    DataValueField="StateProvinceCode" />
            </td>
            <td>Zip</td>
            <td>
                <asp:TextBox ID="txtShippingZip" runat="server" />
                <asp:RegularExpressionValidator ID="reShippingZip"
                    runat="server"
                    ErrorMessage="Invalid Zip format"
                    ControlToValidate="txtShippingZip"
                    Display="Dynamic"
                    ValidationExpression="^\d{5}$|^\d{5}-\d{4}$"
                    CssClass="ValidationError">*
                </asp:RegularExpressionValidator>
            </td>
        </tr>
    </table>
</asp:Panel>
        </td>
    </tr>
```

Notice how this `Panel` control itself contains another table for laying out the controls used to gather the shipping address.

Finally, there is a row to contain the `ValidationSummary` control.

CODE
```
<tr>
    <td colspan="4">
        <asp:ValidationSummary ID="ValidationSummary1" runat="server"
            CssClass="ValidationError" />
    </td>
</tr>
```

And one more row to contain the `Button` for completing the purchase.

CODE
```
<tr>
    <td colspan="4">
        <asp:Button ID="btnBuy" runat="server" Text="Buy Now"
            CssClass="ButtonText" />
    </td>
</tr>
</table>
```

When the Buy Now button is clicked, a real application would process the order, updating the database as necessary. In our simple example, it will stash the order info in `Session` in a Dictionary object, and then call the `Confirm` page for order confirmation. The event handler for the Buy Now button is included in Example 10-11.

Note that in order for the Dictionary object to be properly instantiated, you must include the Imports statement at the top of Example 10-11.

Example 10-11. Purchase.aspx.vb event handlers

```vb
Imports System.Collections.Generic

Protected Sub rblShippingAddress_SelectedIndexChanged(ByVal sender As Object, _
        ByVal e As System.EventArgs) _
        Handles rblShippingAddress.SelectedIndexChanged
    If rblShippingAddress.SelectedValue = "billing" Then
        pnlShippingAddress.Visible = False
    Else
        pnlShippingAddress.Visible = True
    End If
End Sub


Protected Sub btnBuy_Click(ByVal sender As Object, _
        ByVal e As System.EventArgs) _
        Handles btnBuy.Click
    ' stash all the info in a dictionary object going to Session
    Dim dictBuy As Dictionary(Of String, String) = _
        New Dictionary(Of String, String)
    dictBuy.Add("Name", txtName.Text)
    dictBuy.Add("Address", txtAddress.Text)
    dictBuy.Add("City", txtCity.Text)
    dictBuy.Add("State", ddlStates.SelectedValue)
    dictBuy.Add("Zip", txtZip.Text)
    dictBuy.Add("Card", rblCardType.SelectedValue)
    dictBuy.Add("CardNumber", txtCCNumber.Text)
    dictBuy.Add("SecurityCode", txtSecurityCode.Text)

    If rblShippingAddress.SelectedValue = "billing" Then
        dictBuy.Add("ShippingAddress", txtAddress.Text)
        dictBuy.Add("ShippingCity", txtCity.Text)
        dictBuy.Add("ShippingState", ddlStates.SelectedValue)
        dictBuy.Add("ShippingZip", txtZip.Text)
    Else
        dictBuy.Add("ShippingAddress", txtShippingAddress.Text)
        dictBuy.Add("ShippingCity", txtShippingCity.Text)
        dictBuy.Add("ShippingState", ddlShippingStates.SelectedValue)
        dictBuy.Add("ShippingZip", txtShippingZip.Text)
    End If

    Session("BuyerInfo") = dictBuy

    Response.Redirect("Confirm.aspx")
End Sub
```

Now run the web site and navigate to the Purchase page, as shown in Figure 10-12, after filling in most of the fields along with an invalid zip code.

Adventure Works
Purchase
3/9/2007 1:42:20 PM

Logout
Welcome dhurwitz

Home
Products
Shopping Cart
Purchase

Billing Information

Name | Dan Hurwitz

Address | 123 Main Street

City | Worcester | Massachusetts

Zip | 01655-12345 | *

Card | ○ American Express ○ Discover ○ MasterCard ⊙ Visa

CC # | 1234-1234-1234-1234 | **Security Code** | 123

Shipping Information | ○ Ship to Billing Address ⊙ Ship to Different Address

Address | 125b Main Street

City | Worcester | Massachusetts | **Zip** | 01655

- Invalid Zip format

[Buy Now]

Figure 10-12. The Purchase page looks like this after you've entered information, including an invalid zip code, and then clicked Buy Now.

This page would benefit from being wrapped inside an UpdatePanel, as was done for the Products page. However, there is an unwanted interaction between the validation controls and the AJAX control, both of which work with the use of client-side JavaScript. Therefore, we will leave the AJAX off this page.

Confirm Page

The Confirm page in this example does nothing more than retrieve the two Session objects, one containing the cart and one containing the buyer information, and display them on the page. The cart is displayed in a GridView and the buyer information is displayed in a ListBox.

Again, the page contains an HTML table for layout. The first row contains a GridView and its associated data source for the cart information.

CODE▶

```
<table>
    <tr>
        <td valign="top" class="ListHeading">Cart:</td>
        <td valign="top">
            <asp:SqlDataSource ID="sqlCartConfirm" runat="server"
                ConnectionString=
                    "<%$ ConnectionStrings:AdventureWorksConnectionString %>"
```

```
             SelectCommand= "select ProductID, Name, ProductNumber, Color,
                     ListPrice
                     from Production.Product " >
        </asp:SqlDataSource>

        <asp:GridView ID="gvCart" runat="server"
               DataSourceID="sqlCartConfirm"
               AllowPaging="True" AllowSorting="True"
               HeaderStyle-CssClass="TableColumnHeading"
               RowStyle-CssClass="TableCells"
               AutoGenerateColumns="false">
          <Columns>
              <asp:BoundField DataField="ProductID" HeaderText="ID" />
              <asp:BoundField DataField="Name" HeaderText="Name" />
              <asp:BoundField DataField="ProductNumber"
                  HeaderText="Product #" />
              <asp:BoundField DataField="Color" HeaderText="Color" />
              <asp:BoundField DataField="ListPrice" HeaderText="Cost"
                  DataFormatString="{0:F2}"  HtmlEncode="false"/>
          </Columns>
        </asp:GridView>
      </td>
    </tr>
```

The SelectCommand of the SqlDataSource is updated with the contents of the Cart Session object, exactly as was done for the Cart page, using the Selecting event of the SqlDataSource control.

```
    Protected Sub sqlCartConfirm_Selecting(ByVal sender As Object, _
    ByVal e As System.Web.UI.WebControls.SqlDataSourceSelectingEventArgs) _
    Handles sqlCartConfirm.Selecting

        Trace.Warn("sqlCartConfirm_Selecting")    ' aid in debugging

        If Session("Cart") IsNot Nothing Then
            Dim strCart = Session("Cart").ToString
            e.Command.CommandText &= "where ProductID in (" + _
                strCart + ")"
        Else
            e.Cancel = True
        End If

    End Sub
```

After a spacing row, the next row contains a ListBox for the buyer information.

```
        <tr>
          <td colspan="2"> </td>
        </tr>
        <tr>
          <td valign="top" class="ListHeading">Buyer Info:</td>
          <td valign="top">
            <asp:ListBox ID="lbBuyerInfo" runat="server" Rows="12"
                Width="250" />
```

```
            </td>
        </tr>
    </table>
```

The ListBox is populated in Page_Load the first time the page is loaded.

```
CODE▶    Protected Sub Page_Load(ByVal sender As Object, _
                ByVal e As System.EventArgs) Handles Me.Load
            If User.Identity.IsAuthenticated = False Then
                Response.Redirect("login.aspx")
            End If

            Me.Master.PageSubTitle.Text = "Confirmation"

            If Not IsPostBack Then
                lbBuyerInfo.Items.Clear()
                If Session("BuyerInfo") IsNot Nothing Then
                    Dim dictBuyerInfo As Dictionary(Of String, String) = Nothing
                    dictBuyerInfo = CType(Session("BuyerInfo"), _
                        Dictionary(Of String, String))
                    For Each key As String In dictBuyerInfo.Keys
                        lbBuyerInfo.Items.Add(key + ": " + dictBuyerInfo(key))
                    Next
                Else
                    lbBuyerInfo.Items.Add("There is no buyer info.")
                End If
            End If

        End Sub
```

In order for the Dictionary to work in this method, you need to add the following line at the top of the code-behind file to import the proper namespace:

```
CODE▶    Imports System.Collections.Generic
```

The markup for this page is shown in Example 10-14 and the code-behind is in Example 10-15.

Running the site and navigating through the entire purchase process brings you to the confirmation page shown in Figure 10-13.

Custom Error Pages

In case of any errors, you don't want your users to see the ugly generic error page provided by ASP.NET, so you will add some custom error pages, just like you did in Chapter 8. To do so, add the following section to the *web.config* file, within the <system.web> section:

```
CODE▶    <!-- Valid values of customErrors mode: On, Off, RemoteOnly -->
        <customErrors mode="RemoteOnly" defaultRedirect="CustomErrorPage.aspx">
            <error statusCode="400" redirect="CustomErrorPage400.aspx"/>
            <error statusCode="404" redirect="CustomErrorPage404.aspx"/>
            <error statusCode="500" redirect="CustomErrorPage500.aspx"/>
        </customErrors>
```

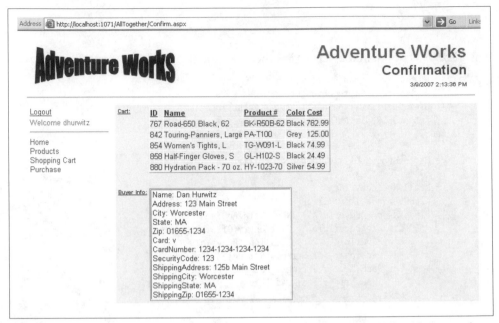

Figure 10-13. Here's the last page the user will see: the confirmation page. All the information from the Cart and the Purchase page is passed here and displayed again.

This will provide for specific error pages to cover errors 400, "Bad Request," the ubiquitous 404, "Not Found," and the dreaded 500, "Internal Server Error." It will also specify a generic error page for any error not specifically covered. Setting the mode to RemoteOnly means while working on your local machine, you will see the generic error page, with all its helpful information, but remote users will see your custom error pages.

 Notice that here the custom error pages have an extension of *.aspx*, rather than the *.htm* used in Chapter 8. This is so they can take advantage of the master pages.

Now you need to actually create those error pages. Add four new pages to the web site called *CustomErrorPage.aspx*, *CustomErrorPage400.aspx*, *CustomErrorPage404. aspx,* and *CustomErrorPage500.aspx*. Be sure to check the checkboxes for "Place code in a separate file" and "Select master page."

In the markup file for each of these new pages, add the following MasterType directive, after the Page directive but before the opening `<asp:Content>` tag:

CODE
```
<%@ MasterType TypeName="MasterPage" %>
```

This will allow each page to modify the master page, setting the page subtitle appropriately. To do this, add the following Page_Load method to each page:

```
Protected Sub Page_Load(ByVal sender As Object, _
        ByVal e As System.EventArgs) Handles Me.Load
    Me.Master.PageSubTitle.Text = "Error"
End Sub
```

Finally, add some content to each page to indicate what the error is and what to do about it. While you are at it, add a HyperLink to take the user back to the Home page.

Summary

There you have it—a functional web site with user registration, data access, session state, and a consistent look and feel, all coded by you. You can now go out and create sites that you didn't dream were possible just a short time ago.

Don't let this be the end of your learning, though. Although you're quite familiar with most of the controls we've discussed, they also have plenty of properties that you can still discover on your own. Experiment with the examples and exercises in this book to see what's possible. The Web is full of ASP.NET resources to continue your education—the AJAX community is adding new extenders all the time, just to pick one example. And, of course, there are other fine books out there, including *Programming ASP.NET*, to help you learn about the advanced controls.

Source Code Listings

The style sheet, *StyleSheet.css*, is listed in Example 10-1.

The site map file, *Web.sitemap*, is listed in Example 10-7.

Cart Page

Example 10-12. Cart.aspx

```
<%@ Page Language="VB" MasterPageFile="~/MasterPage.master" AutoEventWireup="false"
    CodeFile="Cart.aspx.vb" Inherits="Cart" title="Cart" %>
<%@ MasterType TypeName="MasterPage" %>
<asp:Content ID="Content1" ContentPlaceHolderID="ContentPlaceHolder1"
    Runat="Server">
    <asp:SqlDataSource ID="sqlCart" runat="server"
        ConnectionString="<%$ ConnectionStrings:AdventureWorksConnectionString %>"
        SelectCommand= "select product.ProductID, product.Name,
                product.ProductNumber, product.Color,
                subcat.Name as SubcategoryName, cat.Name as CategoryName,
                description.Description
                from Production.Product product
                join Production.ProductSubcategory subcat on
                    product.ProductSubcategoryID = subcat.ProductSubcategoryID
                join Production.ProductCategory cat on
                    subcat.ProductCategoryID = cat.ProductCategoryID
```

Example 10-12. Cart.aspx (continued)

```
                    join Production.ProductModel model on
                        product.ProductModelID = model.ProductModelID
                    join Production.ProductModelProductDescriptionCulture culture
                        on model.ProductModelID = culture.ProductModelID
                    join Production.ProductDescription description on
                        culture.ProductDescriptionID =
                            description.ProductDescriptionID ">
    </asp:SqlDataSource>
    <asp:GridView ID="gvCart" runat="server"
            DataSourceID="sqlCart"
            AllowPaging="True" AllowSorting="True" Width="100%"
            AutoGenerateColumns="False"
            HeaderStyle-CssClass="TableColumnHeading"
            RowStyle-CssClass="TableCells">
        <Columns>
            <asp:CommandField ShowSelectButton="True" SelectText="Remove"
                ControlStyle-CssClass="ButtonSelect" ItemStyle-Width="50px"
                    ItemStyle-HorizontalAlign="Center"/>
            <asp:BoundField DataField="ProductID" HeaderText="ID"
                    ItemStyle-Width="50px"/>
            <asp:BoundField DataField="ProductNumber" HeaderText="Product Number"
                    ItemStyle-Width="90px" />
            <asp:BoundField DataField="Color" HeaderText="Color"
                    ItemStyle-Width="60px" />
            <asp:BoundField DataField="CategoryName" HeaderText="Cat"
                    ItemStyle-Width="75px" />
            <asp:BoundField DataField="SubcategoryName" HeaderText="SubCat"
                    ItemStyle-Width="75px" />
            <asp:BoundField DataField="Description" HeaderText="Description"  />
        </Columns>
    </asp:GridView>
    <br />
    <asp:Button ID="btnPurchase" runat="server" Text="Purchase Items in the Cart"
            CssClass="ButtonText"/>
</asp:Content>
```

Example 10-13. Cart.aspx.vb

```
Partial Class Cart
    Inherits System.Web.UI.Page

    Protected Sub Page_Load(ByVal sender As Object, _
            ByVal e As System.EventArgs) Handles Me.Load
        If User.Identity.IsAuthenticated = False Then
            Response.Redirect("login.aspx")
        End If

        Me.Master.PageSubTitle.Text = "Cart"
    End Sub

Protected Sub sqlCart_Selecting(ByVal sender As Object, _
        ByVal e As System.Web.UI.WebControls.SqlDataSourceSelectingEventArgs) _
        Handles sqlCart.Selecting
```

Example 10-13. Cart.aspx.vb (continued)

```vb
    Trace.Warn("sqlCart_Selecting")

    Dim strCart As String = String.Empty
    If Session("Cart") IsNot Nothing Then
        strCart = Session("Cart").ToString
        e.Command.CommandText &= " where product.ProductID in (" + _
            strCart + _
            ") and culture.CultureID = 'en' "
    Else
        e.Cancel = True
    End If
End Sub

Protected Sub btnPurchase_Click(ByVal sender As Object, _
        ByVal e As System.EventArgs) _
        Handles btnPurchase.Click
    Response.Redirect("Purchase.aspx")
End Sub

Protected Sub gvCart_SelectedIndexChanged(ByVal sender As Object, _
        ByVal e As System.EventArgs) _
        Handles gvCart.SelectedIndexChanged
    Dim strProductID As String = gvCart.SelectedRow.Cells(1).Text
    If Session("Cart") IsNot Nothing Then
        ' remove the selected ProductID from the Session string
        ' Retrieve the session string.
        Dim strCart As String = Session("Cart").ToString()
        Dim arIDs As String() = strCart.Split(New [Char]() {","c})

        ' iterate through the ID's comprising the string array
        ' rebuild the cart string, leaving out the matching ID
        strCart = String.Empty
        For Each str As String In arIDs
            If str <> strProductID Then
                strCart += str + ","
            End If
        Next

        ' remove the trailing comma
        If strCart.Length > 1 Then
            strCart = strCart.Substring(0, strCart.Length - 1)
        End If

        ' put it back into Session
        Session("Cart") = strCart

        ' rebind the GridView, which will force the SqlDataSource to requery
        gvCart.DataBind()
    End If          ' close for test for Session
End Sub

End Class
```

Confirm Page

Example 10-14. Confirm.aspx

```
<%@ Page Language="VB" MasterPageFile="~/MasterPage.master" AutoEventWireup="false"
    CodeFile="Confirm.aspx.vb" Inherits="Confirm" title="Confirm" %>
<%@ MasterType TypeName="MasterPage" %>
<asp:Content ID="Content1" ContentPlaceHolderID="ContentPlaceHolder1"
        Runat="Server">
    <table>
        <tr>
            <td valign="top" class="ListHeading">Cart:</td>
            <td valign="top">
                <asp:SqlDataSource ID="sqlCartConfirm" runat="server"
                    ConnectionString=
                        "<%$ ConnectionStrings:AdventureWorksConnectionString %>"
                    SelectCommand= "select ProductID, Name, ProductNumber, Color,
                                ListPrice
                                from Production.Product " >
                </asp:SqlDataSource>
                <asp:GridView ID="gvCart" runat="server"
                        DataSourceID="sqlCartConfirm"
                        AllowPaging="True" AllowSorting="True"
                        HeaderStyle-CssClass="TableColumnHeading"
                        RowStyle-CssClass="TableCells"
                        AutoGenerateColumns="false">
                    <Columns>
                        <asp:BoundField DataField="ProductID" HeaderText="ID" />
                        <asp:BoundField DataField="Name" HeaderText="Name" />
                        <asp:BoundField DataField="ProductNumber"
                            HeaderText="Product #" />
                        <asp:BoundField DataField="Color" HeaderText="Color" />
                        <asp:BoundField DataField="ListPrice" HeaderText="Cost"
                            DataFormatString="{0:F2}"  HtmlEncode="false"/>
                    </Columns>
                </asp:GridView>
            </td>
        </tr>
        <tr>
            <td colspan="2"> </td>
        </tr>
        <tr>
            <td valign="top" class="ListHeading">Buyer Info:</td>
            <td valign="top">
                <asp:ListBox ID="lbBuyerInfo" runat="server" Rows="12"
                    Width="250" />
            </td>
        </tr>
    </table>
</asp:Content>
```

Example 10-15. Confirm.aspx.vb

```vb
Imports System.Collections.Generic

Partial Class Confirm
    Inherits System.Web.UI.Page

    Protected Sub Page_Load(ByVal sender As Object, _
            ByVal e As System.EventArgs) Handles Me.Load
        If User.Identity.IsAuthenticated = False Then
            Response.Redirect("login.aspx")
        End If

        Me.Master.PageSubTitle.Text = "Confirmation"

        If Not IsPostBack Then
            lbBuyerInfo.Items.Clear()
            If Session("BuyerInfo") IsNot Nothing Then
                Dim dictBuyerInfo As Dictionary(Of String, String) = Nothing
                dictBuyerInfo = CType(Session("BuyerInfo"), _
                    Dictionary(Of String, String))
                For Each key As String In dictBuyerInfo.Keys
                    lbBuyerInfo.Items.Add(key + ": " + dictBuyerInfo(key))
                Next
            Else
                lbBuyerInfo.Items.Add("There is no buyer info.")
            End If
        End If

    End Sub

    Protected Sub sqlCartConfirm_Selecting(ByVal sender As Object, _
        ByVal e As System.Web.UI.WebControls.SqlDataSourceSelectingEventArgs) _
        Handles sqlCartConfirm.Selecting

        Trace.Warn("sqlCartConfirm_Selecting")    ' aid in debugging

        If Session("Cart") IsNot Nothing Then
            Dim strCart = Session("Cart").ToString
            e.Command.CommandText &= "where ProductID in (" + _
                strCart + ")"
        Else
            e.Cancel = True
        End If

End Sub

End Class
```

Home Page

Example 10-16. Home.aspx

```
<%@ Page Language="VB" MasterPageFile="~/MasterPage.master" AutoEventWireup="false"
    CodeFile="Home.aspx.vb" Inherits="Home" title="Home Page" Trace="false"%>
<%@ MasterType TypeName="MasterPage" %>
<asp:Content ID="Content1" ContentPlaceHolderID="ContentPlaceHolder1"
    Runat="Server">
    <h2>This Is Your Home Page</h2>
    <div class="TextNormal">
        You can put some stuff about your company here.  Perhaps some links.
        Of course, in a real world application, the navigation would probably
        much more complex. Also, the buttons would actually do something,
        rather than just wave their arms and say <span class="TextBold">
        Look at me!</span>
    </div>
    <asp:Panel ID="pnlEmployee" runat="server" Visible="false" >
        <h3>Employee Information</h3>
        <div class="TextNormal">
            This panel should only be visible to users are a members of the
            <b>Employee</b> role. Turning on the visibility of this Panel
            occurs in the Page_Load event handler.
        </div>
    </asp:Panel>
    <asp:Panel ID="pnlManager" runat="server" Visible="false" >
        <h3>Manager Information</h3>
        <div class="TextNormal">
            This panel should only be visible to users are a members of the
            <b>Manager</b> role. Turning on the visibility of this Panel
            occurs in the Page_Load event handler.
        </div>
    </asp:Panel>
</asp:Content>
```

Example 10-17. Home.aspx.vb

```
Partial Class Home
    Inherits System.Web.UI.Page

    Protected Sub Page_Load(ByVal sender As Object, _
            ByVal e As System.EventArgs) Handles Me.Load
        Me.Master.PageSubTitle.Text = "Home"

        ' control the visibility of sections restricted to specific roles
        pnlManager.Visible = User.IsInRole("Manager")
        pnlEmployee.Visible = User.IsInRole("Employee")
    End Sub
End Class
```

Login Page

Example 10-18. Login.aspx

```
<%@ Page Language="VB" MasterPageFile="~/MasterPage.master" AutoEventWireup="false"
    CodeFile="Login.aspx.vb" Inherits="Login" title="Login" Trace="false" %>
<%@ MasterType TypeName="MasterPage" %>
<asp:Content ID="Content1" ContentPlaceHolderID="ContentPlaceHolder1"
        Runat="Server">
    <asp:Login ID="Login1" runat="server" DestinationPageUrl="~/home.aspx"
            BackColor="#F7F6F3" BorderColor="#E6E2D8" BorderPadding="4"
            BorderStyle="Solid" BorderWidth="1px" Font-Names="Verdana"
            Font-Size="0.8em" ForeColor="#333333">
        <TitleTextStyle BackColor="#5D7B9D" Font-Bold="True"
            Font-Size="0.9em" ForeColor="White" />
        <InstructionTextStyle Font-Italic="True" ForeColor="Black" />
        <TextBoxStyle Font-Size="0.8em" />
        <LoginButtonStyle BackColor="#FFFBFF" BorderColor="#CCCCCC"
            BorderStyle="Solid" BorderWidth="1px"
            Font-Names="Verdana" Font-Size="0.8em" ForeColor="#284775" />
    </asp:Login>
</asp:Content>
```

Example 10-19. Login.aspx.vb

```
Partial Class Login
    Inherits System.Web.UI.Page

    Protected Sub Page_Load(ByVal sender As Object, _
            ByVal e As System.EventArgs) Handles Me.Load
        Me.Master.PageSubTitle.Text = "Login"
    End Sub
End Class
```

Master Page

Example 10-20. MasterPage.master

```
<%@ Master Language="VB" CodeFile="MasterPage.master.vb"
    Inherits="MasterPage" %>

<!DOCTYPE html PUBLIC "-//W3C//DTD XHTML 1.0 Transitional//EN"
    "http://www.w3.org/TR/xhtml1/DTD/xhtml1-transitional.dtd">

<html xmlns="http://www.w3.org/1999/xhtml" >
<head id="head1" runat="server">
    <title>Adventure Works</title>
    <style type="text/css">@import url(StyleSheet.css); </style>
</head>
```

Example 10-20. MasterPage.master (continued)

```
<body>
    <form id="form1" runat="server">
    <asp:ScriptManager ID="ScriptManager1" runat="server" />
    <div>
        <table border="0">
            <tr>
                <td colspan="4">
                    <table>
                        <tr>
                            <td width="10px"> </td>
                            <td>
                                <asp:ImageButton ID="ibLogo" runat="server"
                                    ImageUrl=
                                        "~/images/AdventureWorksLogo-250x70.gif"
                                    AlternateText="AdventureWorks logo"
                                    PostBackUrl="~/Home.aspx" />
                            </td>
                            <td width="10px"> </td>
                            <td width="500px" align="right">
                                <span class="PageTitle">Adventure Works</span>
                                <br />
                                <asp:Label ID="lblPageSubTitle" runat="server"
                                    CssClass="PageSubTitle" Text="Page SubTitle"/>
                                <br />
                                <asp:Label id="lblTime" runat="server"
                                    CssClass="TextXSmall"/>
                            </td>
                            <td width="10px"> </td>
                        </tr>
                        <tr>
                            <td colspan="5">
                                <hr />
                            </td>
                        </tr>
                    </table>
                </td>
            </tr>
            <tr>
                <td width="5px"> </td>
                <td width="150px" valign="top">
                    <asp:LoginStatus ID="LoginStatus1" runat="server"
                        CssClass="Hyperlink" />
                    <br />
                    <asp:LoginView ID="LoginView1" runat="server" >
                        <LoggedInTemplate>
                            <span class="WarningRoutine">Welcome</span>
                            <asp:LoginName ID="LoginName1" runat="server"
                                CssClass="WarningRoutine"/>
                        </LoggedInTemplate>
```

Example 10-20. MasterPage.master (continued)

```
                            <AnonymousTemplate>
                                <span class="WarningRoutine">
                                    You are not logged in. Please click the login
                                    link to log in to this website.
                                </span>
                            </AnonymousTemplate>
                        </asp:LoginView>
                        <hr />
                        <asp:SiteMapDataSource ID="SiteMapDataSource1" runat="server"
                            ShowStartingNode="false" />
                        <asp:Menu ID="Menu1" runat="server"
                            DataSourceID="SiteMapDataSource1"
                            CssClass="MenuText" />
                    </td>
                    <td width="5px"> </td>
                    <td width="700px" valign="top" bgcolor="yellow">
                        <asp:contentplaceholder id="ContentPlaceHolder1"
                            runat="server" >
                        </asp:contentplaceholder>
                    </td>
                </tr>
            </table>
        </div>
        </form>
</body>
</html>
```

Example 10-21. MasterPage.master.vb

```
Partial Class MasterPage
    Inherits System.Web.UI.MasterPage
Public Property PageSubTitle() As Label
    Get
        Return lblPageSubTitle
    End Get
    Set(ByVal value As Label)
        lblPageSubTitle = value
    End Set
End Property

    Protected Sub Page_Load(ByVal sender As Object, _
            ByVal e As System.EventArgs) Handles Me.Load
        If Page.User.Identity.IsAuthenticated = False Then
            Menu1.Enabled = False
        End If

        lblTime.Text = DateTime.Now.ToString()
    End Sub
End Class
```

Products Page

Example 10-22. Products.aspx

```
<%@ Page Language="VB" MasterPageFile="~/MasterPage.master" AutoEventWireup="false"
    CodeFile="Products.aspx.vb" Inherits="Products" title="Products" %>
<%@ MasterType TypeName="MasterPage" %>
<asp:Content ID="Content1" ContentPlaceHolderID="ContentPlaceHolder1"
        Runat="Server">
    <asp:UpdatePanel id="UpdatePanel1" runat="server">
        <ContentTemplate>

        <asp:SqlDataSource ID="sqlCategories" runat="server"
            ConnectionString=
                "<%$ ConnectionStrings:AdventureWorksConnectionString %>"
            SelectCommand="select Name, ProductCategoryID
                            from Production.ProductCategory
                            order by Name" >
        </asp:SqlDataSource>
        <asp:RadioButtonList ID="rblCategories" runat="server"
            DataSourceID="sqlCategories" RepeatDirection="Horizontal"
            DataTextField="Name" DataValueField="ProductCategoryID"
            CssClass="LabelSmall" AutoPostBack="True">
        </asp:RadioButtonList>
        <asp:SqlDataSource id="sqlProducts" runat="server"
            ConnectionString=
                "<%$ ConnectionStrings:AdventureWorksConnectionString %>">
            <SelectParameters>
                <asp:ControlParameter ControlID="rblCategories"
                    Name="ProductCategoryID"
                    PropertyName="SelectedValue" />
            </SelectParameters>
        </asp:SqlDataSource>
        <asp:GridView id="gvProducts" runat="server"
            DataSourceID="sqlProducts" DataKeyNames="ProductID"
            AllowSorting="True" AllowPaging="True"
            AutoGenerateColumns="False"
            HeaderStyle-CssClass="TableColumnHeading"
            RowStyle-CssClass="TableCells">
            <Columns>
                <asp:CommandField ShowSelectButton="True" ItemStyle-Width="50px"
                    ControlStyle-CssClass="ButtonSelect" />
                <asp:BoundField DataField="ProductID" HeaderText="ID"
                    SortExpression="ProductID">
                    <ItemStyle Width="50px" />
                </asp:BoundField>
                <asp:BoundField DataField="Name" HeaderText="Name"
                    SortExpression="Name">
                    <ItemStyle Width="225px" />
                </asp:BoundField>
                <asp:BoundField DataField="ProductNumber"
                    HeaderText="Product Number"
                    SortExpression="ProductNumber">
                    <ItemStyle Width="90px" />
```

Example 10-22. Products.aspx (continued)

```
        </asp:BoundField>
        <asp:BoundField DataField="ListPrice" HeaderText="Cost"
            SortExpression="ListPrice"
            ItemStyle-CssClass="TableNumberDecimal"
            HeaderStyle-CssClass="TableColumnHeadingRight">
            <ItemStyle Width="60px" />
        </asp:BoundField>
    </Columns>
</asp:GridView>
<asp:Panel id="pnlProduct" runat="server" Visible="false">
    <table width="100%">
        <tr>
            <td valign="top">
                <asp:Button id="btnAddToCart" runat="server"
                    Text="Add To Cart" OnClick="btnAddToCart_Click"
                    CssClass="ButtonText" />
                <div class="ListHeading">Items In Cart</div>
                <asp:Label ID="lblCart" runat="server" CssClass="TextSmall"
                    Width="90"/>
            </td>
            <td valign="top">
                <asp:SqlDataSource id="sqlDetailsView" runat="server"
                    ConnectionString=
                    "<%$ ConnectionStrings:AdventureWorksConnectionString %>">
                    <SelectParameters>
                        <asp:ControlParameter ControlID="gvProducts"
                                Name="ProductID"
                                PropertyName=
                                    "SelectedDataKey.Values['ProductID']" />
                    </SelectParameters>
                </asp:SqlDataSource>
                <asp:DetailsView id="DetailsView1" runat="server"
                    DataSourceID="sqlDetailsView" DataKeyNames="ProductID"
                    AutoGenerateRows="false"
                    CssClass="TableCells" BorderWidth="0"
                    FieldHeaderStyle-CssClass="TableRowHeading"
                    CellSpacing="2" CellPadding="2"
                    Width="500px" Height="50px">
                    <Fields>
                        <asp:BoundField DataField="ProductID"
                                HeaderText="Product ID:"
                                SortExpression="ProductID" />
                        <asp:BoundField DataField="Name" HeaderText="Name:"
                                SortExpression="Name" />
                        <asp:BoundField DataField="ProductNumber"
                                HeaderText="Product #:"
                                SortExpression="ProductNumber" />
                        <asp:BoundField DataField="ListPrice"
                                HeaderText="Cost:"
                                SortExpression="ListPrice"
                                DataFormatString="{0:C}"
                                HtmlEncode="false"/>
```

Example 10-22. Products.aspx (continued)

```
                            <asp:BoundField DataField="Color" HeaderText="Color:"
                                    SortExpression="Color" />
                            <asp:BoundField DataField="CategoryName"
                                    HeaderText="Category:"
                                    SortExpression="CategoryName" />
                            <asp:BoundField DataField="SubcategoryName"
                                    HeaderText="SubCategory:"
                                    SortExpression="SubcategoryName" />
                            <asp:BoundField DataField="Description"
                                    HeaderText="Description:"
                                    SortExpression="Description" />
                    </Fields>
                </asp:DetailsView>
            </td>
        </tr>
    </table>
</asp:Panel>

    </ContentTemplate>
    </asp:UpdatePanel>
</asp:Content>
```

Example 10-23. Products.aspx.vb

```
Partial Class Products
    Inherits System.Web.UI.Page

Protected Sub Page_Load(ByVal sender As Object, _
        ByVal e As System.EventArgs) Handles Me.Load
    If User.Identity.IsAuthenticated = False Then
        Response.Redirect("login.aspx")
    End If
    Me.Master.PageSubTitle.Text = "Products"

    Dim strCommand As String = String.Empty
    strCommand = "select ProductID, Name, ProductNumber, ListPrice from " + _
                "Production.Product "
    strCommand += "where ProductSubcategoryID in "
    strCommand += "(select ProductSubcategoryID from " + _
                "Production.ProductSubcategory "
    strCommand += "where ProductCategoryID = "
    strCommand += "@ProductCategoryID)"
    sqlProducts.SelectCommand = strCommand

    strCommand = String.Empty
    strCommand += "select product.*, subcat.ProductSubcategoryID, " + _
                "subcat.Name as SubcategoryName, "
    strCommand += "cat.ProductCategoryID, cat.Name as CategoryName, "
    strCommand += "model.Name as ModelName, model.CatalogDescription, " + _
                "model.Instructions, "
    strCommand += "description.Description "
    strCommand += "from Production.Product product "
```

Example 10-23. Products.aspx.vb (continued)

```vb
        strCommand += "join Production.ProductSubcategory subcat on " + _
                       "product.ProductSubcategoryID = subcat.ProductSubcategoryID "
        strCommand += _
            "join Production.ProductCategory cat on subcat.ProductCategoryID = " + _
                       "cat.ProductCategoryID "
        strCommand += _
            "join Production.ProductModel model on product.ProductModelID = " + _
                       "model.ProductModelID "
        strCommand += _
            "join Production.ProductModelProductDescriptionCulture culture on " + _
                       "model.ProductModelID = culture.ProductModelID "
        strCommand += "join Production.ProductDescription description on " + _
                       "culture.ProductDescriptionID = " + _
                       "description.ProductDescriptionID "
        strCommand += "where product.ProductID = @ProductID and " + _
                       "Culture.CultureID = 'en' "
        sqlDetailsView.SelectCommand = strCommand

End Sub
Protected Sub btnAddToCart_Click(ByVal sender As Object, _
        ByVal e As System.EventArgs)
    ' the contents of the cart will be saved in a Session object as
    '     a string of comma-delimited values of ProductID's
    Dim strCart As String = String.Empty
    Dim strProductId As String = gvProducts.SelectedDataKey.Value.ToString()

    If Session("Cart") Is Nothing Then
        strCart = strProductId
    Else
        strCart = Session("Cart").ToString() + ", " + strProductId
    End If

    Session("Cart") = strCart
    lblCart.Text = strCart
End Sub


Protected Sub gvProducts_SelectedIndexChanged(ByVal sender As Object, _
        ByVal e As System.EventArgs) _
        Handles gvProducts.SelectedIndexChanged
    pnlProduct.Visible = True
End Sub


Protected Sub gvProducts_RowDataBound(ByVal sender As Object, _
        ByVal e As System.Web.UI.WebControls.GridViewRowEventArgs) _
        Handles gvProducts.RowDataBound
    Dim str As String = String.Empty
    If e.Row.RowType = DataControlRowType.DataRow Then
        Dim cell As TableCell = e.Row.Cells(4)    ' ListPrice cell
        Dim nCost As Decimal
        Try
            nCost = CType(cell.Text, Decimal)
            str = nCost.ToString("##,##0.00", Nothing)
```

Example 10-23. Products.aspx.vb (continued)

```vb
        Catch ex As ApplicationException
            str = "n.a."
        Finally
            cell.Text = str
        End Try
    End If
End Sub

Protected Sub rblCategories_SelectedIndexChanged(ByVal sender As Object, _
        ByVal e As System.EventArgs) _
        Handles rblCategories.SelectedIndexChanged
    pnlProduct.Visible = False
End Sub

End Class
```

Purchase Page

Example 10-24. Purchase.aspx

```asp
<%@ Page Language="VB" MasterPageFile="~/MasterPage.master" AutoEventWireup="false"
    CodeFile="Purchase.aspx.vb" Inherits="Purchase" title="Make Your Purchase" %>
<%@ MasterType TypeName="MasterPage" %>
<asp:Content ID="Content1" ContentPlaceHolderID="ContentPlaceHolder1"
        Runat="Server">
    <table border="0" class="TableRowHeading">
        <tr>
            <td colspan="4">
                Billing Information
            </td>
        </tr>
        <tr>
            <td>Name</td>
            <td colspan="4">
                <asp:TextBox ID="txtName" runat="server" Width="250" />
                <asp:RequiredFieldValidator ID="rfName" runat="server"
                    ControlToValidate="txtName"
                    Display="Dynamic" ErrorMessage="Name is a required field."
                    CssClass="ValidationError">*</asp:RequiredFieldValidator></td>
        </tr>
        <tr>
            <td>Address</td>
            <td colspan="3">
                <asp:TextBox ID="txtAddress" runat="server" Width="250" />
                <asp:RequiredFieldValidator ID="rfAddress" runat="server"
                    ControlToValidate="txtAddress"
                    Display="Dynamic" ErrorMessage="Address is a required field."
                    CssClass="ValidationError">*</asp:RequiredFieldValidator></td>
        </tr>
        <tr>
            <td>City</td>
```

Example 10-24. Purchase.aspx (continued)

```
        <td style="width: 181px">
            <asp:TextBox ID="txtCity" runat="server" />
            <asp:RequiredFieldValidator ID="rfCity" runat="server"
                ControlToValidate="txtCity"
                Display="Dynamic" ErrorMessage="City is a required field."
                CssClass="ValidationError">*</asp:RequiredFieldValidator>
        </td>
        <td>
            <asp:SqlDataSource ID="sqlStates" runat="server"
                ConnectionString=
                    "<%$ ConnectionStrings:AdventureWorksConnectionString %>"
                SelectCommand="SELECT StateProvinceCode, [Name]
                        FROM Person.StateProvince
                        WHERE CountryRegionCode = 'US' order by [Name]">
            </asp:SqlDataSource>
            <asp:DropDownList ID="ddlStates" runat="server"
                DataSourceID="sqlStates"
                DataTextField="Name" DataValueField="StateProvinceCode" />
        </td>
    </tr>
    <tr>
        <td>Zip</td>
        <td style="width: 181px">
            <asp:TextBox ID="txtZip" runat="server" />
            <asp:RequiredFieldValidator ID="rfZip" runat="server"
                ControlToValidate="txtZip"
                Display="Dynamic" ErrorMessage="Zip is a required field."
                CssClass="ValidationError">*</asp:RequiredFieldValidator>
            <asp:RegularExpressionValidator ID="reZip" runat="server"
                ErrorMessage="Invalid Zip format"
                ControlToValidate="txtZip"
                Display="Dynamic"
                ValidationExpression="^\d{5}$|^\d{5}-\d{4}$"
                CssClass="ValidationError">*</asp:RegularExpressionValidator>
        </td>
    </tr>
    <tr>
        <td>Card</td>
        <td colspan="3" >
            <asp:RadioButtonList ID="rblCardType" runat="server"
                    RepeatDirection="Horizontal">
                <asp:ListItem Value="am" Text="American Express" />
                 <asp:ListItem Value="d" Text="Discover" />
                <asp:ListItem Value="mc" Text="MasterCard" />
                <asp:ListItem Value="v" Text="Visa" />
            </asp:RadioButtonList>
            <asp:RequiredFieldValidator ID="rfCreditCard" runat="server"
                ErrorMessage="Credit Card type is missing."
                ControlToValidate="rblCardType" Display="Dynamic"
                InitialValue=""
                CssClass="ValidationError">*</asp:RequiredFieldValidator>
        </td>
    </tr>
```

Example 10-24. Purchase.aspx (continued)

```
<tr>
    <td>CC #</td>
    <td style="width: 181px">
        <asp:TextBox ID="txtCCNumber" runat="server" />
        <asp:RequiredFieldValidator ID="rfCCNumber" runat="server"
            ControlToValidate="txtCCNumber"
            Display="Dynamic"
            ErrorMessage="Credit Card Number is a required field."
            CssClass="ValidationError">*</asp:RequiredFieldValidator>
        <asp:RegularExpressionValidator ID="reCCNumber" runat="server"
            ErrorMessage="Invalid Credit Card Number"
            ControlToValidate="txtCCNumber"
            Display="Dynamic"
            ValidationExpression=
                "^(\d{4}-){3}\d{4}$|^(\d{4} ){3}\d{4}$|^\d{16}$"
            CssClass="ValidationError">*</asp:RegularExpressionValidator>
    </td>
    <td align="right">Security Code</td>
    <td>
        <asp:TextBox ID="txtSecurityCode" runat="server" />
        <asp:RequiredFieldValidator ID="rfSecurityCode" runat="server"
            ControlToValidate="txtSecurityCode"
            Display="Dynamic"
            ErrorMessage="Security Code is a required field."
            CssClass="ValidationError">*</asp:RequiredFieldValidator>
        <asp:RegularExpressionValidator ID="reSecurityCode"
            runat="server"
            ErrorMessage="Invalid Security Code"
            ControlToValidate="txtSecurityCode"
            Display="Dynamic"
            ValidationExpression="^\d{3}$"
            CssClass="ValidationError">*</asp:RegularExpressionValidator>
    </td>
</tr>
<tr>
    <td colspan="2">
        Shipping Information
    </td>
    <td colspan="2">
        <asp:RadioButtonList ID="rblShippingAddress" runat="server"
            AutoPostBack="true" RepeatDirection="Horizontal">
            <asp:ListItem Value="billing" Text="Ship to Billing Address"
                    Selected="True" />
            <asp:ListItem Value="different"
                    Text="Ship to Different Address" />
        </asp:RadioButtonList>
    </td>
</tr>
<tr>
    <td colspan="4">
        <asp:Panel ID="pnlShippingAddress" runat="server" Visible="false" >
            <table border="0">
```

Example 10-24. Purchase.aspx (continued)

```
                    <tr>
                        <td>Address</td>
                        <td colspan="3">
                            <asp:TextBox ID="txtShippingAddress" runat="server"
                                    Width="250" />
                        </td>
                    </tr>
                    <tr>
                        <td>City</td>
                        <td>
                            <asp:TextBox ID="txtShippingCity" runat="server" />
                        </td>
                        <td>
                            <asp:DropDownList ID="ddlShippingStates"
                                    runat="server"
                                    DataSourceID="sqlStates"
                                    DataTextField="Name"
                                    DataValueField="StateProvinceCode" />
                        </td>
                        <td>Zip</td>
                        <td>
                            <asp:TextBox ID="txtShippingZip" runat="server" />
                            <asp:RegularExpressionValidator ID="reShippingZip"
                                    runat="server"
                                    ErrorMessage="Invalid Zip format"
                                    ControlToValidate="txtShippingZip"
                                    Display="Dynamic"
                                    ValidationExpression="^\d{5}$|^\d{5}-\d{4}$"
                                    CssClass="ValidationError">*
                            </asp:RegularExpressionValidator>
                        </td>
                    </tr>
                </table>
            </asp:Panel>
        </td>
    </tr>
    <tr>
        <td colspan="4">
            <asp:ValidationSummary ID="ValidationSummary1" runat="server"
                CssClass="ValidationError" />
        </td>
    </tr>
    <tr>
        <td colspan="4">
            <asp:Button ID="btnBuy" runat="server" Text="Buy Now"
                CssClass="ButtonText" />
        </td>
    </tr>
</table>

</asp:Content>
```

Example 10-25. Purchase.aspx.vb

```vb
Partial Class Products
    Inherits System.Web.UI.Page

Protected Sub Page_Load(ByVal sender As Object, _
        ByVal e As System.EventArgs) Handles Me.Load
    If User.Identity.IsAuthenticated = False Then
        Response.Redirect("login.aspx")
    End If
    Me.Master.PageSubTitle.Text = "Products"

    Dim strCommand As String = String.Empty
    strCommand = "select ProductID, Name, ProductNumber, ListPrice from " + _
                    "Production.Product "
    strCommand += "where ProductSubcategoryID in "
    strCommand += "(select ProductSubcategoryID from " + _
                    "Production.ProductSubcategory "
    strCommand += "where ProductCategoryID = "
    strCommand += "@ProductCategoryID)"
    sqlProducts.SelectCommand = strCommand

    strCommand = String.Empty
    strCommand += "select product.*, subcat.ProductSubcategoryID, " + _
                    "subcat.Name as SubcategoryName, "
    strCommand += "cat.ProductCategoryID, cat.Name as CategoryName, "
    strCommand += "model.Name as ModelName, model.CatalogDescription, " + _
                    "model.Instructions, "
    strCommand += "description.Description "
    strCommand += "from Production.Product product "
    strCommand += "join Production.ProductSubcategory subcat on " + _
                    "product.ProductSubcategoryID = subcat.ProductSubcategoryID "
    strCommand += _
        "join Production.ProductCategory cat on subcat.ProductCategoryID = " + _
                    "cat.ProductCategoryID "
    strCommand += _
        "join Production.ProductModel model on product.ProductModelID = " + _
                    "model.ProductModelID "
    strCommand += _
        "join Production.ProductModelProductDescriptionCulture culture on " + _
                    "model.ProductModelID = culture.ProductModelID "
    strCommand += "join Production.ProductDescription description on " + _
                    "culture.ProductDescriptionID = " + _
                    "description.ProductDescriptionID "
    strCommand += "where product.ProductID = @ProductID and " + _
                    "Culture.CultureID = 'en' "
    sqlDetailsView.SelectCommand = strCommand
End Sub

Protected Sub btnAddToCart_Click(ByVal sender As Object, _
        ByVal e As System.EventArgs)
    ' the contents of the cart will be saved in a Session object as
    '    a string of comma-delimited values of ProductID's
    Dim strCart As String = String.Empty
    Dim strProductId As String = gvProducts.SelectedDataKey.Value.ToString()
```

Example 10-25. Purchase.aspx.vb (continued)

```vb
    If Session("Cart") Is Nothing Then
        strCart = strProductId
    Else
        strCart = Session("Cart").ToString( ) + "," + strProductId
    End If

    Session("Cart") = strCart
    lblCart.Text = strCart
End Sub


Protected Sub gvProducts_SelectedIndexChanged(ByVal sender As Object, _
        ByVal e As System.EventArgs) _
        Handles gvProducts.SelectedIndexChanged
    pnlProduct.Visible = True
End Sub


Protected Sub gvProducts_RowDataBound(ByVal sender As Object, _
        ByVal e As System.Web.UI.WebControls.GridViewRowEventArgs) _
        Handles gvProducts.RowDataBound
    Dim str As String = String.Empty
    If e.Row.RowType = DataControlRowType.DataRow Then
        Dim cell As TableCell = e.Row.Cells(4)      ' ListPrice cell
        Dim nCost As Decimal
        Try
            nCost = CType(cell.Text, Decimal)
            str = nCost.ToString("##,##0.00", Nothing)
        Catch ex As ApplicationException
            str = "n.a."
        Finally
            cell.Text = str
        End Try
    Fnd If
End Sub


Protected Sub rblCategories_SelectedIndexChanged(ByVal sender As Object, _
        ByVal e As System.EventArgs) _
        Handles rblCategories.SelectedIndexChanged
    pnlProduct.Visible = False
End Sub

End Class
```

Web.config

Example 10-26. web.config

```xml
<?xml version="1.0"?>
<configuration xmlns="http://schemas.microsoft.com/.NetConfiguration/v2.0">
    <configSections>
        <sectionGroup name="system.web.extensions"
         type="System.Web.Configuration.SystemWebExtensionsSectionGroup,
         System.Web.Extensions, Version=1.0.61025.0, Culture=neutral,
```

Example 10-26. web.config (continued)

```
            PublicKeyToken=31bf3856ad364e35">
                <sectionGroup name="scripting"
                 type="System.Web.Configuration.ScriptingSectionGroup,
                 System.Web.Extensions, Version=1.0.61025.0, Culture=neutral,
                 PublicKeyToken=31bf3856ad364e35">
                    <section name="scriptResourceHandler"
                     type="System.Web.Configuration.
                     ScriptingScriptResourceHandlerSection, System.Web.Extensions,
                     Version=1.0.61025.0, Culture=neutral,
                     PublicKeyToken=31bf3856ad364e35" requirePermission="false"
                     allowDefinition="MachineToApplication"/>
                    <sectionGroup name="webServices"
                     type="System.Web.Configuration.ScriptingWebServicesSectionGroup,
                     System.Web.Extensions, Version=1.0.61025.0, Culture=neutral,
                     PublicKeyToken=31bf3856ad364e35">
                        <section name="jsonSerialization"
                         type="System.Web.Configuration.
                         ScriptingJsonSerializationSection, System.Web.Extensions,
                         Version=1.0.61025.0, Culture=neutral,
                         PublicKeyToken=31bf3856ad364e35" requirePermission="false"
                         allowDefinition="Everywhere"/>

                        <section name="profileService"
                         type="System.Web.Configuration.ScriptingProfileServiceSection,
                         System.Web.Extensions, Version=1.0.61025.0, Culture=neutral,
                         PublicKeyToken=31bf3856ad364e35" requirePermission="false"
                         allowDefinition="MachineToApplication"/>
                        <section name="authenticationService"
                         type="System.Web.Configuration.
                         ScriptingAuthenticationServiceSection, System.Web.Extensions,
                         Version=1.0.61025.0, Culture=neutral,
                         PublicKeyToken=31bf3856ad364e35" requirePermission="false"
                         allowDefinition="MachineToApplication"/>
                    </sectionGroup>
                </sectionGroup>
            </sectionGroup>
        </configSections>
        <connectionStrings>
     <add name="AdventureWorksConnectionString" connectionString="Data
      Source=DELL380;Initial Catalog=AdventureWorks;Integrated Security=True"
      providerName="System.Data.SqlClient" />
    </connectionStrings>
    <system.web>
        <roleManager enabled="true" />
        <authentication mode="Forms" />
        <pages>
            <controls>
                <add tagPrefix="asp" namespace="System.Web.UI"
                 assembly="System.Web.Extensions, Version=1.0.61025.0, Culture=neutral,
                 PublicKeyToken=31bf3856ad364e35"/>
            </controls>
        </pages>
```

Example 10-26. web.config (continued)

```
        <!--
          Set compilation debug="true" to insert debugging
          symbols into the compiled page. Because this
          affects performance, set this value to true only
          during development.
        -->
    <compilation debug="true">
        <assemblies>
            <add assembly="System.Web.Extensions, Version=1.0.61025.0,
              Culture=neutral, PublicKeyToken=31bf3856ad364e35"/>
        </assemblies>
    </compilation>
    <httpHandlers>
        <remove verb="*" path="*.asmx"/>
        <add verb="*" path="*.asmx" validate="false"
         type="System.Web.Script.Services.ScriptHandlerFactory,
         System.Web.Extensions, Version=1.0.61025.0, Culture=neutral,
         PublicKeyToken=31bf3856ad364e35"/>
        <add verb="*" path="*_AppService.axd" validate="false"
         type="System.Web.Script.Services.ScriptHandlerFactory,
         System.Web.Extensions, Version=1.0.61025.0, Culture=neutral,
         PublicKeyToken=31bf3856ad364e35"/>
        <add verb="GET,HEAD" path="ScriptResource.axd"
         type="System.Web.Handlers.ScriptResourceHandler, System.Web.Extensions,
         Version=1.0.61025.0, Culture=neutral, PublicKeyToken=31bf3856ad364e35"
         validate="false"/>
    </httpHandlers>
    <httpModules>
        <add name="ScriptModule" type="System.Web.Handlers.ScriptModule,
         System.Web.Extensions, Version=1.0.61025.0, Culture=neutral,
         PublicKeyToken=31bf3856ad364e35"/>
    </httpModules>
     <customErrors mode="On" defaultRedirect="CustomErrorPage.aspx">
        <error statusCode="400" redirect="CustomErrorPage400.aspx"/>
        <error statusCode="404" redirect="CustomErrorPage404.aspx"/>
        <error statusCode="500" redirect="CustomErrorPage500.aspx"/>
     </customErrors>
</system.web>
<system.webServer>
        <validation validateIntegratedModeConfiguration="false"/>
        <modules>
            <add name="ScriptModule" preCondition="integratedMode"
             type="System.Web.Handlers.ScriptModule, System.Web.Extensions,
             Version=1.0.61025.0, Culture=neutral,
             PublicKeyToken=31bf3856ad364e35"/>
        </modules>
        <handlers>
            <remove name="WebServiceHandlerFactory-Integrated"/>
            <add name="ScriptHandlerFactory" verb="*" path="*.asmx"
             preCondition="integratedMode"
             type="System.Web.Script.Services.ScriptHandlerFactory,
             System.Web.Extensions, Version=1.0.61025.0, Culture=neutral,
             PublicKeyToken=31bf3856ad364e35"/>
```

Example 10-26. web.config (continued)

```
            <add name="ScriptHandlerFactoryAppServices" verb="*"
             path="*_AppService.axd" preCondition="integratedMode"
             type="System.Web.Script.Services.ScriptHandlerFactory,
             System.Web.Extensions, Version=1.0.61025.0, Culture=neutral,
             PublicKeyToken=31bf3856ad364e35"/>
            <add name="ScriptResource" preCondition="integratedMode"
             verb="GET,HEAD" path="ScriptResource.axd"
             type="System.Web.Handlers.ScriptResourceHandler,
             System.Web.Extensions, Version=1.0.61025.0, Culture=neutral,
             PublicKeyToken=31bf3856ad364e35"/>
        </handlers>
    </system.webServer>
</configuration>
```

Installing the Applications

This book contains lots of practice examples, both ones that you can follow along with, and exercises that you can do yourself. To do them, though, you'll need the right tools: an Integrated Development Environment (IDE), the AJAX extensions, and a database. Fortunately, everything you need is available in free versions from Microsoft, although you can use the fancier paid versions if you want. In this appendix, we'll walk you through getting all the software you need, and installing it. By the end of this appendix, you'll be ready to do all the examples in this book.

What Hardware and Software You'll Need

To build the examples in this book, you'll need a PC running one of the following editions of Windows:

- Windows Vista (any edition)
- Windows XP Home, SP 2
- Windows XP Professional, SP 2
- Windows 2000 Professional, SP 4
- Windows 2000 Server, SP 4
- Windows Server 2003, SP 2
- Windows x64 (any edition with the accompanying service pack)

Microsoft recommends that your computer have (at a minimum) a Pentium III 600 MHz with 1 GHz recommended. Although Microsoft insists you can run with 192 MB of memory, 512 MB is recommended. Many serious programmers find that 1 GB of memory is the minimum for professional work, and the authors have recently stepped up to 4 GB (but this is what we do for a living).

Visual Web Developer, the .NET Framework, the documentation, and SQL Express will require nearly two gigabytes of space on your hard drive. A full install of Visual Studio 2005 will take considerably more.

There are two software environments that will work equally well for this book: Visual Web Developer (VWD) and Visual Studio 2005 (VS). The advantage of VWD is that it is free. The advantage of VS is that it is a full-featured development environment (IDE) widely used for professional development of both web and desktop applications. In addition, you will need to install the ASP.NET AJAX libraries.

Visual Web Developer (VWD)

VWD is a subset of Visual Studio and can be used only to build web sites. That said, it is a full-featured development environment and will be all you'll need if all you are doing is developing web sites or web services (and you can't beat the price).

 Within the realm of creating web sites, we have found only one limitation of VWD, and that is a very advanced topic: It will not let you create your own AJAX extender controls, which are mentioned (but not demonstrated) in Chapter 3.

You can beef up (in my family, that would be "soy up") VWD by downloading the Reporting Add-in, which consists of the ReportViewer control, an integrated report designer, and report programming interface.

Installing VWD

To get started, download *vwdsetup.exe* from *http://msdn.microsoft.com/vstudio/express/vwd/download/* in the language of your choice. After it is downloaded to your machine, double-click it and it will self-install.

Accept the terms of the license and select which additional features you'd like to install along with the development environment, as shown in Figure A-1. You should select both options—the MSDN Express Edition provides documentation that will help you when you get stuck on how to use a control, for example. The SQL Server 2005 Express Edition lets you connect your web applications to databases, and you'll need it for several of the examples in this book, starting in Chapter 4.

 If you already have SQL Server installed on your machine, there is no need to install SQL Server 2005 Express Edition.

You will then be asked to select the destination folder for installation—accepting the default is fine. You'll also be asked to be sure you are connected to the Internet before proceeding with the installation, as shown in Figure A-2.

The installation will proceed, downloading what it needs as it goes. You will be required to restart Windows after the .NET Framework is installed, but other than that (and a request to register the software), the installation should pretty much take care of itself.

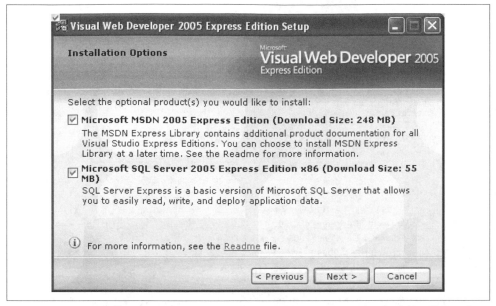

Figure A-1. The Visual Web Developer Installation Options. Be sure to select both checkboxes for this book.

After the installation is complete, it is always a good idea to go to the Microsoft web site at *http://msdn2.microsoft.com/en-us/downloads/default.aspx* to get the latest service packs. Also, if you are running Vista, you want to download and install the Vista Compatibility Pack by going to Windows Update.

Once it is fully installed, fire up the program from the Start menu, and the development environment should open, as shown in Figure A-3. You'll see a number of windows here, most of which are empty right now, but you'll be using them a lot once you start creating web pages. The Start Page occupies most of the middle of the screen, with a lot of news from Microsoft that you can browse or ignore, as you see fit. The "Recent Projects" area gives you shortcuts to create a new project or open an existing one; once you've done a few projects, you'll see them listed here for quick reference.

The bar on the left is the Toolbox. This is where you'll find the *controls* you'll be using in your projects—labels, text boxes, radio buttons, and so on, but that's just the beginning. On the upper right is the Solution Explorer, which is empty now, but you'll be able to use it to access any of the files in your project. Underneath that is the Properties window, which will let you fine-tune your controls, once you have some.

Figure A-2. Before you proceed with the installation, VWD will ask you to select a destination folder; the default works fine. You'll also need to make sure you're connected to the Internet before you click Install.

Configuring SQL Express

During the VWD installation, SQL Express was installed if you checked the appropriate checkbox. To ensure that you can make a connection to your new database, open VWD's Database Explorer window (click View → Database Explorer), right-click Data Connections, and choose Add Connection. You will get the dialog box shown in Figure A-4, asking you to choose your data source. Select Microsoft SQL Server, as shown in Figure A-4, and click Continue.

The Add Connection dialog box shown in Figure A-5 will open.

Either type in a server name, use the drop-down menu, or click Refresh to get all the available servers. Typically, however, your SQL Express installation will not appear in the list. If that is the case, just enter **.\sqlexpress** (that is, "dot slash" before the word "sqlexpress"). Make sure the radio button "Use Windows Authentication" is chosen, and you should then be able to drop down the list of databases that come with your installation of SQL Express. Select one of those databases to connect to. Once you have selected a database to connect to, click the Test Connection button to verify that the connection is good. Click OK in the Add Connection dialog box.

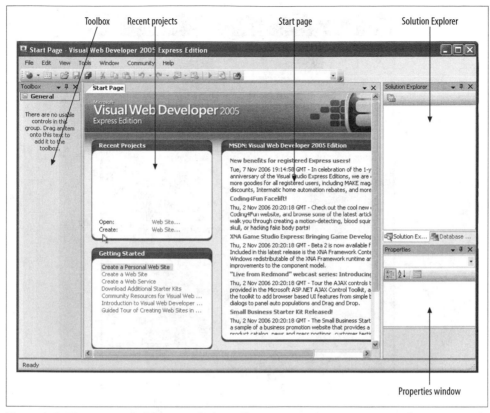

Figure A-3. The VWD Initial Screen, which you'll see every time you open VWD. There's not much here now, but that'll change shortly.

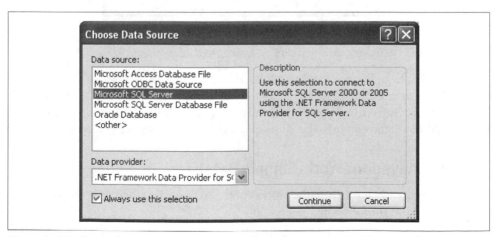

Figure A-4. To begin the connection to your database, select Microsoft SQL Server as your data source.

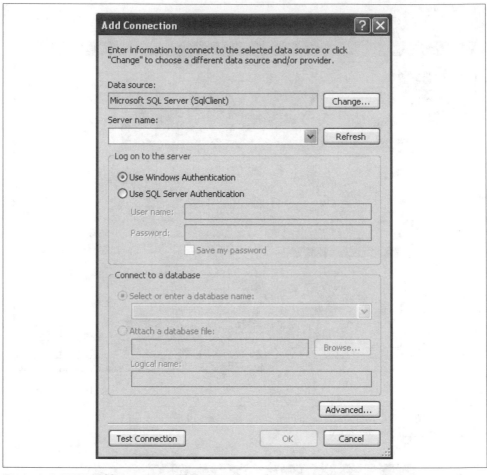

Figure A-5. VWD Add Connection dialog box. Enter the name of the SQL Server instance as the Server name, select Windows Authentication, and select the database name to connect to.

If you're using SQL Express, you won't be able to use the databases in that list until you install or create a database (or databases) to work with. You need a sample database, such as AdventureWorks, but AdventureWorks doesn't come with SQL Express, so you'll have to install it yourself, which we do in the next section.

Using the AdventureWorks Sample Database

If you don't already have the AdventureWorks database installed on your machine, download it from the following:

> *http://www.microsoft.com/downloads/details.aspx?FamilyID=e719ecf7-9f46-4312-af89-6ad8702e4e6e&DisplayLang=en*

There are several different versions of the database you can download, depending on your circumstances and preferences. *AdventureWorksDB.msi* contains the database with case-sensitive indexing. *AdventureWorksDBCI.msi* contains a case-insensitive version. Either works, but the case-insensitive version is easier to work with. If you are running a 64-bit machine, you should download *AdventureWorksDB_x64.msi*.

Download the appropriate file, and double-click the file to copy the sample database to your machine. You next need to attach this sample database to your instance of SQL Express or SQL Server. This is done with a line of SQL script. The exact steps depend on whether you are running SQL Server or SQL Express.

If you are using SQL Server, open a query window in SQL Server Management Studio.

If you are using SQL Express, open a command prompt by clicking Start → Run..., type in cmd, and press Enter. Then, from within that command window, enter the following command to get a query prompt into the database (be careful of your capitalization):

```
sqlcmd -S .\sqlexpress
```

In either case, enter the following SQL command—all on one line. We've broken it up here to fit on the page:

```
exec sp_attach_db @dbname=N'AdventureWorks', @filename1=N'C:\Program
Files\Microsoft SQL Server\MSSQL.1\MSSQL\Data\AdventureWorks_Data.mdf',
@filename2=N'C:\Program Files\Microsoft SQL
Server\MSSQL.1\MSSQL\Data\AdventureWorks_log.ldf'
```

In a Management Studio query window, highlight the line of script and press F5 to execute it. In a SQL Express query prompt, press Enter, then enter the command go, and then press Enter again.

If you are using the query prompt, type exit to quit the program. The database should now be installed and ready to use.

Visual Studio 2005

As an alternative to VWD, you can choose to purchase Visual Studio 2005, which comes in a variety of flavors (Standard, Professional, and Team). Briefly, the Standard edition fully supports the creation of ASP.NET web sites. The Professional edition allows you to develop Windows desktop apps, and comes with Crystal Reports and fuller support for XML. Stepping up to the Team edition brings full support for Office development, all languages, 64-bit support, code profiling, static analysis, unit testing, code coverage, project management, and test case management.

Our recommendation: If money is no object or you are part of an enterprise development team, then purchase the top-of-the-line MSDN subscription (Visual Studio Team Suite with MSDN Premium). The approximate retail cost is $11,000 initially and $3,500 to renew. For developers working on smaller projects, either alone or with one or two team members, Visual Studio Professional with MSDN Premium will probably be all you need, at around $3,000 initially and $2,500 to renew. Both of these subscriptions include almost all the software Microsoft sells, plus four support incidents and a free subscription to *MSDN Magazine*. There are many other subscription plans; check them out at *http://msdn2.microsoft.com/en-us/vstudio/ aa718657.aspx*.

On the other hand, if you don't feel the need to buy a Ferrari, or even a Corvette, to learn to drive, the free Visual Web Developer and SQL Express will be fine.

Installing Visual Studio 2005

Insert your disk, or click the EXE if you've downloaded the file. On the initial splash screen, shown in Figure A-6, click "Install Visual Studio 2005."

Figure A-6. Visual Studio 2005 installation initial splash screen. Select "Install Visual Studio 2005" for now, but you can come back and look for documentation and patches later.

Follow the Wizard. Accept the terms of the License Agreement, and when prompted, enter the product key, as shown in Figure A-7.

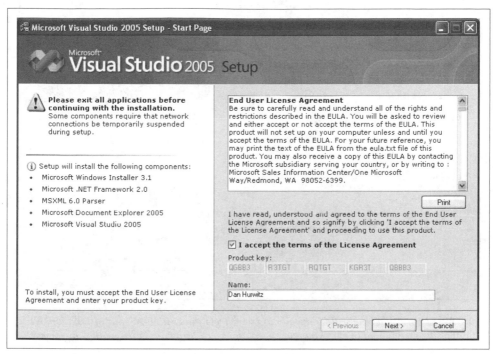

Figure A-7. The License Agreement for Visual Studio 2005. Enter your Product key, and click Next to agree to the terms. You can even read the agreement, if you want.

The next screen in the Wizard, shown in Figure A-8, allows you to select which features to install, as well as the installation location.

The default location is in *c:\Program Files*. In theory, it is possible to install to a different location—say, for example, a hard drive with more space available. This sometimes works, but is often problematic. You will have far fewer problems if you allow the installation to proceed in the default location.

The Default installation requires 2.7 GB of disk space. It installs the most commonly used features, including Visual C#, Visual J#, Visual Basic, Visual Web Developer, the .NET Framework (but without the QuickStart Samples), the Dotfuscator Community Edition, tools for redistributing applications (necessary for deploying desktop applications and creating installation packages), Crystal Reports, and SQL Server Express.

The Full installation requires 3.2 GB of disk space. It includes all of the Default installation, plus adds Visual C++ and the .NET Framework QuickStart Samples.

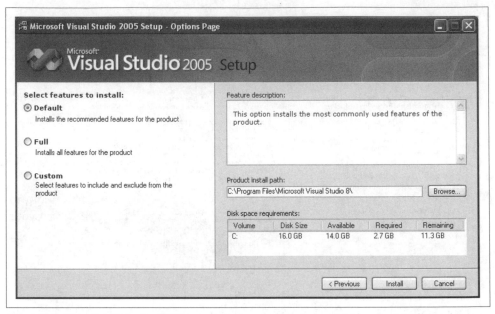

Figure A-8. This Visual Studio 2005 installation screen lets you customize your installation. Even Default probably has a lot of stuff you don't need, so select Custom and remove the languages that aren't C# or VB.NET.

The Custom selection allows you to choose what to install. You would select this option, for example, if you do not want to install all of the default languages or any of the other features included with the Default installation.

We suggest doing the Custom installation, and then deselecting the language(s) and features that you are quite certain you will never be using. You can always go back and add the missing languages and features. However, it is often very useful to have both C# and VB installed at a minimum, since many examples in articles and other books will be presented in either C# or VB, but not both.

Click the Install button to commence the installation process. The installer will restart your system part-way through, after the Framework is installed, and then continue the installation on its own.

After the VS installation completes, you definitely want to install the Product Documentation, which installs the MSDN Library on your machine, if you have the disk space. Do this by clicking the Install Product Documentation link, shown back in Figure A-6. The installation wizard will walk you through the process. Again, you have the choice of a Full (1950 MB of disk space required), Custom, or Minimum (868 MB disk space required) installation. We recommend doing the Full installation, as long as you have the disk space.

ASP.NET AJAX

The next step is to download and install the AJAX libraries from Microsoft, available at no charge at *http://AJAX.asp.net/downloads/*.

ASP.NET AJAX is deployed in three parts, each a separate download:

ASP.NET 2.0 AJAX Extensions 1.0

Installs the framework for developing and running AJAX-enabled web applications, including the libraries that automatically get loaded to the client to perform the AJAX magic. This must be installed prior to installing either of the other two parts required for AJAX.

The AJAX Extensions setup program will configure VWD or Visual Studio to include the ASP.NET AJAX project templates, fully integrating AJAX into your ASP.NET development environment.

ASP.NET AJAX Control Toolkit

An ever-expanding shared-source collection of samples and components, provided by both Microsoft and the ASP.NET community, that make it easy to add client-side functionality to your ASP.NET web site. Our experience is that the Toolkit is incredibly valuable, as demonstrated in Chapter 3. Don't be put off by the fact that it is open source; this is solid code and truly worthwhile.

The included SDK simplifies the creation of your own AJAX controls and extenders and provides a wealth of examples of how to build world-class AJAX controls.

ASP.NET AJAX Futures Community Technology Preview (CTP)

CTPs contain newly evolving features and components that extend the core ASP.NET AJAX 1.0 platform, released by Microsoft every few months. There may be useful features in the latest CTP, but this is prerelease software, so you may want to be cautious about putting this on your computer. We do not use any of the features of the CTP in this book, so it is not necessary to install it to work through any of our examples.

Now you're ready to install the AJAX software.

1. Download the ASP.NET 2.0 AJAX Extensions 1.0 installation file from *http://go. microsoft.com/fwlink/?LinkID=77296*. This is a file called *ASPAJAXExtSetup.msi*. Save it to a convenient folder on your system; then double-click the file in Windows Explorer to start the installation process. Follow the Wizard.

2. Download the AJAX Control Toolkit from *http://www.codeplex.com/ AtlasControlToolkit/Release/ProjectReleases.aspx* and save it to a convenient folder on your machine. This will be a zipped archive file. There are two versions: *AjaxControlToolkit.zip* and *AjaxControlToolkit-NoSource.zip*. The first contains the source code for the components it contains, while the second contains no source code. For this book, all you need is the NoSource file.

This file is updated frequently, so you may want to check back periodically for bug fixes and new features. Be aware that installing a newer version may break stuff that currently works. Usually this is worth the trade-off.

3. Unpack the AJAX Control Toolkit archive folder into a convenient folder on your computer.

4. Create a new web site from the ASP.NET AJAX web site template by opening Visual Studio 2005 or Visual Web Developer (VS/VWD) and clicking File → New Web Site…, and then picking "ASP.NET AJAX-Enabled Web Site" under "Visual Studio installed templates." (Yes, we know this is a strange way to install software, but trust us, it is necessary.) You can use the default name for this new web site because it is not necessary to actually save it.

5. After the web site opens in the IDE, the Toolbox should be visible on the left side of the screen. (If it is not visible, click the View → Toolbox menu item.)

6. The Toolbox comprises a number of groups. Each group's name is in boldface, and each group may have a number of items in it; the items are revealed when the + preceding the group's name is clicked. The first item in the Standard group, for example, is Pointer. What we will do next is to add a new group (tab) to the Toolbox with the name "AJAX Control Toolkit" and then populate that group. (Microsoft has made this somewhat confusing to explain because they refer to these groups as both groups and tabs.)

    a. First, check whether the Toolbox already has a group named AJAX Control Toolkit. If it does, then skip this step.

    b. Right-click any item in the Toolbox and select "Add Tab."

    c. A text box will open on the Toolbox, above the General tab.

    d. Type the name of the new tab into this text box: "AJAX Control Toolkit"; then press Enter.

7. Right-click the new Toolbox tab and select "Choose Items…" from the pop-up menu.

8. When the "Choose Toolbox Items" dialog appears, click the "Browse…" button. Navigate to the folder where you unzipped the ASP.NET AJAX Control Toolkit package. You will find a folder named *SampleWebSite*, and under that another folder named *Bin*. Inside that folder, select *AJAXControlToolkit.dll* and click Open. Click OK to close the Choose Toolbox Items dialog.

9. Close the web site. There is no need to save anything.

10. You can now use the controls from the AJAX Control Toolkit in any of your web sites.

Copying a Web Site

You'll often find it necessary or convenient to make a copy of an existing web site—that is, to make a new web site that is the same as the original except for a different name. We do this frequently in this book when building up examples, layering functionality on to a previous example. In the real world, you might want to make a copy of a web site so you can experiment without breaking something that works. We often copy a web site at various stages of development to have an easy snapshot to refer to without having to go to the bother of restoring from backup.

Before looking at the different ways to copy a web site, it would be helpful to understand a bit about what actually constitutes a web site. However, if all you want is the cookbook recipe—the set of steps you need to follow to copy a web site—you can skip the following discussion and move on to the next two sections, "Copying the Web Site Without Using the IDE" and "Copying the Web Site with the IDE."

Virtual Directories

Physically, what comprises a web site? Answer: a folder on the hard drive of the web server. If the server in question, such as Microsoft IIS (Internet Information Services), is operating outside the bounds of Visual Studio, Visual Web Developer, or some other development tool, then the folder containing the web site must be designated as a *virtual directory*—that is, a directory that is mapped to a web URL by the web server. When a user enters that URL into a browser, the request is passed to the web server and the server looks to the contents of the virtual directory to satisfy the request. How you designate the virtual directory depends on whether you're operating from inside or outside the IDE.

Outside the IDE

You can map any physical directory on the web server to a virtual directory in IIS. There are several ways to do so. Perhaps the easiest is to click the Start button, right-click My Computer, and select Manage, to bring up the Computer Management window. Drill down through Services and Applications, Internet Information Services, and Web Sites to Default Web Site, as shown in Figure B-1. Alternatively, go to Control Panel → Administrative Tools → Internet Information Services, which will bring you to Figure B-1, already drilled in to Internet Information Services.

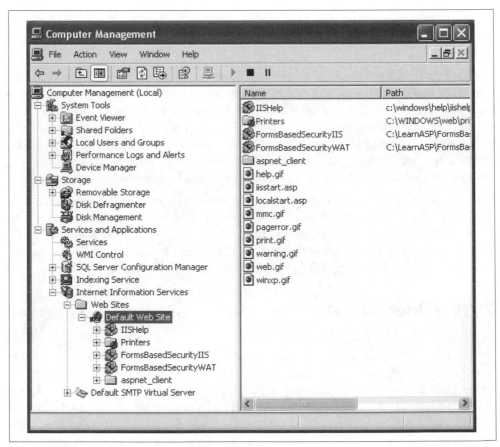

Figure B-1. Computer Management window, showing the contents of the Default Web Site virtual directory.

You can see in Figure B-1 that there are already two virtual directories in the Default Web Site, called FormsBasedSecurityIIS and FormsBasedSecurityWAT. (These correspond to two of the examples in this book from Chapter 9.)

By default, the physical directory corresponding to the Default Web Site virtual directory is located at *c:\inetpub\wwwroot*. You can see this by right-clicking Default Web Site, selecting Properties, and then clicking the Home Directory tab, as shown in Figure B-2.

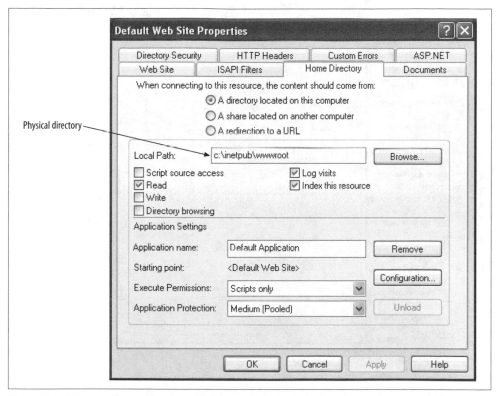

Figure B-2. You can change the physical directory of your default web site with the Default Web Site Properties dialog.

If there were a web page called *Welcome.aspx* in the default web site, and the domain name MyDomain.com was registered to the IP address of the server, then the following URL in a browser would bring up the page:

CODE▶
```
www.MyDomain.com/Welcome.aspx
```

Opening a browser locally on the server, you would use the following equivalent URL:

CODE▶
```
localhost/Welcome.aspx
```

where localhost always refers to the Default Web Site on the local server.

By default in IIS, certain web page names will be the default for each web site. In other words, you do not need to include them as part of the URL. If you enter a URL without a page name, it will automatically look for one of the default names.

You can see the default page names by right-clicking the virtual directory, selecting Properties, and clicking the Documents tab, as shown in Figure B-3, for one of the virtual directories on your test server.

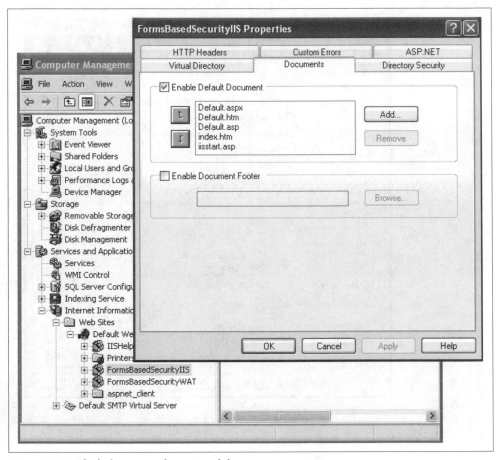

Figure B-3. Default documents for a virtual directory.

So, to access a web site in this virtual directory, a user on the Internet would enter the following URL from a browser, assuming that *Default.aspx* existed:

CODE▶
```
www.MyDomain.com/FormsBasedSecurityIIS
```

The equivalent URL from the local machine would be as follows:

CODE▶
```
localhost/FormsBasedSecurityIIS
```

Inside the IDE

One of the big advantages to using Visual Studio or Visual Web Developer is that you do not need to use IIS to serve your pages, and you do not need to create a virtual directory. Instead, the IDE provides its own web server and temporarily creates any necessary virtual directories.

You create a web site in the IDE either by clicking Create Web Site on the Start Page, or by clicking the File → New Web Site menu item. In either case, you get the New Web Site dialog box shown in Figure B-4.

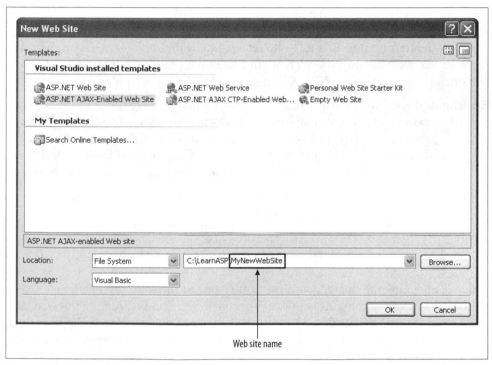

Figure B-4. New Web Site dialog box with web site path entered and the web site name indicated.

The highlighted portion of the path in Figure B-4 has a dual meaning. Physically, it is the folder that contains the web site. (If you want to make this web site accessible via IIS, this is the folder that you would make into a virtual directory.) It also is the name of the web site for the IDE.

In other words, when you click Open Web Site on the Start page or the File → Open Web Site menu item, you navigate to this folder to open the web site. The folder contains all the files comprising the web site.

The default web site name for a new web site is based on the template used with a number appended to the end. For example, if you are creating an AJAX-enabled web site, the default name will be something like *AJAXEnabledWebSite1*. You can change that name to anything you like.

The default location for a new web site will be the location used the last time you created a new web site. If you change the location and name in Figure B-4 to something like *c:\WebSites\OrderEntrySystem*, then the next time you create a new web site, the default location and name will be *c:\WebSites\AJAXEnabledWebSite2* (assuming there is already a web site named *AJAXEnabledWebSite1* in that folder).

There is one more piece of this puzzle that will be helpful to know. The IDE keeps track of files that comprise the web site, the default language, and build information. This information is saved in a text file, referred to as the *solution file*, with the same name as the web site (MyNewWebSite in Figure B-4) and an extension of *.sln*. You can open the web site in the IDE by double-clicking the solution file.

By default, this solution file is created in a folder with the same name as the web site in *c:\Documents and Settings\<username>\My Documents\Visual Studio 2005\Projects*, where <username> is replaced with your user name. You can change this default location by opening the IDE and clicking Tools → Options... → Projects and Solutions → General and changing the Visual Studio projects location, as shown in Figure B-5.

 Be sure to check the Show all settings checkbox in the lower-left corner of the Options dialog box; otherwise, you will not see many of the options, including the default locations shown in Figure B-5.

There is one more file created, with the same name as the solution file and an extension of *.suo*. This file contains developer-specific information relating to the web site, such as which files are displayed in the editing surface, which page is the start page for the web site, breakpoints, and so on. If this file is deleted, or otherwise missing, a new one is automatically created the next time the web site is opened in the IDE.

Now that you know how the files that comprise a web site are organized, you will better understand how to copy a web site. There are at least two different ways to do this: inside the IDE and outside the IDE.

Copying the Web Site Without Using the IDE

To copy a web site without using the IDE, simply copy the web site folder to another location and name, using Windows Explorer. The new copy can be in the same parent folder as the original, or in a totally different location. For example, suppose the original web site is called OrderEntrySystem and is located in the following folder:

    c:\WebSites\OrderEntrySystem

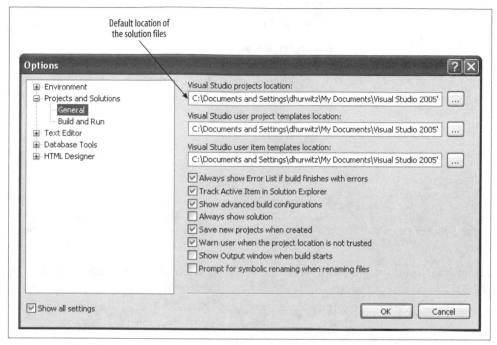

Default location of
the solution files

Figure B-5. *Changing the location of the solution files in the Options dialog box.*

You want to copy it to a new name, say OrderEntrySystemTest. Copy the original folder to the following:

> c:\WebSites\OrderEntrySystemTest

To work with this new web site, open the IDE, click Open Web Site, and navigate to this new folder. That's it.

The IDE will automatically create the necessary solution file and put it in the default location.

Copying the Web Site with the IDE

You can also copy a web site from within the IDE. The advantage of doing it inside the IDE instead of in Windows Explorer is that you have a lot more flexibility. Not only can you copy the site to your local file system, but you can also simultaneously create an IIS virtual directory or copy it to an FTP or remote web site over the Internet.

In this example, we will copy the AdventureWorks web site to another web site, called AdventureWorksRevisited, in the same parent folder.

There are two equivalent ways to begin the process of copying a web site from within the IDE. One is to click the Website → Copy Web Site… menu item. The other is to click the Copy Web Site icon at the top of the Solution Explorer (see Figure B-6).

Figure B-6. The Copy Web Site icon at the top of the Solution Explorer is a quick way to start the copying process.

Either way you do it, the Copy Web Site window will open in the middle window of the IDE, as shown in Figure B-7.

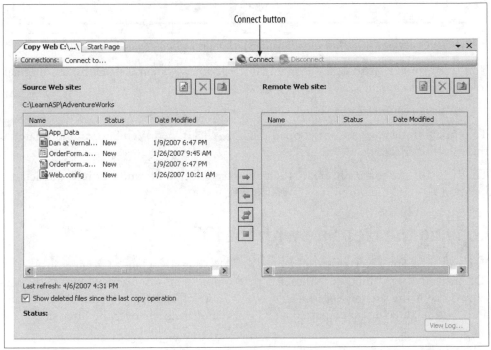

Figure B-7. The Copy Web Site window looks like this when you first open it. You use the Connect button to locate the destination folder.

Click the Connect button, indicated in Figure B-7, to bring up the Open Web Site dialog box shown in Figure B-8. This dialog is used to select the target destination of the copied web site.

 The screen shots in these figures were taken after most of the example web sites in this book were already created. Obviously, the folders you see in your file system will be different.

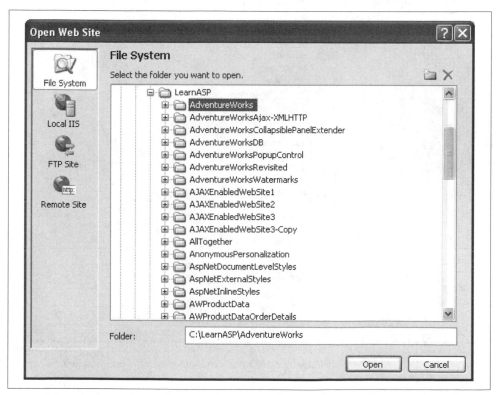

Figure B-8. The Connect button brings up the Open Web Site dialog box, where you choose the destination for the copy.

Notice the four icons down the left side of the dialog box. In Figure B-8, the File System icon is selected and the local file system is shown with the source web site initially highlighted.

Clicking any of the other three location icons will replace the File System browser in Figure B-8 with the appropriate means of specifying the location. For instance, if you click FTP site, you will be offered fields for the name of the FTP server and login credentials.

Because you want to copy the target web site to another location within the same parent folder, click that parent folder, LearnASP, and then click the Create New Folder icon, indicated in Figure B-9. This will create a new folder under LearnASP called WebSite, indicated in Figure B-9, ready to be renamed to something more meaningful.

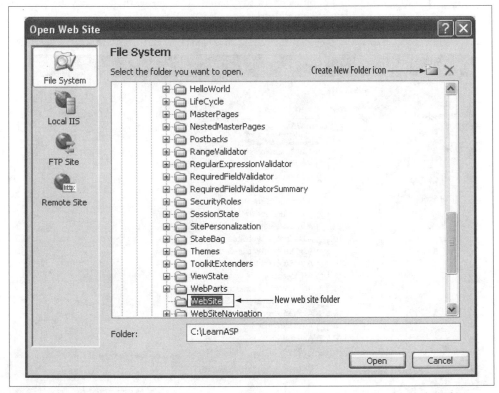

Figure B-9. *In the Open Web Site dialog box, click the New Folder icon to create a new web site folder. You'll be invited to rename it immediately.*

 A very common mistake to make here is to forget to select the parent directory before clicking the Create New Folder icon. Because the dialog initially opens with the source folder selected, this mistake will create the new web site folder as a subdirectory of the source folder, which is almost certainly *not* what you intended.

Replace WebSite with the target name—in this case, AdventureWorksRevisited—and tab off the menu tree. The new folder will be created and the full folder name inserted into the text box, as shown in Figure B-10.

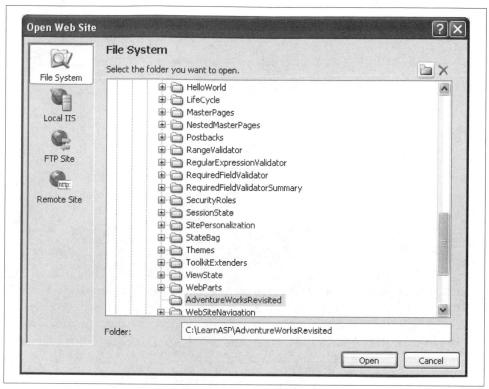

Figure B-10. Open Web Site dialog box with the new web site folder created.

Click the Open button to select the folder you just created as the target.

You will be brought back to the Copy Web Site window, similar to that shown back in Figure B-7, except now the target location will be indicated as the Remote Web Site, as shown in Figure B-11.

Now you can select the items in the grid on the Source side of the window that you want to copy, which is typically all of them. Click the first item in the list, then hold down Shift and click the last one. When items are selected, the buttons in the middle between the two grids become active. Click the right-pointing arrow to copy over the selected files and folders. The finished result will look something like that shown in Figure B-12.

The new web site has now been created and the contents copied over.

To work on this web site, click Open Web Site on the Start page or the File → Open Web Site menu item and select the new web site.

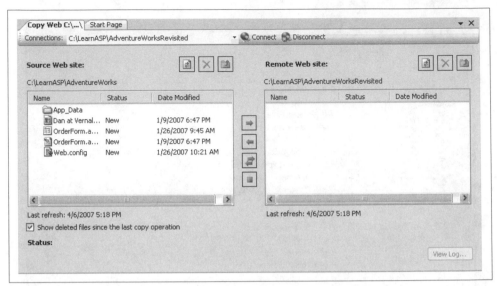

Figure B-11. After you've created the target web site folder, the Copy Web Site window will show the target.

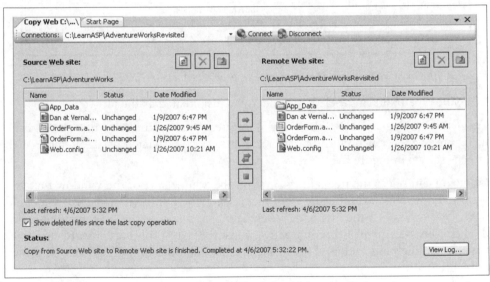

Figure B-12. After you've copied the web site, both project folders should show the same contents.

Answers to Quizzes and Exercises

Chapter 1: Getting Started

Answers to Quiz Questions

1. You can create a new web site by selecting File → New Web Site, or by clicking the "Create: Web Site" link on the Start page.

2. The two views are Design view, which shows you the appearance of your page, and Source view, which shows you the markup.

3. The settings that are specific to each control are called properties, and you can view them in the Properties window of the IDE.

4. The controls are kept in the Toolbox, which is on the left side of the IDE by default.

5. There are three different ways to run your program: click Debug → Start Debugging, press F5, or click the Start Debugging icon on the toolbar.

6. The Click event.

7. The code for the event handler is located in the code-behind file.

8. You can get to the code-behind file by selecting the file in the Solution Explorer, or by double-clicking the control whose default event you want to set up.

9. Use the Label control's Text property to set the content of the label. You'll see that many controls have a Text property that you can set.

10. The web page is kept in a file with the *.aspx* extension.

Answers to Exercises

Exercise 1-1. There is no "right" or "wrong" answer to this exercise; you're just playing around with the properties to get a feel for the range of options you have. If the changes you're making aren't showing up properly, make sure you've selected the label control; you can tell because "Label1" will be displayed at the top of the properties page. If you're having difficulty changing the text of the label, be sure you're looking in the `Default.aspx.vb` code-behind file, which you can access by clicking the tab at the top of the page, or through the Solution Explorer.

If you switch to Source view, you'll see the properties you've assigned reflected in the markup, and you can change the values here as well, of course. Example C-1 shows the markup for one author's page.

Example C-1. One version of the markup for Exercise 1-1

```
<%@ Page Language="VB" AutoEventWireup="false" CodeFile="Default.aspx.vb"
Inherits="_Default" %>

<!DOCTYPE html PUBLIC "-//W3C//DTD XHTML 1.0 Transitional//EN"
"http://www.w3.org/TR/xhtml1/DTD/xhtml1-transitional.dtd">

<html xmlns="http://www.w3.org/1999/xhtml" >
<head runat="server">
    <title>Untitled Page</title>
</head>
<body>
    <form id="form1" runat="server">
    <div>
        <asp:Button ID="Button1" runat="server" Text="Button" />
        <asp:Label ID="Label1" runat="server" BorderStyle="Dotted"
         BorderWidth="2px" Font-Bold="True" Font-Names="Arial"
         Font-Size="Large" ForeColor="Green" ></asp:Label></div>
    </form>
</body>
</html>
```

Chapter 2: Building Web Applications

Answers to Quiz Questions

1. A postback is when the page is returned to the server to evaluate code handlers, and the same page is sent back to the browser afterward.

2. The first type of postback in AJAX is synchronous, in which the entire page is sent back to the server, as with a non-AJAX page. The second type is asynchronous, in which only part of the page is updated, and the rest is unaffected.

3. The ID property. The IDE sets this property for you (although you can change it), and you need it to refer to the control from elsewhere on the page.

4. Use a `TextBox` control with the `TextMode` property set to `Password`.

5. Use a `ListBox` control, which allows multiple selections and is best for long lists.

6. Set the `GroupName` property of each radio button to the same group.

7. A `Panel` control groups other controls together in one place, and enables you to make all the controls visible or invisible as a whole.

8. The `SelectedItem` property retrieves the `Text` property of the currently selected item of the control.

9. Set the control's `Visible` property to false. The control will be present, but won't be rendered until something changes the `Visible` property.

10. Set the `HyperLink` control's `Target` property to _blank.

Answers to Exercises

Exercise 2-1. This exercise isn't too tricky; you're just getting used to adding controls to the page, and seeing how nested `UpdatePanel` controls work. If the labels aren't updating independently of each other, make sure you have the buttons and labels inside the appropriate update panels. If not, you can drag them to their proper places. Also make sure, in the code-behind file, that your event handler is changing the text of the appropriate label. Example C-2 shows the markup for this exercise.

Example C-2. The markup file for Exercise 1-2

```
<%@ Page Language="VB" AutoEventWireup="true" CodeFile="Default.aspx.vb"
Inherits="_Default" %>

<!DOCTYPE html PUBLIC "-//W3C//DTD XHTML 1.1//EN"
"http://www.w3.org/TR/xhtml11/DTD/xhtml11.dtd">
<html xmlns="http://www.w3.org/1999/xhtml">
<head runat="server">
    <title>Exercise 2-1</title>
</head>
<body>
    <form id="form1" runat="server">
        <asp:ScriptManager ID="ScriptManager1" runat="server" />
        <div>
            Page Loaded at:
            <asp:Label ID="lblPageLoad" runat="server" Text="Label"
                Width="200px"></asp:Label>
            <asp:Button ID="btnPostback" runat="server" Text="Postback" />
            <asp:UpdatePanel ID="UpdatePanel1" runat="server">
                <ContentTemplate>
                    Partial-Page update at:<asp:Label ID="lblPartialUpdate"
                        runat="server" Text="Label"
                        Width="200px"></asp:Label>
                    <asp:Button ID="btnPartialUpdate" runat="server"
                        OnClick="btnPartialUpdate_Click"
                        Text="Partial Update" />
                    <asp:UpdatePanel ID="UpdatePanel2" runat="server">
                        <ContentTemplate>
                            Another partial-page update at:<asp:Label
                                ID="lblOtherPartialUpdate" runat="server"
                                Text="Label" Width="200px"></asp:Label>
```

Example C-2. The markup file for Exercise 1-2 (continued)

```
                                <asp:Button ID="btnOtherPartialUpdate" runat="server"
                                    OnClick="btnOtherPartialUpdate_Click"
                                    Text="Another Partial Update" />
                            </ContentTemplate>
                        </asp:UpdatePanel>
                    </ContentTemplate>
                </asp:UpdatePanel>
            </div>
        </form>
    </body>
</html>
```

Example C-3 shows the code-behind file for this exercise.

Example C-3. The code-behind file for Exercise 2-1

```
Partial Class _Default
    Inherits System.Web.UI.Page

    Protected Sub Page_Load(ByVal sender As Object, ByVal e As System.EventArgs) _
      Handles Me.Load
        lblPageLoad.Text = DateTime.Now
    End Sub

    Protected Sub btnPartialUpdate_Click(ByVal sender As Object, ByVal e _
      As System.EventArgs)
        lblPartialUpdate.Text = DateTime.Now
    End Sub

    Protected Sub btnOtherPartialUpdate_Click(ByVal sender As Object, _
      ByVal e As System.EventArgs)
        lblOtherPartialUpdate.Text = DateTime.Now
    End Sub
End Class
```

Exercise 2-2. This exercise isn't too hard, and there are several valid solutions. The only challenge comes in choosing the best controls for the situation. The choice of ice cream type is a somewhat long list, and only allows for one selection, so a DropDownList control is probably best. For the toppings, again it's a long list, but multiple selections are possible, so you could use a ListBox, but you need to make sure to set the SelectionMode property to Multiple. The choice of cone or dish is much simpler; there are only two options, and they're mutually exclusive, so a pair of RadioButton controls is the way to go here. Be sure to give them a common GroupName, so they'll be part of the same group.

Of course, that's not the only way to solve the problem. For an ice-cream parlor, you might think it's good marketing to display all your flavors and toppings for your customers to choose from. In that case, you could use a RadioButtonList for the ice cream, and a CheckBoxList for the toppings. When you're designing a page, you need to consider all the customer's requirements.

One solution to this exercise is shown in Figure C-1. We didn't use much fancy styling here, but we did put the controls in a table to make the layout easier. The markup for this solution is shown in Example C-4.

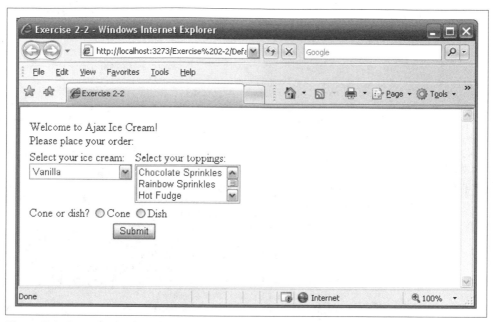

Figure C-1. One solution to Exercise 2-2.

Example C-4. Markup for one solution to Exercise 2-2

```
<%@ Page Language="VB" AutoEventWireup="true" CodeFile="Default.aspx.vb"
Inherits="_Default" %>

<!DOCTYPE html PUBLIC "-//W3C//DTD XHTML 1.1//EN"
"http://www.w3.org/TR/xhtml11/DTD/xhtml11.dtd">
<html xmlns="http://www.w3.org/1999/xhtml">
<head runat="server">
    <title>Exercise 2-2</title>
</head>
<body>
    <form id="form1" runat="server">
        <asp:ScriptManager ID="ScriptManager1" runat="server" />
        <div>
            <table>
                <tr>
                    <td colspan=2>
                        Welcome to Ajax Ice Cream!<br />
                        Please place your order:</td>
                </tr>
                <tr valign=top>
                    <td>
                        Select your ice cream:<br />
```

Example C-4. Markup for one solution to Exercise 2-2 (continued)

```
                <asp:DropDownList ID="ddlIceCream" runat="server">
                    <asp:ListItem Value="Van">Vanilla</asp:ListItem>
                    <asp:ListItem Value="Choc">Chocolate</asp:ListItem>
                    <asp:ListItem Value="Straw">Strawberry</asp:ListItem>
                    <asp:ListItem Value="Mint">Mint Chocolate
                                            Chip</asp:ListItem>
                    <asp:ListItem Value="ButPec">Butter
                                            Pecan</asp:ListItem>
                    <asp:ListItem Value="Coff">Coffee</asp:ListItem>
                    <asp:ListItem Value="Pist">Pistachio</asp:ListItem>
                    <asp:ListItem Value="Coco">Coconut</asp:ListItem>
                    <asp:ListItem Value="Bub">Bubble Gum</asp:ListItem>
                    <asp:ListItem Value="CotCan">Cotton
                                            Candy</asp:ListItem>
                </asp:DropDownList></td>
        <td>
            Select your toppings:<br />
            <asp:ListBox ID="lbToppings" runat="server" Rows="3"
                            SelectionMode="Multiple">
                <asp:ListItem Value="CSprink">Chocolate
                                            Sprinkles</asp:ListItem>
                <asp:ListItem Value="RSprink">Rainbow
                                            Sprinkles</asp:ListItem>
                <asp:ListItem Value="HFudge">Hot Fudge</asp:ListItem>
                <asp:ListItem Value="Carm">Caramel</asp:ListItem>
                <asp:ListItem Value="CDough">Cookie
                                            Dough</asp:ListItem>
                <asp:ListItem Value="Oreo">Oreo Cookies</asp:ListItem>
                <asp:ListItem Value="Pretz">Pretzel bits</asp:ListItem>
                <asp:ListItem Value="Nuts">Crushed
                                            Walnuts</asp:ListItem>
                <asp:ListItem Value="CBean">Coffee beans</asp:ListItem>
                <asp:ListItem Value="Candy">Crushed Candy
                                            Bars</asp:ListItem>
            </asp:ListBox></td>
    </tr>
    <tr>
        <td colspan=2>
            Cone or dish?
            <asp:RadioButton ID="rbCone" runat="server"
                            GroupName="grpConeDish" Text="Cone" />
            <asp:RadioButton ID="rbDish" runat="server"
                            GroupName="grpConeDish" Text="Dish"
                            /></td>
    </tr>
    <tr>
        <td colspan=2 align=center>
            <asp:Button ID="btnSubmit" runat="server" Text="Submit"
                /></td>
    </tr>
</table>
```

Example C-4. Markup for one solution to Exercise 2-2 (continued)

```
            </div>
        </form>
    </body>
    </html>
```

Exercise 2-3. Creating the web page for this exercise is simple; you just need a TextBox, a Label, a Button, and some plain text to tell the user what to do. The only hitch is that you need to remember to set the TextMode property of the TextBox to Password. The next step is writing the event handler for the Submit button. All you want to do is set the Text property of the Label to be the same as the Text property of the TextBox. For that, you need just one line:

```
    lblPassword.Text = txtPassword.Text
```

Notice that even though the user can't see the text that's typed in the TextBox, the page can, and can assign that value to another control (the label, in this case). This is, of course, a terrible security practice, but it illustrates the point. Example C-5 shows the markup file for this exercise, and Example C-6 shows the short event handler for the Submit button.

Example C-5. The markup for Exercise 2-3

```
<%@ Page Language="VB" AutoEventWireup="true" CodeFile="Default.aspx.vb"
Inherits="_Default" %>

<!DOCTYPE html PUBLIC "-//W3C//DTD XHTML 1.1//EN"
"http://www.w3.org/TR/xhtml11/DTD/xhtml11.dtd">
<html xmlns="http://www.w3.org/1999/xhtml">
<head runat="server">
    <title>Exercise 2-3</title>
</head>
<body>
    <form id="form1" runat="server">
        <asp:ScriptManager ID="ScriptManager1" runat="server" />
        <div>
            Enter your password:
            <asp:TextBox ID="txtPassword" runat="server"
                        TextMode="Password"></asp:TextBox><br />
            The password you entered is:
            <asp:Label ID="lblPassword" runat="server"></asp:Label>
            <br />
            <asp:Button ID="btnSubmit" runat="server" Text="Submit" /></div>
    </form>
</body>
</html>
```

Example C-6. The event handler for the Submit button in Exercise 2-3

```
Partial Class _Default
    Inherits System.Web.UI.Page

    Protected Sub btnSubmit_Click(ByVal sender As Object, ByVal e As _
                             System.EventArgs) Handles btnSubmit.Click
        lblPassword.Text = txtPassword.Text
    End Sub
End Class
```

Exercise 2-4. In this exercise, you're combining the assignment you did in Exercise 2-3 with the DropDownList control you learned about earlier. When you create the drop-down list, either with the ListItem editor, or by hand, you assign the ISBN number to the Value property of the ListItem. That way, when the user makes a selection, the user never sees the ISBN number, but it appears in the output anyway. You can see how this would be useful for a database, so that you can hide your internal system from the users, but still allow them to choose by title.

The only twist for this exercise is that it lacks a Submit button. Therefore, to get the postback, you have to set the DropDownList control's AutoPostBack property to true, so that the page posts back every time the user makes a selection. That means you have to put the event handler in the Load event for the page, just as you did in the Postbacks example in this chapter. The event handler works a bit differently than in Exercise 2-3:

CODE▶
```
        lblID.Text = ddlBookList.SelectedValue
        lblTitle.Text = ddlBookList.SelectedItem.Text
```

To assign the text to the ID label, you need to retrieve the Value property of the selected item in the drop-down list—that's the SelectedValue property. Assigning the title text is slightly trickier: You retrieve the Text property of the SelectedItem property of the drop-down list: ddlBookList.SelectedItem.Text.

The markup for this exercise is shown in Example C-7, and the event handler is in Example C-8.

Example C-7. The markup for Exercise 2-4

```
<%@ Page Language="VB" AutoEventWireup="true" CodeFile="Default.aspx.vb" Inherits="_
Default" %>

<!DOCTYPE html PUBLIC "-//W3C//DTD XHTML 1.1//EN"
"http://www.w3.org/TR/xhtml11/DTD/xhtml11.dtd">
<html xmlns="http://www.w3.org/1999/xhtml">
<head runat="server">
    <title>Exercise 2-4</title>
</head>
<body>
    <form id="form1" runat="server">
        <asp:ScriptManager ID="ScriptManager1" runat="server" />
        <div>
            Which book are you interested in?<br />
```

Example C-7. The markup for Exercise 2-4 (continued)

```
        <asp:DropDownList ID="ddlBookList" runat="server" AutoPostBack="true">
            <asp:ListItem Value="00916X">Programming ASP.NET</asp:ListItem>
            <asp:ListItem Value="006993">Programming C#</asp:ListItem>
            <asp:ListItem Value="004385">Programming Visual Basic
                                  .NET</asp:ListItem>
            <asp:ListItem Value="102097">Learning C# 2005</asp:ListItem>
        </asp:DropDownList><br />
            Thank you for your interest in <br />
            <asp:Label ID="lblID" runat="server" Text="ID number"></asp:Label>
        <br />
            <asp:Label ID="lblTitle" runat="server"
                        Text="Title"></asp:Label></div>
    </form>
</body>
</html>
```

Example C-8. The event handler for Exercise 2-4

```
Partial Class _Default
    Inherits System.Web.UI.Page

    Protected Sub Page_Load(ByVal sender As Object, ByVal e As System.EventArgs)
                        Handles Me.Load
        lblID.Text = ddlBookList.SelectedValue
        lblTitle.Text = ddlBookList.SelectedItem.Text
    End Sub
End Class
```

Chapter 3: Snappier Web Sites with AJAX

Answers to Quiz Questions

1. Nothing—when you create an AJAX-enabled web site, the ScriptManager control is included on your page by default.

2. The EnablePartialRendering property is the critical property of the ScriptManager control, which is why it is set to True by default.

3. The UpdatePanel control is the key control that enables asynchronous updates.

4. No, you can't. The extender controls need to have a target control to extend; they don't work alone.

5. All the Extender controls have a property called TargetControlID, which indicates the control that the extender acts on.

6. You have to set the WatermarkText property from Source view; it's not visible from Design view.

7. Yes; style sheets aren't necessary to use TextBoxWatermarkExtender; they're just a nice touch.

8. It allows you to hide choices for a control within an UpdatePanel, saving valuable screen space.

9. The Commit( ) method is the method of the PopUpControlExtender that causes the target control to display the results.

10. A CollapsiblePanelExtender, logically enough, lets you expand or collapse a Panel control.

Answers to Exercises

Exercise 3-1. Start by creating a web site called Exercise 3-1; be sure to select ASP. NET AJAX-Enabled Web Site from the New Web Site dialog box. When the new web site opens, type in "Shipping State," and add a TextBox control called txtState. Set its Text property to "Click Here," its ReadOnly property to True, and its Width property to 70 px. Those are the controls the user will see to start out. Now add an UpdatePanel control below that. Inside the UpdatePanel, place a standard Panel, and name it pnlPopup. Inside the panel, place the DropDownList control, and call it ddlStates. Set the AutoPostBack property of ddlStates to True—this is an important step. Now use the ListItem Editor·to fill in the six items. Be sure to set the Text of each ListItem to the full name of the state, and the Value to the state's postal code.

So far, it's easy. Now add a PopupControlExtender to the page, and call it pceStates. Switch to Source view to set the properties. The target is the TextBox, so set TargetControlID to txtState. The Panel is the control that you want to pop up, so set PopupControlID to pnlPopup. Set Position to Bottom, just to make it neater.

The PopupControlExtender is in place now, and ready to go, but it still needs to know what to do, and for that, you need an event handler for the DropDownList. Double-click ddlStates to open the default event handler, SelectedIndexChanged. You need to call the Commit method of pceStates here, and pass in the value that the user has selected, not the text. So add this line of code to the event handler:

```
Protected Sub ddlStates_SelectedIndexChanged(ByVal sender As Object, _
ByVal e As System.EventArgs)
    pceStates.Commit(ddlStates.SelectedValue)
End Sub
```

Run your application. You should find that the panel is hidden until you click it, and that the value is automatically passed to txtState when you make a selection. Example C-9 shows the markup for *Default.aspx* for this exercise.

Example C-9. The markup file for Exercise 3-1

```
<%@ Page Language="VB" AutoEventWireup="true" CodeFile="Default.aspx.vb"
Inherits="_Default" %>

<%@ Register Assembly="AjaxControlToolkit" Namespace="AjaxControlToolkit"
TagPrefix="cc1" %>
```

Example C-9. The markup file for Exercise 3-1 (continued)

```
<!DOCTYPE html PUBLIC "-//W3C//DTD XHTML 1.1//EN"
"http://www.w3.org/TR/xhtml11/DTD/xhtml11.dtd">
<html xmlns="http://www.w3.org/1999/xhtml">
<head runat="server">
    <title>Exercise 3-1</title>
</head>
<body>
    <form id="form1" runat="server">
        <asp:ScriptManager ID="ScriptManager1" runat="server" />
        <div>
            Shipping State: 
            <asp:TextBox ID="txtState" runat="server" ReadOnly="True"
                     Width="70px">Click Here</asp:TextBox>
            <asp:Panel ID="pnlPopup" runat="server" Height="50px" Width="125px">
                <asp:UpdatePanel ID="UpdatePanel1" runat="server">
                    <ContentTemplate>
                        <asp:DropDownList ID="ddlStates" runat="server"
                          AutoPostBack="True"
                          OnSelectedIndexChanged="ddlStates_SelectedIndexChanged">
                            <asp:ListItem Value="CT">Connecticut</asp:ListItem>
                            <asp:ListItem Value="MA">Massachusetts</asp:ListItem>
                            <asp:ListItem Value="NJ">New Jersey</asp:ListItem>
                            <asp:ListItem Value="NY">New York</asp:ListItem>
                            <asp:ListItem Value="PA">Pennsylvania</asp:ListItem>
                            <asp:ListItem Value="RI">Rhode Island</asp:ListItem>
                        </asp:DropDownList>
                    </ContentTemplate>
                </asp:UpdatePanel>
            </asp:Panel>
        </div>
        <cc1:PopupControlExtender ID="pceStates" runat="server"
            TargetControlID="txtState" PopupControlID="pnlPopup" Position=Bottom>
        </cc1:PopupControlExtender>
    </form>
</body>
</html>
```

Example C-10 shows the very brief code-behind file.

Example C-10. The code-behind file for Exercise 3-1

```
Partial Class _Default
    Inherits System.Web.UI.Page

    Protected Sub ddlStates_SelectedIndexChanged(ByVal sender As Object, _
            ByVal e As System.EventArgs)
        pceStates.Commit(ddlStates.SelectedValue)
    End Sub
End Class
```

Exercise 3-2. This is a fairly simple extender to work with—it does what it says it does. To start, create a new AJAX-enabled web site and call it Exercise 3-2. First add the Panel control, call it pnlRounded, and set its Width to 150, its Height to 100, and its BackColor to LightGray (or whatever you prefer). Add the Label control inside the Panel, call it lblRounded, and set its Width to 50, its BackColor to DarkGray, its ForeColor to White, and its Font.Bold to True.

So far, nothing particularly interesting has happened. Now, add two RoundedCornersExtender controls: rceLabel and rcePanel. The first thing to do is make sure that the TargetControlID for rceLabel is set to lblRounded, and that for rcePanel, it's set to pnlRounded. For the rest, you'll have to check out the online documentation, which will tell you that there's a property called Radius, and one called Corners. Those properties aren't available in Design view, so switch to Source view and set the Radius for rceLabel to 2; for rcePanel, set the Radius to 8, and the Corners to Top, so that the bottom corners of the Panel will be left square. There you go! It's not the most exciting extender, but you can see how you might use it to add a little bit of style to your forms. The markup for this page is in Example C-11. There is no code-behind file for this example.

Example C-11. The markup file for Exercise 3-2

```
<%@ Page Language="VB" AutoEventWireup="true" CodeFile="Default.aspx.vb"
Inherits="_Default" %>

<%@ Register Assembly="AjaxControlToolkit" Namespace="AjaxControlToolkit"
TagPrefix="cc1" %>

<!DOCTYPE html PUBLIC "-//W3C//DTD XHTML 1.1//EN"
"http://www.w3.org/TR/xhtml11/DTD/xhtml11.dtd">
<html xmlns="http://www.w3.org/1999/xhtml">
<head runat="server">
    <title>Exercise 3-2</title>
</head>
<body>
    <form id="form1" runat="server">
        <asp:ScriptManager ID="ScriptManager1" runat="server" />
        <div>
            <asp:Panel ID="pnlRounded" runat="server" Height="100px"
                    Width="150px" BackColor="LightGray">
                 <br />
                 
                <asp:Label ID="lblRounded" runat="server" BackColor="DarkGray"
                        Text="Label" Width="50px" Font-Bold="True"
                        ForeColor="White"></asp:Label>
                <cc1:RoundedCornersExtender ID="rceLabel" runat="server"
                                        TargetControlID="lblRounded" Radius=2 >
                </cc1:RoundedCornersExtender>
            </asp:Panel>
        </div>
```

Example C-11. The markup file for Exercise 3-2 (continued)

```
        <cc1:RoundedCornersExtender ID="rcePanel" runat="server"
                                    TargetControlID="pnlRounded" Radius=8
                                    Corners=top>
        </cc1:RoundedCornersExtender>
    </form>
</body>
</html>
```

If you experiment with this extender, you'll find that it doesn't work on other controls, such as the TextBox or the DropDownList. Sometimes the documentation doesn't tell you everything you need to know, and you can only find out by trial and error.

Exercise 3-3. This exercise is slightly tricky because of the need for two textboxes. Start by creating an AJAX-enabled page. Type "Volume Level:" and then add a TextBox control. This is the TextBox that you want to see in the finished page, so name it txtVolume_Bound. Set its Width to 15px, and its ReadOnly property to True (you don't want users typing in there).

That's the easy part. Now add another TextBox, called txtVolume, on a new line. None of the display properties matter on this TextBox, because users will never see it. Now add the SliderExtender, and call it sleVolume. Switch to Source view, set the TargetControlID to txtVolume, the BoundControlID to txtVolume_Bound, and the Maximum to 10. Run the application, and the slider should work as you'd expect, although you'll only see one TextBox. The markup for this page is shown in Example C-12. There is no code-behind.

Example C-12. The markup for Exercise 3-3

```
<%@ Page Language="VB" AutoEventWireup="true" CodeFile="Default.aspx.vb"
Inherits="_Default" %>

<%@ Register Assembly="AjaxControlToolkit" Namespace="AjaxControlToolkit"
TagPrefix="cc1" %>

<!DOCTYPE html PUBLIC "-//W3C//DTD XHTML 1.1//EN"
"http://www.w3.org/TR/xhtml11/DTD/xhtml11.dtd">
<html xmlns="http://www.w3.org/1999/xhtml">
<head runat="server">
    <title>Exercise 3-3</title>
</head>
<body>
    <form id="form1" runat="server">
        <asp:ScriptManager ID="ScriptManager1" runat="server" />
        <div>
             <div>
            Volume Level:   
            <asp:TextBox ID="txtVolume_Bound" runat="server" Width="15px"
                        ReadOnly="True"></asp:TextBox>
                 <br />
```

Example C-12. The markup for Exercise 3-3 (continued)

```
            <asp:TextBox ID="txtVolume" runat="server">
                        </asp:TextBox>
            <cc1:SliderExtender ID="sleVolume" runat="server"
                            TargetControlID="txtVolume"
                            BoundControlID="txtVolume_Bound"
                            Maximum="10">
            </cc1:SliderExtender>
            </div>
        </div>
    </form>
</body>
</html>
```

As you can imagine, there are many possible uses for a control like this, and for many of them, you would actually want to hide the textbox the control extends. You could use it as an actual volume control, for one thing, or you could use several of them to make a color slider like you find in a drawing application.

Chapter 4: Saving and Retrieving Data

Answers to Quiz Questions

1. A DataSource control.
2. Binding.
3. A connection string is a string that contains the information necessary to connect to a database on a server. You can store the connection string in the *web.config* file for later use.
4. Create (add a new record), Retrieve, Update (edit), and Delete.
5. Use the GridView's Smart Tag and the "Choose Data Source" drop-down list.
6. Turn on paging by clicking the Smart Tag, and selecting Enable Paging.
7. It safeguards your data by only writing changes to the database if none of the records have changed since the records were read.
8. Enable Updating and Deleting, from the Smart Tag.
9. Create an event handler for the RowDataBound event.
10. Use a WHERE clause.

Answers to Exercises

Exercise 4-1. Here's one way to get a page that looks like Figure 4-27:

1. Create a new web site as usual. Name it Exercise 4-1.
2. Drag a SqlDataSource control onto the Design view.

3. Drag a GridView control onto the Design view. Click the GridView's Smart Tag, go to the "Choose Data Source" drop-down list, and select SqlDataSource1.

4. Click "Configure Data Source" in the Smart Tag. The Configure Data Source Wizard starts. You can use the connection string from the other exercises in this chapter. Click Next.

5. On the next page, click the radio button marked "Specify columns from a table or view," and select the Product table from the drop-down list. Check the boxes for ProductID, Name, ProductNumber, Color, and ListPrice. The Wizard should look like Figure C-2.

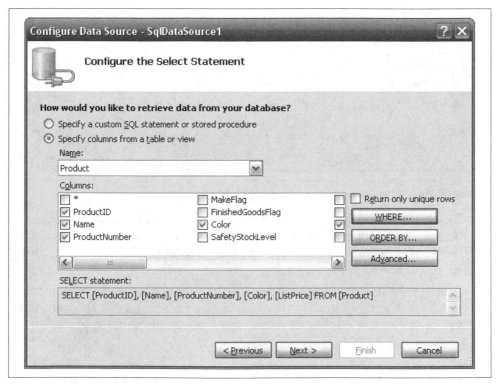

Figure C-2. Creating the Select statement for your GridView.

6. Click the WHERE button. In the Add WHERE Clause dialog, select Weight in the Column drop-down list, select > (greater than) in the Operator drop-down list, and None in the Source drop-down list. The Value field appears on the right side of the box; enter 100 in the field. The dialog should look like Figure C-3. Click Add to add the WHERE clause, and OK to return to the Wizard.

7. Click the Advanced button and check both Generate INSERT, UPDATE, and DELETE statements and Use optimistic concurrency.

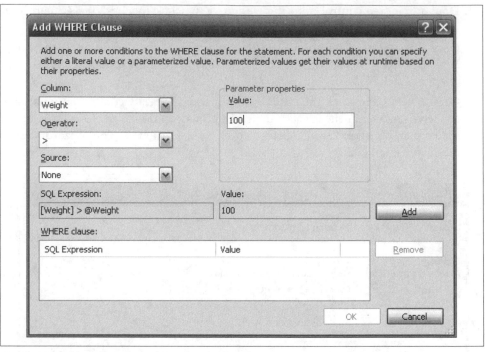

Figure C-3. Adding the Where clause for your GridView.

8. Click Next to go to the next page; then click Finish to close the Wizard. Remember that this query won't work properly right now, so switch to Source view, find the four instances of [Product], and change them to [Production].[Product], like you did earlier in the chapter.

9. Return to Design View, click the Smart Tag for the GridView, and check the boxes for Enable Paging, Enable Sorting, Enable Editing, and Enable Deletion. Click AutoFormat, and select the Professional color scheme. Run your application.

The Source code for this application looks like Example C-13.

Example C-13. The markup for Exercise 4-1

```
<%@ Page Language="VB" AutoEventWireup="true" CodeFile="Default.aspx.vb"
Inherits="_Default" %>

<!DOCTYPE html PUBLIC "-//W3C//DTD XHTML 1.1//EN"
"http://www.w3.org/TR/xhtml11/DTD/xhtml11.dtd">
<html xmlns="http://www.w3.org/1999/xhtml">
<head runat="server">
    <title>Exercise 4-1</title>
</head>
<body>
    <form id="form1" runat="server">
        <asp:ScriptManager ID="ScriptManager1" runat="server" />
```

Example C-13. The markup for Exercise 4-1 (continued)

```
<div>
    <asp:SqlDataSource ID="SqlDataSource1" runat="server"
    ConnectionString=
        "<%$ ConnectionStrings:AdventureWorksConnectionString %>"
    SelectCommand="SELECT [ProductID], [Name], [ProductNumber],
        [Color], [ListPrice] FROM [Production].[Product]
        WHERE ([Weight] > @Weight)"
    ConflictDetection="CompareAllValues"
    DeleteCommand="DELETE FROM [Production].[Product]
        WHERE [ProductID] = @ProductID"
    InsertCommand="INSERT INTO [Production].[Product] ([Name],
        [ProductNumber], [Color], [ListPrice])
        VALUES (@Name, @ProductNumber, @Color, @ListPrice)"
    OldValuesParameterFormatString="original_{0}"
    UpdateCommand="UPDATE [Production].[Product]
        SET [Name] = @Name, [ProductNumber] = @ProductNumber,
        [Color] = @Color, [ListPrice] = @ListPrice
        WHERE [ProductID] = @ProductID">
        <SelectParameters>
         <asp:Parameter DefaultValue="100" Name="Weight" Type="Decimal" />
        </SelectParameters>
        <DeleteParameters>
            <asp:Parameter Name="ProductID" Type="Int32" />
        </DeleteParameters>
        <UpdateParameters>
            <asp:Parameter Name="Name" Type="String" />
            <asp:Parameter Name="ProductNumber" Type="String" />
            <asp:Parameter Name="Color" Type="String" />
            <asp:Parameter Name="ListPrice" Type="Decimal" />
            <asp:Parameter Name="ProductID" Type="Int32" />
        </UpdateParameters>
        <InsertParameters>
            <asp:Parameter Name="Name" Type="String" />
            <asp:Parameter Name="ProductNumber" Type="String" />
            <asp:Parameter Name="Color" Type="String" />
            <asp:Parameter Name="ListPrice" Type="Decimal" />
        </InsertParameters>
    </asp:SqlDataSource>
</div>
<asp:GridView ID="GridView1" runat="server"
    DataSourceID="SqlDataSource1" CellPadding="4"
    ForeColor="#333333" GridLines="None"
    AllowPaging="True" AllowSorting="True">
    <FooterStyle BackColor="#5D7B9D" Font-Bold="True" ForeColor="White" />
    <RowStyle BackColor="#F7F6F3" ForeColor="#333333" />
    <EditRowStyle BackColor="#999999" />
    <SelectedRowStyle BackColor="#E2DED6" Font-Bold="True"
        ForeColor="#333333" />
    <PagerStyle BackColor="#284775" ForeColor="White"
        HorizontalAlign="Center" />
    <HeaderStyle BackColor="#5D7B9D" Font-Bold="True" ForeColor="White" />
    <AlternatingRowStyle BackColor="White" ForeColor="#284775" />
```

Example C-13. The markup for Exercise 4-1 (continued)

```
        <Columns>
            <asp:CommandField ShowDeleteButton="True" ShowEditButton="True" />
        </Columns>
    </asp:GridView>
    </form>
</body>
</html>
```

Exercise 4-2. Adding labels and textboxes to your page is easy. The tricky bit is that you need to change the content of the textboxes whenever the user selects a row in the GridView. Fortunately, you've seen the SelectedIndexChanged event, which makes it easy to send data to controls based on a user's selections in the GridView.

Start by copying the web site from Exercise 4-1 to a new web site, Exercise 4-2, as explained in Appendix B.

Click the GridView's Smart Tag, and check the Enable Selection checkbox. The Select links show up next to the Edit and Delete links that are already there.

Drag a Label onto the Design view, below the GridView. Name it lblName, and change the text to "Name:". Drag a TextBox next to the Label, name it txtName, and set its ReadOnly property to True. Add another Label, named lblColor, with text of "Color:". Finally, add a second TextBox, name it txtColor, and set its ReadOnly property to True.

You're got all the parts in place, but now you need to connect the Select link in the GridView to the two TextBoxes. Double-click one of the Select links to open the SelectedIndexChanged event handler for GridView1. Add the following code:

```
Protected Sub GridView1_SelectedIndexChanged(ByVal sender As Object,_
    ByVal e As System.EventArgs) Handles GridView1.SelectedIndexChanged
    If GridView1.SelectedRow.RowType = DataControlRowType.DataRow Then
        Dim cellName As TableCell = GridView1.SelectedRow.Cells(2) ' Name column
        Dim cellColor As TableCell = GridView1.SelectedRow.Cells(4) ' Color column
        txtName.Text = cellName.Text
        txtColor.Text = cellColor.Text
    End If
End Sub
```

This is very similar to what you did earlier in the chapter. GridView1.SelectedRow represents the currently selected row—the one the user clicked. First, you check to see if SelectedRow is a DataRow. If it is, you create a cell variable called cellName, and set that equal to the cell at index 2 in SelectedRow, because you know that's the Name column (remember that the row starts at index 0). Similarly, you create a cell cellColor, which is set to the cell at index 4. Then you assign the Text properties of each of these cells to the respective TextBoxes.

Run your application and try it out. As you select different rows, the values in the TextBoxes change. You can see how this would be useful for customers to select products on your order form.

Example C-14 shows the source code for Exercise 4-2.

Example C-14. The markup for Exercise 4-2

```
<%@ Page Language="VB" AutoEventWireup="true" CodeFile="Default.aspx.vb" Inherits="_
Default" %>

<!DOCTYPE html PUBLIC "-//W3C//DTD XHTML 1.1//EN" "http://www.w3.org/TR/xhtml11/DTD/
xhtml11.dtd">
<html xmlns="http://www.w3.org/1999/xhtml">
<head runat="server">
    <title>Exercise 4-2</title>
</head>
<body>
    <form id="form1" runat="server">
        <asp:ScriptManager ID="ScriptManager1" runat="server" />
        <div>
            <asp:SqlDataSource ID="SqlDataSource1" runat="server"
                ConnectionString=
                    "<%$ ConnectionStrings:AdventureWorksConnectionString %>"
                SelectCommand="SELECT [ProductID], [Name], [ProductNumber],
                    [Color], [ListPrice] FROM [Production].[Product]
                    WHERE ([Weight] > @Weight)"
                DeleteCommand="DELETE FROM [Production].[Product]
                    WHERE [ProductID] = @original_ProductID
                    AND [Name] = @original_Name
                    AND [ProductNumber] = @original_ProductNumber
                    AND [Color] = @original_Color
                    AND [ListPrice] = @original_ListPrice"
                InsertCommand="INSERT INTO [Production].[Product]
                    ([Name], [ProductNumber], [Color], [ListPrice])
                    VALUES (@Name, @ProductNumber, @Color, @ListPrice)"
                UpdateCommand="UPDATE [Production].[Product]
                    SET [Name] = @Name, [ProductNumber] = @ProductNumber,
                    [Color] = @Color, [ListPrice] = @ListPrice
                    WHERE [ProductID] = @original_ProductID
                    AND [Name] = @original_Name
                    AND [ProductNumber] = @original_ProductNumber
                    AND [Color] = @original_Color
                    AND [ListPrice] = @original_ListPrice"
                ConflictDetection="CompareAllValues"
                OldValuesParameterFormatString="original_{0}">
                <SelectParameters>
                    <asp:Parameter DefaultValue="100" Name="Weight" Type="Decimal" />
                </SelectParameters>
                <DeleteParameters>
                    <asp:Parameter Name="original_ProductID" Type="Int32" />
                    <asp:Parameter Name="original_Name" Type="String" />
                    <asp:Parameter Name="original_ProductNumber" Type="String" />
                    <asp:Parameter Name="original_Color" Type="String" />
                    <asp:Parameter Name="original_ListPrice" Type="Decimal" />
                </DeleteParameters>
```

Example C-14. The markup for Exercise 4-2 (continued)

```
            <UpdateParameters>
                <asp:Parameter Name="Name" Type="String" />
                <asp:Parameter Name="ProductNumber" Type="String" />
                <asp:Parameter Name="Color" Type="String" />
                <asp:Parameter Name="ListPrice" Type="Decimal" />
                <asp:Parameter Name="original_ProductID" Type="Int32" />
                <asp:Parameter Name="original_Name" Type="String" />
                <asp:Parameter Name="original_ProductNumber" Type="String" />
                <asp:Parameter Name="original_Color" Type="String" />
                <asp:Parameter Name="original_ListPrice" Type="Decimal" />
            </UpdateParameters>
            <InsertParameters>
                <asp:Parameter Name="Name" Type="String" />
                <asp:Parameter Name="ProductNumber" Type="String" />
                <asp:Parameter Name="Color" Type="String" />
                <asp:Parameter Name="ListPrice" Type="Decimal" />
            </InsertParameters>
        </asp:SqlDataSource>
    </div>
    <asp:GridView ID="GridView1" runat="server" DataSourceID="SqlDataSource1"
        CellPadding="4" ForeColor="#333333" GridLines="None"
        AllowPaging="True" AllowSorting="True" AutoGenerateColumns="False"
        DataKeyNames="ProductID">
        <FooterStyle BackColor="#5D7B9D" Font-Bold="True" ForeColor="White" />
        <RowStyle BackColor="#F7F6F3" ForeColor="#333333" />
        <EditRowStyle BackColor="#999999" />
        <SelectedRowStyle BackColor="#E2DED6" Font-Bold="True"
            ForeColor="#333333" />
        <PagerStyle BackColor="#284775" ForeColor="White"
            HorizontalAlign="Center" />
        <HeaderStyle BackColor="#5D7B9D" Font-Bold="True" ForeColor="White" />
        <AlternatingRowStyle BackColor="White" ForeColor="#284775" />
        <Columns>
            <asp:CommandField ShowDeleteButton="True" ShowEditButton="True"
                ShowSelectButton="True" />
            <asp:BoundField DataField="ProductID" HeaderText="ProductID"
                InsertVisible="False" ReadOnly="True"
                SortExpression="ProductID" />
            <asp:BoundField DataField="Name" HeaderText="Name"
                SortExpression="Name" />
            <asp:BoundField DataField="ProductNumber"
                HeaderText="ProductNumber" SortExpression="ProductNumber" />
            <asp:BoundField DataField="Color" HeaderText="Color"
                SortExpression="Color" />
            <asp:BoundField DataField="ListPrice" HeaderText="ListPrice"
                SortExpression="ListPrice" />
        </Columns>
    </asp:GridView>
    <asp:Label ID="lblName" runat="server" Text="Name:"></asp:Label>
    <asp:TextBox ID="txtName" runat="server" ReadOnly="True"></asp:TextBox>
    <asp:Label ID="lblColor" runat="server" Text="Color:"></asp:Label>
    <asp:TextBox ID="txtColor" runat="server" ReadOnly="True"></asp:TextBox>
```

Example C-14. The markup for Exercise 4-2 (continued)

```
    </form>
</body>
</html>
```

Exercise 4-3. This is mostly a simple exercise, but it shows you how the AJAX Update panels interact with GridViews.

1. Create an AJAX-enabled web site called Exercise 4-3.

2. Drag an UpdatePanel onto your page first. Everything else goes inside the UpdatePanel.

3. Add some text inside the UpdatePanel, "Select the table you would like to see:". Drag two radio buttons into the UpdatePanel beneath that text. Name the first one rbEmployee, set its text to "Show Employees," and set its GroupName to grpEmployeeCustomer. Name the second radio button rbCustomer, set its text to "Show Customers," and set its GroupName to grpEmployeeCustomer as well. Now both buttons are part of the same group.

4. Drag a regular Panel into the UpdatePanel, and name it pnlEmployee. Put a SQLDataSource inside pnlEmployee, and name it sdsEmployee. Add a GridView to pnlEmployee, and call it gvEmployee.

5. Time to give gvEmployee something to do. Click its Smart Tag, select sdsEmployee as the data source, and configure sdsEmployee to retrieve the EmployeeID, ManagerID, and Title columns from the Employee table. Remember to go to source view and add the schema. In this case, you need to replace [Employee] with [HumanResources].[Employee]. Enable paging and sorting on gvEmployee, and give it whatever formatting you like.

6. Now drag another regular Panel into the UpdatePanel, and name it pnlCustomer. Add another SQLDataSource (sdsCustomer) and another GridView (gvCustomer) to pnlCustomer.

7. gvCustomer needs some data as well. Click its Smart Tag, select sdsCustomer as the data source, and configure sdsCustomer to retrieve the CustomerID, AccountNumber, and CustomerType fields from the Customer table. Again, go to source view and change [Customer] to [Sales].[Customer]. Enable paging and sorting, and format it, if you want.

8. Everything's easy so far, right? Now for the only tricky bit. You want pnlEmployee to be visible when the rbEmployee radio button is clicked; when rbCustomer is clicked, only pnlCustomer should be visible. You've seen how to do that in Chapter 2.

9. Start out with neither panel visible. Click each panel, and set its Visible property to false.

10. Double-click `rbEmployee`, which creates the `rbEmployee_CheckChanged` event handler for you. You want to change the visibility of `pnlEmployee` to be the same as the `Checked` value of `rbEmployee`, and you want `rbCustomer.Visible` to have the same value as `rbCustomer.Checked`. Since you know that `rbEmployee` and `rbCustomer` can't both be checked at the same time (because they're part of the same radio button group), you know that only one table will be visible. Here's the code to add to `rbEmployee_CheckChanged`:

```
Protected Sub rbEmployee_CheckedChanged(ByVal sender As Object, _
ByVal e As System.EventArgs)
    pnlEmployee.Visible = rbEmployee.Checked
    pnlCustomer.Visible = rbCustomer.Checked
End Sub
```

11. Go back to the *.aspx* file, click `rbEmployee`, and set its `AutoPostBack` property to true, so that the table will show as soon as the button is clicked.

12. Now double-click `rbCustomer` to create the `rbCustomer_CheckChanged` event handler, and add the exact same code. Also make sure to set `rbCustomer`'s `AutoPostBack` property to true.

13. Test out your application. As you click each radio button, the table displayed should change. You will see some delay the first time you click the radio button, because the data for the `GridView` is being sent to the client, but after that, there's no postback, even if you change the page or sort the `GridView`.

Example C-15 shows the markup file for Exercise 4-3.

Example C-15. The markup file for Exercise 4-3

```
<%@ Page Language="VB" AutoEventWireup="true" CodeFile="Default.aspx.vb"
Inherits="_Default" %>

<!DOCTYPE html PUBLIC "-//W3C//DTD XHTML 1.1//EN"
"http://www.w3.org/TR/xhtml11/DTD/xhtml11.dtd">
<html xmlns="http://www.w3.org/1999/xhtml">
<head runat="server">
    <title>Exercise 4-3</title>
</head>
<body>
    <form id="form1" runat="server">
        <asp:ScriptManager ID="ScriptManager1" runat="server" />
        <asp:UpdatePanel ID="UpdatePanel1" runat="server">
            <ContentTemplate>
                Select the table you would like to see:<br />
                <asp:RadioButton ID="rbEmployee" runat="server"
                    GroupName="grpEmployeeCustomer"
                    OnCheckedChanged="rbEmployee_CheckedChanged"
                    Text="Show Employees" AutoPostBack="True" />
                 
                <br />
```

Example C-15. The markup file for Exercise 4-3 (continued)

```
            <asp:RadioButton ID="rbCustomer" runat="server"
                GroupName="grpEmployeeCustomer"
                OnCheckedChanged="rbCustomer_CheckedChanged"
                Text="Show Customers" AutoPostBack="True" />
        <br />  
        <asp:Panel ID="pnlEmployee" runat="server" Height="50px"
                Width="125px" Visible="False">
            <asp:SqlDataSource ID="sdsEmployee" runat="server"
                ConnectionString=
             "<%$ ConnectionStrings:AdventureWorksConnectionString %>"
                SelectCommand="SELECT [EmployeeID], [ManagerID], [Title]
                    FROM [HumanResources].[Employee]"></asp:SqlDataSource>
            <asp:GridView ID="gvEmployee" runat="server"
                AllowPaging="True" AllowSorting="True"
                DataSourceID="sdsEmployee" AutoGenerateColumns="False"
                DataKeyNames="EmployeeID" BackColor="White"
                BorderColor="#E7E7FF" BorderStyle="None" BorderWidth="1px"
                CellPadding="3" GridLines="Horizontal">
                <Columns>
                    <asp:BoundField DataField="EmployeeID"
                        HeaderText="EmployeeID" InsertVisible="False"
                        ReadOnly="True" SortExpression="EmployeeID" />
                    <asp:BoundField DataField="ManagerID"
                        HeaderText="ManagerID" SortExpression="ManagerID" />
                    <asp:BoundField DataField="Title" HeaderText="Title"
                        SortExpression="Title" />
                </Columns>
                <FooterStyle BackColor="#B5C7DE" ForeColor="#4A3C8C" />
                <RowStyle BackColor="#E7E7FF" ForeColor="#4A3C8C" />
                <SelectedRowStyle BackColor="#738A9C" Font-Bold="True"
                    ForeColor="#F7F7F7" />
                <PagerStyle BackColor="#E7E7FF" ForeColor="#4A3C8C"
                    HorizontalAlign="Right" />
                <HeaderStyle BackColor="#4A3C8C" Font-Bold="True"
                    ForeColor="#F7F7F7" />
                <AlternatingRowStyle BackColor="#F7F7F7" />
            </asp:GridView>
        </asp:Panel>
          
        <asp:Panel ID="pnlCustomer" runat="server" Height="50px"
                Width="125px" Visible="False">
            <asp:SqlDataSource ID="sdsCustomer" runat="server"
                ConnectionString=
             "<%$ ConnectionStrings:AdventureWorksConnectionString %>"
                SelectCommand="SELECT [CustomerID], [AccountNumber],
                    [CustomerType]
                    FROM [Sales].[Customer]">
            </asp:SqlDataSource>
            <asp:GridView ID="gvCustomer" runat="server"
                DataSourceID="sdsCustomer" AllowPaging="True"
                AllowSorting="True" AutoGenerateColumns="False"
                DataKeyNames="CustomerID" BackColor="White"
```

Example C-15. The markup file for Exercise 4-3 (continued)

```
                        BorderColor="#E7E7FF" BorderStyle="None"
                        BorderWidth="1px" CellPadding="3" GridLines="Horizontal">
                        <Columns>
                            <asp:BoundField DataField="CustomerID"
                                HeaderText="CustomerID" InsertVisible="False"
                                ReadOnly="True" SortExpression="CustomerID" />
                            <asp:BoundField DataField="AccountNumber"
                                HeaderText="AccountNumber" ReadOnly="True"
                                SortExpression="AccountNumber" />
                            <asp:BoundField DataField="CustomerType"
                                HeaderText="CustomerType"
                                SortExpression="CustomerType" />
                        </Columns>
                        <FooterStyle BackColor="#B5C7DE" ForeColor="#4A3C8C" />
                        <RowStyle BackColor="#E7E7FF" ForeColor="#4A3C8C" />
                        <SelectedRowStyle BackColor="#738A9C" Font-Bold="True"
                          ForeColor="#F7F7F7" />
                        <PagerStyle BackColor="#E7E7FF" ForeColor="#4A3C8C"
                          HorizontalAlign="Right" />
                        <HeaderStyle BackColor="#4A3C8C" Font-Bold="True"
                          ForeColor="#F7F7F7" />
                        <AlternatingRowStyle BackColor="#F7F7F7" />
                    </asp:GridView>
                </asp:Panel>
                   
            </ContentTemplate>
        </asp:UpdatePanel>
        <div>
             </div>
    </form>
</body>
</html>
```

Example C-16 shows the code-behind file for Exercise 4-3.

Example C-16. The code-behind file for Exercise 4-3

```
Partial Class _Default
    Inherits System.Web.UI.Page

    Protected Sub rbEmployee_CheckedChanged(ByVal sender As Object, _
                        ByVal e As System.EventArgs)
        pnlEmployee.Visible = rbEmployee.Checked
        pnlCustomer.Visible = rbCustomer.Checked
    End Sub

    Protected Sub rbCustomer_CheckedChanged(ByVal sender As Object, _
                        ByVal e As System.EventArgs)
        pnlEmployee.Visible = rbEmployee.Checked
        pnlCustomer.Visible = rbCustomer.Checked
    End Sub
End Class
```

Solution to Exercise 4-4. You're going to need several `DataSource` controls for this exercise—one for each of the drop-down lists, and another for the `GridView`.

1. Call the first `DataSource` `sdsCategorySource`, and the first drop-down list `ddlCategory`. Configure `sdsCategorySource` to retrieve the `ProductCategoryID` and `Name` columns from the `ProductCategory` table (remember to go to Source view and add the `[Production]` schema).

2. Click the Smart Tag on `ddlCategory` and select "Choose Data Source." For the "Select a data source" field, choose `sdsCategorySource`. For "Select a data field to display in the DropDownList," select the Name column—this is what you want the user to see in the drop-down list. For "Select a data field for the value of the DropDownList," select `ProductCategoryID`. The control will automatically associate each name with its appropriate value within the control, so you can use them later. The Choose Data Source page should look like Figure C-4.

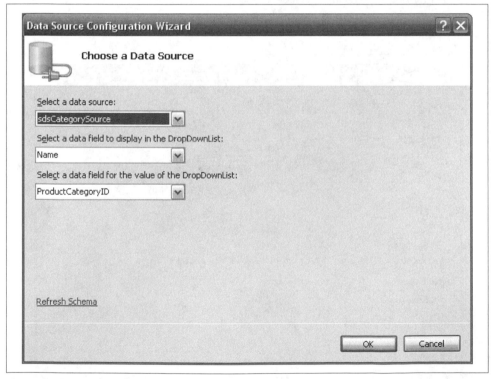

Figure C-4. Select the source, name, and value properties for ddlCategory.

3. That's one control set up. Add a label for the drop-down list if you like, and test the application now to make sure everything is working. Your drop-down list won't do much of anything yet, but if the product categories appear in the list, you'll know you configured your data source properly.

For the Subcategory drop-down list, you want to only show the subcategories that are connected to the category the user chose. That's only slightly trickier—you'll need a WHERE clause.

1. Add a SqlDataSource (call it sdsSubcategorySource), a DropDownList (ddlSubcategory), and a label for the drop-down list. Configure sdsSubcategorySource to retrieve the ProductSubcategoryID and Name columns from the ProductSubcategory table.

2. Click the WHERE button, to add a WHERE clause. You want to display the subcategories of the category in the first drop-down list, which means you want to match on the ProductCategory column. Specifically, you want to select the rows where the ProductCategoryID column is the same as whatever the user selected in ddlCategory. The Wizard can do that for you. Select ProductCategoryID for the Column, = for the Operator, and Control for the Source. The Control ID field on the right becomes visible; select ddlCategory. You don't need a default value, because ddlCategory will always have some value. When you have all that set, your WHERE clause dialog will look like Figure C-5.

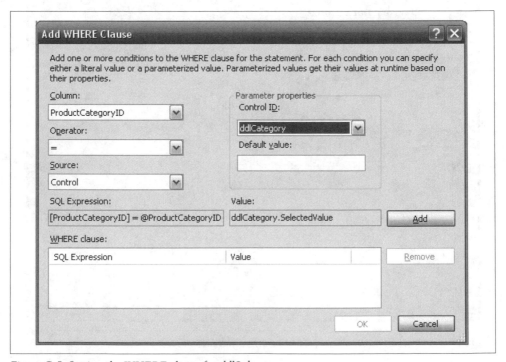

Figure C-5. Setting the WHERE clause for ddlSubcategory.

3. Click Add to add the WHERE clause; then click OK to return to the Wizard. On the Wizard, click Next, and then Finish. Remember to go to Source view and add the [Production] schema.

4. You've got the data, so now you need to tell the drop-down list how to use it. Click ddlSubcategory and select Choose Data Source. When the dialog appears, select sdsSubcategorySource for the data source, select Name for the field to display, and select ProductSubcategoryID for the field to use for the value. Click OK.

5. Back in Design view, click ddlCategory, and set its AutoPostBack property to true. You want ddlSubcategory to change as soon as the user makes a selection in ddlCategory, so you want it to post back right away.

6. Save everything and test it. When you make a selection in the Category drop-down list, the Subcategory drop-down list should change automatically. If it doesn't, go back and check the WHERE statement for ddlSubcategory.

Two drop-down lists are set now; time for the third.

1. Add another SqlDataSource (sdsColorSource) and another DropDownList (ddlColor). Add a Label too. It would be nice if AdventureWorks had a Color table with colors and IDs for each, but it doesn't. The colors are stored in the Product table, so you need to retrieve them from there. That's not hard, but it requires a little SQL trick to make it look good. Configure sdsColorSource to retrieve just the Color column from the Product table—no need for WHERE clauses this time. Remember to add the [Production] schema in Source view.

2. Click ddlColor and select Choose Data Source. In the dialog, select sdsColorSource for the data source, and select Color for both the field to display and the value. Click OK.

3. If you were to run your application right now, you'd see that ddlColor would have a long list of colors—many repeated, and many blank. This actually works fine, but it doesn't look very good. What you want is to only retrieve colors that aren't already in the list. The easiest way to do that is to use an extra bit of SQL code called DISTINCT. DISTINCT does exactly what it sounds like—it makes sure that each data item in the list is unique, by discarding the repeats. To make this work, switch to source view and find this line, which contains the Select statement for sdsColorSource:

```
SelectCommand="SELECT [Color] FROM [Production].[Product]"></asp:SqlDataSource>
```

Just add DISTINCT, like this:

```
SelectCommand="SELECT DISTINCT [Color] FROM _
[Production].[Product]"></asp:SqlDataSource>
```

4. Now test your application. You should see a much shorter list in ddlColor, and each item is unique.

Now you have all the tools the user needs to make a selection, so all you need to do is give them a way to see the results.

1. Add one more SqlDataSource (call it sdsProducts), and a GridView (gvProducts).

2. Configure the Data source to retrieve the ProductID, Name, ProductNumber, and Color from the Product table.

3. Click the WHERE button. This time, you want two WHERE clauses: one for the subcategory, and one for the color. (The category doesn't matter; it's only there to populate the subcategory list.) For the first WHERE, set the Column to ProductSubcategoryID, the Operation to =, and the Source to Control. On the right, set the Control ID to ddlSubcategory. Click Add.

4. For the second WHERE clause, set the Column to Color, the Operation to =, and the Source to Control. On the right, set the Control ID to ddlColor. The dialog should look like Figure C-6.

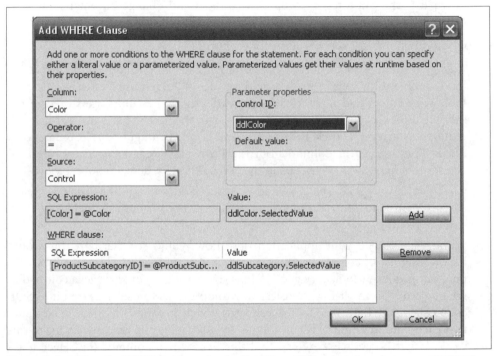

Figure C-6. Adding the WHERE clauses for the GridView. Notice that the subcategory WHERE clause is already added.

5. Click Add to add the second WHERE, and OK to return to the Wizard. Click Next and Finish in the Wizard; then switch to Source view to add the [Production] schema.

6. Back in Design view, click gvProducts, and enable sorting and paging. Apply a nice format if you like.

You don't want to set either ddlSubcategory or ddlColor to Auto-postback, because you want users to be able to make both choices before the GridView does anything. The drop-down lists have AutoPostBack set to false by default, so that's no problem. You need something to trigger the postback, though, so add a Button, and change its text to "Submit." Buttons are set to post back whenever they're clicked, and that's all you want it to do, so you don't even need an event handler for this button. Easy!

Run your application and try it out. Try selecting black gloves or yellow jerseys to see the full effect. Note that if there are no items in the color you've chosen, the GridView will not appear.

Well done! You've taken a long and confusing product list, and with just a handful of drop-down lists, you've made it much friendlier and easier for readers to navigate. With the selection tools you learned about in this chapter, you can imagine that you could enable the user to select items from the GridView to see product details, or add it to a shopping cart, but that's a subject for later on.

Example C-17 shows the markup file for Exercise 4-4.

Example C-17. The markup file for Exercise 4-4

```
<%@ Page Language="VB" AutoEventWireup="true" CodeFile="Default.aspx.vb"
Inherits="_Default" %>

<!DOCTYPE html PUBLIC "-//W3C//DTD XHTML 1.1//EN"
"http://www.w3.org/TR/xhtml11/DTD/xhtml11.dtd">
<html xmlns="http://www.w3.org/1999/xhtml">
<head runat="server">
    <title>Exercise 4-4</title>
</head>
<body>
    <form id="form1" runat="server">
        <asp:ScriptManager ID="ScriptManager1" runat="server" />
        <div>
            <asp:SqlDataSource ID="sdsCategorySource" runat="server"
                ConnectionString=
                  "<%$ ConnectionStrings:AdventureWorksConnectionString %>"
                SelectCommand="SELECT [Name], [ProductCategoryID]
                  FROM [Production].[ProductCategory]">
            </asp:SqlDataSource>
            <asp:SqlDataSource ID="sdsSubcategorySource" runat="server"
                ConnectionString=
                  "<%$ ConnectionStrings:AdventureWorksConnectionString %>"
                SelectCommand="SELECT [ProductSubcategoryID], [Name]
                  FROM [Production].[ProductSubcategory]
                  WHERE ([ProductCategoryID] = @ProductCategoryID)">
                <SelectParameters>
                    <asp:ControlParameter ControlID="ddlCategory"
                        Name="ProductCategoryID" PropertyName="SelectedValue"
                        Type="Int32" />
                </SelectParameters>
            </asp:SqlDataSource>
            <asp:SqlDataSource ID="sdsColorSource" runat="server"
                ConnectionString=
                  "<%$ ConnectionStrings:AdventureWorksConnectionString %>"
                SelectCommand="SELECT DISTINCT [Color]
                  FROM [Production].[Product]">
            </asp:SqlDataSource>
```

Example C-17. The markup file for Exercise 4-4 (continued)

```
            <asp:SqlDataSource ID="sdsProducts" runat="server"
                ConnectionString=
                    "<%$ ConnectionStrings:AdventureWorksConnectionString %>"
                SelectCommand="SELECT [ProductID], [Name], [ProductNumber],
                    [Color] FROM [Prioduction].[Product]
                    WHERE ([ProductSubcategoryID] = @ProductSubcategoryID)
                    AND ([Color] = @Color))">
                <SelectParameters>
                    <asp:ControlParameter ControlID="ddlSubcategory"
                        Name="ProductSubcategoryID" PropertyName="SelectedValue"
                        Type="Int32" />
                    <asp:ControlParameter ControlID="ddlColor" Name="Color"
                        PropertyName="SelectedValue"
                        Type="String" />
                </SelectParameters>
            </asp:SqlDataSource>
            <br />
            <asp:Label ID="lblCategory" runat="server"
                 Font-Bold="True" Text="Category: "></asp:Label>
        <asp:DropDownList ID="ddlCategory" runat="server"
            DataSourceID="sdsCategorySource" DataTextField="Name"
            DataValueField="ProductCategoryID" AutoPostBack="True">
        </asp:DropDownList>
            <asp:Label ID="lblSubcategory" runat="server" Font-Bold="True"
                    Text="Subcategory:"></asp:Label>
            <asp:DropDownList ID="ddlSubcategory" runat="server"
                DataSourceID="sdsSubcategorySource" DataTextField="Name"
                DataValueField="ProductSubcategoryID">
            </asp:DropDownList>
            <asp:Label ID="lblColor" runat="server" Font-Bold="True"
                Text="Color:"></asp:Label>
            <asp:DropDownList ID="ddlColor" runat="server"
                DataSourceID="sdsColorSource" DataTextField="Color"
                DataValueField="Color">
            </asp:DropDownList>
            <asp:Button ID="btnSubmit" runat="server" Text="Submit" /><br />
    </div>
        <br />
<asp:GridView ID="gvProducts" runat="server" AllowPaging="True"
    AllowSorting="True"
    CellPadding="4" DataSourceID="sdsProducts" ForeColor="#333333"
    GridLines="None" AutoGenerateColumns="False" DataKeyNames="ProductID">
    <FooterStyle BackColor="#507CD1" Font-Bold="True" ForeColor="White" />
    <RowStyle BackColor="#EFF3FB" />
    <EditRowStyle BackColor="#2461BF" />
    <SelectedRowStyle BackColor="#D1DDF1" Font-Bold="True"
        ForeColor="#333333" />
    <PagerStyle BackColor="#2461BF" ForeColor="White"
        HorizontalAlign="Center" />
    <HeaderStyle BackColor="#507CD1" Font-Bold="True" ForeColor="White" />
    <AlternatingRowStyle BackColor="White" />
```

Example C-17. The markup file for Exercise 4-4 (continued)

```
        <Columns>
            <asp:BoundField DataField="ProductID" HeaderText="ProductID"
                InsertVisible="False"
                ReadOnly="True" SortExpression="ProductID" />
            <asp:BoundField DataField="Name" HeaderText="Name"
                SortExpression="Name" />
            <asp:BoundField DataField="ProductNumber"
                HeaderText="ProductNumber" SortExpression="ProductNumber" />
            <asp:BoundField DataField="Color" HeaderText="Color"
                SortExpression="Color" />
        </Columns>
    </asp:GridView>
</form>
</body>
</html>
```

Chapter 5: Validation

Answers to Quiz Questions

1. You need validation because users make mistakes. The wrong input could result in misplaced orders, inaccurate records, and can even corrupt your database. Validation gets the user to fix those errors before they get anywhere near your data.

2. Set the button's `CausesValidation` property to false.

3. The `RequiredFieldValidator`—in the case of a radio button list, you've already defined the choices for the user, so you don't need to validate the form or type of input; you just need to make sure that they chose something.

4. When the `Display` property is set to `Static`, the validator takes up a fixed amount of room, even if it's not displaying a message. When it's set to `Dynamic`, the control is only rendered when there's a validation error, which can cause other controls to move around.

5. Use a `RequiredFieldValidator`, and set the `InitialValue` property to "Choose a payment method."

6. It enables you to place all the validation error messages in one spot on the page, instead of next to each control.

7. Use a `CompareValidator`. You can compare the quantity the user ordered with the amount of inventory in your database, and make sure that the amount the user wants is equal to or less than the amount you have.

8. Use a NoSnoreValidation control, to make sure none of the guests snore too loudly. Just kidding. Use a `RangeValidator`. Set the `MinimumValue` to 2, and the `MaximumValue` to 5.

9. Use a `RegularExpressionValidator`. The Regular Expression Editor has an option that provides you with a regular expression to validate the form of an email address.

10. You'd need to use a `CustomValidator`. The `RangeValidator` can only check values in a single range. With a `CustomValidator`, though, you could write code to check that the age the user entered either falls between 6 and 12, or is greater than 65.

Answers to Exercises

Exercise 5-1. This one is fairly simple to start out with. Just make a table with five labels, five textboxes, and five Required Field Validators. We specified that you didn't need to worry about the format of the data, so a `RequiredFieldvalidator` is all you need right now. Just make sure you have the validators targeting the correct controls, add some appropriate error messages, and you're done. Example C-18 shows the markup file for this exercise.

Example C-18. The markup file for Exercise 5-1

```
<%@ Page Language="VB" AutoEventWireup="false" CodeFile="Default.aspx.vb"
Inherits="_Default" %>

<!DOCTYPE html PUBLIC "-//W3C//DTD XHTML 1.0 Transitional//EN"
"http://www.w3.org/TR/xhtml1/DTD/xhtml1-transitional.dtd">

<html xmlns="http://www.w3.org/1999/xhtml" >
<head runat="server">
    <title>Untitled Page</title>
</head>
<body>
    <form id="form1" runat="server">
    <div>
        <H1>Phone Survey Participation Form</H1>
        <p>
            <table>
                <tr>
                    <td align="right">
                        <asp:Label ID="lblName" runat="server" Text="Name:">
                        </asp:Label></td>
                    <td style="width: 100px">
                        <asp:TextBox ID="txtName" runat="server">
                        </asp:TextBox></td>
                    <td style="width: 100px">
                        <asp:RequiredFieldValidator ID="reqFieldName"
                            runat="server"
                            ControlToValidate="txtName">
                        Please enter your name</asp:RequiredFieldValidator>
                    </td>
                </tr>
                <tr>
                    <td align="right">
```

Example C-18. The markup file for Exercise 5-1 (continued)

```
                    <asp:Label ID="lblAddress" runat="server"
                        Text="Street address:"></asp:Label></td>
        <td style="width: 100px">
            <asp:TextBox ID="txtAddress" runat="server">
            </asp:TextBox></td>
        <td style="width: 100px">
            <asp:RequiredFieldValidator ID="reqFieldAddress"
                runat="server"
                ControlToValidate="txtAddress">
                Please enter the street address
            </asp:RequiredFieldValidator></td>
    </tr>
    <tr>
        <td align="right">
            <asp:Label ID="lblCity" runat="server" Text="City:">
            </asp:Label></td>
        <td style="width: 100px">
            <asp:TextBox ID="txtCity" runat="server">
            </asp:TextBox></td>
        <td style="width: 100px">
            <asp:RequiredFieldValidator ID="reqFieldCity"
                runat="server"
                ControlToValidate="txtCity">
                Please enter the city
            </asp:RequiredFieldValidator></td>
    </tr>
    <tr>
        <td align="right">
            <asp:Label ID="lblState" runat="server" Text="State:">
            </asp:Label></td>
        <td style="width: 100px">
            <asp:TextBox ID="txtState" runat="server">
            </asp:TextBox></td>
        <td style="width: 100px">
            <asp:RequiredFieldValidator ID="reqFieldState"
                runat="server"
                ControlToValidate="txtState">
                    Please enter the state
            </asp:RequiredFieldValidator></td>
    </tr>
    <tr>
        <td align="right">
            <asp:Label ID="lblZip" runat="server"
                Text="ZIP code"></asp:Label></td>
        <td style="width: 100px">
            <asp:TextBox ID="txtZip" runat="server"></asp:TextBox></td>
        <td style="width: 100px">
            <asp:RequiredFieldValidator ID="reqFieldZip" runat="server"
                ControlToValidate="txtZip">
                Please enter the Zip code
            </asp:RequiredFieldValidator></td>
    </tr>
```

Example C-18. The markup file for Exercise 5-1 (continued)

```
                <tr>
                    <td></td>
                    <td align="center">
                        <asp:Button ID="btnSubmit" runat="server" Text="Submit" />
                    </td>
                    <td></td>
                </tr>
            </table>
        </p>
    </div>
    </form>
</body>
</html>
```

Exercise 5-2. This exercise also isn't too difficult. You saw how to add a ValidationSummary control earlier in the chapter. All you need to do is change the text of the other validator controls to ErrorMessage properties, and the messages will display automatically in the summary control.

To check the user's age, you need two controls: A RequiredFieldValidator, to make sure the user can't leave the field blank, and a CompareValidator to make sure that the user is over 18 (or that they say they are, anyway). The RequiredFieldValidator is the same as the ones in Exercise 5-1. For the CompareValidator, be sure to set the ControlToValidate property to txtAge (or whatever you called the age TextBox), set the Type property to Integer, set the Operator property to GreaterThanEqual, and set the ValueToCompare property to 18.

You want to make sure that the user enters a date when they'd like you to call, and that the date is sometime in July. Sounds like a job for the RangeValidator. You need to make sure the user enters a date, so add a RequiredFieldValidator that validates txtCallDate first. Then add a RangeValidator that also validates txtCallDate. Make sure you set the Type to Date, or you'll get unexpected results. Set the MaximumValue to 07/31/2007, and the MinimumValue to 07/01/2007. Add appropriate text and error messages, and you're done. Try it out, and you'll see that the user can only enter dates in July. Example C-19 shows the markup file for this exercise.

Example C-19. The markup file for Exercise 5-2

```
<%@ Page Language="VB" AutoEventWireup="false" CodeFile="Default.aspx.vb"
Inherits="_Default" %>

<!DOCTYPE html PUBLIC "-//W3C//DTD XHTML 1.0 Transitional//EN"
"http://www.w3.org/TR/xhtml1/DTD/xhtml1-transitional.dtd">

<html xmlns="http://www.w3.org/1999/xhtml" >
<head runat="server">
    <title>Untitled Page</title>
</head>
```

Example C-19. The markup file for Exercise 5-2 (continued)

```
<body>
    <form id="form1" runat="server">
    <div>
        <H1>Phone Survey Participation Form</H1>
        <p>
            <table>
                <tr>
                    <td align="right">
                        <asp:Label ID="lblName" runat="server" Text="Name:">
                        </asp:Label></td>
                    <td style="width: 100px">
                        <asp:TextBox ID="txtName" runat="server">
                        </asp:TextBox></td>
                    <td style="width: 100px">
                        <asp:RequiredFieldValidator ID="reqFieldName"
                            runat="server" ErrorMessage="Please enter your name"
                            ControlToValidate="txtName">*
                        </asp:RequiredFieldValidator></td>
                </tr>
                <tr>
                    <td align="right">
                        <asp:Label ID="lblAddress" runat="server"
                            Text="Street address:"></asp:Label></td>
                    <td style="width: 100px">
                        <asp:TextBox ID="txtAddress" runat="server">
                        </asp:TextBox></td>
                    <td style="width: 100px">
                        <asp:RequiredFieldValidator ID="reqFieldAddress"
                            runat="server"
                            ErrorMessage="Please enter the street address"
                            ControlToValidate="txtAddress">*
                        </asp:RequiredFieldValidator></td>
                </tr>
                <tr>
                    <td align="right">
                        <asp:Label ID="lblCity" runat="server" Text="City:">
                        </asp:Label></td>
                    <td style="width: 100px">
                        <asp:TextBox ID="txtCity" runat="server">
                        </asp:TextBox></td>
                    <td style="width: 100px">
                        <asp:RequiredFieldValidator ID="reqFieldCity"
                            runat="server" ErrorMessage="Please enter the city"
                            ControlToValidate="txtCity">*
                        </asp:RequiredFieldValidator></td>
                </tr>
                <tr>
                    <td align="right">
                        <asp:Label ID="lblState" runat="server" Text="State:">
                        </asp:Label></td>
```

Example C-19. The markup file for Exercise 5-2 (continued)

```
        <td style="width: 100px">
            <asp:TextBox ID="txtState" runat="server">
            </asp:TextBox></td>
        <td style="width: 100px">
            <asp:RequiredFieldValidator ID="reqFieldState"
                runat="server" ErrorMessage="Please enter the state"
                ControlToValidate="txtState">*
            </asp:RequiredFieldValidator></td>
    </tr>
    <tr>
        <td align="right">
            <asp:Label ID="lblZip" runat="server" Text="ZIP code">
            </asp:Label></td>
        <td style="width: 100px">
            <asp:TextBox ID="txtZip" runat="server"></asp:TextBox></td>
        <td style="width: 100px">
            <asp:RequiredFieldValidator ID="reqFieldZip" runat="server"
                ErrorMessage="Please enter the Zip code"
                ControlToValidate="txtZip">*
            </asp:RequiredFieldValidator></td>
    </tr>
    <tr>
        <td align="right">
            <asp:Label ID="lblAge" runat="server" Text="Age:">
            </asp:Label></td>
        <td>
            <asp:TextBox ID="txtAge" runat="server"></asp:TextBox></td>
        <td>
            <asp:CompareValidator ID="compareValidatorAge"
                runat="server"
                ErrorMessage="You must be over 18 to participate"
                ControlToValidate="txtAge" Operator="GreaterThanEqual"
                Type="Integer" ValueToCompare="18">*
            </asp:CompareValidator>
            <asp:RequiredFieldValidator ID="reqFieldAge" runat="server"
                ControlToValidate="txtAge"
                ErrorMessage="Please enter your age.">*
            </asp:RequiredFieldValidator></td>
    </tr>
    <tr>
        <td align="right">
            <asp:Label ID="lblCallDate" runat="server"
                Text="Enter a date for us to call you, in July,
                    2007 (format m/d/yyyy):"
                Width="150px"></asp:Label></td>
        <td>
            <asp:TextBox ID="txtCallDate" runat="server">
            </asp:TextBox></td>
        <td>
            <asp:RequiredFieldValidator ID="reqFieldCallDate"
                runat="server" ControlToValidate="txtCallDate"
                ErrorMessage="Please enter a date for your call">*
            </asp:RequiredFieldValidator>
```

Example C-19. The markup file for Exercise 5-2 (continued)

```
                              <asp:RangeValidator ID="rangeValCallDate" runat="server"
                                  ControlToValidate="txtCallDate"
                                  ErrorMessage="The date must be between 7/1/2007
                                               and 7/31/2007"
                                  MaximumValue="07/31/2007"
                                  MinimumValue="07/01/2007" Type="Date">*
                              </asp:RangeValidator></td>
                  </tr>
                  <tr>
                  <td colspan=3>
                      <asp:ValidationSummary ID="valSummary" runat="server"
                          HeaderText="The following errors were found:" />
                  </td>
                  </tr>
                  <tr>
                      <td></td>
                      <td align="center"style="width: 100px">
                          <asp:Button ID="btnSubmit" runat="server"
                              Text="Submit" /></td>
                      <td></td>
                  </tr>
              </table>
          </p>
      </div>
      </form>
  </body>
  </html>
```

Exercise 5-3. This time around, you need three validators on a single TextBox. The RequiredFieldValidator and RangeValidator work the same as they do in Exercise 5-2—you can even copy-and-paste the appropriate markup in Source view to make the new row. However, be sure to change the ControlToValidate properties of both validators to txtFollowup (or whatever you call the follow-up text box).

Now you need to add a third validator—this time, a CompareValidator. You're not comparing to a constant value, though, like you were with the age text box. This time, you want to make sure that the date in txtFollowup is later than the date in txtCallDate, which means you want the value in txtFollowup to be greater. Add your CompareValidator, set its ControlToValidate property to txtFollowup, and set the ControlToCompare property to txtCallDate. Be sure not to get the two properties backwards, or you'll get unexpected results. Now set the Operator property to GreaterThan, and make sure to set the Type to Date. Add the appropriate text and error messages, and try it out. You'll see that the follow-up date still has to be in July, but also that it must be later than the date of the original call. (If you want to be extra helpful, you can change the RangeValidator for txtCallDate so that the latest date is July 30, which leaves time for a follow-up on July 31.) Example C-20 shows the markup file for Exercise 5-3.

Example C-20. The markup file for Exercise 5-3

```
<%@ Page Language="VB" AutoEventWireup="false" CodeFile="Default.aspx.vb"
Inherits="_Default" %>

<!DOCTYPE html PUBLIC "-//W3C//DTD XHTML 1.0 Transitional//EN"
"http://www.w3.org/TR/xhtml1/DTD/xhtml1-transitional.dtd">

<html xmlns="http://www.w3.org/1999/xhtml" >
<head runat="server">
    <title>Untitled Page</title>
</head>
<body>
    <form id="form1" runat="server">
    <div>
        <H1>Phone Survey Participation Form</H1>
        <p>
            <table>
                <tr>
                    <td align="right">
                        <asp:Label ID="lblName" runat="server" Text="Name:">
                        </asp:Label></td>
                    <td style="width: 100px">
                        <asp:TextBox ID="txtName" runat="server">
                        </asp:TextBox></td>
                    <td style="width: 100px">
                        <asp:RequiredFieldValidator ID="reqFieldName"
                            runat="server" ErrorMessage="Please enter your name"
                            ControlToValidate="txtName">*
                        </asp:RequiredFieldValidator></td>
                </tr>
                <tr>
                    <td align="right">
                        <asp:Label ID="lblAddress" runat="server"
                            Text="Street address:">
                        </asp:Label></td>
                    <td style="width: 100px">
                        <asp:TextBox ID="txtAddress" runat="server">
                        </asp:TextBox></td>
                    <td style="width: 100px">
                        <asp:RequiredFieldValidator ID="reqFieldAddress"
                            runat="server"
                            ErrorMessage="Please enter the street address"
                            ControlToValidate="txtAddress">*
                        </asp:RequiredFieldValidator></td>
                </tr>
                <tr>
                    <td align="right">
                        <asp:Label ID="lblCity" runat="server" Text="City:">
                        </asp:Label></td>
                    <td style="width: 100px">
                        <asp:TextBox ID="txtCity" runat="server">
                        </asp:TextBox></td>
```

Example C-20. The markup file for Exercise 5-3 (continued)

```
                    <td style="width: 100px">
                        <asp:RequiredFieldValidator ID="reqFieldCity"
                            runat="server" ErrorMessage="Please enter the city"
                            ControlToValidate="txtCity">*
                        </asp:RequiredFieldValidator></td>
                </tr>
                <tr>
                    <td align="right">
                        <asp:Label ID="lblState" runat="server" Text="State:">
                        </asp:Label></td>
                    <td style="width: 100px">
                        <asp:TextBox ID="txtState" runat="server">
                        </asp:TextBox></td>
                    <td style="width: 100px">
                        <asp:RequiredFieldValidator ID="reqFieldState"
                            runat="server" ErrorMessage="Please enter the state"
                            ControlToValidate="txtState">*
                        </asp:RequiredFieldValidator></td>
                </tr>
                <tr>
                    <td align="right">
                        <asp:Label ID="lblZip" runat="server" Text="ZIP code">
                        </asp:Label></td>
                    <td style="width: 100px">
                        <asp:TextBox ID="txtZip" runat="server"></asp:TextBox></td>
                    <td style="width: 100px">
                        <asp:RequiredFieldValidator ID="reqFieldZip" runat="server"
                            ErrorMessage="Please enter the Zip code"
                            ControlToValidate="txtZip">*
                        </asp:RequiredFieldValidator></td>
                </tr>
                <tr>
                    <td align="right">
                        <asp:Label ID="lblAge" runat="server" Text="Age:">
                        </asp:Label></td>
                    <td>
                        <asp:TextBox ID="txtAge" runat="server"></asp:TextBox></td>
                    <td>
                        <asp:CompareValidator ID="compareValidatorAge"
                            runat="server"
                            ErrorMessage="You must be over 18 to participate"
                            ControlToValidate="txtAge" Operator="GreaterThanEqual"
                            Type="Integer" ValueToCompare="18">*
                        </asp:CompareValidator>
                        <asp:RequiredFieldValidator ID="reqFieldAge" runat="server"
                            ControlToValidate="txtAge"
                            ErrorMessage="Please enter your age.">*
                        </asp:RequiredFieldValidator></td>
                </tr>
```

Example C-20. The markup file for Exercise 5-3 (continued)

```
<tr>
    <td align="right">
        <asp:Label ID="lblCallDate" runat="server"
            Text="Enter a date for us to call you, in
                    July, 2007 (format m/d/yyyy):"
            Width="150px"></asp:Label></td>
    <td>
        <asp:TextBox ID="txtCallDate" runat="server">
        </asp:TextBox></td>
    <td>
        <asp:RequiredFieldValidator ID="reqFieldCallDate"
            runat="server" ControlToValidate="txtCallDate"
            ErrorMessage="Please enter a date for your call">*
        </asp:RequiredFieldValidator>
        <asp:RangeValidator ID="rangeValCallDate" runat="server"
            ControlToValidate="txtCallDate"
            ErrorMessage="The date must be between 7/1/2007
                        and 7/31/2007"
            MaximumValue="07/31/2007"
            MinimumValue="07/01/2007" Type="Date">*
        </asp:RangeValidator></td>
</tr>
<tr>
    <td align="right">
        <asp:Label ID="lblFollowup" runat="server"
            Text="Enter a date for us to make a follow-up call,
                in July, 2007 (format m/d/yyyy):"
            Width="150px"></asp:Label></td>
    <td>
        <asp:TextBox ID="txtFollowup" runat="server">
        </asp:TextBox></td>
    <td>
        <asp:RequiredFieldValidator ID="reqFieldFollowup"
            runat="server" ControlToValidate="txtFollowup"
            ErrorMessage="Please enter a date for your
                        follow-up call">*
        </asp:RequiredFieldValidator>
        <asp:RangeValidator ID="rangeValFollowup" runat="server"
            ControlToValidate="txtFollowup"
            ErrorMessage="The date must be between 7/1/2007 and
                7/31/2007"
            MaximumValue="07/31/2007"
            MinimumValue="07/01/2007" Type="Date">*
        </asp:RangeValidator>
        <asp:CompareValidator ID="compareValFollowup"
            runat="server" ControlToCompare="txtCallDate"
            ControlToValidate="txtFollowup"
            ErrorMessage="Please select a date after your
                first call."
            Operator="GreaterThan" Type="Date">*
        </asp:CompareValidator></td>
</tr>
```

Example C-20. The markup file for Exercise 5-3 (continued)

```
                    <tr>
                    <td colspan=3>
                        <asp:ValidationSummary ID="valSummary" runat="server"
                            HeaderText="The following errors were found:" />
                    </td>
                    </tr>
                    <tr>
                        <td></td>
                        <td align="center"style="width: 100px">
                            <asp:Button ID="btnSubmit" runat="server"
                                Text="Submit" /></td>
                        <td></td>
                    </tr>
                </table>
            </p>
        </div>
        </form>
</body>
</html>
```

Exercise 5-4. Adding another couple rows to the table is old hat for you by now, and so is adding the `RequiredFieldValidator` controls for each of the new text boxes. To check the format for the phone number and email address, though, you'll need to use a `RegularExpressionValidator` for each. This isn't too tricky: for the phone number, drag a `RegularExpressionValidator` next to the `RequiredFieldValidator`. Set its `ControlToValidate` to `txtPhone` (or whatever you called the text box), click the `ValidationExpression` property, and then click the ellipsis button to open the Regular Expression Editor. Select "U.S. phone number" from the list (or whatever country you'd like to validate for), and click OK. Add text and error message properties, and it's good to go. The `RegularExpressionValidator` for the email field works the same way, except that the `ControlToValidate` is `txtEmail` (or whatever you called that text box), and you select "Internet e-mail address" in the Regular Expression Editor. Try it out, and you'll see that the page works. You can try a few different variations on phone numbers, and the most common ones will be accepted. Example C-21 shows the markup for Exercise 5-4.

Example C-21. The markup file for Exercise 5-4

```
<%@ Page Language="VB" AutoEventWireup="false" CodeFile="Default.aspx.vb"
Inherits="_Default" %>

<!DOCTYPE html PUBLIC "-//W3C//DTD XHTML 1.0 Transitional//EN"
"http://www.w3.org/TR/xhtml1/DTD/xhtml1-transitional.dtd">

<html xmlns="http://www.w3.org/1999/xhtml" >
<head runat="server">
    <title>Untitled Page</title>
</head>
```

Example C-21. The markup file for Exercise 5-4 (continued)

```
<body>
    <form id="form1" runat="server">
    <div>
        <H1>Phone Survey Participation Form</H1>
        <p>
            <table>
                <tr>
                    <td align="right">
                        <asp:Label ID="lblName" runat="server" Text="Name:">
                        </asp:Label></td>
                    <td style="width: 100px">
                        <asp:TextBox ID="txtName" runat="server">
                        </asp:TextBox></td>
                    <td style="width: 100px">
                        <asp:RequiredFieldValidator ID="reqFieldName"
                            runat="server" ErrorMessage="Please enter your name"
                            ControlToValidate="txtName">*
                        </asp:RequiredFieldValidator></td>
                </tr>
                <tr>
                    <td align="right">
                        <asp:Label ID="lblAddress" runat="server"
                            Text="Street address:"></asp:Label></td>
                    <td style="width: 100px">
                        <asp:TextBox ID="txtAddress" runat="server">
                        </asp:TextBox></td>
                    <td style="width: 100px">
                        <asp:RequiredFieldValidator ID="reqFieldAddress"
                            runat="server"
                            ErrorMessage="Please enter the street address"
                            ControlToValidate="txtAddress">*
                        </asp:RequiredFieldValidator></td>
                </tr>
                <tr>
                    <td align="right">
                        <asp:Label ID="lblCity" runat="server" Text="City:">
                        </asp:Label></td>
                    <td style="width: 100px">
                        <asp:TextBox ID="txtCity" runat="server">
                        </asp:TextBox></td>
                    <td style="width: 100px">
                        <asp:RequiredFieldValidator ID="reqFieldCity"
                            runat="server" ErrorMessage="Please enter the city"
                            ControlToValidate="txtCity">*
                        </asp:RequiredFieldValidator></td>
                </tr>
                <tr>
                    <td align="right">
                        <asp:Label ID="lblState" runat="server" Text="State:">
                        </asp:Label></td>
```

Example C-21. The markup file for Exercise 5-4 (continued)

```
            <td style="width: 100px">
                <asp:TextBox ID="txtState" runat="server">
                </asp:TextBox></td>
            <td style="width: 100px">
                <asp:RequiredFieldValidator ID="reqFieldState"
                    runat="server" ErrorMessage="Please enter the state"
                    ControlToValidate="txtState">*
                </asp:RequiredFieldValidator></td>
    </tr>
    <tr>
        <td align="right">
            <asp:Label ID="lblZip" runat="server"
                Text="ZIP code"></asp:Label></td>
        <td style="width: 100px">
            <asp:TextBox ID="txtZip" runat="server"></asp:TextBox></td>
        <td style="width: 100px">
            <asp:RequiredFieldValidator ID="reqFieldZip" runat="server"
                ErrorMessage="Please enter the Zip code"
                ControlToValidate="txtZip">*
            </asp:RequiredFieldValidator></td>
    </tr>
    <tr>
        <td align="right">
            <asp:Label ID="lblAge" runat="server" Text="Age:">
            </asp:Label></td>
        <td>
            <asp:TextBox ID="txtAge" runat="server"></asp:TextBox></td>
        <td>
            <asp:CompareValidator ID="compareValidatorAge"
                runat="server"
                ErrorMessage="You must be over 18 to participate"
                ControlToValidate="txtAge" Operator="GreaterThanEqual"
                Type="Integer" ValueToCompare="18">*
            </asp:CompareValidator>
            <asp:RequiredFieldValidator ID="reqFieldAge" runat="server"
                ControlToValidate="txtAge"
                ErrorMessage="Please enter your age.">*
            </asp:RequiredFieldValidator></td>
    </tr>
    <tr>
        <td align="right">
            <asp:Label ID="lblPhone" runat="server" Text="Phone:">
            </asp:Label></td>
        <td>
            <asp:TextBox ID="txtPhone" runat="server">
            </asp:TextBox></td>
        <td>
            <asp:RequiredFieldValidator ID="reqFieldPhone"
                runat="server" ControlToValidate="txtPhone"
                ErrorMessage="Please enter your phone number.">*
            </asp:RequiredFieldValidator>
```

Example C-21. The markup file for Exercise 5-4 (continued)

```
                    <asp:RegularExpressionValidator ID="regExpValPhone"
                        runat="server" ControlToValidate="txtPhone"
                        ErrorMessage="Please enter a valid phone number"
                ValidationExpression="((\(\d{3}\) ?)|(\d{3}-))?\d{3}-\d{4}">*
                    </asp:RegularExpressionValidator></td>
        </tr>
        <tr>
            <td align="right">
                <asp:Label ID="lblEmail" runat="server"
                    Text="E-mail address:"></asp:Label></td>
            <td>
                <asp:TextBox ID="txtEmail" runat="server">
                </asp:TextBox></td>
            <td>
                <asp:RequiredFieldValidator ID="reqFieldEmail"
                    runat="server" ControlToValidate="txtEmail"
                    ErrorMessage="Please enter your e-mail address">*
                </asp:RequiredFieldValidator>
                <asp:RegularExpressionValidator ID="regExpValEmail"
                    runat="server" ControlToValidate="txtEmail"
                    ErrorMessage="Please enter a valid e-mail address"
                    ValidationExpression=
                        "\w+([-+.']\w+)*@\w+([-.]\w+)*\.\w+([-.]\w+)*">*
                </asp:RegularExpressionValidator></td>
        </tr>
        <tr>
            <td align="right">
                <asp:Label ID="lblCallDate" runat="server"
                    Text="Enter a date for us to call you, in July,
                        2007 (format m/d/yyyy):"
                    Width="150px"></asp:Label></td>
            <td>
                <asp:TextBox ID="txtCallDate" runat="server">
                </asp:TextBox></td>
            <td>
                <asp:RequiredFieldValidator ID="reqFieldCallDate"
                    runat="server" ControlToValidate="txtCallDate"
                    ErrorMessage="Please enter a date for your call">*
                </asp:RequiredFieldValidator>
                <asp:RangeValidator ID="rangeValCallDate" runat="server"
                    ControlToValidate="txtCallDate"
                    ErrorMessage="The date must be between 7/1/2007
                            and 7/31/2007"
                    MaximumValue="07/31/2007" MinimumValue="07/01/2007"
                    Type="Date">*
                </asp:RangeValidator></td>
        </tr>
        <tr>
            <td align="right">
                <asp:Label ID="lblFollowup" runat="server"
                    Text="Enter a date for us to make a follow-up call,
                        in July, 2007 (format m/d/yyyy):"
                    Width="150px"></asp:Label></td>
```

Example C-21. The markup file for Exercise 5-4 (continued)

```
                        <td>
                            <asp:TextBox ID="txtFollowup" runat="server">
                            </asp:TextBox></td>
                        <td>
                            <asp:RequiredFieldValidator ID="reqFieldFollowup"
                                runat="server" ControlToValidate="txtFollowup"
                                ErrorMessage=
                                    "Please enter a date for your follow-up call">*
                            </asp:RequiredFieldValidator>
                            <asp:RangeValidator ID="rangeValFollowup" runat="server"
                                ControlToValidate="txtFollowup"
                                ErrorMessage=
                                    "The date must be between 7/1/2007 and 7/31/2007"
                                MaximumValue="07/31/2007"
                                MinimumValue="07/01/2007" Type="Date">*
                            </asp:RangeValidator>
                            <asp:CompareValidator ID="compareValFollowup"
                                runat="server" ControlToCompare="txtCallDate"
                                ControlToValidate="txtFollowup" ErrorMessage=
                                    "Please select a date after your first call."
                                Operator="GreaterThan" Type="Date">*
                            </asp:CompareValidator></td>
                    </tr>
                    <tr>
                    <td colspan=3>
                        <asp:ValidationSummary ID="valSummary" runat="server"
                            HeaderText="The following errors were found:" />
                    </td>
                    </tr>
                    <tr>
                        <td></td>
                        <td align="center"style="width: 100px">
                            <asp:Button ID="btnSubmit" runat="server"
                                Text="Submit" /></td>
                        <td></td>
                    </tr>
                </table>
            </p>
        </div>
        </form>
</body>
</html>
```

Chapter 6: Style Sheets, Master Pages, and Navigation

Answers to Quiz Questions

1. The best way to apply styles on your page is to use an external style sheet. You can use inline or document-level styles, but these are error-prone and difficult to maintain.

2. The style for the specific paragraph applies. Style rules are always applied from least to most specific.

3. You use the @import command to apply a style sheet to your page, and it must be placed in the <head> element. If you place it anywhere else, the style sheet will be ignored.

4. A master page acts as a shell inside of which the content of your individual pages is displayed. This allows you to have a consistent look to all the pages on your site.

5. There's no limit to the number of nested master pages you can apply to a single content page, but if you use too many, your content will be difficult to read.

6. The child content page needs a reference to the class of the master page, contained in a @MasterType directive, immediately following the @Page directive for the child page.

7. You can use the Response.Redirect method.

8. You need to add a site map file, which is an XML file. You can use Website → Add New Item to add a new site map with an automatically generated skeleton, but you need to add the content of the XML file yourself.

9. You place a SiteMapDataSource control on the page to enable the navigation controls. In the case of a TreeView or Menu control, you use the Smart Tag to point the control to the SiteMapDataSource.

10. You don't have to do anything. The SiteMapPath control automatically finds the SiteMapDataSource control on the page and uses it.

Answers to Exercises

Exercise 6-1. There are a few different ways to create the pages shown in Exercise 6-1; here's one of them. Create a new web site called Exercise 6-1. Add a new master page called *AjaxTravel.master*, and be sure to put the code in a separate file. Rename the content placeholder something like cphAjaxMaster. Add an <h1> with the appropriate message, and a footer with the copyright message. Check it out in Design view to make sure it looks the way you want.

Use Website → Add New Item to add a new Web Form called *Home.aspx* to your site, and select *AjaxMaster.master* as its master page. Add a `<ul>` with two `<li>` items that each consist of a link: One that reads "Sun and surf packages" with an `href` of `Sun.aspx`, and one that reads "Snow and ski packages" with an `href` of `Snow.aspx`.

Add a new master page to the site; call it *SunMaster.master*. As in Example 6-7, remove everything except the `Master` directive, and add the following code to the `Master` directive:

```
MasterPageFile="AjaxTravel.master"
```

Next, add a `Content` section with a `ContentPlaceHolderID` attribute of `cphAjaxMaster`. Add some content for the header and footer, and be sure to include another `ContentPlaceHolder` called `cphSunContent`.

Create another new master page called *SnowMaster.master*, and set it up in the same way as *SunMaster.master*.

Add a new Web Form, and set its master page to be *SunHome.aspx*. Create another `<ul>` with links to the Bermuda and Maui pages.

Add a new Web Form, and set its master page to be *SnowHome.aspx*. Create another `<ul>` with links to the St. Moritz and Vail pages.

Create content pages for Bermuda and Maui with simple sample text, both of which use *SunMaster.master* as their master page.

Create content pages for St. Moritz and Vail with simple sample text, both of which use *SnowMaster.master* as their master page.

Now you've got a fully functional web site that changes its content depending on where the user wants to go, but maintains brand identity. If this were a real site, of course, you'd use style sheets to jazz up the content, add your company logo, and such. And of course, you'd also have real content on the destination pages. You can imagine that you'd probably have a link in the footers to your honeymoon and ski vacation packages that would take the user to the appropriate pages.

Exercise 6-2. Copy Exercise 6-1 to a new web site, Exercise 6-2. Open *AjaxTravel. master*, and add some text underneath the `<h1>`. Type "Welcome," and then drag a `Label` onto the page after the text. Name the label `lblName`, and change its `Text` property to "Guest." Then add an exclamation point. If you run the site now, you'll see that each page says "Welcome, Guest!"

You need *AjaxTravel.master* to implement a public property to display the label, so open *AjaxTravel.master.vb*, and enter the following code:

```
Private lbl As Label
Public Property MessageLabel() As Label
    Get
        Return lblName
    End Get
```

```
        Set(ByVal value As Label)
            lbl = value
        End Set
    End Property
```

Now, on the *Home.aspx* page, below the <ul>, add some text saying "Enter your name:". Then add a Textbox control (txtName), and a Submit button. The page needs to know about the AjaxTravel page class, so that it can make changes to the master page. Add the following line of code to *Home.aspx*, just after the Page directive:

CODE

```
<%@ MasterType TypeName="AjaxTravel" %>
```

Now you need to wire up the Submit button so that the text in txtName gets copied to the label on the master page. Double-click the Submit button, and when the event handler opens, add the following code:

CODE

```
Me.Master.MessageLabel.Text = txtName.Text
```

Try it out. You'll see the control on the home page where you'll be able to enter your name, and it should be transferred to the master page. Unfortunately, if you navigate to any other page, the greeting goes back to being "Hello, Guest!" To save that information, you'll need to use session state, which you'll see in Chapter 7.

Exercise 6-3. We won't use the user greeting for this web site, so copy Exercise 6-1 to a new web site called Exercise 6-3. The first thing you need to do is add a Site Map, so select Website → Add New Item, select Site Map, and accept the default name. The skeleton of *web.sitemap* is created for you automatically, but you need to fill in the nodes. The results should look like this:

CODE

```
<?xml version="1.0" encoding="utf-8" ?>
<siteMap xmlns="http://schemas.microsoft.com/AspNet/SiteMap-File-1.0" >
  <siteMapNode url="~/Home.aspx" title="Home"  description="Home page">
    <siteMapNode url="~/SunHome.aspx" title="Sun"  description="Sunny
                                                        destinations">
      <siteMapNode url="~/Bermuda.aspx" title="Bermuda" description="Bermuda" />
      <siteMapNode url="~/Maui.aspx" title="Maui" description="Maui" />
    </siteMapNode>
    <siteMapNode url="~/SnowHome.aspx" title="Snow"  description="Snow
                                                        destinations">
      <siteMapNode url="~/StMoritz.aspx" title="St. Moritz" description="St.
                                                                Moritz" />
      <siteMapNode url="~/Vail.aspx" title="Vail" description="Vail, Colorado" />
    </siteMapNode>
  </siteMapNode>
</siteMap>
```

Next, open up *AjaxTravel.master*, and add a SiteMapDataSource control to the master page. It doesn't matter where you put it, and the data source will find *Web.sitemap* automatically.

Now add two radio buttons, rbTree and rbMenu, with Text properties of "Tree View" and "Menu." Be sure to set the GroupName property of each control to the same value, such as grpNavView. Now add two panels below the radio button list, pnlTree and

---

pnlMenu. Set the Visible property of each panel to False. Add a TreeView control to pnlTree, and a Menu control to pnlMenu. Set the data source of the TreeView and menu controls to point to the SiteMapDataSource you added earlier.

Now you need to set the event handler for the radio buttons. Double-click rbTree to be taken to the CheckChanged event. You want pnlTree to be visible when this button is checked, and pnlMenu to be invisible, so add this code to the event handler:

```
pnlTree.Visible = rbTree.Checked
pnlMenu.Visible = rbMenu.Checked
```

Create an event handler for pnlMenu's CheckChanged event, and add the same code.

Now run the site. You should be able to select the TreeView or Menu navigation control on each page. You may need to rearrange the content of your pages so that the menus will fit. Unfortunately, you can't retain the user's choice from page to page, but again, you'll see how to do that in Chapter 7.

Exercise 6-4. This last exercise is very simple. Simply open *AjaxTravel.master*, and drag a SiteMapPath control onto the page. The SiteMapPath will automatically find the SiteMapDataSource and implement the bread crumbs for you.

Chapter 7: State and Life Cycle

Answers to Quiz Questions

1. A session is the period of time in which a single user interacts with an application, no matter how many individual pages he or she visits.

2. The state of a page refers to the current values of all controls on the page, including any changes made by the user.

3. Add the Trace="True" attribute to the Page directive to see the page Trace, including the stages of the page life cycle, and the control hierarchy.

4. The postback mode is determined in the Start phase of the life cycle.

5. The Page_Load event is the most common event to handle if you want to take actions during the Load phase.

6. ASP.NET manages Control state, View state, Session state, and Application state. You cannot affect the management of the Control state.

7. The EnableViewState="false" attribute disables view state for more complex controls. Simpler controls, such as text boxes, retain their state no matter what.

8. Use the state bag to store the value of a counter that increments each time the page is loaded. If you navigate to a separate page, the counter will reset, but not if you click the browser's Refresh button.

9. Save the user's name in session state.

10. Use the syntax Session("username") = <user's name>.

Answers to Exercises

Exercise 7-1. The trick to this exercise isn't the code—it's where you put it. You want to evaluate the IsPostBack attribute, and take action based on its value, so the best place to do that is in the Page_Load event. Just a simple bit of code in the Page_Load event handler does what you want:

```
Protected Sub Page_Load(ByVal sender As Object, _
        ByVal e As System.EventArgs) Handles Me.Load
    If Not IsPostBack Then
        lblPostBack.Text = "You're seeing this page for the first time!"
    Else
        lblPostBack.Text = "Welcome back to the page."
    End If
End Sub
```

Exercise 7-2. This exercise isn't all that different from Exercise 7-1, except that you need to use the state bag. The button and the label aren't anything special. The key to this exercise is in the code-behind file, specifically the event handler for the Page_Load event.

The first thing you need to do is create an empty string to hold the message that you'll put in the label:

```
Dim message As String = ""
```

If this is the first time the page has been loaded, you add a message to the string saying that. You use an If statement that checks whether the page is a postback, just as in Exercise 7-1. Notice that you use DateTime.Now to insert the current time, and then add a line break just to make things look nice:

```
If Not IsPostBack Then
    message += "Page first accessed at " + DateTime.Now + ".<br/>"
End If
```

Then you assign the string to the Text property of the label:

```
lblMessage.Text = message
```

That's all easy enough, but you need that string for the next time the page is posted, so you need to store it in the state bag. You simply create a new item in the dictionary, give it a name, and then assign the string to it:

```
ViewState("message") = message
```

Now you need to account for when the page is posted back, so you have to go back up and add an Else clause to your If statement. This time, you want to retrieve the previous message first, so you get it back from the state bag, and use CType to convert it to a string. Then you can add the rest of the message just as you did in the first half of the If:

```
Else
    message = CType(ViewState("message"), String) + "Page posted back at " _
            + DateTime.Now + ".<br/>"
```

The statements to assign the message to the label and then store the message back in the state bag happen outside the If, so there's no need to repeat them here.

The entire event handler is shown in Example C-22.

Example C-22. The event handler for the Page_Load event in Exercise 7-3

```
Protected Sub Page_Load(ByVal sender As Object, ByVal e As System.EventArgs) _
Handles Me.Load

    Dim message As String = ""
    If Not IsPostBack Then
        message += "Page first accessed at " + DateTime.Now + ".<br/>"
    Else
        message = CType(ViewState("message"), String) + "Page posted back at " _
                    + DateTime.Now + ".<br/>"

    End If
    lblMessage.Text = message
    ViewState("message") = message

End Sub
```

As a bonus, try adding EnableViewState = "False" to the Page directive, and then run the application again. Instead of appending each new line to the string, every postback will overwrite the existing string.

Exercise 7-3. For this exercise, you need to use the Session dictionary instead of the state bag. Start by adding the two new buttons to *Default.aspx*, and give each of them a handler that uses Response.Redirect to point to *SecondPage.aspx* and *ThirdPage.aspx*.

You'll need to make some changes to the code-behind file of *Default.aspx*. First, replace the ViewState methods with Session. In addition, you have to make a change to the first half of the If statement:

```
        If Not IsPostBack Then
            message += "Page first accessed at " + DateTime.Now + ".<br/>"
```

If you navigate to another page, and then return to the Home page, the message will be defined again as a blank string. If that happens, you need to retrieve Session("message") from the session state, even the first time the page loads, when Session("message") will be empty:

```
        If Not IsPostBack Then
            message = CType(Session("message"), String) + _
                    "Home page first accessed at " + DateTime.Now + ".<br/>"
```

The entirety of the code-behind for *Default.aspx* should now look like Example C-23.

Example C-23. The code-behind file for Default.aspx in Exercise 7-3

```
Partial Class _Default
    Inherits System.Web.UI.Page

    Protected Sub Page_Load(ByVal sender As Object, ByVal e As System.EventArgs)_
    Handles Me.Load

        Dim message As String = ""
        If Not IsPostBack Then
            message = CType(Session("message"), String) + _
                      "Home page first accessed at " + DateTime.Now + ".<br/>"
        Else
            message = CType(Session("message"), String) + _
                      "Home page posted back at " + DateTime.Now + ".<br/>"
        End If
        lblMessage.Text = message
        Session("message") = message

    End Sub

    Protected Sub btnPage2_Click(ByVal sender As Object, ByVal e As _
    System.EventArgs) Handles btnPage2.Click
        Response.Redirect("SecondPage.aspx")
    End Sub

    Protected Sub btnPage3_Click(ByVal sender As Object, ByVal e As _
    System.EventArgs) Handles btnPage3.Click
        Response.Redirect("ThirdPage.aspx")
    End Sub
End Class
```

Now create *SecondPage.aspx* and *ThirdPage.aspx*. These two pages need the same controls as *Default.aspx*, and the same code-behinds, but be sure to change the messages and the `Response.Redirect` targets accordingly.

This time, if you add `EnableViewState = "False"` to the `Page` directive, the application doesn't change, because the string is stored in state instead. If you disable session state and try to run the application, you'll get an error.

Chapter 8: Errors, Exceptions, and Bugs, Oh My!

Answers to Quiz Questions

1. Add `Trace="true"` to the @Page directive of the page you want to trace.
2. The only difference is that `Trace.Warn` writes to the trace log in red.
3. `Trace.Write` and `Trace.Warn` can both take a category string, a message string, and an exception object.

4. Click in the left column of any code file to set a breakpoint. A red dot will appear on the line where you set the breakpoint.

5. Simply hover the mouse over the variable, and a pop-up will appear, showing its value.

6. When the application is stopped at a breakpoint, you can use the Immediate window to change the value of a variable.

7. The Locals window shows the variables in the current context, and their values.

8. Syntax errors are errors in the code that violate the rules of the language. The IDE can catch most of these for you. Logic errors occur when the syntax of code is correct, but the code does not provide the results that the programmer expected.

9. In the *web.config* file, you need to create a `<customErrors>` section, and set the mode attribute to `On`.

10. Add the `ErrorPage` attribute to the `@Page` directive, where you can specify the error page that will apply only to errors generated by the current page.

Answers to Exercises

Exercise 8-1. After you've downloaded the file, open *Default.aspx*, and add the attribute `Trace="true"` to the `@Page` directive. You've now enabled tracing on this file. Open *Default.aspx.vb*, where you'll find the event handler for the drop-down list. Insert a line of code similar to the following:

```
Trace.Warn("In event handler.")
```

Now run the application. You'll see the trace information immediately, but you won't see your trace message until you select an item from the drop-down list. Once you do, the message will show up in the trace.

Exercise 8-2. In debugging, there are always many different ways to identify a problem. You could try to trace to solve this problem, but it probably won't tell you much. The best thing to do is to set a breakpoint somewhere, and have a look at the local variables. The problem is with the text being written to the label, so placing a breakpoint where the text is assigned would be a good idea. Open the *Default.aspx. vb* file, and place a breakpoint on this line:

```
lblProduct.Text = ddlProduct.SelectedItem.Value + "<br />" + description
```

Now run the application. Nothing happens until you make a selection in the drop-down list, which triggers the event handler. Still nothing happens in the application, because the breakpoint halted execution before the text was written to the label.

In the Locals window, you should now see the value of several variables. You can see the value of `description` there, but that's not the problem. If you hover over `ddlProduct.SelectedItem.Value`, you'll see that the value is "ox" in this case, which isn't what you want. You might know just from looking at it that `SelectedItem.Value` isn't what you want to write to the label, but if you didn't, there's still more information available. In the Locals window, you'll see that the value of "sender" is {System. Web.UI.WebControls.DropDownList}. The problem is with the drop-down list, so that looks promising. If you click the plus sign to expand that item, you'll see another heading at first, but if you click that plus sign, you'll see a list of properties for the DropDownList. There's a lot of them, but if you scroll down to "SelectedItem," you'll see that you can expand that too. Once you do, you'll see that SelectedItem.Value is set to "ox," which you don't want, but right above it, SelectedValue.Text is set to "Oxford shirt," which is what you want. Therefore, if you change this:

CODE►
```
lblProduct.Text = ddlProduct.SelectedItem.Value + "<br />" + description
```

to this:

CODE►
```
lblProduct.Text = ddlProduct.SelectedItem.Text + "<br />" + description
```

you'll resolve the problem.

It's not obvious that you'd find the answer to the problem three levels deep in the Locals window. A large part of debugging is experience, along with knowing where to look. The important part is learning to put the breakpoints at the right spots to give you the best leads you can get.

Exercise 8-3. One of the most frustrating troubleshooting situations is trying to work out why your application is not doing something. In this case, you can see that the checkbox is checked, but the panel isn't appearing as expected. Something must be wrong in the event handler. Open *Default.aspx.vb*, and place a breakpoint at the beginning of the event handler:

CODE►
```
Protected Sub ddlProduct_SelectedIndexChanged(ByVal sender _
    As Object, ByVal e As System.EventArgs) Handles ddlProduct.SelectedIndexChanged
```

Run the application. When it stops at the breakpoint, there isn't much to see in the Locals window. If you click the plus sign next to the Me item in the Locals window, you'll see a very lengthy list of everything related to the page, including all the controls on it. You need to narrow down the information some. Open the Watch window next to the Locals window (you may need to drag the Watch tab to some other part of the UI to see it). Scroll down in the Locals window until you find pnlProduct. Click the plus sign next to it to see the panel's properties. Drag the Visible property into the Watch window, so you can watch it all by itself.

Now that you know what you're watching, you need the application to continue. Use the Step Into button on the Debugging toolbar, or press F11 to step through the event handler line-by-line. When you reach the end of the event handler, you'll see that the panel's Visible property is still False—nothing ever changed it. That means that a line is missing from the event handler; specifically, this one:

CODE►
```
pnlProduct.Visible = cbProduct.Checked
```

Without that line, the panel stays at its initial value of Visible = False. Once you insert that line, the application runs properly.

Exercise 8-4. The first thing you need to do is modify the *Web.config* file to indicate that you'll be using a custom error page. Insert the following code between the `<system.web>` tags:

CODE▶
```
<customErrors mode="On" defaultRedirect="Error.htm">
  <error statusCode="404" redirect="Error404.htm"/>
```

This code creates a default error page, *Error.htm*, and a page specifically for 404 errors, *Error404.htm*.

The next step is creating error file. Select Website → Add New Item, and select an HTML file, naming it *Error404.htm*. Open the file and add some HTML similar to the following:

CODE▶
```
<html>
<head>
    <title>Bad Link Error</title>
</head>
<body>
    <h1>Error</h1>
    We're sorry, the page you're looking for does not exist. Please notify
    the webmaster.
    Click <a href="Default.aspx">here</a> to return to the product page.
</body>
</html>
```

Return to *Default.aspx*, run the application, and click the link. You'll be taken to your custom error page. You can even use the link to get back to the product page, which probably won't make the user very happy, so it would be a good idea to get the customer assistance page created right away, or delegate it to a subordinate.

Chapter 9: Security and Personalization

Answer to Quiz Questions

1. You can create users by hand, using the WAT, or you can allow users to create accounts programmatically with the `CreateUserWizard` control.

2. Forms-based security grants privileges to users based on credentials, such as username and password, which are gathered from the user via a web page. With Windows authentication, user privileges are based on their Windows login.

3. User information is stored in a database named ASPNETDB.MDF within the App_Data directory of your site.

4. You need to provide a CreateUserWizard control so that users can specify their own account information.

5. You can add users to roles by using the WAT.

6. Use the `User.IsInRole` property to test whether a user is a member of a role before granting access to a page.

7. You need to add a line to *web.config*, setting `profile` enabled to true. You also need to add a `<properties>` section within the profile section, and use the `<add>` property to specify the names of the properties you want to retain.

8. Use an anonymous profile by setting `<anonymousIdentification enabled="true">` in the *web.config* file.

9. Style sheet themes are functionally equivalent to CSS style sheets, and can be overridden by the page or by the control. Customization themes are applied last, and therefore cannot be overridden.

10. You define the settings for a skin in a *.skin* file, which resides inside a folder named after the theme, which in turn is located with the `App_Themes` folder of your site.

Answers to Exercises

Exercise 9-1. Create your new web site. Start off by deleting *Default.aspx*. Add a new page *Home.aspx*, set it as the start page, give it a title and an `<h1>`, and then add a `LoginStatus` control. Add a `LoginView` control, and set the Logged In and Logged Out templates to the appropriate messages. Add a `LoginName` control to the Logged In template to greet the user by name.

If you're not going to use the WAT to create any users, you need to add the following line to your *web.config* file, in the `<system.web>` section:

CODE▶
```
<authentication mode="Forms" />
```

Add a new page to your site, *login.aspx*. Give it a title and an `<h1>`, and then drag a Login control onto the page. Give it whatever formatting you like.

At the moment, though, the only way to create a new user is with the WAT. Add a page where users can create their own user accounts. Create a new page, *CreateAccount.aspx*. Give it a title and an `<h1>`, and then add a `CreateUserWizard` control to the page. Set the `ContinueDestination` property to *Home.aspx* to take users back to the front of the site when they've created their accounts. Go back to the *Login. aspx* page, and add a `Hyperlink` control with a `NavigateUrl` property of `CreateAccount. aspx`, so that users can create an account if they don't already have one.

Run your site and create a handful of users to populate your database. Be sure to write down the passwords because you'll need them later.

Exercise 9-2. Create the content pages first, *fishforum.aspx* and *siteadmin.aspx*. The next thing you'll need to do is define roles for your existing users. You can only do that from the WAT, so start up the WAT (Website → ASP.NET Configuration), select Security, click "Enable Roles," click "Create or Manage Roles," and add two roles for "Moderator" and "User." Then go back, click Manage Users, and add some of your users to the "Moderator" group, and all of them to the "User" group. Close the WAT.

Open *siteadmin.aspx.vb*. You want to restrict access to this page to just users who have the Moderator role. Create an event handler for the Page Load event as usual, and add this code:

CODE►
```
If User.IsInRole("Moderator") = False Then
    Response.Redirect("Home.aspx")
End If
```

This allows Moderators to view the page, but plain users will be sent back to the home page.

Open *siteadmin.aspx* and add some text indicating that this is a placeholder page for content to come. Add a hyperlink and set the NavigateUrl property to *Home.aspx*.

Now open *fishforum.aspx.vb*. You want only people in the User role to be able to access this page, so create a Page Load event for this page and add the following code:

CODE►
```
If User.IsInRole("User") = False Then
    Response.Redirect("Home.aspx")
End If
```

Users who are in the "User" role will be able to view this page, but anyone else will be sent back to the home page.

Open *fishforum.aspx* and also add some text indicating that this is a placeholder page for content to come. Add a hyperlink and set the NavigateUrl property to *Home.aspx*.

Open up *Home.aspx* and add two hyperlinks—one that points to *fishforum.aspx*, and one that points to *siteadmin.aspx*.

Test out your site. You'll find that your users in the Moderator role can visit both content pages, but users in the User role can only visit the Fish Forum. Users who aren't logged in, or don't have a role, are returned to the home page. Of course, in practice, you'd redirect users to a "No permissions" page, but returning them to the home page is fine for now.

Exercise 9-3. If you're going to use profiles, the first thing you need to do is make a modification to the *web.config* file. Open *web.config* and add the following code to enable profiles and store the four data elements you want to save:

CODE►
```
<profile enabled="true" defaultProvider="AspNetSqlProfileProvider">
  <properties>
    <add name="userName" />
    <add name="numFish" />
    <add name="fishType" />
    <add name="favFish" />
  </properties>
</profile>
```

Next, add a new page, *ProfilePage.aspx*, to the site. Use a table for layout, and enter the standard controls as shown in the figure. Be sure to add the Save button at the bottom of the table.

Double-click the Save button to create a handler for the Click event. You need to record the string values from the form into the Profile object.

CODE▶

```
Protected Sub btnSave_Click(ByVal sender As Object, ByVal e
                 As System.EventArgs) Handles btnSave.Click
    If Profile.IsAnonymous = False Then
        Profile.userName = Me.txtUserName.Text
        Profile.numFish = Me.txtNumFish.Text
        If rbTropical.Checked = True Then
            Profile.fishType = "Tropical"
        Else
            Profile.fishType = "Freshwater"
        End If
        Profile.favFish = ddlFavFish.SelectedItem.Text
    End If
    Response.Redirect("Home.aspx")
End Sub
```

You have to write a little bit of code to extract the text values from the radio button pair, and the drop-down list, and then enter them into the Profile attributes.

Notice that this handler redirects to *Home.aspx* when it's done. The next thing you need to do is make some modifications to *Home.aspx* so that users can see their profiles. First, switch the LoginView control to the logged-in template, and add a hyperlink directing users to the Profile page.

Now add a panel, pnlProfileInfo, so that users can see the current contents of their profile. The markup for this panel and its contents should look like this:

CODE▶

```
<asp:Panel ID="pnlProfileInfo" runat="server" Height="50px" Visible="False"
Width="250px">
    <table>
        <tr align=left>
            <td>User Name:</td>
            <td style="width: 100px">
                <asp:Label ID="lblName" runat="server"></asp:Label>
            </td>
        </tr>
        <tr align=left>
            <td>Number of fish:</td>
            <td style="width: 100px">
                <asp:Label ID="lblNumFish" runat="server"></asp:Label></td>
        </tr>
        <tr align=left>
            <td>Tropical or Fresh?</td>
            <td style="width: 100px">
                <asp:Label ID="lblFishType" runat="server"></asp:Label></td>
        </tr>
```

```
            <tr align=left>
                <td>Favorite Fish</td>
                <td style="width: 100px">
                    <asp:Label ID="lblFavFish" runat="server"></asp:Label></td>
            </tr>
        </table>
    </asp:Panel>
```

Now you just have to write an event handler to populate the labels in the table in the panel. Add the following code to the Page_Load event handler:

```
Protected Sub Page_Load(ByVal sender As Object, ByVal e As System.EventArgs) _
        Handles Me.Load
    If Not IsPostBack And _
            Profile.UserName IsNot Nothing And _
            Profile.IsAnonymous = False Then
        Me.pnlProfileInfo.Visible = True
        Me.lblName.Text = Profile.userName
        Me.lblNumFish.Text = Profile.numFish
        Me.lblFishType.Text = Profile.fishType
        Me.lblFavFish.Text = Profile.favFish
    Else
        Me.pnlProfileInfo.Visible = False
    End If

End Sub
```

Exercise 9-4. Start by creating the App_Themes folder in Solution Explorer. Now add the two theme folders for Angelfish and Clownfish. Create the *Button.skin* and *Label. skin* files in the Angelfish folder. Here's the markup for the *Button.skin* file in the Angelfish theme:

```
<asp:Button runat="server"
    ForeColor="Yellow"
    BackColor="Black"
    Font-Size="Large" />
```

The other skin files are similar, but with different colors, of course.

Next, you have to enable themes in the properties element of the profile section in *web.config*:

```
<add name="Theme" />
```

Now open up *Home.aspx.vb* and add the overrides StyleSheetTheme( ) method as follows:

```
Public Overrides Property StyleSheetTheme( ) As String
    Get
        If Profile.IsAnonymous = False And Profile.Theme IsNot Nothing Then
            Return Profile.Theme
        Else
            Return "Angelfish"
        End If
    End Get
```

```
    Set(ByVal value As String)
        Profile.Theme = value
    End Set
End Property
```

When the user logs in, the theme stored in the user's profile will be loaded. The anonymous users will get the Angelfish theme.

Next, you need to provide a way for users to choose their theme. Add two buttons to *Home.aspx*—one labeled Clownfish Theme and the other Angelfish Theme, with IDs of btnClownfish and btnAngelfish, respectively. Because you don't want these buttons to be visible unless the user is logged in, add the following two lines to the Page_Load method of *Home.aspx.vb*:

CODE▶
```
btnAngelFish.Visible = Not Profile.IsAnonymous
btnClownfish.Visible = Not Profile.IsAnonymous
```

Create an event handler to use for the Click event for both buttons. Call it Theme_Click and add the highlighted code from the following snippet:

CODE▶
```
Protected Sub Theme_Click(ByVal sender As Object, ByVal e As System.EventArgs) _
            Handles btnClownfish.Click, btnAngelFish.Click
    Dim btn As Button = CType(sender, Button)
    If btn.Text = "Clownfish Theme" Then
        Profile.Theme = "Clownfish"
    Else
        Profile.Theme = "Angelfish"
    End If

    Server.Transfer(Request.FilePath)
End Sub
```

If the button that raises the Click event has the text "Clownfish Theme," the Clownfish theme is set. Otherwise, the Angelfish theme is set.

Finally, create an event handler for the PreInit event and add the highlighted code from the following snippet:

```
Protected Sub Page_PreInit(ByVal sender As Object, ByVal e As System.EventArgs) _
        Handles Me.PreInit
    If Profile.IsAnonymous = False Then
        Page.Theme = Profile.Theme
    End If
End Sub
```

Now when you run the app, the default theme on the home page will be Angelfish, and if you log in and change the theme for user, that theme will be remembered the next time the user logs in.

Index

Symbols

+= operator, 237
> (greater-than symbol), 213
@import command, 180

A

access
    databases, security, 288
    files, 4
    modifiers, 193
    restricting, 298–304
    site map nodes
        programmatically, 209–212
Accordion control, 72
Add Connection dialog box, 100, 287, 404
Add New Item dialog box, 73
Add ORDER BY Clause dialog box, 126
Add WHERE Clause dialog box, 125, 127
adding
    AJAX, 363
    asynchronous postbacks, 29–31
    bread crumbs, 212
    content pages, 184–187
    controls, 8–13
        with Item Editor, 42
    custom error pages, 377
    Hyperlink controls, 199
    images, 51–52
    items
        to lists, 42
        in Source view, 43
    Label controls to master pages, 192
    LinkButton controls, 53

links, 52
master pages, 183
navigation tools, 351–353
PopupControlExtender, 76–82
profiles, 308
schema names, 106
ScriptManager controls, 67–71
site maps, 203–212
skins, 325
styles, 340–343
tables, 48
themes, 324, 327
trace logs, 256–259
UpdatePanel controls, 69
validation controls, 143
    CompareValidator, 154–159
    CustomValidator, 162–164
    RangeValidator, 159
    RegularExpressionValidator, 160–162
    RequiredFieldValidator, 144–151
    ValidationSummary, 152
watermarks, 72–76
Web Forms, 186
Advanced SQL Generation Options dialog
    box, 114
AdventureWorks database
    applying, 406
    getting data from, 97–116
AJAX
    adding, 363
    Control Toolkit, 22, 72–87
    controls, 22
    installing, 411
    overview of, 66

We'd like to hear your suggestions for improving our indexes. Send email to *index@oreilly.com*.

C

G

Garrett, Jesse James, 66
global.asax file, custom error pages, 276
Globally Unique Identifier (GUID), 317
glyphs, breakpoints, 265
Gould, Lee, 362
graphical user interfaces (see GUIs)
greater-than symbol (>), 213
GridView control, 98
   applying, 107–113
   building, 99
   data, selecting from, 123
   modifying, 119
GUID (Globally Unique Identifier), 317
GUIs (graphical user interfaces), 19

H

handlers, event, 28
   calling, 11
   Page_Load, 26–29
handling
   errors, 250, 271
      error pages, 273–277
      unhandled errors, 272
   events
      postbacks, 23
      RowDataBound, 120
Hansel and Gretel, 200
hardware requirements, 401
Has changed radio button, 264
<head> element, 180
Hello World, 2
   controls, adding, 8–13
   creating, 6–8
helper methods, 232
Hit Count button, 264
Home page
   source code, 384
Home.aspx file, 346
hosting web sites, 5
HoverMenuExtender control, 72
HTML (HyperText Markup Language), 17
   controls, 19
   tables, 37
      creating within panels, 41–45
HTTP (Hypertext Transfer Protocol)
   status codes, 256
   web sites, hosting, 5

hyperlinks, 196–200
   controls, 52
HyperText Markup Language (see HTML)
Hypertext Transfer Protocol (see HTTP)

I

icons
   breakpoints, 265
   Debug toolbar, 260
ID property, 46
IDE (Integrated Development
      Environment), 2
   controls, adding, 8–13
   Debug toolbar, 260
   Debug windows, 268–271
   error handling, 271
      error pages, 273–277
      unhandled errors, 272
   Hello World, creating, 6–8
   web sites
      copying with the, 419–424
      copying without using the, 418
      creating, 2–5
If statements, 120, 121
IIS (Internet Information Server), 5
image controls, 51–52
ImageControlID property, 85
Immediate window, 268
initializing arrays, 235
InitialValue attribute, 147
inline styles, 171–173
inner joins, 362
Insert statement, 112–116
Insert Table dialog box, 38
Insert Table Wizard, 48
installing applications
   AJAX, 411
   hardware/software requirements, 401
   Visual Studio 2005, 407–410
   VWD, 402–407
instances, 21
Int event, 224
Integrated Development Environment (see
      IDE)
IntelliSense properties, searching, 32
interacting with databases, 97–116
interfaces
   GUIs, 19
   (see also browsers)

Internet Information Server (IIS), 5
intranet web sites, WAT, 283
Is true radio button, 264
IsAnonymous property, 307
Item Editor, adding controls with, 42
items
    lists, adding, 42
    Source view, adding in, 43

J
joins, 362

K
Kennedy, Bill, 19
keywords
    Session, 239
    ViewState, 234
Kline, Kevin, 362

L
Label controls, adding to master pages, 192
labels, adding, 9
lblRadioButtonList label, 330
length units, styles, 177
life cycles
    trace logs, 256
    web pages, 221–227
LinkButton controls, 53
links, controls, 52
ListBox control, 40
ListItem Collection Editor, 42, 239
lists
    items, adding, 42
    selection controls, 46
literals, 160
Load event, 226
loading web pages, life cycles of, 224
localhost, 298
Locals window, 270
Location field, 4
Location menu, 263
LoggedInTemplate view, 291
login, 348–351
    controls, 21
    status, testing, 300
login pages
    creating, 293
    source code, 385
LoginName control, 291
LoginStatus control, 291

logs, trace, 256, 256–259
loops
    For, 253
    For Each, 211

M
MakeFlag column, 108, 119, 122
ManagersPage.aspx file, 301
managing
    skins, 323
    state, 227
        application, 244
        session, 238–244
        view, 228–238
    themes, 323
    user accounts, 285, 299
maps, site, 203–212
markup
    AWProductData site, 128–136
    CompareValidator control, 155
    Home.aspx file, 346
    ManagersPage.aspx file, 301
    PopupControlExtender control, 81
    TextBoxwaterMarkExtender control, 75
Master directive, 189
master pages, 22
    applying, 343–346
    formatting, 180–195
    modifying, 191–195
    nested, applying, 187–191
    source code, 387
MasterType directive, 344
Me object, 196
membership, testing role-based
        authentication, 300
Menu control, 208
menus, 200–203
    Disable, 263
    Location, 263
messages
    customizing, 292
    trace logs, sending to, 258
metacharacters, 160
methods, 21, 28
    CType, 123
    DisplayStuff( ), 242
    helper, 232
    Page_Load, 252
    Warn, 256, 259
    Write, 256
MigrateAnonymous event handlers, 320

About the Authors

Jesse Liberty, Microsoft .NET MVP, is the best-selling author of O'Reilly Media's *Programming ASP.NET*, *Programming C#*, *Programming Visual Basic 2005*, and over a dozen other books on web and object-oriented programming. He is president of Liberty Associates, Inc., where he provides contract programming, consulting, and on-site training in .NET.

Jesse is a frequent contributor to O'Reilly Network web sites, as well as many industry publications, and he has spoken at numerous events. He is a former Distinguished Software Engineer at AT&T, and Vice President for technology development at CitiBank.

Dan Hurwitz is the president of Sterling Solutions, Inc., where for nearly two decades he has been providing contract programming and database development to a wide variety of clients. He has coauthored three editions of *Programming ASP.NET*.

Brian MacDonald is an editor of programming and networking books. He has edited books for several major publishers on topics ranging from securing Windows servers to PHP web programming to running an eBay business. His work for O'Reilly includes *Programming WCF Services* and *Programming ASP.NET*. He also coauthored *Learning C# 2005* with Jesse Liberty. He lives in southeastern Pennsylvania with his wife and son.

Colophon

The animal on the cover of *Learning ASP.NET 2.0 with AJAX* is a pelagic stingray (*Pteroplaytrygon violacea*). The pelagic stingary is found worldwide in temperate to tropical seas, in both open bays and deep ocean waters. While many other varieties of rays live near the sandy ocean floor, the pelagic stingray primarily swims in open water. It has many small sharp teeth and is sometimes seen feeding upside-down or using its pectoral fins to push food into its mouth. It eats crustaceans, jellyfish, octopus, squid, and small fish such as mackerel and herring.

Pelagic stingrays can grow up to five feet long and almost three feet wide. This is small relative to other rays, which can be as long as 14 feet, yet is substantial enough that its only predators are large marine creature, such as hammerhead and oceanic whitetip sharks. Its coloring, dark purple or gray on top with a paler underside, serves to camouflage the stingray from predators above. The pelagic stingray wards off these predators with serrated, venomous spines, which protrude about one-third of the way down its tail.

Pups, or baby stingrays, are born in small litters after a two- to four-month gestational period. At birth, they are between 6 and 10 inches long, and they are able to feed and take care of themselves. Though pelagic stingrays are often caught unintentionally in fishing nets, they are not currently endangered, and some scientists have noted a recent increase in pelagic stingray populations.

Try the online edition free for 45 days

Get the information you need when you need it, with Safari Books Online. Safari Books Online contains the complete version of the print book in your hands plus thousands of titles from the best technical publishers, with sample code ready to cut and paste into your applications.

Safari is designed for people in a hurry to get the answers they need so they can get the job done. You can find what you need in the morning, and put it to work in the afternoon. As simple as cut, paste, and program.

To try out Safari and the online edition of the above title FREE for 45 days, go to www.oreilly.com/go/safarienabled and enter the coupon code ZZLJTYG.

To see the complete Safari Library visit:
safari.oreilly.com

Related Titles from O'Reilly

.NET

ADO.NET Cookbook

ASP.NET 2.0 Cookbook, *2nd Edition*

ASP.NET 2.0: A Developer's Notebook

C# Cookbook, *2nd Edition*

C# in a Nutshell, *2nd Edition*

C# Language Pocket Reference

Learning C# 2005, *2nd Edition*

Learning WCF

MCSE Core Elective Exams in a Nutshell

.NET and XML

.NET Gotchas

Programming .NET Components, *2nd Edition*

Programming .NET Security

Programming .NET Web Services

Programming ASP.NET, *3rd Edition*

Programming Atlas

Programming C#, *4th Edition*

Programming MapPoint in .NET

Programming Visual Basic 2005

Programming WCF Services

Programming Windows Presentation Foundation

Visual Basic 2005: A Developer's Notebook

Visual Basic 2005 Cookbook

Visual Basic 2005 in a Nutshell, *3rd Edition*

Visual Basic 2005 Jumpstart

Visual C# 2005: A Developer's Notebook

Visual Studio Hacks

Windows Developer Power Tools

XAML in a Nutshell